SECRECY & PRIVILEGE

Also by Robert Parry

Fooling America
Trick or Treason
October Surprise X-Files
Lost History

SECRECY & PRIVILEGE

~~~~~

Rise of the Bush Dynasty
from Watergate to Iraq

ROBERT PARRY

The Media Consortium Inc.
Arlington, Virginia

To Samuel, Nathaniel, Elizabeth, Jeffrey, Claudia and Diane

Grateful acknowledgement is made to Samuel and Nathaniel Parry for their
assistance in preparation of this book. Thanks is also given to Diane Duston for
her support and assistance throughout this project.

Parry, Robert, 1949-

Secrecy & Privilege: Rise of the Bush Dynasty from Watergate to Iraq

Included index.

ISBN 1-893517-01-2

Printed in the United States of America

CONTENTS

"Earn this. Earn it."

**The dying words of Army Captain Miller
to Private Ryan in the movie "Saving Private Ryan"**

Introduction

The idea of this book was to examine how the two George Bushes intersected with important turning points of recent American history, not just what they did but how the surrounding events affected them and how they affected the course of the American democratic experiment. While other authors have examined aspects of this extraordinary family dynasty, I wanted to take a journalist's eye view of how the Bushes fit into various scandals and other momentous political events from Watergate to Iraq.

At times, the two George Bushes were leading players; other times, they had smaller roles; sometimes, they were the beneficiaries of actions taken by others. Often the mix of these roles surprised me. In the end, however, it became clear that how George H.W. and George W. Bush blended with events of the last three decades has changed the American political process in fundamental ways, especially how information – the sustenance of democracy – is rationed to the American people and how the government leads the people.

The book also became a way to explore how the United States got to where it is today, with a political process that often is impervious to fact or driven by fear. Indeed, one interpretation of the 30 years since the Watergate scandal is that the secrecy and dirty tricks that were the hallmarks of Richard Nixon's political style have simply become the daily routine of today's politics. Certainly, the post-Watergate demands for greater government openness and limits on executive authority seem like a distant echo, more a memory than a legacy.

It's perhaps ironic that the two George Bushes, who sprang from the privileged background that Nixon so disdained, would have emerged as the chief beneficiaries of the cut-throat politics that Nixon pioneered. But the Bushes' social, economic and political connections may have been Nixon's missing ingredient. While the lowly born Nixon was a stranger to the protections afforded by Establishment credentials, the Bushes possessed important contacts from two powerful spheres of influence, the "Ivy League/Wall Street East" and the "Texas Oil/Sunbelt South." These connections guarded the two George Bushes as they pushed – and elbowed – their way through their political careers. When the chips were down, they could count on their friends and their allies coming through.

The elder George Bush also injected another new element into American politics, his background as director of the Central Intelligence Agency. His year running the spy agency earned him the allegiance of talented American spies and gave them an entrée into U.S. domestic politics that they had never had. The CIA's tradecraft of secrecy and compartmentalization helped Bush – as Vice President and then President – shield many politically dangerous secrets from the American people, preventing anything approaching full public knowledge of historic events.

George H.W. Bush's greatest impact on U.S. politics may have been that he infused the process with CIA theory and practice, from covert diplomacy in dealing with other countries to "perception management" in controlling how the American people perceive events. Secrecy became a trademark, too, of George W. Bush's administration.

Buttressing the Bush family's political power was a potent conservative news media that took shape in the late 1970s and early 1980s, partly as a reaction to Nixon's Watergate debacle. While this conservative infrastructure was not created with the two George Bushes in mind, it benefited them more than any other political leaders. Between the family's own powerful connections and the conservative media's ability to shape the news, the elder George Bush and his son enjoyed a buffer of protection that few American politicians have ever had. Investigations of their activities or challenges to their power often collapsed into retreat like an undermanned attack force charging up hill against a well-entrenched enemy with superior firepower.

This book examines, too, the strange relationship between one of the principal financiers of the conservative infrastructure – Korean theocrat Sun Myung Moon – and the Bush family. Possibly more than any other figure on the Right, Moon has lavished money on U.S. conservative causes and political leaders. Yet, the source of that money remains one of the most troubling mysteries of modern American politics though interestingly one of the least investigated. The evidence points to significant illegal activity surrounding Moon's fortune, including first-hand accounts of money laundering and longstanding connections to organized-crime figures.

Since Moon's conviction on tax evasion in the early 1980s, however, U.S. government investigators have turned a blind eye to this evidence of a continued criminal conspiracy. The decline in law enforcement's interest in

Moon's financial activities has corresponded with the rise in Moon's influence-buying among conservatives, including his funding of *The Washington Times* and his funneling of speaking fees and other payments to conservative politicians, including George H.W. Bush.

By covering a 30-year swath of history, this book allows seemingly disconnected events to be placed in context, to make sense out of behavior that otherwise might appear anomalous. To understand the chip-on-the-shoulder attitude of today's ascendant conservative movement, for instance, one must look back at the twin catastrophes of Watergate and Vietnam. Out of the bitter ashes of those defeats rose the modern American conservative movement, which has kept alive the flame of that anger even as conservatives came to dominate all branches of the U.S. government and to hold great sway over the U.S. news media.

This book also gave me the opportunity to research the Bush family's role in some scandals, like Watergate, that I did not personally cover, as well as to revisit stories that I did cover. Those stories include the Iran-Contra scandal, which I investigated for the Associated Press and *Newsweek*, and the October Surprise controversy, which I was asked to examine by the PBS *Frontline* documentary program. I've pulled together, too, more recent material about the Clinton administration and the second Bush administration that I developed for the Web site, *Consortiumnews.com*, which I have operated with two of my sons, Sam and Nat, since 1995.

In recent years, a number of books have examined aspects of how the United States reached this historical juncture. Some books, such as Kevin Phillips's *American Dynasty* and Craig Unger's *House of Bush, House of Saud*, have looked at the financial underpinnings of the Bush family. *The Clinton Wars* by Sidney Blumenthal and *The Hunting of the President* by Joe Conason and Gene Lyons have studied how and why the national news media went after the Clinton administration with such ferocity. Other books, such as Eric Alterman's *What Liberal Media?* and David Brock's *Blinded by the Right* and *The Republican Noise Machine* have explored the development of the conservative media infrastructure.

This book won't try to recreate what those authors have already done. Instead it will explore a series of historical mysteries that have defined the modern political era – and will show how the two George Bushes emerged from these shadowy controversies to gain a dynastic hold over the highest office in the United States.

Chapter 1: The Wedding

The light from the setting sun streamed through the windows of the East Room after the first White House wedding in more than two decades. Guests were picking desserts from a buffet table and conversing, some gesturing with crystal champagne flutes in hand. Despite the formality of the surroundings, the event had a relaxed air. Earlier, President Bill Clinton had given a gracious toast in honor of the wedding couple – Tony Rodham and Nicole Boxer – and played the saxophone to entertain their families and friends. The groom was Clinton's brother-in-law; the bride was the daughter of his political ally, Senator Barbara Boxer of California. Many other guests had supported his campaign for the White House two years earlier.

Clinton, a tall man renowned for his personal magnetism and ability to focus on each individual he meets at least for a few fleeting seconds, was moving among the guests like a host at the latter stages of a house party. Unlike many of the guests sipping from crystal or drinking from coffee cups, Clinton carried in his large hands a mug with the presidential seal. As he came upon one knot of guests, Clinton started talking like one might chat with neighbors about troubles at work. He complained about how rancorous Washington had become, how beleaguered he felt, how horribly the press was treating him.

"He was unburdening himself," recalled Stuart Sender, a Los Angeles-based documentary filmmaker who was one of the guests.

Sixteen months into his Presidency, Clinton was learning about the hard-knuckled realities of the new Washington where campaigns never stop, where there is no respite for governance between elections. Clinton was getting clobbered by the Republicans and by the news media over an old real-estate deal in Arkansas, known as Whitewater. The political heat had gotten so searing that Clinton had consented to the appointment of a special prosecutor.

There had been a firestorm, too, over allegations from Arkansas state troopers about Clinton's philandering as governor. A woman named Paula Jones had emerged from that controversy with claims that Clinton had crudely propositioned her. He also was taking flak over the firing of employees in the White House Travel Office, and there were bizarre suspicions circulating about the suicide of White House deputy counsel Vincent Foster, who had come with the Clintons from Arkansas. Foster shot himself in the head after growing despondent over the harsh press criticism he had received for his role in the Travel Office affair, but some conservatives were spreading rumors of a deeper mystery.

Clinton felt besieged not only by aggressive Republicans but by the national press corps. Since the last Democratic President, Jimmy Carter, left office in 1981, a powerful conservative media had come into its own. Every day, radio talk show host Rush Limbaugh regaled his millions of listeners with three hours of ridicule directed at Clinton and his wife, Hillary. Besides Limbaugh, there were scores of imitators and wannabes all over talk radio, such as Watergate convict G. Gordon Liddy and Iran-Contra figure, retired Marine Lieutenant Colonel Oliver North.

Right-wing print outlets also were growing in number and in influence, the likes of the *American Spectator* and *The Washington Times*, not to mention *The Wall Street Journal's* editorial pages and conservative columnists in newspapers across the country. Many of the commentators also appeared on TV political chat shows to reprise their opinions for millions of more Americans nationwide. Anti-Clinton books and videos were selling fast, too. The annual Conservative Political Action Conference in February 1994 looked like a trade show for "I-hate-Clinton" paraphernalia.

Many mainstream journalists at outlets such as NBC News and *The New York Times* also joined in the Clinton bashing, seemingly eager to prove that they could be tougher on a Democrat than any Republican. They were determined to show they weren't the "liberal media" that the conservatives had railed against since the U.S. defeat in Vietnam and the Watergate scandal that sank Richard Nixon's presidency in 1974. Indeed, it was *The Washington Post*, the newspaper credited with unraveling the Watergate mystery, which had led the charge on the Whitewater case with front-page stories that put Clinton in a public relations corner, forcing him to acquiesce to a special prosecutor.

So, on that warm spring day of May 28, 1994, Clinton hosted the Rodham-Boxer wedding – the first at the White House since Nixon hosted the nuptials of his daughter Tricia and Edward Cox in 1971. The Boxer-Rodham wedding had started 90 minutes behind schedule because Clinton returned late from a golf game. The anxious bride and groom learned that nothing happens at the White House until the President is ready. But the nervousness was put into historical perspective by Clinton's toast. He recalled that the last time a wedding reception was planned for the East Room was 1814, when the event was interrupted by the British attack on Washington and the burning of the White House.

Almost 180 years later, the White House was under siege again – or so it felt to Clinton – only this time the guys with the torches were the Republicans and the target of their flames was the first Democratic President in 12 years. As the spring sun was setting and the wedding event was winding down, Clinton's mind was gearing back up. He was thinking about the nasty political battles all around him. Making the rounds at the party at his White House home, he was looking for a sympathetic hearing.

Stuart Sender and his wife Julie Bergman Sender were admiring the glorious scene in the ornate East Room. "All of a sudden we looked up and there was President Clinton," Stuart Sender said. The chitchat soon turned to Clinton's complaints about his ill treatment at the hands of the news media. "He started the conversation by saying how horrible the press is being to him," said Julie Bergman Sender, a Hollywood producer, political activist and daughter of songwriters Alan and Marilyn Bergman. "I was looking around at the planters. I was thinking, 'you're not standing in your living room, really.'"

Stuart Sender, who had worked as a journalist on the Reagan-Bush-era Iran-Contra and Iraqgate scandals, had a different reaction. He wondered why Clinton had never pursued those investigations of Republican wrongdoing when he became President in January 1993. After all, Sender thought, those were real scandals, involving secret dealings with unsavory regimes. Top Republicans allegedly had helped arm Iraq's Saddam Hussein as well as the radical Islamic mullahs of Iran, violations both of law and constitutional principles. Those actions had then been surrounded by stout defenses by Republicans and their media allies. The protection had taken on the look of systematic cover-ups, sometimes even obstruction of justice, to spare the top echelons of the Reagan-Bush administrations from accountability. These weren't like the trivial allegations besetting Clinton's Presidency.

Indeed, as Clinton was heading into office at the start of 1993, four investigations were underway that implicated senior Republicans in potential criminal wrongdoing. The Iran-Contra arms-for-hostages case was still alive, with special prosecutor Lawrence Walsh furious over new evidence that President George H.W. Bush may have obstructed justice by withholding his own notes from investigators and then ducking an interview that Walsh had put off until after the 1992 elections. Bush also had sabotaged the investigation by pardoning six Iran-Contra defendants on Christmas Eve 1992, possibly the first presidential pardon ever issued to protect the same President from criminal liability. In granting the pardons, Bush had denigrated the Iran-Contra charges as the "criminalization of policy differences."

In late 1992, Congress also was investigating Bush's alleged role in secretly aiding Iraq's Saddam Hussein during and after Hussein's eight-year-long war with Iran. Representative Henry Gonzalez, a Democrat from Texas who had served three decades in Congress, led the charge in exposing intricate financial schemes that the Reagan-Bush administrations had employed to assist Hussein. There also were allegations of indirect U.S.

military aid through third countries, claims that Bush and other Republican leaders emphatically denied.

Lesser known investigations were examining two other sets of alleged wrongdoing: the so-called October Surprise issue (allegations that Bush and other Republicans had interfered with Jimmy Carter's hostage negotiations with Iran during the 1980 campaign) and the Passportgate affair (evidence that Bush operatives had improperly searched Clinton's passport file in 1992, looking for dirt that could be used to discredit his patriotism and secure reelection for Bush).

All told, the four sets of allegations, if true, would paint an unflattering portrait of the 12-year Republican rule, with two illegal dirty tricks (October Surprise and Passportgate) book-ending ill-considered national security schemes in the Middle East (Iran-Contra and Iraqgate). Had the full stories been told, the American people might have perceived the legacies of Ronald Reagan and George H.W. Bush quite differently than they do today.

But the Clinton administration and congressional Democrats dropped all four investigations beginning in early 1993, either through benign neglect – by failing to hold hearings and keeping the issues alive in the news media – or by actively closing the door on investigative leads. Clinton's disinterest in these scandals had mystified some activists in the Democratic base and some investigators who, like Stuart Sender, had watched as the rug was pulled from under these historic inquiries.

After the investigations died, some Democrats in Congress, who had participated in the aborted probes, came under nasty Republican attacks as did journalists who had pursued the stories. Gonzalez had raised the ire of the Bush administration by revealing that Bush and other senior Republicans had followed an ill-fated covert policy of coddling Saddam Hussein, disclosures that had rained on Bush's parade after the U.S. military victory over Iraq in the first Persian Gulf War in 1991. Now, Gonzalez was left looking like a foolish old man, a kind of modern-day Don Quixote tilting at windmills.

The same could be said of Lawrence Walsh, a lifelong Republican who crossed his own party by challenging the cover stories that had shielded top Republicans caught up in the Iran-Contra Affair. In pressing investigations into alleged obstructions of justice, Walsh had found his reputation under *ad hominem* attacks from *The Washington Times* and other parts of the conservative news media for petty matters such as ordering room-service meals and flying first-class. Walsh was so stunned by the ferocity of the Republican defensive strategy that he entitled his memoirs *Firewall* in recognition of the impenetrable barrier that was built to keep the Iran-Contra scandal away from Reagan and Bush. Walsh, too, was dismissed by many Washington insiders as a foolish old man, though the literary metaphor for Walsh was *Moby Dick*'s Captain Ahab, obsessively pursuing the white whale.

But letting the outgoing Reagan-Bush team off the hook hadn't earned the Democrats any measure of bipartisan reciprocity. In spring 1994, in the weeks before the Rodham-Boxer wedding, Clinton had begun to sense the rising tide of political danger that the non-stop attacks against him represented. By damaging Clinton's public image, the Republicans were also undercutting his legislative plans on economic, budget and health-care policies. He was looking for allies and some sympathy.

***

As waiters poured coffee at the wedding reception and Clinton voiced his complaints about the media hostility, Stuart Sender saw his chance to ask Clinton why he hadn't pursued leads about the Reagan-Bush secret initiatives in the Middle East.

"I had this moment to say to him, 'What are you going to do about this? Why aren't you going after them about Iran-Contra and Iraqgate?'" Sender said. "If the shoe were on the other foot, they'd sure be going after our side. ... Why don't you go back after them, their high crimes and misdemeanors?"

But Clinton brushed aside the suggestion. "It was very clear that that wasn't what he had in mind at all," Sender said. "He said he felt that Judge Walsh had been too strident and had probably been a bit too extreme in how he had pursued Iran-Contra. Clinton didn't feel that it was a good idea to pursue these investigations because he was going to have to work with these people. To me what was amazingly telling was his dig at Walsh, this patrician Republican jurist who had been put in charge of this but even the Democratic President had decided that this was somewhere that he couldn't go. He was going to try to work with these guys, compromise, build working relationships."

Sender, like others who had been in the trenches of the national security scandals of the 1980s, thought the retreat on the investigations by Clinton and the Democrats after they won the 1992 elections was wrong for a host of reasons. Most importantly, it allowed an incomplete, even false history to be written about the Reagan-Bush era, glossing over many of the worst mistakes. The bogus history denied the American people the knowledge needed to assess how relationships had evolved between the United States and Middle East leaders, including Iraq's Saddam Hussein, the Saudi royal family and the Iranian mullahs. The corruption was left to fester.

Though the Middle East crises had receded by the time Clinton took office in 1993, the troubles had not gone away and were sure to worsen again. When that time came, the American people would have only a sanitized version of how the country got where it was. Even government officials responsible for the policies would have only a partial history of how these entangling alliances crisscrossed through the deals and betrayals of the prior two decades.

The Democratic retreat from the investigative battles in 1993 would have another profound effect on the future of American politics. By letting George H.W. Bush leave the White House with his reputation intact – and even helping Bush fend off accusations of serious wrongdoing – the Democrats unwittingly cleared the way for a restoration of the Bush political dynasty eight years later.

If investigators had dug out the full truth about alleged secret operations involving George H.W. Bush, the family's reputation would have been badly tarnished, if not destroyed. Since that reputation served as the foundation for George W. Bush's political career, it's unlikely that he ever would have gained the momentum to propel him to the Republican presidential nomination, let alone to the White House.

***

The political future of the Bush family was at a crossroads as Bill Clinton was taking office in January 1993. The Bushes' fate also was largely in the hands of Democrats who controlled both houses of Congress, the White House and the Justice Department. Beyond that, the Democrats had a potential Republican ally in Iran-Contra special prosecutor Walsh. A different set of decisions by the Democrats in those months could have set the nation on a very different course. The Democratic control of the Executive Branch might not have ended after eight years. Conceivably, the calamities of the last four years, including a renewed war in Iraq, might have been averted.

But, in 1993, Clinton and the Democratic congressional leadership concluded that pursuit of these "old" scandals would only embitter the Republicans, make the Democratic Party look vindictive and endanger the bipartisanship that Clinton saw as essential for his domestic policy agenda. The scandals also were complicated affairs, requiring detailed understanding of the underlying facts. Much of what happened had occurred in secret and involved foreign witnesses spread over several continents. The events covered more than a decade in time.

An outsider to Washington, Clinton also didn't comprehend how the nation's capital had changed, how nasty the partisan conflict had become, and how effectively the Republicans were building a media machine that could churn out a coordinated message day-in, day-out, 365 days a year. Besides serving Republican political interests, this machine had taken on a life of its own. With 24-hour news cycles and endless hours to fill on talk radio shows, it needed controversy to survive. When no longer playing defense for the Republicans, the conservative media machine was freed up to go on the offensive. Clinton and his wife would become its primary targets.

Rather than his hoped-for bipartisan cooperation on domestic issues, Clinton soon encountered a solid wall of Republican opposition. In a break with tradition, every Republican in the House and Senate voted against Clinton's budget plan, which included tax increases aimed mostly at the wealthy. Backed with only Democratic votes, Clinton managed to push through his plan by the narrowest of margins. Some Democrats sacrificed their political careers in the House by supporting the tax provisions and Vice President Al Gore was needed to break a tie vote in the Senate. By spring 1994, Clinton's health care plan also was under fierce Republican attack.

"He really did have this idea that he'd be able to work with these guys," Sender recalled about his White House encounter with Clinton. "It seemed even at the time terribly naïve that these same Republicans were going to work with him if he backed off on congressional hearings or possible independent prosecutor investigations. How ironic that he decides he's not going to pursue this when later on they impeach him for the Monica Lewinsky scandal."

***

Though the Bush family wasn't intimately associated with the building of the Republican attack machine that so bedeviled Clinton in the 1990s, the rise of the Bush Dynasty paralleled the growth of what some observers have called the conservative Counter-Establishment.

Pieces of this Counter-Establishment date back to the 1950s and 1960s, but it gained powerful motivation from the political disasters of the 1970s. By the middle of that decade, embattled conservatives were cursing the fates that had plagued them through the Watergate scandal, the U.S. defeat in Vietnam and the exposure of intelligence abuses inside the CIA. Those reversals, particularly the forced resignation of Richard Nixon over Watergate, had devastated the Republican Party. By 1977, Republicans were shut out of the White House and both houses of Congress. Conservatives also viewed the federal courts and the national news media as bastions of liberalism that had aided and abetted the Republican reversals of the mid-1970s.

Watergate also was where George H.W. Bush entered this picture, as Republican National Committee chairman during the latter half of the scandal. A clean-cut former Texas congressman with ties both to Texas oil money and Wall Street financiers, Bush was given the task of containing the spreading political cancer of Watergate after the initial cover-up of the White House role in the break-in had bought Nixon enough time to secure his reelection in 1972.

In his RNC post, Bush tested out some of the tactics that would recur throughout his career. He used counter-disclosures to throw Democratic investigators on the defensive. He pushed Nixon's argument that there was nothing new about the covert political espionage at the heart of the Watergate scandal. Bush also tried to cajole members of the Washington Establishment into agreeing that the disorder from Nixon's impeachment would hurt the nation. But eventually the evidence of Nixon's guilt grew too overwhelming even for the cleverest of tricks to overcome. Bush was one of Nixon's last loyalists to conclude that the President had no choice but to resign and hand over the White House to Vice President Gerald Ford on August 9, 1974.[*]

A little more than a year later, as another flood of scandals lapped around the foundations of the Central Intelligence Agency, Bush got the call again to perform damage control. This time, to keep the dikes around the CIA's most sensitive secrets from giving way, Bush alternately cooperated with Congress in limited oversight and attacked the spy agency's critics for jeopardizing the nation's security. When new scandals emerged on his watch, such as the Chilean junta's assassination of political opponent Orlando Letelier on the streets of Washington in September 1976, Bush again demonstrated his skills, stonewalling investigators and diverting the worst of the damage away from the CIA. His performance during the year made Bush something of a hero to the beleaguered intelligence officers at Langley, Virginia.[†]

With the election of Democrat Jimmy Carter in 1976, conservatives surveyed a bleak landscape left by the rubble of the Nixon resignation and the Vietnam defeat. Some felt desperation that – like a hangman's noose – concentrated their minds. Others saw opportunities. Whatever the motivations, the next four years marked the start of a historic comeback for American conservatism, both in the construction of a new political infrastructure and the emergence of a fighting style that would transform the tone of the nation's political discourse.

Led by former Treasury Secretary William Simon, conservative foundations banded together to direct tens of millions of dollars into strategic investments in a network of think tanks, media outlets and pressure groups that went after perceived enemies in the news media, academia and politics. Though this network would eventually become famous for taking the fight to its adversaries, particularly Bill and Hillary Clinton, its original purpose was essentially defensive. It was built to ensure that the Republican Party would never suffer another catastrophe like Watergate.[‡]

By 1980, the Republicans were fighting fiercely to regain the White House that many conservatives felt was unjustly taken from them in 1976. President Carter struggled with a slumping economy, rising inflation and energy shortages. His reelection campaign also played out against the backdrop of an international crisis with Islamic fundamentalists in Iran holding 52 Americans hostage.

---

[*] See Chapter Three.
[†] See Chapter Four.
[‡] See Chapter Five.

This early experience with Islamic extremism captivated the interest of the American people – and incited their anger. Every day, CBS News anchor Walter Cronkite reported the number of days that America had been "held hostage." ABC's Ted Koppel launched a nightly news show about the hostage crisis that would later turn into *Nightline*. Many world leaders, including Israeli Prime Minister Menachem Begin and the Saudi royal family, felt that Carter was making a mess of policy in the Middle East and elsewhere. Carter was unpopular at the CIA, too, where his CIA Director Stansfield Turner had cashiered scores of covert operatives. Longtime CIA officers, such as associate deputy director for operations Ted Shackley, saw their careers abruptly come to an end.

Shackley and other former CIA officers saw a hope for redemption in Election 1980 as their ex-boss, George H.W. Bush, sought the Republican presidential nomination. Though Bush lost to Ronald Reagan in the Republican primaries, Bush accepted the second spot on the ticket at the GOP convention in Detroit. In merging the two campaigns, Bush brought into the Reagan-Bush team many retired CIA officers who had been part of Bush's political operation. They began putting to use their intelligence skills against Carter. Former CIA officers took on the job of monitoring Carter's attempts to gain the release of the hostages before Election Day. Some of their intelligence reports went through Bush.

In the months before the 1980 election, Carter failed to gain the hostages' freedom. The public's frustration over the humiliating standoff helped turn a close race in October into a Reagan landslide in November. The hostages were finally released just as Reagan was sworn in as the nation's 40th President on January 20, 1981. Bush became Vice President and served as the administration's chief national security expert.

Over the next decade, a mixed bag of intelligence operatives, arms dealers and Iranian officials began to allege that the Republicans had gone beyond monitoring Carter's hostage negotiations and had engaged in parallel negotiations behind Carter's back. Some witnesses claimed that Bush had personally participated in these so-called "October Surprise" contacts. Those clandestine Republican-Iranian relationships allegedly merged by the mid-1980s with the secret Iran-Contra deals.

When those Iran-Contra arms-for-hostage swaps surfaced in late 1986, the Reagan-Bush team suffered its worst scandal of its 12-year reign. Some investigators viewed Bush as the well-protected *eminence grise* behind the secret operations. New suspicions about Bush arose in 1991 as other allegations bubbled to the surface about secret dealings with Iraq's Saddam Hussein during the 1980s. Faced with these investigative threats to continued Republican rule, conservatives mounted powerful rearguard defenses, made possible by the new infrastructure that had been built in the years since

Watergate. Soon, it was the investigators who found themselves on the defensive, often labeled "conspiracy theorists" or worse.[*]

The other Bush-related scandal pending at the start of the Clinton Presidency came directly from Campaign 1992. It had the look of a classic dirty trick out of Richard Nixon's playbook. Desperate for a "silver bullet" to kill Clinton's electoral viability, State Department political appointees pawed through the passport files of Clinton and his mother, looking for information that could be used to challenge Clinton's patriotism. The goal of the search was a rumored letter in which Clinton supposedly sought to renounce his citizenship during the Vietnam War.

The search failed to find such a letter but administration officials noticed a torn corner of Clinton's passport application and cited that to fashion a criminal referral to the FBI, suggesting that someone may have tampered with the file to remove the supposed letter. The existence of the criminal referral was then leaked to the press allowing President Bush to question Clinton's loyalty. However, when the weakness of Bush's case was revealed, the passport search boomeranged on Bush, creating political embarrassment and leading to appointment of a special prosecutor.[†]

If President Clinton's motive for turning his back on those four investigations – October Surprise, Iran-Contra, Iraqgate and Passportgate – was to curry favor with the Republicans, it didn't work. Senator Bob Dole and other Republicans even cited a lack of incriminating findings against Reagan and Bush as justification for aggressively investigating the Clinton administration. The reasoning went that since the Democrats had investigated "bogus" scandals and found no wrongdoing, Republican probes of seemingly minor infractions by the Clinton administration were only a fair turnabout. The conservative news media, which had lambasted investigations of the Republicans as excessive, also flipped sides, arguing that it was the duty of journalists to explore every suspicion raised about the Clintons.

Those investigations of Clinton would consume the next eight years, although ultimately the Whitewater probe would be closed with no charges against either Bill or Hillary Clinton. The suspicions about Vincent Foster's death also would come to nothing. But the confluence of Clinton scandals eventually led to Clinton's deceptive testimony in a civil lawsuit that delved into his dalliance with former White House intern Monica Lewinsky. The House Republican leadership then pushed through an impeachment resolution against Clinton in December 1998, making him the first U.S. President to be impeached since Andrew Johnson after the Civil War. Like Johnson, Clinton prevailed in a trial before the U.S. Senate. But the impeachment will forever stain his legacy.

---

[*] See Chapters Six to Twelve.
[†] See Chapter Seventeen.

The so-called "Clinton fatigue" that the nation felt from the eight years of "scandal" also would take a toll on the candidacy of Vice President Al Gore, who stood behind Clinton during the impeachment but tried to distance himself from the tainted President during Campaign 2000.

***

The Clinton "scandals" – and the damage they would inflict on the Democratic Party – set the stage for the most remarkable dynastic comeback in American history, the ascension of George W. Bush, the eldest son of the 41st President.

During his early adulthood, the younger George Bush epitomized the wastrel son of a successful father. Given every opportunity at elite schools and spared a tour in Vietnam by latching onto a prized spot in the Texas Air National Guard, Bush was better known for his partying than for any accomplishments. He drank heavily though he denied he was an alcoholic. In business, as an oil man, Bush squandered the financial backing of his patrons but always failed up, with new investors – including some from Saudi Arabia – arriving to bail him out of one foundering business after another. Bush also dabbled in politics, losing a congressional race and working on some of his father's campaigns.

When Bush did set his sights on his own political career after his father's 1992 defeat, the younger Bush's principal qualification for office – one might say his only qualification – was his family pedigree. When people had doubts about the younger George Bush, they would comfort themselves with the knowledge that his father was a decent man who could give his son guidance as needed.

George W. Bush's rise also tracked with the arc of the Clinton "scandals." By November 1994, after months of sordid allegations about Clinton's personal life, there was already a public longing for the good old days of the first Bush administration, a kind of buyer's regret for making the switch to the Democrat. That attitude helped Republicans across the country score major victories in the mid-term elections. Bush won the Texas governorship in a surprise landslide over the popular Democratic Governor Ann Richards. National Republicans also gained control of the House and Senate.

In 1998, Governor Bush won a resounding reelection amid the congressional Republican drive to impeach Clinton. Bush soon was aiming at the Presidency with a promise that he would restore "honor and dignity" to the White House. Everyone understood that the pledge was a coded reference to Clinton's sexual shenanigans with Monica Lewinsky.

In Campaign 2000, the increasingly powerful conservative news media – now bolstered by Rupert Murdoch's highly rated Fox News cable network – would again play a decisive role, often aided and abetted by mainstream journalists who intuitively understood that their careers could be helped by slapping around Democrats. The news media's hostility toward Vice President Al Gore also may have reflected a residual frustration over Clinton somehow surviving all the scandal reporting of the prior eight years.[*]

The press corps' tilt toward Bush continued through the disputed Florida election even though Gore built a lead in the national popular vote of more than 500,000. Little media outrage was expressed when national Republicans dispatched to Florida demonstrators who staged a minor riot in Miami that apparently intimidated voting officials into scrapping their recount plans. Led by Bush family lawyer James Baker III, the Bush-Cheney campaign also took its hardball strategies into the federal courts to stop Florida state courts from ordering a recount to determine who actually got the most legally cast ballots. Five conservative Republicans on the U.S. Supreme Court agreed to stop the vote counting, effectively handing Florida's 25 electoral votes and the Presidency to George W. Bush.

Upon taking office, one of Bush's first acts was to clamp down on release of historic records from the 12 years when his father was Vice President and then President.

***

The first three-plus years of the second Bush administration didn't work out with the smoothness and competence that many Washington commentators had expected.

On September 11, 2001, just short of nine months into the second Bush Presidency, 19 terrorists working with Osama bin Laden's al-Qaeda organization hijacked four commercial jets. The terrorists then crashed two jetliners into the World Trade Center towers, one into the Pentagon and one into a field in Pennsylvania, after passengers apparently battled the hijackers for control. The attacks, which killed about 3,000 people, again turned the nation's attention to the Middle East, but Americans had only a limited understanding of the cross-currents of secret history that connected the new President's family to the region's dangerous intrigue. Few citizens had more than an inkling about the Bush family ties to Iran, Iraq and Saudi Arabia – even to Osama bin Laden's family.

By 2001, many chapters of that history had been lost in a haze of conflicting claims, withheld documents and failed investigations. Out of that confusion, it wasn't hard for George W. Bush and his administration to persuade large numbers of Americans to merge the images of Iraq's Saddam Hussein and al-Qaeda's Osama bin Laden into a composite enemy, even though the two men were themselves bitter adversaries in the Arab world. After attacking al-Qaeda base of operation in Afghanistan, the Bush

---

[*] See Chapters Twenty and Twenty-one.

administration turned its attention to Saddam Hussein and Iraq with Bush ordering a U.S.-led invasion on March 19, 2003.

Today, as U.S. and Iraqi casualties from the Iraq War continue to mount, the historical questions still hang in the air: Did the Reagan-Bush administration help Hussein get the chemical weapons that George W. Bush would later cite to justify an invasion? Were secret Republican-Iranian negotiations in 1980 the start of entangling relationships that drew the United States deeper into the Middle East violence? Did the subterranean financial tunnels connecting the Bush family and the Saudi royal family contribute to al-Qaeda's determination to strike at the United States in 2001? Would American history have taken a very different course if the investigations of the Reagan-Bush era had gone forward and the archives of secret documents been thrown open? Did the pattern of suppressing fair-minded inquiry in the 1980s and 1990s contribute to the shallowness of the Iraq War debate in 2002 and 2003?

In a May 23, 2004, article, *Washington Post* associate editor Robert Kaiser observed that the catastrophic developments in the Iraq War, including the international opprobrium from photographs of U.S. soldiers humiliating Iraqi prisoners at Abu Ghraib prison, had finally brought unease to the Washington Establishment. "We have come to a delicate moment in an absorbing drama," Kaiser wrote. "The actors seem unsure of their roles. The audience is becoming restless with the confusion on stage. But the scriptwriters keep trying to convince the crowd that the ending they imagined can still, somehow, come to pass. The authors stick to their plotline even as its plausibility melts away, and why not? For months the audience kept applauding, many of the reviewers were admiring, while many others kept still."

A goal of this book is to explain why so many of Kaiser's reviewers swooned over the second Bush administration's policies for so long while so many other Americans who should have joined a critical debate about war and peace stayed silent. Those reasons can only be understood if viewed in the sweep of events over the past three decades and by examining the secret history of the Bush family dynasty.

Chapter 2: Front Row

My own perspective on how the U.S. government stumbled from the Watergate scandal to the Iraq War comes from more than a quarter century as a Washington journalist. In fall 1977, I arrived in the nation's capital as a reporter for the Associated Press, the leading U.S. wire service, known for its terse, no-nonsense style in stories distributed to print and broadcast outlets across the country and around the world. After three years editing on the AP night desk and covering economic issues on Capitol Hill, I was assigned to the AP's investigative unit in the days after Ronald Reagan's 1980 election.

Given the new administration's interest in Central America, I concentrated much of my initial investigative efforts on those emerging policies. It soon became apparent that there was a widening gap between the reality on the ground and the way the Central American conflicts were presented to the American people. In the region, the conflicts looked like local civil wars, pitting established economic elites and their security forces against leftist peasants and students demanding social change. But in Washington, the conflicts were pitched as Cold War proxy battles between the Soviet Union and the United States.

The brutality of those wars was shocking. Hundreds of people in El Salvador and Guatemala were being murdered each week, although back in Washington, the human rights violations were soft-pedaled unless they were politically useful, such as abuses by Marxist-led guerrillas in El Salvador or the leftist Sandinista government in Nicaragua.

The Reagan-Bush administration was developing a strategy that became known inside the government as "perception management," which set as a national security priority the ability of U.S. officials to manage how Americans perceived events. "Perception management" was a response to the Vietnam War and the student protests that had undermined that war effort. It had become conservative orthodoxy that the combination of negative media coverage of the Vietnam War, massive public protests and crumbling congressional support had prevented the United States from winning in Vietnam. The administration saw as a strategic goal the reversal of what was known as the Vietnam Syndrome, a national hesitancy about using military force in distant countries. As Reagan-Bush officials dipped their toes back into the waters of international conflict, they wanted to make sure that they kept the American people behind them.

Sometimes outright lying was considered necessary. To counter congressional opposition to the CIA's covert support for the Nicaraguan contra rebels fighting to overthrow the Sandinista government, the Reagan-Bush administration misled both Congress and the public. After Congress first restricted and then blocked military aid to the contras, Reagan-Bush officials took the contra supply operations underground in defiance of the congressional ban. White House aide Oliver North – an energetic Marine officer known for his close-cropped hair and gap-toothed smile – was made the point man for a clandestine network of weapons depots and a small air force to deliver the supplies inside Nicaragua. Secretly, North coordinated with CIA officers in the field and with intelligence operatives, such as former CIA officer and Cuban exile Felix Rodriguez who was close to the office of Vice President George H.W. Bush, the former CIA director.

North's operation was hidden from Congress and even some senior members of the Reagan-Bush administration. In 1985, I wrote the first story mentioning the secretive activities of North. Later that year, another AP reporter Brian Barger and I also discovered that some contra units were supplementing their finances with funds from cocaine smuggling, a dirty secret that the administration tried desperately to keep from the American people, who were assured that the "war on drugs" was a top administration priority. Part of the administration's propaganda strategy for Nicaragua had been to portray the Sandinistas as drug traffickers, not the contras.[1]

By mid-1986, Barger and I had pieced together a great deal about North's contra supply operation in Central America, but the Reagan-Bush administration kept denying that North's network existed. One of our stories that had cited 24 sources finally prompted an investigation by the House Intelligence Committee, then headed by Representative Lee Hamilton, an Indiana Democrat with an assiduously maintained reputation for moderation. In August 1986, Hamilton and committee members – including Republican Representatives Dick Cheney and Henry Hyde – met with North in the White House Situation Room. They asked the Marine lieutenant colonel if there was truth to the contra supply allegations. North and his superiors denied the story. That was good enough for Hamilton and the other committee members who agreed that there was no need for further investigation.

After the meeting, a Democratic staff aide called me. "Your story didn't check out," the aide said. "Congressman Hamilton had the choice of accepting the word of honorable men or the word of your sources. It wasn't a close call."

For me, that moment in August 1986 was one of the lowest of our investigation of the secret contra supply operation. It meant that Reagan-Bush officials and their conservative allies in the news media could cite a bipartisan consensus that our stories were wrong. That made it harder to persuade our AP superiors that a continued commitment of resources was justified. Facing an extended assignment to the AP's overnight desk, Barger resigned. Though my job wasn't at risk, I found myself in a journalistic doghouse for pursuing a now-discredited story. Only an unlikely event in Nicaragua several months later shattered this first cover-up, revealing some of the secrets that would become known as the Iran-Contra Affair.

***

On October 5, 1986, a quiet Sunday morning, a C-123 cargo plane, one of the last planned flights of North's secret contra supply network, was rumbling through the skies over Nicaragua. In the previous weeks, the Reagan-Bush administration had succeeded in wresting from Congress approval for a resumption of military and non-military aid to the contra rebels. So North's ragtag air force of aging cargo planes was closing down. The C-123 was preparing to dump one of its last loads of AK-47s and other equipment to contra bands below. One of the crewman, Eugene Hasenfus, had opened the cargo door and was preparing to kick the pallets of guns out of the plane. He was wearing the only parachute on board.

On the ground, a teen-age Sandinista draftee fumbled with a shoulder-fired, surface-to-air missile. He had never fired one before and wasn't sure what to expect. He pulled the trigger and was surprised when the Russian-made missile soared directly at the cargo plane. The missile struck the plane below the wing, sending the plane into a death spiral. Knocked to the floor by the impact, Hasenfus struggled to the door, climbed through it and parachuted to the ground, the plane's only survivor. He was soon captured by the Sandinistas and was taken to Managua. There, before the international press corps, Hasenfus told his story about being recruited into the supply operation managed by CIA operatives working with the office of Vice President George H.W. Bush.

Bush and other administration officials denied Hasenfus's story, but his account, along with documents that the Sandinistas recovered from the plane, began the unraveling of a first layer of the cover-up, confirming the existence of what Barger and I had called the North network. The next month, a disclosure by the Lebanese newspaper *Al-Shiraa* about U.S. arms-trading with Iran ruptured another compartment of secrets. Several weeks later, when evidence surfaced that North had crossed the two covert operations by diverting money from the Iranian arms sales to the Nicaraguan contras, the Iran-Contra scandal was born.

For me, there was a brief period of vindication. Our "discredited" story had turned out to be true. In early 1987, I was offered a job at *Newsweek* and took it. By then, I also was reporting that a new cover-up was underway, with the White House trying to lay the blame on North; his boss, National Security Adviser John Poindexter; and CIA Director William Casey, who collapsed and was dying of brain cancer. That group of suddenly expendable officials became known as the "men of zeal" or "cowboys" in the White

House. The new White House story was that the "cowboys" had operated without the knowledge of the administration's top echelon. My sources were telling me, however, that the evidence actually implicated officials at the highest levels, including President Reagan and Vice President Bush, as well as the CIA institutionally.

Within months of the original Iran-Contra disclosures, the pressure was back on to cap off the eruptions of national security secrets. I began to encounter resistance from senior *Newsweek* editors about pursuing stories that followed the scandal up the chain of command. A similar disinclination soon pervaded the Washington press corps.

A joint House-Senate investigation, co-chaired by Representative Lee Hamilton, also chose not to challenge the "men of zeal" explanation of the scandal. The congressional report in fall 1987 largely blamed North and his cohorts while scolding President Reagan for inattention to what his subordinates were doing. That version was satisfactory for most of the Washington news media, though I kept insisting that a new cover story simply had been substituted for the old one, that a major historical event was being misreported. I pushed especially hard to investigate Bush's role as he sought the Presidency in 1988. My relations with *Newsweek*'s editorial hierarchy soured, especially after Bush secured the White House and access to his inner circle became a high priority for the magazine.

In 1990, I left *Newsweek* and began work on my first book, a look at the declining quality of the national press corps, entitled *Fooling America*. A few weeks into that project, I was approached by the Public Broadcasting System's *Frontline* documentary program. One of *Frontline*'s senior producers, Martin Smith, asked me if I would be interested in examining allegations that the Reagan-Bush campaign had manipulated the 1980 Iranian hostage crisis for political gain, a prequel to the Iran-Contra scandal.

I had largely steered clear of this so-called October Surprise story, recognizing that it held the potential for even worse career damage than the Iran-Contra story. But *Frontline*'s interest did offer a chance to explore one of the intriguing mysteries of the Iran-Contra Affair: the origins of the contacts between the Reagan-Bush administration and the Iranian mullahs. I had come to suspect that the connections between the Republicans and the Iranian leadership did predate the 1984 contacts that were cited by the official histories as the start of the Iran-Contra Affair. So, in summer 1990, I agreed to take the *Frontline* assignment.

The October Surprise investigation would lead even deeper into a world of hidden national security secrets. After Saddam Hussein sent his army into Kuwait in August 1990, our investigation stumbled upon allegations of another set of clandestine contacts – between the Reagan-Bush administration and Iraq. Some of the witnesses claiming knowledge of the October Surprise operation, including Israeli intelligence officer Ari Ben-Menashe, also described secret deals that the CIA had managed between Iraq and third-country cut-outs, such as Chilean arms manufacturer Carlos Cardoen.

Ben-Menashe, whom I first interviewed in a federal jail in Manhattan where he was facing charges of illegal aircraft sales to Iran, was the first witness I had heard mention Cardoen's alleged role in funneling military-related equipment to Iraq. Ben-Menashe, a cocky fellow who was later acquitted of the federal charges against him, told me that the Israeli government had tried to block Cardoen's shipments because they included material that Saddam Hussein could use for chemical warfare. At the time, there was scant corroborating evidence to support Ben-Menashe's allegations.

But my major work for *Frontline* centered on the October Surprise mystery. In the course of the documentary, producer Robert Ross and I uncovered more than two dozen witnesses who alleged that Republicans did negotiate with Iranians behind Carter's back during the 1980 campaign. We also obtained documentary evidence showing that the shipments of U.S. arms to Iran, through Israel, dated back to the earliest days of the Reagan-Bush administration, more than three years before the arms sales that were part of the Iran-Contra Affair.

Though we reached no firm conclusion about whether the October Surprise story was true or not, the documentary, which aired in April 1991, contributed to renewed interest in conducting an official investigation. Also adding to that momentum, former Carter NSC official Gary Sick wrote an Op-Ed piece for *The New York Times* endorsing the October Surprise allegations as most likely true. Over Republican opposition, the House and Senate agreed to undertake limited reviews of the issue, with Lee Hamilton assigned to head the House Task Force.

The October Surprise investigation prompted a sustained attack against the allegations from journalists with close ties to the Bush administration or to the Likud Party in Israel. One of the most aggressive was Steven Emerson, who wrote attack pieces against the October Surprise case for several publications, including *The New Republic*. My old adversaries in senior editorial posts at *Newsweek* also joined the fray, in part, I was told out of personal animosity toward me.

Emerson's *New Republic* article in the November 18, 1991, issue claimed to disprove the October Surprise allegations by presenting an alibi for Ronald Reagan's campaign chief William Casey that would have excluded a trip to Madrid in July 1980 for one of the alleged Republican meetings with Iranians. Supposedly Casey had been at a historical conference in London, according to Emerson's reading of conference attendance records. The same week as *The New Republic* article, *Newsweek* published a matching attack story that also adopted the Casey alibi as the conclusive proof that the October Surprise case was a "myth." Those twin stories effectively killed the October Surprise as a topic for serious discussion in Washington.

At *Frontline*, however, we took another look at the Casey alibi and discovered that Emerson and *Newsweek* were mistaken in their interpretation of the London attendance records. Our key interview was with the historian who spoke at the morning session on July 28, 1980, a time period that was central to the Casey alibi. The historian, Robert Dallek, said he had looked for Casey that morning in the conference room and the Reagan-Bush campaign chief wasn't there. Other American participants agreed with Dallek, effectively debunking the *New Republic-Newsweek* debunkings.

But the fact that the Casey alibi had collapsed was little known outside the small world of people following this complex issue. As far as the larger political-journalistic community of Washington was concerned, the October Surprise story was still "debunked."

For its final report in January 1993, the House October Surprise Task Force cobbled together a new alibi for Casey's whereabouts in late July 1980. Though that alibi was even more unsound than the false *New Republic-Newsweek* alibi, it was added to the mix of supposed proof against the October Surprise allegations. Even last-minute arrival of new evidence supporting the October Surprise suspicions didn't make the Task Force reconsider its conclusions. Hamilton released the House Task Force report, again "debunking" the October Surprise allegations on January 13, 1993.[*]

***

After elaborating on my experiences with the *Frontline* investigation in a book entitled *Trick or Treason*, I left the story behind, I hoped, forever. In 1993, I worked on a *Frontline* documentary about the political crisis in Haiti and spent time in 1994 investigating the strange assortment of allegations about Bill Clinton's past in Arkansas. With the Republican congressional election victory in November 1994, however, I decided that the final weeks of Democratic leadership in the House might be my last chance to inspect the unpublished October Surprise files of the House Task Force. So I scheduled a time to go through what I was told were the unclassified records that had been left behind.

The file boxes were in an office off the Rayburn House Office Building parking garage. After arriving at the office, I was led back to an abandoned Ladies Room where the taped-up boxes were piled up along a wall. When I began opening the boxes, I was stunned to find that a number of "secret" and even "top secret" documents were among the records. In their haste to wrap up business, the House Task Force apparently had failed to separate out some

---

[*] See Chapters Six to Twelve.

of the classified material, much of which buttressed the October Surprise suspicions and contradicted the Task Force's conclusions.

After copying as many of the classified pages as I could, I next wrote up a summary of the material and shopped the paper around to several magazine editors. But I found no interest. The October Surprise story had become such a topic of ridicule by then that it seemed that no one wanted to hear about it even if the evidence included secret government documents of historical significance. By 1995, the attention of the Washington media was glued to "scandals" about Bill Clinton's Whitewater investments and other alleged wrongdoing. There was no space for some revisionist examination of a supposedly discredited story of Reagan-Bush skullduggery.

The recognition that there was no room in Washington journalism for such stories led to the creation of the *Consortiumnews.com* Web site in fall 1995. My eldest son Sam had encouraged me to test out this relatively new medium, the Internet, as a way to put the October Surprise and other unwanted information in the public domain. So, over the years, *Consortiumnews.com* became something of a time capsule for well-documented historical stories with the thought that in the future, some free-thinking readers and maybe even historians might find the information useful. In recognition of how disbelieving many editors had been about the October Surprise files, I dubbed the first series "The October Surprise X-Files." When I ran short of money in early 2000, we put the Web site on a part-time basis. I took a decent-paying job as an editor at Bloomberg News.

In the back of my mind, however, I always thought there might come a time when I should revisit the journalism about the Reagan-Bush era. Then, in early 2004, Kevin Phillips published *American Dynasty*, an unflattering look at the rise of the Bush political dynasty. Phillips, a traditional conservative whose best-known work was *The Emerging Republican Majority* published in 1969, had come upon *Consortiumnews.com* during his research. Our articles about the 1980 hostage crisis had helped Phillips fill in an important gap in his thesis about the high-handedness that the Bush Dynasty took toward the popular will. Phillips cited the "considerable evidence" supporting the October Surprise allegations. He called that information relevant to a "discussion of the Bush family's commitment to the democratic election process," questions that had been raised anew by how George W. Bush blocked a full counting of votes in Florida.

I concluded that the time had come for me to tell the fuller story of the October Surprise mystery as part of a broader account of the political ascension of the two George Bushes, from Watergate to Iraq.

Chapter 3: Surreptitious Entry

It is an iconic moment in U.S. political history: In the early morning hours of June 17, 1972, Frank Wills, a 24-year-old night watchman at the Watergate complex in Washington, notices that a door at the garage level has been taped so it won't lock. Wills calls the Washington Metropolitan Police who catch five burglars inside the offices of the Democratic National Committee. The arrests touch off a historic political scandal, revealing a broad conspiracy by Richard Nixon's reelection committee to sabotage the Democrats and clear the way for a second term. Barely two years after the Watergate break-in, Nixon becomes the only U.S. President to resign from office.

In the three decades since, the comforting conventional wisdom has been that Watergate proved the system works: a free press acting as the people's watchdog, constitutional checks and balances stopping abuses by the executive, the legal process demonstrating that no man is above the law. Political historians also see Watergate as a milestone for government reform: rules limiting donations to candidates, public disclosure of financial conflicts of interest, a system of independent counsels to ensure that sensitive investigations are free of political pressure. In the popular culture – immortalized by the movie "All the President's Men" – Watergate was a case where the good guys – scrappy journalists and principled government officials – won, while the bad guys – led by a sinister and foul-mouthed Richard Nixon – lost. Ever since, the suffix "-gate" has been attached to scandals, big and small.

But Watergate represented another historic marker of a very different sort. It was the beginning of a conservative backlash against what many Republicans viewed as an over-zealous "liberal" news media and misguided congressional "reforms." This reaction turned Watergate into a rallying cry for the birth of a right-wing infrastructure that would come to remake American politics and reestablish Republican dominance in ways that not even the Machiavellian Nixon could envision. Out of the ashes of Nixon's resignation would rise a powerful network of think tanks, attack groups and media outlets, a Counter-Establishment financed by wealthy conservatives determined to protect a future Republican President from "another Watergate." That network's political significance eventually would tower over any good-government reforms that Watergate inspired.

Indeed, three decades after Watergate, money sloshed through the political process to an extent unimagined by Richard Nixon's men. By 2004, money influenced politics not only through donations to campaigns and political parties but more importantly in investments into ideological media and a permanent infrastructure of political operatives. Other Watergate reforms also were negated. In the 1990s, the special prosecutor law was first neutralized as an instrument of neutral investigations – by being put under the control of partisan judges – and then was allowed to die an unmourned death as a case study of misguided reform. By the first years of the second Bush administration, government secrecy also had reasserted itself with a vengeance, with new executive orders keeping even historical documents away from the public and raising doubts that a thorough understanding of recent U.S. political history would ever be possible.

So, the epilogue of Watergate wasn't so much that Richard Nixon and his allies were routed in 1973-74 as that they regrouped – and counter-attacked. Watergate would reveal, too, the early cross-currents within the Democratic Party – between Democrats who favor accommodation with Republicans at almost any cost and those who would fight for accountability even if that provokes partisan bitterness. Though the "accountability" Democrats prevailed in Watergate, the "accommodationists" surfaced during the scandal's early stages counseling an avoidance of confrontation. Over the next three decades, the "accommodationist" wing overpowered the "accountability" wing, even as Republicans grew more brazen in savaging Democratic political leaders.

***

Watergate served as a historical marker in another little-recognized way: It was the personal introduction of George H.W. Bush into the world of Washington scandal, a preview of how he and his family would fend off future scandals. Bush was implicated in an early phase of the White House financial abuses (while seeking a Texas Senate seat in 1970) and later worked to contain the Watergate scandal (as Republican national chairman in 1973-1974). In both episodes, Bush demonstrated the powerful connections that have made him something of a political untouchable, the well-liked, well-bred guy who always gets the benefit of the doubt.

In the early 1970s, George H.W. Bush emerged as one of Nixon's chief loyalists, though a contrast from Nixon in physical appearance, political style and social background. Nixon was the angry outsider, Bush the congenial insider. While Nixon was born to a poor family in rural California, Bush belonged to a family anchored in the clubby world of international finance and national politics. While the hunched Nixon was a man his enemies loved to hate, the rangy Bush was someone many adversaries felt kindly toward. But Nixon and Bush shared the same manipulative view of power.

Nixon notoriously resented people of privilege who got the breaks he didn't, but he was openly fond of Bush, particularly enjoying Bush's deferential side. Bush was an Ivy Leaguer with an Establishment pedigree, but he knew how to take orders. Some Bush watchers traced that characteristic to the subordinate position that the paternal side of the Bush family had to the Walker maternal side. Though the Bushes had achieved moderate success in business and were known for public service, the greater wealth and power had come from the high-rolling Walkers and especially Bush's grandfather, George H. Walker.

The product of English schooling, George Herbert Walker was a St. Louis-based investment banker who founded an investment firm, G.H. Walker and Company in 1900, building it into a major financial player in the Mississippi Valley by 1914. Walker jumped into a new league in 1919 when he teamed up with Averell Harriman of the Harriman railroad fortune. Walker helped Harriman found a new investment banking firm, W.A. Harriman Company, which was backed by the Rockefellers' National City Bank and the Morgan family's Guaranty Trust. Walker also assisted in assembling the Harriman family's overseas business investments, including Germany's Hamburg-Amerika steamship line and mineral interests in the Russian Caucasus.[1] Some of the Walker-Harriman foreign holdings were linked to industrialists behind the rise of Adolf Hitler's Nazi regime.

In 1921, Walker's favorite daughter, Dorothy, married Prescott Bush, a Yale graduate and a member of the school's exclusive Skull and Bones society. Handsome and athletic, admired for his golf and tennis skills, Prescott Bush was a young man with the easy grace of someone born into the comfortable yet competitive world of upper-crust contacts. Three years later, Dorothy gave birth to George Herbert Walker Bush in Milton, Massachusetts.

Lifted by the financial boom of the 1920s, the family of Prescott and Dorothy Bush was on the rise. By 1926, George H. Walker had brought his son-in-law in on a piece of the Harriman action, hiring him as a vice president in the Harriman firm. By the mid-Thirties, Prescott Bush was a managing partner at the merged firm of Brown Brothers Harriman.[2] But Prescott Bush found that these international business interests came with the whiff of scandal. Harriman's investments in Germany turned sour after Japan and Germany went to war against the United States in 1941.

The U.S. government seized the property of the Hamburg-Amerika line under the Trading with the Enemy Act in August 1942. The government also moved against affiliates of the Union Banking Corporation where Nazi financial backer Fritz Thyssen had placed money. UBC was run by Brown Brothers Harriman, and Prescott Bush was a UBC director. In November 1942, the U.S. government also seized the assets of the Silesian-American Corporation, another company connected to Harriman, Walker and Bush.[3]

For many public personages allegations of trading with the enemy would have been a political kiss of death, but the disclosures barely left a lipstick smudge on Averell Harriman, Prescott Bush and others implicated in the Nazi business dealings.

"Politically, the significance of these dealings – the great surprise – is that none of it seemed to matter much over the next decade or so," wrote Kevin Phillips in *American Dynasty*. "A few questions would be raised, but Democrat Averell Harriman would not be stopped from becoming federal mutual security administrator in 1951 or winning election as governor of New York in 1954. ... Nor would Republican Prescott Bush (who was elected senator from Connecticut in 1952) and his presidential descendants be hurt in any of their future elections. It is almost as if these various German embroilments, despite their potential for scandal, were regarded as unfortunate but in essence business as usual."[4]

But the quick dissipation of the Nazi financial scandal was only a portent of the Bush family's future. Unlike politicians of modest backgrounds, the Bushes seemed to travel in a bubble impervious to accusations of impropriety.

George H.W. Bush – also a Yale graduate and a member of the Skull and Bones secret society – would double the thickness of the bubble when he moved his young family to Texas after World War II to pursue a career as an oil man and then a politician. Beyond the layer of protection from the old school ties of the GOP's Eastern Establishment, Bush gained regional backing from the Republicans' expanding base in the Sun Belt. Possibly unmatched by any other U.S. politicians, the Bush family soon could count on support across a varied political landscape, from the tree-lined playing fields of Andover, Massachusetts, to the parched oil fields of Midland, Texas. Few rivals could count on as friendly – or at least as respectful – a reception from so many editorial boards and political organizations across the country as could the Bushes.

***

An admirer of Prescott Bush, Richard Nixon took notice of his son, George H.W. Bush after this scion of the Bush-Walker clan won a congressional seat from Texas in 1966. To Nixon, Bush was a promising and presentable Sun Belt Republican who also knew his way around the corridors of Eastern power. After winning the Presidency in 1968, Nixon pondered how to expand Republican clout in the U.S. Senate and advance his "Southern Strategy" of wresting the South away from the Democrats. In 1970, Nixon selected Congressman Bush as the best candidate to challenge liberal Democratic Senator Ralph Yarborough. To help pay for Bush's campaign, Nixon dipped into one of his slush funds.

The vehicle for funneling money to Bush's Senate campaign was called the Town House Project, a secretive Nixon financing scheme for the mid-term elections so named because the money was disbursed out of a back room at a townhouse at 1310 19th St. N.W., near DuPont Circle in Washington, D.C. *The Wall Street Journal* would later describe the operation as "a dress rehearsal for the campaign finance abuses of Watergate."

The project was run by Nixon's personal lawyer and longtime fund-raiser Herbert W. Kalmbach, whom Nixon once described to White House counsel John Dean as not "a lawyer in the sense that most people have a lawyer." Kalmbach served as Nixon's man to see on the West Coast, operating out of the top floor of the Irvine Towers overlooking yachts bobbing in the Pacific Ocean off Newport Beach, California. Kalmbach watched over Nixon's San Clemente home and filled out the annual tax returns, but mostly he oversaw cash slush funds. In March 1970, Nixon's chief of staff H.R. Haldeman and other White House political advisers decided to set up a fund that would finance House and Senate races of favored candidates. Haldeman tapped Kalmbach to lead the fund-raising with the advice, "get cash whenever you can get it."[5]

Kalmbach, working with Nixon aides Harry Dent and Jack A. Gleason, oversaw the secret operation which pulled in $3.9 million. Kalmbach reported in a confidential memo to Haldeman that Chicago insurance executive W. Clement Stone pledged $250,000 as did PepsiCo Chairman Donald Kendall and Texas tycoon H. Ross Perot. The money went into congressional campaigns in at least 19 states, making it an illegal fund since laws at the time required public disclosures by a political committee that supported candidates in two or more states.[6]

Bush's Senate campaign got $106,000 from the Town House Project.[7] But the Texas Senate race took a surprising turn when conservative Democrat, Lloyd Bentsen, defeated Yarborough in the Democratic primary. Instead of facing a liberal who could be portrayed as out of the Texas mainstream, Bush was facing Bentsen, a man of tall, aristocratic bearing – like Bush – but who possessed a more legitimate-sounding Texas accent. The nomination of a conservative Democrat also took some of the wind out of Bush's fund-raising sails. "Money is not available in the quantities heretofore counted on" from conservative Wall Street sources, wrote Town House Project manager Gleason to his colleague Dent. Bush trimmed his campaign budget to $1.7 million from $2 million.[8]

To the dismay of some Nixon men who favored a negative campaign against Bentsen, Bush's campaign stressed his own positive image as an athletic 46-year-old congressman who bounded down stairs. Bush used the slogan: "He's in step with the Texas of today." The genial tone of the campaign fueled criticism from the Nixon White House. "He refused to allow us to use some very derogatory information about Bentsen," White House political aide Charles Colson wrote to Nixon. "We probably should have forced him to do more." Bentsen won with 53.4 percent of the vote out of 2.15 million votes cast.[9]

When the Town House Project was exposed during the Watergate scandal, Kalmbach, Gleason and Dent were convicted for their roles in the illegal operation. Kalmbach served six months in jail and was fined $10,000. Dent was sentenced to one-month probation, and Gleason got a suspended sentence.[10] Bush acknowledged that his campaign received the $106,000 from the Town House Project, while denying that he had been a direct recipient.[11] Though he was the principal beneficiary of the illegal operation, Bush wasn't charged in the criminal case.

Despite losing the Senate race in Texas in 1970, Bush remained a Nixon favorite. In the days after the defeat, Nixon recommended Bush to be the new Republican national chairman, citing his "enthusiasm and better image," according to Nixon's chief of staff Haldeman. But Haldeman wrote in his diaries that Attorney General John Mitchell objected to the choice of Bush and the idea was nixed.[12]

Haldeman also portrayed Nixon as sensitive about offending Bush over the impending appointment of former Democratic Texas Governor John Connally to be Treasury Secretary, the top-ranking job in the Cabinet next to Secretary of State. Trying to sort out the post-election job changes, Nixon next suggested giving Bush a job in the White House, but this time it was Bush who balked. The defeated Senate candidate requested the United Nations ambassadorship, which Nixon gave him. "This really does work out better, because it gives Bush a more prestigious appointment and a seat in the Cabinet, which will help when the Connally blow strikes," Haldeman wrote.[13] Nixon, however, was not always so solicitous of Bush's feelings. The President would sometimes disparage "Ivy League bastards" in front of Bush.[14]

Ensconced in the United Nations, Bush would consult frequently with Nixon on the President's global strategies of balancing war in Vietnam against opening the doors to China and negotiating with the Soviet Union. Nixon relished these intricacies of world power politics. But his obsession with domestic challenges – his Vietnam War critics and his insecurities about possible electoral defeat – merged as Campaign 1972 grew near. Nixon searched for new ways to destroy domestic adversaries, the likes of former Defense Department official Daniel Ellsberg, who had leaked the secret Pentagon Papers history of the Vietnam War.

After the Pentagon Papers were published, revealing deceptions used to lead the United States into war, Nixon demanded a more aggressive strategy to stop leaks. On July 1, 1971, Nixon lectured chief of staff Haldeman and National Security Adviser Henry Kissinger about the need to do whatever it takes, including break-ins at sites such as the Brookings Institution where Nixon suspected incriminating information might be found about Ellsberg.

Nixon criticized Attorney General Mitchell for worrying about what "is technically correct" in countering those who leaked the secret history.

"We're up against an enemy, a conspiracy," Nixon fumed. "They're using any means. We are going to use any means. Is that clear? Did they get the Brookings Institute raided last night? No. Get it done. I want it done. I want the Brookings Institute safe cleaned out and have it cleaned out in a way that makes somebody else" responsible.[15] "Now, how do you fight this [Ellsberg case]?" Nixon continued. "You can't fight this with gentlemanly gloves ... We'll kill these sons of bitches." Nixon then referred to an obscure White House official named Cooke, who had given Ellsberg some papers when Ellsberg worked at the Rand Corporation. "I want to get him [Cooke] killed," Nixon said. "Let him get in the papers and deny it. ... Get a story out and get one to a reporter who will use it. Give them the facts and we will kill him in the press. Isn't that clear? And I play it gloves off. Now, Goddammit, get going on it."[16]

One of Nixon's schemes for discrediting the Pentagon Papers release was to transform it into a spy scandal, like the Alger Hiss case of the 1940s where Nixon made his national reputation. He saw a role for the successor to the House Un-American Activities Committee, the House subcommittee on internal security. "Don't you see what a marvelous opportunity for the committee," Nixon said on July 2, 1971. "They can really take this and go. And make speeches about the spy ring. ... But you know what's going to charge up an audience. Jesus Christ, they'll be hanging from the rafters... Going after all these Jews. Just find one that is a Jew, will you."[17]

Nixon's men did "play it gloves off." Under Nixon's supervision, a Plumbers unit was recruited, drawing from the ranks of former CIA officers and operatives. Digging for dirt on Ellsberg, the Plumbers broke into the office of Ellsberg's psychiatrist. The secret Plumbers unit that was used to crank down on leaks soon merged with Nixon's reelection strategy. The goal was to cripple or eliminate Nixon's strongest Democratic challengers and smooth the President's way to a second term. The Plumbers were reassigned from national security break-ins to searching for the inside dope on the latest Democratic strategies and other intelligence that could be exploited. Nixon's paranoia would lead his men to Watergate.

**

Three times in May 1972, burglars working for Richard Nixon's reelection committee tried to enter the Watergate complex, an elegant new building with curved exterior lines situated along the Potomac River, roughly equidistant between downtown Washington and Georgetown. The target was the Democratic National Committee, which had rented space there at a bargain price because the Watergate was in a newly developed part of the city. Known for its hotel, apartments and restaurant, the Watergate had yet to catch on as a prime location for offices.

For the Watergate burglars, the third try was the charm. Armed with an array of burglary tools, two of the Cuban-Americans on the team – Virgilio Gonzalez and Frank Sturgis – entered the building through the B-2 garage level. They climbed the stairs and taped open the doors behind them. Reaching the sixth floor where the DNC offices were located, Gonzalez made quick work of the door lock and the burglars were finally inside.

"The horse is in the house," they reported over a walkie-talkie back to team leaders across Virginia Avenue at a Howard Johnson's hotel. The leaders included G. Gordon Liddy, a former FBI agent who had devised the spying plan called Gemstone, and E. Howard Hunt, an ex-CIA officer and part-time spy novel writer. At word that the break-in had finally succeeded, Liddy and Hunt embraced. From a balcony at the Howard Johnson's, James McCord, another former CIA officer and the security chief for the Committee to Re-elect the President known as CREEP, could see the burglars' pencil flashlights darting around the darkened offices.[18]

McCord, an electronics specialist, made his way over to the Watergate and was let in by one of the Cuban burglars. Upon reaching the DNC offices, McCord placed one tap on the phone of a secretary of Democratic National Chairman Larry O'Brien and a second on the phone of R. Spencer Oliver, a 34-year-old Democratic operative who was executive director of the Association of State Democratic Chairmen. While some of the burglars rifled through DNC files and photographed documents, McCord tested the bugs on the two phones. His little pocket receiver showed that they worked.[19]

The choice of the two phones has never been fully explained. O'Brien's might seem obvious since he was party chairman, while Oliver was a well-placed insider in Democratic politics, though little known to the general public. Some *aficionados* of the Watergate mystery have speculated that Oliver's phone was chosen because his father worked with Robert R. Mullen whose Washington-based public relations firm had employed Hunt. The firm also served as a CIA front in the 1960s and early 1970s, and did work for industrialist Howard Hughes, who, in turn, had questionable financial ties to Nixon's brother, Donald. Because Oliver's father also represented Hughes, one theory held that Nixon's team wanted to know what derogatory information the Democrats might possess about money to Nixon's brother from Hughes, evidence that might be sprung during the fall campaign.[20]

After returning to the Howard Johnson's hotel from the Watergate, the burglary team's glow of success faded fast. The Gemstone team discovered that their receivers only could pick up conversations on one of the phones, the tap in Oliver's office. Though upset about the limited information that might flow from that single tap, the Gemstone team began transcribing the mix of personal and professional calls by Oliver and other members of his staff who used his phone when he wasn't there. One of the Nixon operatives,

Alfred Baldwin, said he transcribed about 200 calls, including some dealing with "political strategy," passing the transcripts on to McCord, who gave them to Liddy. The intercepts then went to Jeb Stuart Magruder, CREEP's deputy chairman who said he passed the material to reelection chairman John Mitchell, who had left the Justice Department to run CREEP.[21]

Whatever other mysteries might surround the Watergate operation, one Gemstone goal was clear: to pick up intelligence on Democratic strategies as part of the larger plan to ensure that a weakened Democratic Party led by the least appealing candidate would face President Nixon in November 1972.

How useful the material turned out to be is another point in historical dispute. Since the intercepts violated strict federal wiretapping statutes, the contents were never fully disclosed and the recipients of the intercepts had both legal and political reasons to insist that they either hadn't seen the material or that it wasn't very useful. Magruder said Mitchell personally chastised Liddy over the limited political value of the information. Some of the material was little more than gossip or personal details about the break-up of Oliver's marriage. "This stuff isn't worth the paper it's printed on," Mitchell told Liddy, according to Magruder. Mitchell, however, called Magruder's account "a palpable, damnable lie."[22]

***

Oliver has his own theory about what insights the wiretap on his phone could have given the Republicans: a window into the end game of the Democratic nomination. As it turned out, Oliver was in the middle of the last-ditch effort by Democratic state chairmen to head off the nomination of liberal South Dakota Senator George McGovern.

"The California primary was the first week of June," Oliver recalled in an interview with me 22 years later. "The state chairs were very concerned about the McGovern candidacy," foreseeing the likelihood of an electoral debacle. So they commissioned a hard count of delegates to see whether McGovern's nomination could be headed off, even if the anti-Vietnam War senator secured California's bounty of delegates with a victory in the state's winner-take-all primary.

Other Democratic campaigns had failed to catch fire or blew up in the early months. Secretly, Nixon's reelection team had targeted former front-runner, Maine Senator Edmund Muskie, with dirty tricks like stink bombs exploded at Muskie events, bogus pizza orders and fake mailings that spread dissension between Muskie and other Democrats. In summer 1971, White House political aide Patrick Buchanan had written a memo identifying Muskie as "target A." Buchanan's memo said "Our specific goals are (a) to produce political problems for him, right now, (b) to hopefully help defeat him in one or more of the primaries (Florida looks now to be the best early bet, California, the best later bet), and (c) finally, to visit upon him some political wounds that would not only reduce his chances for nomination – but damage him as a candidate, should he be nominated."[23]

Though knocked from contention in the early primaries, Muskie still had a bloc of delegates in early June as did former Vice President Hubert Humphrey and Washington Senator Henry "Scoop" Jackson. Scores of other delegates were uncommitted or tied to favorite sons. Oliver hoped that his personal favorite, Duke University President Terry Sanford, might emerge from a deadlocked convention as a unity candidate.

"Muskie had some votes though he had been finished off early," Oliver said. "Hubert Humphrey and Scoop Jackson had a lot of votes. Terry had nearly 100 votes scattered over 22 states and including some influential delegates. McGovern was having a hard time getting a majority. The state chairmen wanted to know whether or not, if he won the California primary, he would have the nomination wrapped up or whether there was still a chance he could be stopped."

"The best way to find out was through the state chairmen because in those days not all primaries were binding and not all delegates were bound," Oliver said. "Don Fowler, the state chairman in South Carolina, took the lead in trying to use the state chairmen's network to get an accurate assessment. Most of the information was gathered by me and Margaret Bethea, a member of Fowler's staff. We called every state chairman or party executive director to find out where their uncommitted delegates would go. We were doing a real hard count. We knew better than anybody else how many delegates could be influenced, who were really anti-McGovern. We had the best count in the country and it was all coordinated through my telephone."

So, while Nixon's political espionage team listened in, Oliver and his little team canvassed state party leaders to figure out how the Democratic delegates planned to vote. "We determined on that phone that McGovern could still be stopped even if he won the California primary," Oliver said. "It would be very close whether he could ever get a majority."

After McGovern did win the California primary, the stop-McGovern battle focused on Texas and its Democratic convention, scheduled for June 13. "The one place he could be stopped was at the Texas State Democratic Convention," Oliver said.

A Texan himself, Oliver knew the Democratic Party there to be a bitterly divided organization, with many conservative Democrats sympathetic to Nixon and hostile to McGovern and his anti-Vietnam War positions. One of the best known Texas Democrats, former Governor John Connally, had joined the Nixon administration in 1970 as Treasury Secretary and was helping the Nixon campaign in 1972. Many other Texas Democrats were loyal to former President Lyndon Johnson who had battled anti-war activists before deciding against a reelection bid in 1968.

"There had been a major fight in Texas between the Left and the Right, between the liberals and the conservatives," Oliver said. "They hated each other. It was one of these lifetime things." Between the strength of the conservative Democratic machine and the history of hardball Texas politics, the Texas convention looked to Oliver like the perfect place to push through a solid anti-McGovern slate, even though nearly one-third of the state delegates listed McGovern as their first choice. Since there was no requirement for proportional representation, whoever controlled a majority at the state convention could take all the presidential delegates or divide them up among other candidates, Oliver said.

At Sanford's suggestion, Oliver decided to fly to Texas. When he reached the Texas convention in San Antonio, Oliver said he was stunned by what he found. The Johnson-Connally wing of the party appeared uncharacteristically generous to the McGovern campaign. Also arriving from Washington was one of Connally's Democratic protégés, the party's national treasurer Bob Strauss.

"I'm in the hotel and I'm standing in the lobby the day before the convention," Oliver said. "The elevator opens and there's Bob Strauss. I was really surprised to see him and he makes a bee-line straight for me. He says, 'Spencer, how you doing?' I say, 'Bob, what are you doing here?' He says, 'I'm a Texan, you're a Texan. Here we are. Who would miss one of these state conventions? Maybe we ought to have lunch.' He was never that friendly to me before."

Oliver was curious about Strauss's sudden appearance because Strauss had never been a major figure in Texas Democratic politics. "He was a Connally guy and had no background in politics except his personal ties to Connally," Oliver said. "He hadn't been active in state politics except as Connally's fund-raiser. He wasn't a delegate to the state convention." Plus, Strauss's chief mentor, Connally, was a member of Nixon's Cabinet and was planning to head up Democrats for Nixon in the fall campaign.

Known as a smooth-talking lawyer, Strauss had made his first major foray into politics as a principal fund-raiser for Connally's first gubernatorial race in 1962. Connally then put Strauss on the Democratic National Committee in 1968. Two years later, Connally agreed to join the Nixon administration. "I wouldn't say that Connally and Strauss are close," one critic famously told *The New York Times*, "but when Connally eats watermelon, Strauss spits seeds."[24]

Other Connally guys held other key positions at the state convention, including state chairman Will Davis. So, presumably the liberal, anti-war McGovern would have looked to be in a tight spot, opposed not only by Davis but also by much of the conservative state Democratic leadership and organized labor. "It was clear that 70 percent of the delegates were anti-McGovern, so they very easily could have coalesced, struck a deal and blocked McGovern," Oliver said. "That probably would have blocked him from the nomination."

Oliver told some political allies at the convention, including party activists R.C. "Bob" Slagle III and Dwayne Holman, about the plan that had been hatched in Washington to shut McGovern out of Texas delegates. "They thought it might work and agreed to promote it with the state Democratic leadership," Oliver said. "Bob went to lay out this plan to stop McGovern and I waited for him. (After he emerged from the meeting,) we went around the corner, and he said, 'It's not going to work.' He said, 'Will Davis thinks we ought to give McGovern his share of the delegates.' I said, 'What? Will Davis, John Connally's guy? Does he know that this will give McGovern the nomination?' He [Davis] said, 'We shouldn't have a big fight. We should all agree that everyone gets the percentage they had in the preference. We'll just let it go.'"

Oliver said, "That was the most astonishing thing I had heard in all my years of Texas politics. There's never been any quarter given or any asked in this sort of thing. Seventy percent of the delegates were against McGovern. Why did those die-hard conservatives and organized labor want to give him 30 percent of the votes? I was stunned."

News articles at the time described a convention dominated by an unusual alliance between Democrats loyal to liberal George McGovern and others backing populist George Wallace, though the alliance nearly fell apart when Wallace delegates took to the floor with Confederate flags. After a 17-hour final session, the convention gave 42 national delegates to Wallace and 34 to McGovern, with Hubert Humphrey getting 21 and 33 listed as uncommitted. According to *The New York Times*, the Texas results put McGovern about two-thirds of the way toward 1,509 needed for a first-round nomination.[25]

Although failing at his Texas mission, Oliver continued to pursue his strategy of promoting Terry Sanford as a compromise Democratic nominee. He proceeded to Mississippi where Hodding Carter, a rising star among moderate Mississippi Democrats, agreed to nominate Sanford at the national convention. Oliver then returned to Washington, where he discussed the delegate situation by telephone with Fowler and other state chairmen before traveling to his father's summer home on the Outer Banks of North Carolina.

***

On June 14, back in Washington, the Gemstone team began planning a return to the DNC's Watergate office to install new eavesdropping equipment. Liddy, famous for his tough-guy reputation, was under pressure from higher-ups to get more information, Hunt said later. When Hunt suggested to Liddy that targeting the Miami hotels to be used during the upcoming Democratic National Convention made more sense, Liddy checked with his "principals" and reported that they were adamant about sending the team back into the Watergate.[26]

One person in the White House who was demanding continued vigilance over the Democrats was Richard Nixon. Though it's never been established that Nixon had prior knowledge about the Watergate break-in, the President was continuing to demand that his political operatives keep collecting whatever information they could about the Democrats. "That business of the McGovern watch, it just has to be – it has to be now around the clock," Nixon told presidential aide Charles Colson on June 13, according to a White House taped conversation. "You never know what you're going to find."[27]

Facing demands from the "principals," Hunt contacted the Cuban-Americans in Miami on June 14. The burglars reassembled in Washington two days later. For this entry, James McCord taped six or eight doors between the corridors and the stairwells on the upper floors and three more in the sub-basement. But McCord applied the tape horizontally instead of vertically, leaving pieces of tape showing when the doors were closed.

Around midnight, security guard Frank Wills came on duty. An African-American high school dropout, Wills was new to the job. About 45 minutes after starting work, he began his first round of checking the building. He discovered a piece of tape over a door latch at the garage level. Thinking that the tape was probably left behind by a building engineer earlier in the day, Wills removed it and went about his business. A few minutes after Wills passed by, Gonzalez, one of the Cuban-American burglars, reached the now-locked door. He managed to open it by picking the lock. He then re-taped the latch so others could follow him in. The team then moved to the sixth floor, entered the DNC offices and got to work installing the additional equipment.

Shortly before 2 a.m., Wills was making his second round of checks at the building when he spotted the re-taped door. His suspicions aroused, the security man called the Washington Metropolitan Police. A dispatcher reached a nearby plainclothes unit, which pulled up in front of the Watergate. After telling Wills to wait in the lobby, the police officers began a search of the building, starting with the eighth floor and working their way down to the sixth. The hapless burglars tried to hide behind desks in the DNC's office, but the police officers spotted them and called out, "Hold it!" McCord and four other burglars surrendered. Hunt, Liddy and other members of the Gemstone crew – still across the street at the Howard Johnson's – hurriedly stashed their equipment and papers into suitcases and fled.[28]

***

Oliver was at his father's cottage on North Carolina's Outer Banks when the news broke that five burglars had been caught inside the Democratic national headquarters in Washington. "I heard about it on the television news," Oliver said. "I thought that was strange, why would anybody break into the Democratic National Committee? I mean we don't have any money; the convention's coming up and everybody's moved to Miami; the delegates have been picked and the primaries are over. So why would anybody be in there? I didn't think anything of it."

After returning to Washington, Oliver – like other Democratic staffers – was asked some routine questions by the police and the FBI, but the whole episode remained a mystery. "People were buzzing about it, talking about it, but people thought it was just crazy that anyone would have gone in there," Oliver recalled. In July, along with other Democratic officials, Oliver went to the national convention in Miami, where McGovern barely managed to secure a majority of delegates to win the nomination. After the victory, McGovern loyalists were installed at the DNC in the Watergate offices. Jean Westwood replaced Larry O'Brien as national chairman and focused on unifying the party, which remained deeply divided between the McGovernites and party regulars.

"One of the problems we had was how do you get the state party people to work with the McGovern people," said Oliver, who was one of the officials trying to mend the schism. At a meeting of the Democratic executive committee in early September at the Watergate, Oliver was to give a report about cooperation on voter registration between the McGovern campaign and state party organizations.

"Someone brought me a note that Larry O'Brien called and wants you to call him," Oliver said. "I put the note in my pocket. The meeting went on. They brought a second note and said, 'Larry O'Brien wants you to call.' At the lunch break, I went upstairs to call O'Brien a little after 12 o'clock. I asked to speak to Larry. Stan Gregg, his deputy, came on the line: 'Spencer, Larry's at lunch, but he wanted me to tell you that he's going to have a press conference at 2 o'clock and he's going to announce that the burglars that they caught in the Watergate were not in there for the first time. They had been in there before, in May.'

"I was saying to myself, 'Why's he telling me all this?' He said, 'and they put taps on at least two phones. One of the phones was Larry's and one was yours.' I said, 'What?' And he said, 'the tap on Larry's didn't work. He's going to announce all this at 2 o'clock.'"

After digesting the news of the May break-in, Oliver called Gregg back, telling him, "'Stan, take my name out of that press release. I don't know why they tapped my phone, but I don't want my name involved in it. Let Larry say, there were two taps involved and one was on his. But I don't want to become embroiled in this.' He said, 'it's too late. The press releases have already gone out.'"

Oliver suddenly found himself at the center of a political maelstrom as the DNC moved to file a civil lawsuit accusing the Republicans of violating the federal wiretap statute. "Immediately, I became the object of all sorts of speculation," Oliver recalled. "The worst thing about it was that other people on the national committee were jealous that my phone was tapped, not theirs.

One of the worst was Strauss, who was reportedly saying things like 'I don't know why they tapped his phone. He didn't mean anything. He was an unimportant guy. ' Everybody wanted to be the celebrity victim."

The wording of the wiretap statute, however, made Oliver a legally significant player, since only the bug on his phone worked and his conversations were the ones intercepted. "If somebody put a tap on your phone and if nobody listened to it, then you have no cause of action," said Oliver, a lawyer by profession. "You have to be able to prove interception and use. So I was crucial to the lawsuit."

The statute also created legal dangers for anyone who got information, even indirectly, from the wiretaps. "I realized that anybody who received the contents of the intercepted telephone conversation and passed them on, in other words, the fruits of the criminal act, was also guilty of a felony," Oliver said. "So that meant that if someone listened to my phone, wrote a memo like McCord had done and sent it to the White House or to CREEP, everybody who got those memos and either read them or passed them on was a felon. It was a strict statute. Wherever the chain led, anybody who got them, used them, discussed them, sent them on to someone else was guilty of a felony and subject to criminal as well as civil penalties."

After the Democratic lawsuit was filed, lawyers for CREEP immediately took Oliver's deposition. Some of the questions were trolling for any derogatory information that might be used against him, Oliver recalled. "CREEP asked if I was a member of the Communist Party, Weather Underground, 'were you ever arrested? '" But some questions reflected facts that would have been contained in Gemstone memos, Oliver said, such as "Who is Terry Sanford?"

The FBI also launched a full field investigation of Oliver. "They tried to tie me to radical groups and asked questions of my neighbors and my friends about whether I had ever done anything wrong, whether I drank too much, whether I was an alcoholic, whether I had a broken marriage, whether I had had any affairs," Oliver said. "It was a very intrusive and obnoxious assault on my private life."

Initially, Nixon's Justice Department denied that the bug on Oliver's phone had been installed by the Watergate burglars, implying that the Democrats may have tampered with the crime scene by installing the wiretap themselves to create a bigger scandal. In a television interview, Attorney General Richard Kleindienst said the device on Oliver's phone must have been put on after June 17 because FBI agents had found nothing during "a thorough sweep" of the office. "Somebody put something on that telephone since the FBI was there," declared Kleindienst.[29]

Meanwhile, Democrats encountered solid stonewalls when they tried to crack the Watergate mystery through discovery in the wiretap case. "Our guys couldn't get anybody's deposition; everybody was stalling," Oliver said. "It was clear to me that what's going on was that the Justice Department was fixed, the FBI was fixed, and the only way we were going to get to the bottom of this was to have an independent investigation."

In October 1972, Oliver wrote a memo to Senator Sam Ervin, a moderate Democrat from North Carolina, recommending an independent congressional investigation as the only way to get to the bottom of Watergate, a task Ervin couldn't undertake until the next year. In the meantime, Nixon's Watergate cover-up held. The White House successfully tagged the incident as a "third-rate burglary" that didn't implicate the President or his top aides. On Election Day, Nixon rolled to a record victory over his preferred Democratic opponent, George McGovern, who only won one state, Massachusetts.

***

The McGovern debacle had immediate repercussions inside the Democratic National Committee, where the party regulars moved to purge McGovern's people in early December. "Labor, conservatives, party establishment and others wanted to get rid of the McGovernites and they wanted Jean Westwood to resign," Oliver said. "We had a bruising battle for the chairmanship. It ended up being between George Mitchell [of Maine] and Bob Strauss."

The Strauss candidacy was strange to some Democrats, given his close ties to John Connally, who had led Nixon's drive to get Democrats to cross party lines and vote Republican. Two Texas labor leaders, Roy Evans and Roy Bullock, urged the DNC to reject Strauss because "his most consistent use of his talents has been to advance the political fortune and career of his life-long friend, John B. Connally."[30] Another Texan, former Senator Ralph Yarborough, said anyone who thinks Strauss could act independently of Connally "ought to be bored for the hollow horn," a farm hand's expression for being crazy.[31]

For his part, Connally offered to do what he could to help his best friend Strauss. Connally said he would "endorse him or denounce him," whichever would help more. Strauss "displays in my judgment the reasonableness that the [Democratic] party has to have," Connally said.[32] The fight to oust the McGovernites from the DNC leadership also brought to the fore a group of conservative Democrats, such as Michael Novak and Ben Wattenberg, who would support the Reagan-Bush campaign in 1980 and become known as neoconservatives.

"After a terribly hard-fought battle, Strauss won," Oliver recalled. "Strauss came to the national committee the next week."

Strauss's immediate priority was to give the Democratic Party new direction as it tried to traverse the political landscape reshaped by the Nixon landslide. Strauss's strategy called for putting the Watergate scandal into the past both by moving the DNC out of the Watergate complex and by trying to settle the Watergate civil lawsuit.

"Within a few days of his being there, I was called and told he wanted to see me," Oliver said. "He said, 'Spencer, you know I want to work with the state party chairs, but now that I'm here there's something I want you to do. I want to get rid of this Watergate thing. I want you to drop that lawsuit.' I said, 'What?' I didn't think he knew what he was talking about. I said, 'But, Bob, you know that's the only avenue we have for discovery. Why would we want to get out of the lawsuit?' He replied, 'I don't want that Watergate stuff anymore. I want you to drop that lawsuit.' I said, 'Bob, without me, there is no lawsuit under the law.' He said, 'I'm the chairman and I want you to do it.' I said, 'Bob, I work for the state chairmen's association and I see no reason to do that.' It was very unpleasant at the end."

Oliver also found himself cut adrift by the DNC lawyers who said they had to follow Strauss's orders and back off the Watergate case, though privately they expressed hope that Oliver would find another lawyer and continue pursuing the case, Oliver recalled. "I said, 'I can't afford that.'" Oliver was then studying for the bar, supporting three children and working two jobs (for the state chairmen and for the American Council of Young Political Leaders). Plus, his marriage was on the rocks.

Oliver began a search for a new attorney willing to take on the powerful White House. He faced a string of rejections from other lawyers partly because so many Watergate figures had already hired attorneys at major firms that it created conflicts of interests for other law partners. Finally, at a dinner party in Potomac, Maryland, a personal injury lawyer named Joe Koonz offered to take the case on a contingency basis. "They can't do anything to me," Koonz said, according to Oliver. "I'm a plaintiff's lawyer, a personal injury lawyer. You won't have to pay a thing. If we win, I'll get one-third and you'll get two-thirds, and I guarantee you if I get this thing before a jury, we'll win."

Oliver's success in keeping the civil suit alive represented a direct challenge to Strauss, who continued to seek an end to the DNC's legal challenge to the Republicans over Watergate. While Oliver didn't directly work for Strauss, the national chairman could force Oliver off the payroll. "He couldn't fire me as executive director of the state chairmen's association, but he could cut off my pay, which he did after a big, nasty, ugly fight," Oliver said. "The state chairmen then paid my salary out of their own funds."

Strauss also moved the DNC out of Watergate, despite the favorable terms on the rent and the building's usefulness as a reminder of Republican wrongdoing. "Strauss said, 'I don't care what it costs to move. I want to get this Watergate thing behind us,'" Oliver said. "It was ridiculous. They moved the office across the city to a worse location for less space at more cost. Plus, they lost the symbol of Watergate."

***

While Democratic leaders were debating whether to fold their hand on Watergate, Nixon was reshuffling his personnel deck for a second term. George H.W. Bush's credentials as a Nixon loyalist made him a top candidate for several senior administration jobs. "A total Nixon man – first," Nixon said in a discussion of Bush's future. "Doubt if you can do better than Bush." In one denigrating compliment, Nixon told Bush that he was high on the job lists because the administration needed "not brains but loyalty."[33]

Nixon concluded that Bush would fit best as chairman of the Republican National Committee, replacing Senator Bob Dole, whom Nixon considered too independent and acerbic. "Bush was perfect for the RNC," wrote Bush's biographer Herbert S. Parmet, "whistle-clean, a tonic for the GOP's public image, a nice guy to everyone, but tough. How else could he have built a career in oil and politics? A great combination: respectability and strength, able to firm up the administration's lines of control. He could be handy at the money-raising, too."[34]

With more Watergate troubles looming in federal criminal court (over the five burglars) and in Congress (with Ervin's plans for public hearings), Nixon told Bush, "The place I really need you is over at the National Committee running things." Bush accepted though he was less than thrilled with the new job.[35]

Bush's genial demeanor helped in negotiations with Strauss, a fellow Texan whom Bush also counted as a friend. By mid-April 1973, Strauss appeared on the verge of achieving his goal of putting the Watergate civil lawsuit into the past. "I'm driving into work one day and I hear that Strauss and George Bush were holding a press conference at the National Press Club to announce that they were settling the Watergate case, putting it behind them," Oliver said. "I said he can't settle that suit without me. The Republicans were holding out $1 million dollars to settle that suit, but they couldn't settle it without me."

On April 17, 1973, Strauss disclosed that CREEP had offered $525,000 to settle the case. "There has been some serious discussion for many months" between Democratic and CREEP lawyers, Strauss said. "It has become intense in the past several weeks." Strauss explained his interest in a settlement partly because the Democratic Party was saddled with a $3.5 million debt and could not afford to devote enough legal resources to the case.[36] But two days later, Strauss backed off the settlement talks because Oliver and Common Cause, another organization involved in the civil case, balked. "We haven't the slightest intention of settling short of what we set out to get," said Common Cause chairman John Gardner. "I think that the Democratic National Committee suit and ours are the two that are least susceptible to control."[37]

At a press conference, Oliver declared, "I am appalled at the idea of ending the civil suit in the Watergate case through a secretly negotiated settlement and thereby destroying what may be an important forum through which the truth about those responsible may become known. I do not know what motivated Robert Strauss to even contemplate such a step." For his part, Strauss said he had discussed a settlement with former Attorney General Mitchell "with the knowledge and approval of the Democratic leadership on the Hill after talking to a number of Democratic governors and with eight or 10 members of the Democratic National Committee." Asked if he was compromising the interests of the Democratic Party, Strauss responded, "If I was doing so, I was doing so with a lot of company."[38]

Though in retrospect, the idea of leading Democrats shying away from the Watergate scandal may seem odd, the major breaks in the cover-up had yet to occur. At the time, the prospect that the scandal might lead to Nixon's removal from office appeared remote. (As late as April 1974, Strauss would chastise Democratic governors for calling for Nixon's resignation.[39]) The pattern of prominent Democrats seeking to avoid confrontation with Republicans is also one that would recur in subsequent scandals that threatened the political survival of senior Republicans.

After the public flare-up over the aborted Watergate settlement, the strained relationship between Oliver and Strauss grew even worse. "Strauss started calling around to state chairs, saying 'Did you see what that little SOB said about me? He's accusing me of being a crook.' He really launched a campaign against me."

Oliver said it was not until spring 1973 that he began putting the pieces of the Watergate mystery together, leading him to believe that the events around the Texas convention were not simply coincidental but rather the consequence of Republican eavesdropping on his telephone. If that were true, Oliver suspected, Strauss may have been collaborating with his old mentor Connally both in arranging a Texas outcome that would ensure McGovern's nomination and later in trying to head off the Watergate civil lawsuit. That would not mean that Connally and Strauss necessarily knew about the bugging, only that they had been used by Republicans who had access to the information from the Gemstone wiretappers, Oliver said.

"In my opinion, they were listening to me on that phone do a vote count and they're listening to us start a project to block McGovern's nomination," Oliver said. "They were scared to death that it would be Scoop Jackson or Terry Sanford (emerging as the Democratic nominee). This strategy is about to work and we're about to stop McGovern. Now, how do you block that? Well, the man who Nixon admired the most in the world, who he wanted to be his Vice President was John Connally. And who could block it in Texas? John Connally. Who was the state party chairman? Who controlled the machinery? John Connally's people. No Republican could have done it. Only

Connally. They had to go directly to him because he's the only one who could fix it.

"But Connally wasn't somebody who could be called by just anybody. So I believe what happened was that they went to Connally – Haldeman or Nixon, maybe Mitchell or Colson – but it had to be one of them. They must have briefed him on what they knew, and what they knew is what they got off the interception of my telephone. Nixon wanted Connally to be his successor, but this is in jeopardy if Nixon doesn't get reelected. So Connally may have contacted Will Davis and may have sent Strauss to Texas."

McGovern got his share of the Texas delegates after a marathon session that ended at 3:31 a.m. on June 14, 1972. That same day, according to Hunt, Liddy was told by his "principals" that the burglars needed to return to the Democratic offices at the Watergate to install more eavesdropping equipment. Three days later, the Watergate burglars were arrested.

"Once they were caught, they [Nixon and his men] had to cut off our avenue of discovery, which of course was the civil suit," Oliver said. "I think Strauss may have run for national chairman for that purpose. Strauss wanted to kill the Wategate thing because he may have been part of this conspiracy to help nominate McGovern, part of the conspiracy to cover up the Watergate matter and put it behind us. In desperate fear of exposure later on, he tried to crush me. Somebody told me about a conversation with Strauss when someone said, 'Spencer's never going to give in on the Watergate thing,' and Strauss said, 'When he doesn't have any more income, he'll be a lot more reasonable.'"[*]

***

Nixon's White House had fended off the Watergate allegations through the 1972 election, but the pressure on Nixon built in the early months of 1973. As Republican national chairman, George H.W. Bush was one of Nixon's staunchest defenders. "I don't think for a moment that he condoned it," Bush said of Nixon and Watergate. "No responsible people will believe the

---

[*] Over the next quarter century, Strauss would come to epitomize the national Democratic leader who cultivated friendly relations with Republicans. His friendship with Bush confidante James Baker III was cemented when Strauss headed President Jimmy Carter's failed reelection bid in 1980, while Baker held a top job in the Reagan-Bush campaign. After Carter's loss in 1980, the defeated Democratic President joked to his staff that "Bob is a very loyal friend – he waited a whole week after the election before he had dinner with Ronald Reagan." Strauss also counted himself one of George H.W. Bush's closest friends, accepting an appointment as Bush's ambassador to Moscow in 1991. A senior Bush administration official explained the appointment to *The New York Times* by saying, "The President wants to send one of his best friends" to Moscow. Strauss did not respond to requests for an interview for this book.

President had anything to do with it."[40] But Nixon began to have doubts about Bush's toughness, telling Haldeman on April 20, that Bush is a "worrywart."[41]

Yet as the Watergate scandal continued to spread, Nixon took action himself to pull the plug on some of his closest aides who had protected him by fending off the Watergate suspicions in the months before the election. On April 30, 1973, declaring there would be "no whitewash at the White House," Nixon announced the resignations of chief of staff Haldeman, domestic policy chief John Ehrlichman and White House counsel John Dean. Nixon also shook up the leadership of the Justice Department – replacing Attorney General Kleindienst – because of Watergate taint. Bush hailed Nixon's actions as a "most statesmanlike and courageous appeal to principle."[42] The next day, Bush gushed to Nixon, "I want you to know that Republicans everywhere are strongly supporting you."[43]

As the waves of scandal kept pounding closer and closer to Nixon, Bush loyally positioned himself as the President's breakwater. He used one tactic that later would reappear in his own battles against scandal. He tried to turn the tide against a key Democrat in the case, Senate Watergate Committee's chief investigator, Carmine Bellino, by accusing him of offenses similar to Watergate. On July 24, 1973, Bush released affidavits from two private eyes and a retired police inspector suggesting that Bellino had tried to hire operatives to undermine Nixon's 1960 presidential campaign through clandestine tactics. Those tactics allegedly included putting eavesdropping devices in a Washington hotel where Nixon was preparing for a televised debate with John F. Kennedy.

While saying "I cannot and do not vouch for the veracity of the statements contained in the affidavits," Bush said the alleged bugging of Nixon's debate preparations "could very well have affected the outcome of the 1960 presidential race. The Nixon-Kennedy election was a real cliff-hanger, and the debates bore heavily on the outcome of the people's decision." Bush also said he wasn't trying "to justify Watergate" nor was he trying to disrupt the Watergate investigation. He said he simply was making the information available in the name of "fair play." Still, the obvious point was that, if true, the Democrats were guilty of the same kind of electronic spying that they were alleging in the Watergate break-in.[44]

Bush's allegations proved tenuous and murky, however. One affidavit was from John W. Shimon, a retired Washington police inspector who said another man, Oliver Angelone, had asked him to arrange access to two floors of the hotel prior to Nixon's arrival so the bugs could be planted. Shimon said Angelone claimed to work for Bellino, who was then an aide to the Kennedy campaign. Shimon said he refused Angelone's request.

In a second affidavit, private investigator John W. Leon said he was retained by Bellino during the 1960 campaign "to infiltrate the operations" of Albert B. "Ab" Hermann, a longtime Republican National Committee staff aide. Failing that, Leon said he watched Hermann's office through field glasses and aimed an electronic ear at his window. Leon also said another private eye, Edward Murray Jones, tapped the telephones of three ministers at the Mayflower Hotel in Washington in fall 1960 because Bellino suspected they were distributing anti-Catholic literature against Kennedy. Leon said he was "confident" that Angelone and private eye Jones "had bugged the Nixon space or tapped his phone prior to the television debate." But Jones's affidavit said he participated only in physical surveillance of "subjects" in downtown Washington, not electronic surveillance.[45]

In an interview with *The Washington Post* in 1973, Angelone denied Shimon's story about trying to bug Nixon's debate preparations. Angelone said his work for Bellino related to another issue: tracing the source of anti-Catholic mail about Kennedy that was circulating during the 1960 campaign. The *Post* also reported that former police inspector Shimon and private eye Leon had been convicted in 1964 in a wire-tapping case after a lawyer for El Paso Natural Gas Company found an electronic bug under a coffee able in his suite at the Mayflower. Follow-up on Bush's allegations against Bellino also were complicated by the fact that Leon had died 11 days before Bush released the affidavits and Jones had moved to the Philippines.[46]

For his part, Bellino "categorically and unequivocally" denied that he had "ever ordered, requested, directed or participated in any electronic surveillance whatsoever in connection with any political campaign." Bellino said only that he once tried – and failed – to have a former Republican congressman tailed to a ministerial conference. "By attacking me on the basis of such false and malicious lies," Bellino told reporters outside a Senate Watergate hearing, "Mr. Bush has attempted to distract me from carrying out what I consider one of the most important assignments of my life. I shall continue to exert all my efforts to ascertain the facts and the truth pertaining to this [Watergate] investigation."[47]

Though Bush's allegations had only a tenuous relevance to the Watergate investigation, they did force the Watergate committee to appoint a special subcommittee to investigate Bellino. The panel later released an investigative memo that found no evidence to support the allegations of electronic eavesdropping. Columnists Jack Anderson and Les Whitten revisited the case in early 1976 when Bush was awaiting Senate confirmation as CIA director. "As the Republican National Committee chairman during the Watergate uproar, Bush did a little extracurricular spying on the Senate Watergate Committee's respected chief investigator, Carmine Bellino," Anderson and Whitten wrote. "To get the evidence, Bush relied upon an undercover operative named John Buckley – a Damon Runyon character whom the [subcommittee's] memo identifies 'as a political spy with the code name Fat Jack.' Buckley had gained a measure of notoriety earlier for directing a snooping operation against Senator Edmund S. Muskie."

Anderson and Whitten wrote that although Bush's affidavits didn't lead to a conclusion against Bellino, they did force creation of the special subcommittee, "which wasted hundreds of hours investigating Bush's alleged findings." The subcommittee's investigative memo also noted that after getting the ball rolling, "Bush ducked out on the Senate investigation," Anderson and Whitten wrote. The memo said Bush "was not allowed by (the Republican Party counsel Jerris) Leonard to be questioned by staff members." By avoiding questioning, Bush protected himself against queries about his motives or the circumstances behind his decision to put Bellino on the defensive.[48] Bush's avoidance of formal testimony would become a pattern over the years.

During his time as RNC chief, Bush drew criticism, too, from Nazi-hunters for tolerating Nixon's plans to absorb anticommunist émigrés into the Republican Party structure despite allegations that many had collaborated with Hitler's war machine. "Bush's tenure as head of the Republican National Committee exactly coincided with Laszlo Pasztor's 1972 drive to transform the Heritage Groups Council into the party's official ethnic arm," wrote former Justice Department official John Loftus and his associate Mark Aarons. "The groups Pasztor chose as Bush's campaign allies were the émigré Fascists whom (CIA Director Allen) Dulles had brought to the United States. It seems clear that George Bush, as head of the Republican National Committee in 1972, must have known who these 'ethnics' really were. Columns by Jack Anderson and others had already made it clear, in 1971, that Nixon was a little too close to the Fascist groups. The Nazis for Nixon problem was one of those scandals that Bush inherited when he took over the Republican National Committee."[49]

***

But the most pressing issue before Bush was managing the fallout from the seemingly endless string of Watergate explosions, as one investigative bomb after another rocked Washington. The scandal took a dangerous turn for Nixon when the Senate Watergate Committee discovered that the President had installed a taping system to record his conversations. Through torturous maneuvering in the early months of 1974, Nixon tried to keep control of the tape recordings while offering limited transcripts to investigators.

As Democratic demands for Nixon's resignation mounted, Democratic National Chairman Strauss was one of the party's dissenters. At a meeting of Democratic governors in Chicago on April 22, 1974, Strauss called for toning down the rhetoric to avoid future retribution from Nixon and the Republicans. "I ask you what horrors await this nation if he is able to portray himself as a resigned martyr," Strauss declared.[50] (The DNC also agreed to settle the Watergate lawsuit in 1974. Though the precise terms were sealed, Strauss said publicly that the Democrats were willing to accept about $1.25

million.[51] Oliver eventually settled separately with the Republicans, with those terms also under court seal.)

Throughout the extended struggle over the tapes, Bush remained Nixon's loyal cheerleader. On April 29, 1974, for instance, Nixon offered to supply selected transcripts of White House tape recordings to the House Judiciary Committee for its impeachment proceedings. Bush praised Nixon's proposal as "a bold move" and "a major step in putting the impeachment proceedings behind us and in laying to rest the charges against the President."[52] Bush said the President had the right to protect "private and highly confidential talks with some of his closest aides."

But the U.S. Supreme Court compelled Nixon to surrender the tapes, which established beyond doubt that Nixon had participated in a criminal conspiracy to obstruct investigations into the Watergate scandal. On August 5, 1974, the White House released a tape from June 23, 1972 – six days after the Watergate arrests – showing that Nixon had ordered the FBI investigation stopped for political reasons. Bush began to recognize the inevitable. He was one of about 10 senior Republicans shown the transcripts before they were made public. Political adviser Dean Burch told congressional liaison William Timmons about Bush's reaction: "He broke out into assholes and shit himself to death," Burch said about Bush.[53]

Two days later, Bush delivered a letter to Nixon recommending that he resign. "I expect in your lonely embattled position this would seem to you an act of disloyalty from one you have supported and helped in so many ways," Bush wrote. "Until this morning, resignation has been no answer at all, but given the impact of the latest development, and it will be a lasting one, I now firmly feel resignation is best for this country, best for this President."[54] That same day, Nixon told his family he intended to quit. The next night, Nixon gave a farewell address to the nation. On August 9, Nixon resigned, handing the presidency to Gerald Ford.

Some Republican insiders viewed Bush as a possible choice to become Ford's Vice President. But *Newsweek* disclosed in its August 26, 1974, issue that Bush's 1970 senatorial campaign had received $106,000 from the Watergate forerunner, the Town House Project. Of that money, $40,000 had not been reported, a potential violation of the Corrupt Practices Act. The matter came under the purview of Watergate special prosecutor Leon Jaworski, a Texas lawyer who was considered close to Bush. Jaworski eventually accepted the Bush campaign's explanation that it had been unclear the money was going to Bush and that therefore it was left off his finance report. Jaworski gave Bush a "full clearance" on any wrongdoing, though by then Bush's chance of getting Ford's vice presidential nod had passed. That job instead went to Nelson Rockefeller.[55]

The storm over Nixon's scandals might have sunk the career of a politician without the ballast of Bush's many influential supporters. But Bush soon steadied himself and was back on course. Ford offered Bush a posting as ambassador in the U.S. liaison office in China, which sent Bush literally to the opposite side of the world from the Watergate mess. He also wasn't left holding the political bag when the Republicans were trounced in congressional elections of November 1974.

***

The Nixon resignation in 1974 and the collapse of the South Vietnamese government in 1975 were not only watershed historical events. They also were low water marks for the Republican/conservative movement in the United States. George H.W. Bush assessed the political situation from his post in Beijing. "As he thought about it in 1975, it was hard to figure the duration of the post-Watergate damage," wrote Bush biographer Parmet.[56]

"Watergate was the most devastating blow that any political party has suffered in modern history," Spencer Oliver told me in an interview in 1992 when he was serving as chief counsel for the House International Affairs Committee. "The President was driven out of office. The Republicans were repudiated at the polls. They took enormous losses in Congress. What they learned from Watergate was not 'don't do it,' but 'cover it up more effectively.' They have learned that they have to frustrate congressional oversight and press scrutiny in a way that will avoid another major scandal."

Chapter 4: Containing the Secrets

Halfway around the world in China, George H.W. Bush soon found his skills at defusing and deflecting scandal in demand again back in Washington.

After the scandals over the Pentagon Papers and Watergate, investigators in the press and in Congress turned their attention to the Central Intelligence Agency. Richard Nixon had put the CIA in the line of fire by trying to shield himself from Watergate by claiming the probe must be curtailed to protect national security secrets involving the CIA. The collapse of that cover story made the CIA a tempting target for investigators interested in other abuses of U.S. government power. After a quarter century fighting the clandestine battles of the Cold War behind a screen of secrecy, the CIA suddenly found itself exposed to public scrutiny.

The rupture of secrets began the month after Nixon's resignation with disclosures by investigative reporter Seymour Hersh in *The New York Times* that the Nixon administration had authorized $8 million for a clandestine operation to "destabilize" the democratically elected Marxist government of Salvador Allende in Chile. The CIA-sponsored chaos from 1970 to 1973 ended in a bloody coup with General Augusto Pinochet seizing power and Allende shot to death as Pinochet's forces stormed the Presidential Palace. Thousands of political dissidents – including Americans and other foreigners – were rounded up and executed. The CIA initially had denied any role in the coup. But CIA Director William Colby revised that account, acknowledging that the agency had misled Congress about the destabilization project, though Colby continued to insist that the CIA had not organized the coup.

Other embarrassing CIA disclosures followed, including articles about assassination plots against foreign leaders and reports of drug experimentation on unwitting subjects. In December 1974, *The New York Times* published perhaps the most sensational of the allegations, another Hersh exposé about illegal CIA spying on U.S. anti-war protesters and other dissidents. Hersh reported that the CIA collected files on 10,000 American citizens and engaged in break-ins, wiretaps and mail openings, despite its charter prohibiting domestic operations. Colby said the story "triggered a firestorm." It fed off the tinder-dry kindling of historical resentments against the arrogant CIA[1]

Colby's strategy of relative openness with Congress in acknowledging CIA misdeeds distressed many conservative Republicans and prompted

President Ford to fire Colby as CIA director. Donald Rumsfeld, Ford's Secretary of Defense, recommended Bush as Colby's replacement. In a July 1975 memo to Ford, Rumsfeld praised Bush's qualifications as a man with a keen political sense and friends in the intelligence community. Though Rumsfeld anticipated that Bush would come under fire for the "undesirable political cast" from his tenure as Nixon's Republican national chairman, the Defense Secretary said Bush's political savvy could prove useful in fending off attacks on the CIA. Bush's candidacy was helped, too, by the fact that the prime alternative candidate, former Attorney General Elliot Richardson, was opposed by Secretary of State Henry Kissinger, who was worried that Richardson would prove too independent of the Executive Branch.[2] Kissinger still had many secrets to keep.

Ford took Rumsfeld's recommendation and nominated Bush, who accepted with some reluctance because of the potential damage the job could cause his political ambitions. But there was little doubt that Bush had the acumen to know how to handle sensitive issues and how to put critics on the defensive. His Establishment contacts could be counted on, too, to assist in quelling any choppy waves of CIA scandals that might otherwise disrupt Ford's electoral course toward November 1976.

The choice of Bush, however, ran into immediate opposition from Democrats who were demanding congressional oversight of the U.S. intelligence community. The CIA had long functioned beyond the institutional purview of Congress, except for some informal briefings that Presidents would grant a few senior committee chairmen. Since Bush's most prominent political job had been to protect Richard Nixon's flanks in Watergate, Democrats questioned whether Bush would see his new job as protecting Nixon's successor from damaging disclosures. Democrats also worried that Bush might use his position at the CIA to shape intelligence analyses in ways pleasing to his political allies. Both concerns proved prescient.

"We need a CIA that can resist all the partisan pressures, which may be brought to bear by various groups inside and outside government," said Senator Frank Church of Idaho, who was spearheading the Senate's CIA investigations. Church said he doubted Bush would face down President Ford if he needed something from the CIA in an election year.[3] "It is one thing to choose an individual who may have had political experience, say someone like Elliot Richardson or John Sherman Cooper, two men whose whole public life tended to demonstrate a proven independence as a muted partisan background, and quite another to choose someone whose principal political role has been chairman of the Republican National Committee," Church said. In a televised interview on CBS's "Face the Nation," Church stressed that point again. "Whoever is chosen should be one who has demonstrated a capacity for independence, who has shown he can stand up to principle at the cost of public office," the senator said.[4]

Given the perception during the "détente" days of the mid-1970s that the Cold War was ending, another question about Bush's fitness for the job was whether he had the creativity to redirect the CIA in addressing new challenges. "Mr. Bush will encounter an agency that, nearly everyone agrees, has a vital national security role, but is being asked to set out on a new, post-Cold War tack," wrote Nicholas M. Horrock of *The New York Times*. "The agency will have to concentrate on intelligence gathering and analysis and not on secret wars and assassination plots."[5] At least, that was the thinking in 1975.

Returning from China, Bush turned his political charms on senators whose votes he needed for confirmation. In private meetings, he assured them that he would put politics aside and uphold the awesome duties of running the nation's wide-ranging intelligence community. But skepticism remained. During his confirmation hearings, Bush faced a hypothetical question about whether he would give President Ford political dirt about a challenger if requested. Bush answered, "If I were put in that kind of position where you had a clear moral issue, I would simply say no. I have the advantages as everyone on this committee of 20-20 hindsight – that this agency must stay in the foreign intelligence business and must not harass American citizens . ... I really believe, I am putting politics behind me on this." Bush's nomination was approved on a 64-27 vote. On January 30, 1976, he was sworn in at CIA headquarters by Supreme Court Justice Potter Stewart, a close friend.[6]

Speaking at his swearing in, Bush told an audience of CIA officers that he was on their side. He vowed to rein in public disclosures about the CIA and take the offensive against political enemies who exposed secrets that damaged CIA operations. Bush promised to take steps to protect the identity of covert agents who risk their lives "only to have some people bent on destroying this agency expose their names." Bush declared, "This must stop." Several weeks earlier, gunmen had murdered Richard Welch, the CIA's station chief in Greece.[7]

***

When George H.W. Bush took over the CIA, the agency's Old Boys network had been rattled more than at any time in the CIA's quarter century as the secret foreign policy instrument of Presidents. The aging CIA officers – many whom had been with the spy agency since its creation in 1947 – viewed themselves as the protectors of the most vital U.S. national security interests. These intelligence professionals saw their duties as vital enough to justify operating outside the constraints of normal government rules, even beyond conventional morality. They did what they deemed they had to do, certain that they knew best. From Cuba to Iran, from Guatemala to Laos, they had cut deals with unsavory leaders; sponsored coups; spread propaganda and disinformation; and neutralized adversaries, either with lies or, when necessary, by violent means. As legendary CIA officer Miles Copeland was fond of saying, "They were the CIA within the CIA," the inner-most core of the U.S. security defenses.

As the new age of intelligence oversight dawned in 1976, however, the proud agency was often the butt of jokes about crazy spy shenanigans. Many of the CIA spooks looked to George H.W. Bush to refurbish their image and turn the table on their critics.

By all accounts, George H.W. Bush took the job of defending the CIA very seriously. Once in office, Bush directed counter-attacks against not just anti-CIA activists, who were publishing the names of agents, but against a broad range of public disclosures. Bush rallied CIA supporters on Capitol Hill to block the official release of classified sections of a report on the CIA by a panel headed by Congressman Otis Pike, a New York Democrat. The Ford administration warned that Congress was endangering CIA "sources and methods" by publishing the report. The strategy worked, leading to a rejection of the report's release by a 2-to-1 margin in the Democratic-controlled House. Repudiated even by many members of his own party, Pike called the vote a "travesty of the whole doctrine of separation of powers." Bitterly, he said the vote made the panel's work "an exercise in futility."[8]

The congressional decision against releasing the Pike report put CBS correspondent Daniel Schorr in a bind, since he found himself the only journalist to have obtained an actual copy of the full report. Schorr decided that he had no choice but to place the information in the public domain. "Not to publish was to me the unacceptable decision," Schorr said. "To try to arrange publication was the natural duty of a reporter." Schorr told his bosses at CBS that "we owe it to history to publish it." CBS executives, however, were already growing sensitive to the political backlash against disclosure of national security secrets. There were also allegations of operational alliances between the CIA and CBS. Former CBS News President Sig Mickelson said two ex-CBS stringers had worked for the CIA with the approval of CBS Chairman Bill Paley, an allegation that Paley denied.[9]

CIA Director Bush also was working his Establishment contacts behind the scenes. He arranged a meeting with Paley. "If CBS was not, at this point, part of the answer to suppression of CIA secrets, was CBS perhaps part of the problem?" Schorr wondered. CBS's disinterest in releasing the Pike report led Schorr to slip the document to the *Village Voice* newspaper, which trumpeted its exclusive under the headline: "The CIA Report the President Doesn't Want You to Read."

The leak touched off a deluge of criticism against Schorr as a representative of "irresponsible" journalism. "The media's shift in attention from the report's charges to their premature disclosure was skillfully encouraged by the Executive Branch," wrote author Kathryn Olmstead. "[Mitchell] Rogovin, the CIA's counsel, later admitted that the Executive

Branch's 'concern' over the report's damage to national security was less than genuine. 'No one really felt that Western Civilization was at risk.'"[10] The controversy led to Schorr's firing at CBS and the delivery of a powerful message on the limits that the Ford-Bush team would tolerate in the disclosure of CIA secrets.

In the months that followed, the Ford administration pressed its advantage. Ford announced an intelligence reorganization that incorporated only limited reforms, such as a prohibition on assassinations, but he legalized some other questionable activities, such as spying on domestic targets when there was suspicion of foreign espionage. Overall, the CIA came out of Ford's revision as having stronger powers of secrecy, rather than weaker ones. Church and Pike criticized Ford's CIA reform package as a move in the wrong direction. Ford also proposed a bill, strongly supported by Bush, seeking jail terms for government employees who disclosed intelligence "sources and methods" to journalists and other people unauthorized to have the information.[11]

Bush's success in parrying the thrust of the congressional and journalistic investigators won the CIA director admiration at Langley. Bush also earned praise for exercising a light but firm management touch, according to more than a dozen CIA veterans I interviewed about Bush's year at the agency.

"For that period, Bush did a remarkable job," said Theodore Shackley, a senior official in the clandestine division. "He was very warm, very human, very interested. You could get in to see him without difficulty."

John Horton, another senior CIA official, said Bush "was good for morale" at a time when CIA employees felt they were looked down on by many of their countrymen. "He didn't treat them like animals, which they weren't," Horton said.

Thomas Polgar, who was then CIA station chief in Mexico, called Bush "very charming, personable, very friendly, very enthusiastic about everything [but] never with a direct hand in operations. He was more like the Queen of England. He ruled but he didn't govern."[12]

Bush demonstrated his solidarity with embattled Langley veterans by asking at one meeting, "What are they trying to do to us?"[13]

***

While Bush quieted criticism of the CIA, Ford still recognized the daunting political challenges ahead. The plain-talking former college football player had hurt his political standing with many voters by issuing an unconditional pardon of Richard Nixon. Ford said his action was needed to end "our long national nightmare." But many Americans saw the pardon as more proof that the well-connected got special favors and that indeed some men were above the law.

Still, Ford, a centrist Republican from Michigan, was reasonably well positioned to overcome any Democrat who might emerge from a generally weak field of candidates. That field included the brainy former Georgia Governor Jimmy Carter; Senator Henry "Scoop" Jackson, a hard-line Cold Warrior; and Senator Church, who had chaired the CIA investigations. Another threat, however, loomed on Ford's Republican right from former California Governor Ronald Reagan, an ex-movie star who viewed the Nixon-Ford détente strategy toward the Soviet Union as foolhardy.

In the opinion of the Reagan Republicans and many of the rising neoconservatives around the Scoop Jackson campaign, the Soviet Union was not the foundering superpower seeking any port in the storm, as some CIA analysts believed. Instead, to these conservatives, the Soviet Union was an ascendant colossus pursuing a ruthless strategy of paralyzing the United States with an offensive nuclear threat while deploying guerrillas, terrorists and other so-called asymmetrical forces to weaken, surround and ultimately defeat the United States. Instead of seeing the Soviet Union as some bloodied, outmatched boxer staggering back to his corner, these conservatives viewed Moscow as a powerful and clever adversary piling up points on the way to a technical knockout.

The influential conservatives – led by the likes of Richard Pipes, Paul Nitze, William Van Cleave, Max Kampelman, Eugene Rostow, Elmo Zumwalt and Richard Allen – claimed that the CIA's Soviet analysts were ignoring Moscow's strategy for world domination. In essence, the conservatives were saying the CIA analysts had woefully misunderstood the threat posed by its primary intelligence target: the Soviet Union. This political assault challenged a founding principle of the CIA's intelligence assessments – objective analysis.

Since its creation in 1947, the CIA had taken pride in maintaining an analytical division that stayed above the political fray. The CIA analysts – confident if not arrogant about their intellectual skills – prided themselves on bringing unwanted news to the President's door. Those reports included an analysis of Soviet missile strength that contradicted John F. Kennedy's "missile gap" rhetoric and the debunking of Lyndon Johnson's assumptions about the effectiveness of bombing in Vietnam. While the CIA's operational division often got itself into trouble with risky schemes, the analytical division maintained a fairly good record of scholarship and objectivity.

But that tradition came under attack in 1976 with the conservative challenge to the CIA's strategic intelligence on the Soviet Union. The conservatives saw the CIA's tempered analysis of Soviet behavior as the underpinning of Kissinger's détente strategy, the gradual normalizing of relations with the Soviet Union. Détente was, in effect, a plan to negotiate an end to the Cold War or at least its most dangerous elements. It signaled not only a possible reduction in East-West tensions but held out the promise of budget savings by eliminating the need for expensive new weapons programs. Détente, therefore, threatened many powerful interests around Washington.

The CIA's view of a tamer Soviet Union had influential enemies inside Gerald Ford's administration. Hard-liners, such as William J. Casey, John Connally, Clare Booth Luce and Edward Teller, sat on the President's Foreign Intelligence Advisory Board. The PFIAB first raised the idea of letting a team of conservative outsiders inside the CIA to conduct a competitive threat assessment in 1975, but CIA Director Colby shot down the plan by arguing that a new national intelligence estimate was underway and would be disrupted. "It is hard for me to envisage how an *ad hoc* 'independent' group of government and non-government analysts could prepare a more thorough, comprehensive assessment of Soviet strategic capabilities – even in two specific areas – than the intelligence community can prepare," Colby said.[14]

In 1976, with Bush as the new CIA director, the political situation had changed. In March, facing the Reagan challenge from the Right, Ford ordered his White House aides "to forget the use of the word détente." The same month, Allen, Kampelman, Nitze, Rostow and Zumwalt created the "Committee on the Present Danger" to warn the public of the "growing Soviet threat." Putting another scare into the Ford campaign, Reagan pulled off an upset in the North Carolina primary on March 23.[15]

Ford was ready to toss the conservatives a bone by giving them access to the CIA's raw data and permission to prepare a competing analysis of Soviet power. But the project represented a test for George H.W. Bush. As a CIA director who considered himself a defender of the agency's interests, he would have to undercut the proud analytical division. But as a Republican with political ambitions, he – like Ford – needed to win some points with an increasingly influential bloc of Republicans, those who wanted a more confrontational approach toward the Soviet Union.

"Although his top analysts argued against such an undertaking, Bush checked with the White House, obtained an O.K. and by May 26 [1976] signed off on the experiment with the notation, 'Let her fly!!,'" wrote researcher Anne Hessing Cahn after reviewing documents released in response to a Freedom of Information Act request.[16]

Bush offered the rationale that the conservative analysts, known as Team B, would represent an intellectual challenge to the CIA's official assessments. His rationale, however, assumed that Team B didn't have a preset agenda to fashion a worst-case scenario for launching a new and intensified Cold War. To fill out Team B's roster, Harvard professor Pipes picked other like-minded conservatives, including arms negotiator Paul H. Nitze; arms control specialist Paul Wolfowitz; and General Daniel O. Graham, who had been director of the Defense Intelligence Agency.

Not surprisingly, the hard-liners concluded that their notions about Soviet capabilities and intent were correct. "The principal threat to our nation, to world peace and to the cause of human freedom is the Soviet drive for dominance based upon an unparalleled military buildup," wrote three Team B members: Pipes, Nitze and William Van Cleave. Access to secret CIA data gave Team B extra credibility in challenging the assessment of CIA professionals. [17]

According to this conservative counter-analysis, the Nixon-Kissinger détente was a game for suckers, or as Team B put it, détente was just "a particular strategy vis-à-vis the United States" while the Soviet Union pursued its methodical strategy for world domination. "The emergence of a worldwide 'socialist' order is seen by the Soviet leadership as a continuous process, inexorable in nature but not without its pitfalls and temporary reverses," Team B concluded in its final section. [18]

Team B denounced the CIA for a consistent underestimation of the "intensity, scope and implicit threat" from the Soviet Union. The CIA was faulted for basing its analysis on "hard" data, rather than "contemplat[ing] Soviet strategic objectives in terms of the Soviet conception of 'strategy' as well as in light of Soviet history, the structure of Soviet society, and the pronouncements of Soviet leaders." In her analysis of the Team B report for the *Bulletin of Atomic Scientists*, Anne Hessing Cahn said the report's tone represented the vintage "stridency and militancy of the conservatives in the 1970s." [19]

When Team B did cite its own "hard" data, only the most extreme interpretation could be accepted. As Cahn noted, Team B's estimate of Soviet production of the Backfire bomber was off by more than 100 percent. The report said the Soviets would have "perhaps 500 aircraft" manufactured by early 1984, when the real number turned out to be 235. "Team B found the Soviet Union immune from Murphy's law," Cahn wrote. [20] Yet, in reality, the Soviet system was beset by Murphy's law. Whatever could go wrong, did go wrong – consistently – as the Soviets stumbled farther and farther behind the West in technological advances and the economic strength needed to pay for a world-class military.

Beyond the alarmist hypothesis of unbridled Soviet power, the right-wing analysts got key facts wrong. Team B briefer, Air Force General George Keegan, cited the Soviet nuclear test range at Semipalatinsk as the site where the Soviets were trying out supposed nuclear-powered beam weapons. But it turned out to be a place to test rocket engines. "We had overestimated both their capability and their [technical] understanding," said a Los Alamos physicist who toured the facilities, according to Cahn's report.

Team B also engaged in selective translations of Russian phrases to exaggerate the Soviet offensive threat. The supposed Soviet "science of conquest" was taken from the Russian words "nauka pobezhdat," which actually means "the science of winning" or "the science of victory," hardly a novel concept for training military leaders. "Our own military writings are devoted to winning victories, but this is not commonly viewed as a policy of conquest," Cahn wrote. "Neither Team B nor the multibillion-dollar intelligence agencies could see that the Soviet Union was dissolving from within."

Though Team B's analysis of the Soviet Union as a rising power on the verge of overwhelming the United States is now recognized by intelligence professionals and many historians as a wild fantasy, it helped shape the national security debate in the late 1970s and into the 1980s. American conservatives and neoconservatives wielded the analysis like a club against more moderate Republicans and Democrats, who saw a declining Soviet Union desperate for arms control and other negotiations. Hundreds of billions of dollars in taxpayers' money – and IOUs left for their grandchildren – were poured into a U.S. military buildup to counter a Soviet military escalation that never existed.

In the wake of Team B's alarmist presentation and under Bush's leadership, chastened CIA analysts adopted a harsher tone for their own Soviet threat assessments. In November 1976, Bush approved a new National Intelligence Estimate, entitled "Soviet Forces for Intercontinental Conflict Through the Mid-1980s." Bush's cover letter declared that "to the extent that this Estimate presents a starker appreciation of Soviet strategic capabilities and objectives, it is but the latest in a series of estimates that have done so as evidence has accumulated on the continuing persistence and vigor of Soviet programs in the strategic offensive and defensive fields."[21]

Robert Gates, one of the CIA's hard-line Soviet analysts whose personal star brightened as détente's star dimmed, described the significance of Bush's new NIE. A "conclusion of the estimate that would draw much comment was its judgment that the strength of the Soviet offensive strategic forces might be at its greatest relative to the U.S. forces in the early 1980s and would pose an increasing threat to U.S. missile silos," Gates wrote in his book, *From the Shadows.* "This was what came to be known then as 'the window of vulnerability' projected for the early 1980s, that is, a limited period of time – several years – when a theoretical possibility existed that the Soviets might be able to launch a disarming first strike against the United States, destroying enough of our ICBMs in their silos to cripple a retaliatory strike and either prevent a U.S. response or allow the USSR to emerge from a war in significantly better condition than the United States."[22]

Gates acknowledged that the actual threat from this theoretical "window of vulnerability" was remote. "You didn't have to believe that the Soviets actually might start a war for this to be of concern," Gates wrote. "In fact, very few in Washington thought there was even a remote chance that the Soviets would suicidally throw the dice that way." Still, Gates argued there was a chance that the hypothetical Soviet build-up could embolden Moscow in other areas of its foreign policy. "The window of vulnerability came to be accepted by a substantial part of the political spectrum interested in such matters – both Republicans and Democrats – and greatly influenced the strategic debate for a number of years," Gates wrote.[23]

The reality, however, was that this CIA analysis, like Team B's worst-case scenario, never came to pass; "the window of vulnerability" stayed shut. Indeed, in 1983, Deputy CIA Director Gates testified that the Soviets didn't undertake a significant military expansion after 1976. "The rate of growth of overall defense costs is lower because procurement of military hardware – the largest category of defense spending – was almost flat in 1976-1981 [and that trend] appears to have continued also in 1982 and 1983."[24]

Though perhaps factually misguided, the concessions to the hard-line Right made political sense for Ford, buying the embattled President some protection from Reagan's sniping. Reagan came on strong in the later rounds of Republican primaries, but his challenge to the incumbent President fell short. Ford won the Republican nomination and a match-up against former Georgia Governor Carter gave the Michigan Republican a reasonable shot at winning the Presidency on his own. But Ford had to make sure no new scandals emerged.

Bush assured Ford that all was quiet at the Langley front. On August 3, 1976, Bush reported to Ford that "the CIA is a disciplined organization – trained to support the director." Bush observed, too, that it was important to "get the CIA off the front pages and at some point out of the papers altogether."[25] So far, Bush had made good on that goal. Having stopped the hemorrhaging of the CIA's reputation, Bush simply had to make sure the agency avoided any new wounds before the November elections.

***

Throughout George H.W. Bush's year in charge of the CIA, a major intelligence scandal bubbled beneath the surface threatening to erupt. Buoyed by a series of anticommunist military coups in South America's Southern Cone, right-wing forces were stepping up operations across Latin America against their enemies on the Left. The project of assassinations and bombings presented a political danger to President Ford's election campaign because its exposure could put the CIA back on the front pages and remind the nation of the dark days of the Nixon Presidency.

In Chile, the fiercely anticommunist general, Augusto Pinochet, held power after engineering the violent coup that killed the elected Marxist President Salvador Allende on September 11, 1973. The Nixon administration had helped set the stage for the bloody insurrection by aggressively opposing the Allende government and shaking its stability with a wide-ranging covert operation. Washington had blocked international loans, sabotaged Chile's economy and turned major Chilean news outlets, such as the daily newspaper *El Mercurio*, into CIA propaganda organs.

Though the Nixon administration had tried to play down its responsibility for the coup, the documents told a different story. One "secret" CIA memo, written in early 1974, described the success of "the Santiago Station's propaganda project." The memo said, "The project, which used a variety of propaganda mechanisms to inform the Chilean and foreign public of the Allende government's efforts to impose a Marxist totalitarian government, played a significant role in setting the stage for the military coup of 11 September 1973. Prior to the coup the project's media outlets maintained a steady barrage of anti-government criticism, exploiting every possible point of friction between the government and the democratic opposition, and emphasizing the problems and conflicts that were developing between the government and the armed forces. Since the coup, these media outlets have supported the new military government. They have tried to present the Junta in the most positive light."[26]

By summer 1974, despite Chile's appalling human rights record, the CIA was expanding its liaison ties to Pinochet's secret police, the Directorate of National Intelligence, known as DINA. The CIA's deputy director, General Vernon Walters, struck up a personal relationship with DINA chief Manuel Contreras. "Colonel Manuel Contreras considers himself a bosom buddy of the general," observed a State Department memo from the Chilean desk officer. Though principally responsible for ongoing atrocities in Chile, Contreras was put on the CIA's payroll at least briefly in 1975, the CIA has acknowledged in recent years.[27]

By 1975, however, press disclosures and congressional investigations had made the coziness between the Pinochet regime and the Nixon-Ford administration a political embarrassment – and prompted a review of U.S. interference in the affairs of other countries. "The scandal over covert operations to undermine Chilean democracy, coupled with the Nixon-Ford administration's embrace of Pinochet's violent regime, contributed to a dramatic national reevaluation of U.S. foreign policy," wrote historian Peter Kornbluh in *The Pinochet File*. "For the first time, CIA intervention became subject to public debate over the propriety of such practices – a debate that would endure and influence U.S. operations in countries from Angola to Nicaragua to Iraq in the last quarter of the Twentieth Century."[28]

Pinochet and other Latin American dictators didn't make matters any easier by dressing up and acting like a casting agent's idea of Fascist bullies. The dour Pinochet was known for his fondness for wearing a military cloak that made him resemble a well-dressed Nazi SS officer. "Internationally, the Latin generals look like our guys," observed Assistant Secretary of State Harry Shlaudeman in a "secret" briefing paper for Secretary of State Kissinger. "We are especially identified with Chile. It cannot do us any good."[29]

But Pinochet and other right-wing military dictators who dominated South America in 1976 had their own priorities, one of which was the elimination of political opponents who were living in exile in other countries. Though many of these dissidents weren't associated with violent revolutionary movements, the anticommunist doctrines then in vogue among the region's right-wing military made few distinctions between armed militants and political activists. The hard-line views of Pinochet and the other generals matched with the extremism of anticommunist Cuban-Americans, still burning with fury over Fidel Castro. Some of these exiles had dedicated their lives to this anticommunist cause. In 1960 and 1961, many had enlisted in the CIA's Bay of Pigs invasion of Cuba. After the invasion failed, some of these Cuban exiles continued working with the CIA, smuggling caches of weapons into Cuba to support possible insurrections. Other Cubans fought in Vietnam or joined counter-insurgency operations in South America. Others slid into the nether world of terrorism, launching attacks on Cuban diplomats and freighters.

By 1974, Chilean intelligence had begun collaborating with anti-Castro Cuban extremists and with other South American security forces to eliminate opponents. The first prominent victim of these cross-border assassinations was former Chilean General Carlos Prats, who was living in Argentina and was viewed as a potential rival to Pinochet because Prats had opposed Pinochet's coup that overthrew Chile's long history as a constitutional democracy. Learning that Prats was writing his memoirs, Pinochet's secret police chief Contreras dispatched Michael Townley, an assassin trained in explosives, to Argentina. Townley planted a bomb under Prats's car, detonating it in the early morning hours of September 30, killing Prats at the door and incinerating Prats's wife who was trapped inside the car. Pinochet's government denied any responsibility for the terrorist act.[30]

Pinochet's reputation for brutality made him a hero to violent anti-Castro Cubans. In December 1974, extremists Orlando Bosch, Guillermo Novo and Dionesio Suarez traveled to Chile to offer their services to the Chilean secret police, DINA. Assassin Townley began to develop a working relationship with Novo, who led the New Jersey wing of the Cuban National Movement, which the FBI described as an anti-Castro "terrorist group." Meanwhile, DINA's Contreras also linked up with right-wing European terrorists, including Italian Stefano Delle Chiaie.[31] A violent front for anticommunist terrorism was taking shape.

These international relationships gave Chile's intelligence service a reach outside South America. In July 1975, Townley met with Della Chiaie, enlisting his assistance in targeting Chilean exiles in Italy.[32] On October 6, 1975, a gunman approached Christian Democratic leader Bernardo Leighton who was walking with his wife on a street in Rome. The gunman shot both Leighton and his wife, severely wounding both of them. The CIA, aware of Chile's involvement in cross-border operations, warned Portugal and France of two other assassinations planned in those countries, prompting diplomatic actions to head off the killings.

In November 1975, the loose-knit collaboration among the Southern Cone dictatorships took on a more formal structure during a covert intelligence meeting in Santiago, Chile. Delegates from the security forces of Chile, Argentina, Uruguay, Paraguay and Bolivia committed themselves to a regional strategy against "subversives." In recognition of Chile's leadership, the conference named the project after Chile's national bird, the giant vulture that traverses the Andes Mountains. The project was called "Operation Condor." The U.S. Defense Intelligence Agency confidentially informed Washington that the operation had three phases and that the "third and reportedly very secret phase of 'Operation Condor' involves the formation of special teams from member countries who are to carry out operations to include assassinations." The Condor accord formally took effect on January 30, 1976,[33] the same day George H.W. Bush was sworn in as CIA director.

Part of Bush's job was to spare Ford any fresh embarrassments at the CIA. But in Bush's first few months, right-wing violence across the Southern Cone surged. On March 24, 1976, the Argentine military staged a coup, ousting the ineffectual President Isabel Peron and escalating a brutal internal security campaign against both violent and non-violent opponents on the Left. The Argentine security forces became especially well-known for grisly methods of torture and the practice of "disappearing" political dissidents who would be snatched from the streets or from their homes, undergo torture and never be seen again.

Like Pinochet and his regime, the new Argentine dictators saw themselves on a mission to save Western Civilization from the clutches of leftist thought. They took pride in the "scientific" nature of their repression. They were clinical practitioners of anticommunism – refining torture techniques, erasing the sanctuary of international borders and collaborating with right-wing terrorists and organized-crime elements to destroy leftist movements. Later Argentine government investigations discovered that its military intelligence officers advanced Nazi-like methods of torture by testing the limits of how much pain a human being could endure before dying. Torture methods included experiments with electric shocks, drowning, asphyxiation and sexual perversions, such as forcing mice into a woman's vagina.

The Argentine coup was led by General Jorge Rafael Videla, a dapperly dressed ideologue known for his English-tailored suits and his ruthless counter-insurgency theories. Videla, known as the "Bone" or "Pink Panther" because of his slight build, rose to power amid Argentina's political and economic unrest of the early-to-mid 1970s, with the slogan: "As many people as necessary must die in Argentina so that the country will again be secure."[34]

Though armed leftist groups had been shattered before the 1976 coup, the Argentine generals saw the need to eradicate any vestiges of political subversion, what Videla called a "process of national reorganization" which required "the profound transformation of consciousness." Part of the transformation would be achieved through selective use of terror, but it also called for sophisticated manipulation of language to manage popular perceptions of reality. The general held international conferences on public relations and hired the powerful U.S. firm, Burson Marsteller, for $1 million to cultivate journalists at elite publications.[35]

Videla saw control of perceptions and spreading of confusion as vital to his strategy. Since jailings and executions of dissidents were rarely acknowledged, Videla would deny a government role and insist that the missing Argentines must have run away to live comfortably in another country. "I emphatically deny that there are concentration camps in Argentina, or military establishments in which people are held longer than is absolutely necessary in this ... fight against subversion," he told British journalists.[36]

The totalitarian nature of the anticommunism gripping much of South America revealed itself in one particularly perverse Argentine practice, which was used when pregnant women were captured as suspected subversives. The women were kept alive long enough to bring the babies to full term. The women then were subjected to forced labor or Caesarian section. The newborns were given to military families to be raised in the ideology of anticommunism while the mothers were executed. Many were taken to an airport near Buenos Aires, stripped naked, shackled to other prisoners and put aboard a plane. As the plane flew over the Rio Plata or out over the Atlantic Ocean, the prisoners were shoved through a cargo door, sausage-like, into the water. Years later, a group called the Grandmothers of the Plaza de Mayo documented the identities of 256 missing babies. All told, the Argentine war against subversion would claim an estimated 10,000 to 30,000 lives.[37]

***

The 1976 Argentine *coup d'etat* allowed the pace of cross-border executions under Operation Condor to quicken. On May 21, gunmen killed two Uruguayan congressmen on a street in Buenos Aires. On June 4, former Bolivian President Juan Jose Torres was slain also in Buenos Aires. On June 11, armed men kidnapped 23 Chilean refugees and one Uruguayan who were under United Nations protection. After interrogation and torture by a team of Argentine, Uruguayan and Chilean security agents, the captives were ordered to leave Argentina. The U.S. Embassy reported to Washington that the case pointed to fresh evidence of collaboration among Southern Cone security forces.[38]

As the violence mounted in South America, Washington's focus had turned to the presidential election. By late summer, the two parties had picked their candidates, matching President Ford against Democratic challenger Jimmy Carter. The folksy Carter with his toothy smile and his pledge that he would never lie to the American people started out with a formidable lead in the polls, but Ford gained ground as the novelty of Carter's born-again Christianity began to wear thin.

Pinochet also had his eye on Washington, where his government was facing condemnation for its human rights violations. One of the most eloquent voices making the case against Pinochet's regime was Chile's former Foreign Minister Orlando Letelier, who was operating out of a liberal think tank in Washington, the Institute for Policy Studies. Earlier in their government careers, when Letelier was briefly defense minister in Allende's government, Pinochet had been his subordinate. After the coup, Pinochet imprisoned Letelier at a desolate concentration camp on Dawson Island off the south Pacific coast. International pressure won Letelier release a year later.

Now, Pinochet was chafing under Letelier's rough criticism of the regime's human rights record. Letelier was doubly infuriating to Pinochet because Letelier was regarded as a man of intellect and charm, even impressing CIA officers who observed him as "a personable, socially pleasant man" and "a reasonable, mature democrat," according to biographical sketches. Pinochet fumed to U.S. officials, including Secretary of State Kissinger, that Letelier was spreading lies and causing trouble with the U.S. Congress. Soon, Pinochet was plotting with DINA chief Contreras how to silence Letelier's criticism for good.[39]

By summer 1976, Bush's CIA was hearing a lot about Operation Condor from South American sources who had attended a second organizational conference of Southern Cone intelligence services. These CIA sources reported that the military regimes were preparing "to engage in 'executive action' outside the territory of member countries." In intelligence circles, "executive action" is a euphemism for assassination. On July 30, a CIA official briefed State Department officials about these "disturbing developments in [Condor's] operational attitudes." The information was passed to Kissinger in a "secret" report on August 3, 1976. The 14-page report from assistant secretary Shlaudeman said the military regimes were "joining forces to eradicate 'subversion,' a word which increasingly translates into non-violent dissent from the left and center left."[40]

While information about the larger Condor strategy was spreading through the upper levels of the Ford administration, Pinochet and Contreras were putting in motion their most audacious assassination plan yet: to eliminate Orlando Letelier in his safe haven in Washington, D.C.

In July 1976, two DINA operatives – Michael Townley and Armando Fernandez Larios – went to Paraguay where DINA had arranged for them to get false passports and visas for a trip to the United States. Townley and Larios were using the false names Juan Williams and Alejandro Romeral and a cover story claiming they were investigating suspected leftists working for

Chile's state copper company in New York. Townley and Larios said their project had been cleared with the CIA's Station Chief in Santiago. A senior Paraguayan official, Conrado Pappalardo, urged U.S. Ambassador George Landau to cooperate, citing a direct appeal from Pinochet in support of the mission. Supposedly, the Paraguayan government claimed, the two Chileans were to meet with CIA Deputy Director Vernon Walters.[41]

An alarmed Landau recognized that the visa request was highly unusual, since such operations are normally coordinated with the CIA station in the host country and are cleared with CIA headquarters in Langley, Virginia. Though granting the visas, Landau took the precaution of sending an urgent cable to Walters and photostatic copies of the fake passports to the CIA. Landau said he received an urgent cable back signed by CIA Director Bush, reporting that Walters, who was in the process of retiring, was out of town. When Walters returned a few days later, he cabled Landau that he had "nothing to do with this" mission. Landau immediately canceled the visas.

Landau also alerted senior State Department officials. In a cable to assistant secretary Shlaudeman, Landau said the "Paraguayan caper" had "troublesome aspects" and recommended that the two Chileans be barred from entering the United States. "If there is still time, and if there is a possibility of turning off this harebrained scheme," Shlaudeman wrote in reply, "you are authorized to go back [to Paraguayan officials] to urge that the Chileans be persuaded not – repeat not – to travel."

But the Ford administration dithered over delivering a formal *demarche* demanding that Pinochet's government cease and desist in its cross-border assassinations. Though a plan for warning Santiago was developed, the State Department could not agree how to carry it out without offending the prickly Pinochet.[42]

It also remains unclear what – if anything – Bush's CIA did after learning about the "Paraguayan caper." Normal protocol would have required senior CIA officials to ask their Chilean counterparts about the supposed trip to Langley. However, even with the declassification of more records in recent years, that question has never been fully answered. The CIA also demonstrated little curiosity over the August 22, 1976, arrival of two other Chilean operatives using the names, Juan Williams and Alejandro Romeral, the phony names that were intended to hide the identity of the two operatives in the aborted assassination plot. When these two different operatives arrived in Washington, they made a point of having the Chilean Embassy notify Walters's office at CIA.

"It is quite beyond belief that the CIA is so lax in its counterespionage functions that it would simply have ignored a clandestine operation by a foreign intelligence service in Washington, D.C., or elsewhere in the United States," wrote John Dinges and Saul Landau in their 1980 book, *Assassination on Embassy Row*. "It is equally implausible that Bush, Walters,

Landau and other officials were unaware of the chain of international assassinations that had been attributed to DINA."[43]

Apparently, DINA had dispatched the second pair of operatives, using the phony names, to show that the initial contacts for visas in Paraguay were not threatening. In other words, the Chilean government had the replacement team of Williams and Romeral go through the motions of a trip to Washington with the intent to visit Walters to dispel any American suspicions or to spread confusion among suspicious U.S. officials. But it's still unclear whether Bush's CIA contacted Pinochet's government about its mysterious behavior and, if not, why not.

***

As for the Letelier plot, DINA was soon devising another way to carry out the killing. In late August, DINA dispatched a preliminary team of one man and one woman to do surveillance on Letelier as he moved around Washington. Then, Townley was sent under a different alias to carry out the murder. After arriving in New York on Sept. 9, 1976, Townley contacted Cuban National Movement leader Guillermo Novo in Union City, New Jersey, and then headed to Washington. Townley assembled a remote-controlled bomb using parts bought at Radio Shack and Sears.

On September 18, joined by Cuban extremists Virgilio Paz and Dionisio Suarez, Townley went to Letelier's home in Bethesda, Maryland, outside Washington. The assassination team attached the bomb underneath Letelier's Chevrolet Chevelle. Three days later, on the morning of September 21, Paz and Suarez followed Letelier as he drove to work with two associates, Ronni Moffitt and her husband Michael. As the Chevelle proceeded down Massachusetts Avenue, through an area known as Embassy Row because many of the city's embassies line the street, the assassins detonated the bomb. The blast ripped off Letelier's legs and punctured a hole in Ronni Moffitt's jugular vein. She drowned in her own blood at the scene; Letelier died after being taken to George Washington University Hospital. Michael Moffitt survived.

At the time, the attack represented the worst act of international terrorism on U.S. soil. Adding to the potential for scandal, the terrorism had been carried out by a regime that was an ostensible ally of the United States, one that had gained power with the help of the Nixon administration and the CIA. Senior officials in the Ford administration, including Secretary of State Kissinger, were implicated in those events. Though initially treated in the press as a murder mystery, the facts behind the Letelier bombing threatened to unleash a major political scandal at just the wrong time for President Ford's campaign.

Bush's reputation was also at risk. As authors Dinges and Landau noted in *Assassination on Embassy Row,* "the CIA reaction was peculiar," after the cable from Ambassador Landau arrived disclosing a covert Chilean intelligence operation and asking Deputy Director Walters if he had a meeting scheduled with the DINA agents. Ambassador "Landau expected Walters to take quick action in the event that the Chilean mission did not have CIA clearance," authors Dinges and Landau wrote. "Yet a week passed during which the assassination team could well have had time to carry out their original plan to go directly from Paraguay to Washington to kill Letelier. Walters and Bush conferred during that week about the matter. "[44]

"One thing is clear," Dinges and Landau wrote, "DINA chief Manuel Contreras would have called off the assassination mission if the CIA or State Department had expressed their displeasure to the Chilean government. An intelligence officer familiar with the case said that any warning would have been sufficient to cause the assassination to be scuttled. Whatever Walters and Bush did – if anything – the DINA mission proceeded."[45]

Within hours of the bombing, Letelier's associates accused the Pinochet regime, citing its hatred of Letelier and its record for brutality. The Chilean government, however, heatedly denied any responsibility.[46] That night, at a dinner at the Jordanian Embassy, Senator James Abourezk, a South Dakota Democrat, spotted Bush and approached the CIA director. Abourezk said he was a friend of Letelier's and beseeched Bush to get the CIA "to find the bastards who killed him." Abourezk said Bush responded: "I'll see what I can do. We are not without assets in Chile."[47]

A problem, however, was that one of the CIA's best-placed assets – DINA chief Manuel Contreras – would turn out to be the mastermind of the assassination. Wiley Gilstrap, the CIA's Santiago Station Chief, did approach Contreras with questions about the Letelier bombing and wired back to Langley Contreras's assurance that the Chilean government wasn't involved. Following the strategy of public misdirection already used in hundreds of "disappearances," Contreras pointed the finger at the Chilean Left. Contreras suggested that leftists had killed Letelier to turn him into a martyr.

The Ford administration, of course, had plenty of evidence that Contreras was lying. Like a quarter century later, when the U.S. government immediately recognized al-Qaeda's hand in the September 11, 2001, terrorist attacks on New York and Washington because U.S. officials knew about Osama bin Laden's intentions, there were signs everywhere in September 1976 that DINA had been plotting some kind of attack inside the United States. If anything, the Letelier assassination should have been even easier to solve since the Pinochet government had flashed its intention to mount a suspicious operation inside the United States by involving the U.S. Embassy in Paraguay and the deputy director of the CIA. Bush's CIA even had in its files a photograph of the leader of the terrorist squad, Michael Townley.

"The CIA had substantive evidence to show that Contreras was lying," Kornbluh wrote in *The Pinochet File*. "The Agency had concrete knowledge that DINA had murdered other political opponents abroad, using the same *modus operandi* as the Letelier case. The Agency had substantive intelligence on Condor, and Chile's involvement in planning murders of political opponents in Europe."[48]

Rather than fulfilling his promise to Abourezk to "see what I can do," Bush ignored the leads. The CIA either didn't put the pieces together or chose to avoid the obvious conclusions that the evidence presented. Indeed, the CIA didn't seem to want any information that might implicate the Pinochet regime. On October 6, a CIA informant in Chile went to the CIA Station in Santiago and relayed an account of Pinochet denouncing Letelier. The informant said the dictator had called Letelier's criticism of the government "unacceptable." The source "believes that the Chilean Government is directly involved in Letelier's death and feels that investigation into the incident will so indicate," the CIA field report said.[49]

But Bush's CIA chose to accept Contreras's denials and even began leaking information that pointed away from the real killers. *Newsweek* reported in the magazine's October 11, 1976, issue that "the Chilean secret police were not involved. …. The [Central Intelligence] agency reached its decision because the bomb was too crude to be the work of experts and because the murder, coming while Chile's rulers were wooing U.S. support, could only damage the Santiago regime." Similar stories ran in other newspapers, including *The New York Times.*[50]

Despite the lack of help from Washington, the FBI's legal attaché in Buenos Aires, Robert Scherrer, began putting the puzzle together only a week after the Letelier bombing. Relying on a source in the Argentine military, Scherrer reported to his superiors that the assassination was likely the work of Operation Condor, the assassination project organized by the Chilean government. "It is not beyond the realm of possibility that the recent assassination of Orlando Letelier in Washington, D.C., may have been carried out as a third phase of Operation Condor," Scherrer wrote.[51]

Another break in the case came two weeks after the Letelier assassination on October 6, 1976, when anti-Castro terrorists planted a bomb on a Cubana Airlines DC-8 before it took off from Barbados. Nine minutes after takeoff, the bomb exploded, plunging the plane into the Caribbean and killing all 73 people on board including the Cuban national fencing team. Two Cuban exiles, Hernan Ricardo and Freddy Lugo, who had left the plane in Barbados, confessed that they had planted the bomb. They named two prominent anti-Castro extremists, Orlando Bosch and Luis Posada Carriles, as the architects of the attack. A search of Posada's apartment in Venezuela turned up Cubana Airlines timetables and other incriminating documents. Although Posada was a CIA-trained Bay of Pigs veteran and stayed in close touch with some former CIA colleagues, senior CIA officials again pleaded ignorance. For the second time in barely two weeks, Bush's CIA had done nothing to interfere with terrorist attacks implicating anticommunist operatives with close ties to the CIA.

The Cubana Airlines bombing put federal investigators on the right track toward solving the Letelier assassination, however. They began to learn more about the network of right-wing terrorists associated with Operation Condor and its international Murder Inc. Over the next two years, the investigators would crack the case, successfully bringing charges against Townley and several other conspirators.

But other conspirators would escape U.S. justice. Contreras, though indicted, was never extradited to the United States to stand trial. As a head of state favored by Washington, Pinochet was never charged. Though the key facts of the case would eventually become clear, the Chilean government's role was kept under wraps through the 1976 presidential election. Bush and Ford were able to avoid any last-minute revival of the controversy over the CIA's role in Chile. There were no scandalous headlines about how the military dictator who rose to power with the Nixon administration's help returned the favor by bringing his violence to the streets of Washington.

Prosecutor Eugene Propper told me that the CIA did provide some information about the background of suspects, but didn't volunteer the crucial information about the Paraguayan gambit or supply the photo of the chief assassin, Townley. "Nothing the agency gave us helped us break this case," Propper said.

On November 1, 1976, the day before the election, *The Washington Post* was the latest news outlet to report the CIA's assessment that Pinochet was innocent. "Operatives of the present Chilean military Junta did not take part in Letelier's killing," the *Post* wrote, citing CIA officials. "CIA Director Bush expressed this view in a conversation late last week with Secretary of State Kissinger."[52]

On November 2, Democrat Jimmy Carter, whose lead in the polls once had reached 30 percentage points, held off a late surge from President Ford and captured a narrow victory.

***

After Ford's defeat, CIA Director Bush finally showed some concern about the danger from anti-Castro terrorism at least inside the United States. In early November, Bush and a senior FBI official, James Adams, flew to Miami to listen to field reports about the problem of anti-Castro terrorism from FBI and CIA officers. Bush then visited Little Havana, though it's unclear whom he talked with or what his message was. One anti-Castro Cuban activist told me that the CIA's message at the time was to carry out no more attacks inside the United States, although the activist said, the CIA put no bars on anti-Castro attacks outside the United States.[53]

Regarding the Letelier murder, neither Bush nor Walters was ever pressed to provide a full explanation of their activities. When I submitted questions to Bush in 1988 – while he was Vice President and I was a

Newsweek correspondent preparing a story on his year as CIA director –
Bush's chief of staff Craig Fuller responded, saying "the Vice President
generally does not comment on issues related to the time he was at the
Central Intelligence Agency and he will have no comment on the specific
issues raised in your letter." My editors at *Newsweek* subsequently decided
not to publish any story about Bush's year at the CIA though he was then
running for President and citing his CIA experience as an important element
of his resumé.[54] Walters also rebuffed interview requests on the Letelier topic
prior to his death on February 10, 2002, in West Palm Beach, Florida.

As for Pinochet, Bush didn't appear to hold a grudge against this
foreign leader who had sponsored a terrorist attack under the nose of the U.S.
government at a time when Bush was in charge of the U.S. intelligence
services. In 1998, when Pinochet was detained in Great Britain on an
extradition request from Spanish Judge Baltasar Garzon, who was pursuing
Pinochet for his role in killing Spanish citizens, one of the world leaders who
rallied to Pinochet's defense was George H.W. Bush, then the former
President of the United States. Bush called the case against Pinochet "a
travesty of justice" and urged that Pinochet be sent home to Chile "as soon as
possible," a position ultimately endorsed by the British courts.

Chapter 5: First Interregnum

The national Republican Party might have taken solace from Gerald Ford's comeback. He had risen from the political dead to nearly beat Jimmy Carter. The Electoral College vote was one of the closest in modern American history: Carter 297, Ford 241. As *New York Times* analyst Tom Wicker wrote, a switch of only a relatively small number of votes in a couple of key states could have kept Ford in the White House.[1] The near victory showed that the Republican strategy of assailing Big Government and tapping into resentment of social changes offered a route toward a sustainable national majority.

But Ford's narrow defeat also taught the Republicans a painful lesson. As much as George H.W. Bush had succeeded in stanching the flow of damaging secrets out of the CIA and Gerald Ford had rebounded from his unpopular pardon of Richard Nixon, American conservatism faced some daunting challenges. The Republicans saw a Democratic advantage in an array of liberal activist groups and left-of-center think tanks, from Common Cause to the Brookings Institution, that helped set the national agenda.

Conservatives also suspected that the New York- and Hollywood-based national media were something akin to a liberal conspiracy bent on betraying the United States to its enemies. At the center of this despised "liberal media" sat powerful news outlets, including CBS News, *The Washington Post* and *The New York Times*. The Republicans blamed these media forces for exploiting the Watergate scandal to oust Nixon and for losing the Vietnam War by undermining public support.

Many of these suspicions of bias were not supported by fact, but they were powerful beliefs nonetheless. Regarding the war in Indochina, conservatives were right that television images of death and destruction in Vietnam eroded domestic support for the war in the 1960s. But that was not because of biased reporting; it was because cameras accurately captured the horrors of the war and the hopelessness of a war strategy that even its architects, including Defense Secretary Robert McNamara, have since acknowledged was flawed and unworkable. The official U.S. military history on the press and the Vietnam War agrees that the conflict was lost because of an unrealistic strategy and an unending return of American coffins, not because of the press corps and its supposed bias.

"Most of the public affairs problems that confronted the United States in South Vietnam stemmed from the contradictions implicit in Lyndon Johnson's strategy for the war," wrote U.S. Army historian William M. Hammond in *The Military and the Media: 1962-1968*. "What alienated the American public, in both the Korean and Vietnam Wars, was not news coverage but casualties." Military critics of the press focused too much on isolated reporting mistakes while ignoring "the work of the majority of reporters, who attempted conscientiously to tell all sides of the story," Hammond wrote in his book published by the U.S. Army Center of Military History. "It is undeniable … that press reports were still often more accurate than the public statements of the administration in portraying the situation in Vietnam."[2]

On Watergate, while it may have been true that many members of the Washington Establishment were uncomfortable with Nixon's chip-on-the-shoulder hostility, only an overt favoritism toward Nixon could have spared him from his largely self-inflicted political destruction. As Nixon's Watergate tapes were released over the years, they showed that Nixon was his own worst enemy, a political paranoid who abused the powers of his office with the goal of essentially rigging the 1972 election to assure his own victory. His behavior was neither within the traditions of American conservatism nor within the bounds of the sometimes checkered history of U.S. presidential politics.

Nixon's demands for illegal break-ins and other dirty tricks put his aides in the untenable position of either defying the President of the United States or violating the law. Out of ambition and fear, many followed his orders and went to jail. But Nixon's demise could hardly be blamed on a national press corps that basically got the story right and uncovered an abuse of power at the highest level of the U.S. government.

The conservatives may have had a stronger argument about a "liberal press" during the 1950s, when Northern reporters traveled to the South to report on the civil rights struggle. Indeed, the national coverage of the civil rights movement could be viewed as the origin of the conservative grievance against the "liberal media." At the time, Southern segregationists believed that the very idea of giving African-Americans equal time or equal treatment was itself proof of bias.

Southern whites pointed to examples of the national press corps reporting critically about segregationist policies of the South. It was certainly true that many journalists cast a harsh light on the lynching of black men, brutality toward civil rights activists and abuse of black children attending previously all-white schools. Northern reporters, for example, descended on Tallahatchie County, Mississippi, for the trial and acquittal of two white men for the 1955 murder of Emmett Till, a young black man who supposedly had boasted about dating a white woman. The negative press coverage of the trial and the acquittals led some of the state's whites to plaster their cars with bumper stickers reading, "Mississippi: The Most Lied About State in the Union."[3]

While the coverage of the civil rights movements may have sparked conservative anger toward the news media, the press corps was, by any reasonable measure, doing its job. It was holding up a mirror to a way of life based on the repression of millions of Americans because of the color of their skin. Understandably, segregationists would have preferred the news media pay no heed to this unpleasant story or to report on it from the whites' point of view, but the case for condemning the news media for paying attention to the violence sweeping the South was a weak one.

More recently, the core of the conservative complaint about the "liberal media" has come from surveys purportedly showing that a majority of working journalists vote Democratic in presidential elections. Conservatives have argued that the surveys prove a pro-Democratic bias permeates the American news media. Conservatives then bolster this claim of liberal bias with anecdotes, such as the inflections of an anchorman's voice or the supposed overuse of the word "ultra-conservative" in news columns.

Over the years, however, other surveys on the views of individual journalists suggest a more complicated picture. Journalists generally regard themselves as centrists with more liberal views on social issues and more conservative ones on economic issues, when compared with the broader American public, these surveys indicate. For example, journalists might be more likely to favor abortion rights, while less likely to worry about cuts in Social Security and Medicare than other Americans.[4]

But the larger fallacy of the "liberal media" argument is the idea that reporters and mid-level editors set the editorial agenda at their news organizations. In reality, most journalists don't have much more say over what is presented by newspapers and TV news programs than factory workers and foremen do over what a factory manufactures. While factory workers may have limited input in a company's product – making suggestions about improvements and ensuring the product is built soundly – top executives have a much bigger say. The news business is essentially the same. News organizations are hierarchical institutions often run by strong-willed men and a few women who insist that their editorial vision be dominant within their news companies. Media owners historically have enforced their political views and other preferences by installing senior editors whose careers depend on delivering a news product that fits with the owner's prejudices.

Within the framework established by top management, some concessions are made to the broader professional standards of journalism, such as the principles of objectivity and fairness, but working reporters are rarely allowed to wander off in directions opposed by the executives. Mid-level editors and reporters who stray too far from the prescribed path can expect to be demoted or fired. Editorial employees intuitively understand the career risks of going beyond the boundaries.

These limitations were true a century ago when William Randolph Hearst famously studied every day's paper from his publishing empire looking for signs of leftist attitudes among his staff. It has remained true in the more recent media era, dominated by the likes of TV tycoon Rupert Murdoch. Spanning the century, from Hearst to Murdoch, most American newspapers have favored Republican candidates for President over Democrats, often by margins of two- or three-to-one. Even in the 1960s and 1970s, when complaints about the "liberal press" were reaching a boil, most news organizations were run by executives with a conservative bias, not a liberal one.

Still, the oft-repeated notion of the "liberal media" was well on its way to becoming an article of conservative faith by the late 1970s. The final straws had come when conservatives blamed shaggy-haired reporters for "hounding" Nixon out of office over Watergate, followed by the CIA scandals and the collapse of the South Vietnamese government. Beyond the reality of who was at fault for those fiascos, influential conservatives recognized that this new breed of scrappy investigative reporters, personified by the often-abrasive Seymour Hersh, presented a new political threat.

But conservatives gained new public support in some constituencies in the late 1970s because liberal advances in public policy had rubbed many Americans the wrong way. They found their traditions disrupted, saw their social status reduced or felt the intrusion of Big Government on their businesses. In particular, Southern white men felt threatened by the rapidly changing society. But that resentment reached into many blue-collar neighborhoods in the North, too. There was anger toward the "hippie counter-culture," school busing and "social engineering." Many Americans worried about what Nixon's Vice President Spiro Agnew had dubbed the three A's: "acid, abortion and amnesty."

On balance, however, the liberals seemed to have the bulk of the advantages. They could reasonably expect to benefit from their standing on the right side of history on many issues in the years since the Great Depression: supporting the end of racial segregation, equality for women, environmental protections, respect for human rights in international affairs, union protections, and a social safety net for the elderly and the sick. Though having to deal with schisms on the far Left and rivalries among Democratic interest groups, the liberals had earned the allegiance of many blacks, Hispanics, Jews, professional women, elderly and environmentalists.

So, the conservatives and the Republicans had their work cut out for them after losing the White House in 1977. They needed organization, planning and money – lots of money. Distrusting the national press corps, the Republicans and conservatives would set their sights on building their own news media. They also would challenge the dominance of the Brookings

Institution and other left-of-center think tanks by creating or expanding their conservative think tanks. The conservatives also saw the need for a fulltime political attack machine that could gear up quickly to punish some crusading congressman uncovering CIA abuses or some muckraking journalist with an eye toward breaking another Watergate story.

In short, while lost in the political wilderness of President Carter's young administration, the Republicans and conservatives were searching for a route back to power – and eventually to political dominance. At the beginning of this search, at the start of this road, was the idea of creating a Counter-Establishment, a concept that went back at least to Nixon's fulminations in the early 1970s when he ranted about anti-war protesters and the lack of a reliable political infrastructure to counter them.

***

On September 12, 1970, while at Camp David, Nixon arose late one morning and began barking orders. He "has several plots he wants hatched," wrote Nixon's chief of staff H.R. Haldeman in *The Haldeman Diaries*. "One to infiltrate the John Gardner 'Common Cause' deal and needle them and try to push them to left. ... Next, a front group that sounds like SDS to support the Democratic candidates and praise their liberal records, etc., publicize their 'bad' quotes in guise of praise." Then, Nixon turned to one of his pet plans. Nixon was "pushing again on [his] project of building OUR establishment in [the] press, business, education, etc.," Haldeman wrote.

That same year, conservative political theorist Richard Whalen had raised the same alarm in a letter to Nixon. "Our side is woefully short of the institutional resources necessary to complement and consolidate our present political strength," Whalen wrote. "On our side there is no Ford Foundation, no Brookings Institution, no Kennedy Institute; and yet we have intelligent, resourceful men, instinctively aware of the deficiency, who need only inspiration, leadership, and a strategy to do what is required."[5]

In the months that followed, Nixon would be frustrated by what he saw as a shortage of allies in Washington. While he could plant stories in a few right-of-center newspapers, such as the *Washington Star*, he struggled against a Washington Establishment that viewed him with fear, loathing or a mix of the two. Nixon despaired that the press corps was harder to manipulate than it was during the early years of the Cold War when a straightforward Red Scare would do the trick. Now, he lectured his staff on the need to bully journalists into line. Nixon believed "the press and TV don't change their attitude and approach unless you hurt them," Haldeman recounted on April 21, 1972. "The only way we can fight the whole press problem, [Nixon] feels, is through the [Charles] Colson operation, the nut-cutters, forcing our news and in a brutal vicious attack on the opposition."

Nixon's combative political instincts led him to compile "enemies lists" and organize *ad hoc* structures, such as the White House Plumbers, to strike back at his liberal adversaries. One month after his lecture about "the nut-cutters," burglars working for his reelection committee were breaking into the Watergate to plant bugs on phones at the Democratic National Committee. A month after that, his team was caught during a second break-in and the cover-up had begun. As the Watergate scandal engulfed the Nixon Presidency in 1973, conservatives rallied to Nixon's defense. Beer magnate Joseph Coors and heir to the Mellon fortune Richard Mellon Scaife christened the Heritage Foundation as a conservative flagship by donating more than $1 million.

But the Right discovered that it lacked the political clout to save Nixon. Republicans watched in horror as Nixon's Presidency disintegrated. After his resignation on August 9, 1974, the disgraced President retreated to his estate in San Clemente, California, leaving the task of picking up the pieces to Gerald Ford and rising Republican leaders, such as George H.W. Bush.

While ending Nixon's public political life, the Watergate catastrophe actually proved his point that the old strategies for containing scandals – by enlisting a few Wise Men who presumably would understand the larger national interests and clamp down on disclosures – no longer worked, at least not alone. Containment of scandal would require a dedicated infrastructure of permanent operatives who would have as a principal duty the responsibility of protecting a future Republican President from "another Watergate."

Taking the lead in this endeavor was Nixon's former Treasury Secretary William Simon, a hard-bitten conservative who had prospered earlier in life as part of the cut-throat Wall Street world. As a partner at the investment firm of Salomon Brothers, Simon had made millions of dollars a year. He then was lured into public service as Nixon's energy czar and Treasury chief. After leaving government, Simon took a post as president of the John M. Olin Foundation, one of a handful of conservative foundations. In the late 1970s, Simon began pulling those foundations together with the goal of fulfilling Nixon's "project" of building "OUR establishment."

In 1978, Simon argued in his book, *A Time for Truth*, that only a strong conservative ideological movement could break the back of the dominant Liberal Establishment, which he accused of enforcing misguided concepts of "equality" and of being "possessed of delusions of moral grandeur." Simon saw the Liberal Establishment and other parts of that "powerful political intelligentsia" as "as stubborn and ruthless a ruling elite as any in history."

To combat this insidious Liberal Establishment and transform the Republican Party, the conservatives would need a "counter-intelligentsia," Simon said. "Funds generated by business ... must rush by the multimillion to the aid of liberty ... to funnel desperately needed funds to scholars, social scientists, writers and journalists who understand the relationship between political and economic liberty," Simon wrote.[6]

Simon's Olin Foundation soon allied itself with like-minded foundations – associated with Lynde and Harry Bradley, Smith Richardson, the Scaife family and the Coors family – to advance the conservative cause. This network of conservative foundations began to create the nucleus of a national infrastructure of think tanks, media organizations and pressure groups.

In 1980, Simon published *A Time for Action*, which demanded that the "death grip" of the Liberal Establishment and its "New Despotism" be broken. Simon saw the news media as part of the enemy camp. He especially targeted journalists who, Simon charged, "have been working overtime to deny liberty to others."[7]

"The members of the 'counter-intelligentsia' Simon cultivated would assail the conventional wisdom of an antiquated system," observed author Sidney Blumenthal in 1986 in his seminal book on modern conservatism, *The Rise of the Counter-Establishment*. "The Bastille to which they laid siege was the fortress of liberalism, the hollow doctrine of the old regime. These [conservative] intellectuals impressed their thoughts on public activity, staffing the new institutes, writing policy papers and newspaper editorials, and serving as political advisers, lending the power of the word to the defense of ideology."[8]

Though other conservative benefactors, such as Joseph Coors and Richard Mellon Scaife, put more of their own fortunes into building the Counter-Establishment, Simon understood the value of coordinating the movement's resources. "By controlling the wellsprings of funding, Simon makes the movement green," Blumenthal wrote.[9]

Years later, a limited study by the National Committee for Responsive Philanthropy – looking at the investments of 12 "core" conservative foundations – would find that those foundations alone poured $210 million into right-wing ideological activities from 1992 to 1994. The study concluded that these "core" foundations anchored a comprehensive strategy for advancing conservative goals by investing in institutions, from universities and think tanks to media and pressure groups.

Leading recipients of this largesse included top conservative think tanks: the Heritage Foundation, the American Enterprise Institute, the Hudson Institute and the Manhattan Institute. Large sums also went to conservative legal groups pressing "tort reform" and other rightist judicial policies, including the Institute for Justice, the Washington Legal Foundation and the Federalist Society. High on the list, too, were conservative and neoconservative foreign policy organizations, such as the Hoover Institution, Freedom House, and the Ethics and Public Policy Center.

Big chunks of cash went to media outlets as well. Among conservative magazines, major recipients included neoconservative Irving Kristol's *National Interest/Public Interest*; *Commentary*, edited by another neoconservative Norman Podhoretz; and the *American Spectator*, which published over-the-top anti-liberal screeds that especially appealed to younger white men. The conservative foundations invested millions more in organizations that bashed perceived "liberals" in the mainstream media.

Looking to the future, the 12 "core" foundations devoted large sums to support conservative scholars and to train young activists in the nation's universities. Besides paying for scholarships and endowing chairs at prestigious colleges, such as Harvard and Yale, the foundations invested heavily in lesser-known schools, such as George Mason University in Fairfax, Virginia, just outside Washington, D.C. At GMU, the foundations backed the Institute of Humane Studies and the Center for Study of Market Processes, both promoting "free market" principles.

While capturing a sense of this comprehensive infrastructure that Nixon had wished for and Simon had envisioned, the NCRP's study of the 12 "core" foundations examined only a slice of the vast conservative network. It didn't count hundreds of millions of dollars more from corporations, Christian Right groups, smaller foundations, and foreign interests. But the study underscored how the conservative foundations had sprung from the early priming of the pump in the late 1970s.

***

The "bosses" of this new political machine were an odd mix of political moneymen and ideological strategists. They included embittered ex-leftists Kristol and Podhoretz; ultra-conservative tycoons Scaife, Coors and Simon; right-wing apparatchiks Paul Weyrich and Michael Joyce; and libertarian oil men Charles and David Koch. But the machine benefited from cooperation among these leading figures. The "bosses" often coordinated by giving to the same think tanks; they sat on each others' boards; and they adopted broad strategies through organizations such as the Philanthropy Roundtable. "This is a highly networked group," noted Sally Covington, who directed the NCRP study.

By the late 1970s, while the conservative foundations bankrolled the training of the Right's brain trust, televangelists Jerry Falwell and Pat Robertson were recruiting Christian Right foot soldiers for the political trenches. In effect, the conservatives were deploying a political army, with intellectual strategists at the rear, an intimidating battery of artillery in a right-wing news media and an infantry drawn from the ranks of fundamentalist Christianity. Much of what was happening – while in one sense out in the open – was taking shape beneath the surface, like an army surreptitiously digging closer and closer to an enemy's defenses. Within a few years, John Saloma, a moderate Republican, was warning in his book, *Ominous Politics*, that "the conservative labyrinth is a major new presence in American politics."

The conservative strategy would have even a greater impact because of the corresponding failure of liberals to recognize in a timely way what the Right was doing and to respond with a similar financial commitment. "The role that conservative foundations have played in reinvigorating the institutional base of American conservatism simply has no parallel in the liberal funding community," concluded the NCRP's Covington.

In another study in the 1990s looking back at the conservative success, the liberal group People for the American Way noted that – in contrast to the conservative benefactors – progressive foundations devote most of their money to service programs, such as buying park land, seeking an AIDS cure or supplying food to the poor, not the ideological "war of ideas." "Progressive groups, local and national, have over the years sought to fill in the gaps in the ever more frayed social safety net," that report said. "Conservative groups have invested their resources, by and large, in efforts to further shred that net."

As the conservative foundation funding was beginning to tilt the balance of American politics to the Right, the conservative scramble for money didn't stop at the nation's shoreline. Other sources of funding – seeking to influence the direction of U.S. politics – were coming from abroad, perhaps not surprisingly given how many countries are dependent on U.S. military protection or financial assistance.

One of those foreign financial angels of the Right was the Reverend Sun Myung Moon, the leader of a South Korean religious cult who considered himself the new Messiah. Over three decades, starting in the mid-1970s, Moon would spend hundreds of millions of dollars in the U.S. political system, from rallies to defend Richard Nixon in 1974 to backing George W. Bush in both Campaign 2000 and his bid for a second term in 2004 through Moon's media empire, anchored by its flagship newspaper, *The Washington Times*. The source of Moon's money – and his real motives – would represent their own dark mysteries.

***

Sun Myung Moon may have the distinction of being the most unusual person ever to wield substantial influence in the capital of the United States.

Known for crowning himself at lavish ceremonies and ranting for hours in Korean about the proper use of sex organs, Moon demonstrated how almost anyone can secure something akin to respectability in Washington if he's willing to spend enough money. In Moon's case, the ticket to influence in Washington was purchased at the price of hundreds of millions of dollars.

When Moon became a major benefactor of the American conservative movement starting in the latter half of the 1970s, it was a time when the conservatives desperately needed money to augment the limited funds from William Simon's network of conservative foundations. Moon stepped forward to fill that gap. From a mysterious and seemingly bottomless slush fund, Moon ladled out cash to sponsor lavish conferences, to finance political interest groups and eventually to publish one of the capital's two daily newspapers, *The Washington Times.*

Despite his controversial goals – such as replacing democracy and individuality with his own personal theocratic rule over the most intimate details of every person's life – Moon lured into his circle some of the most prominent political figures of the modern era. One was George H.W. Bush who grasped Moon's value as a deep pocket for the conservative movement and for the Bush family.

Moon began building his political influence in Washington at a time when he was best known to most Americans as the leader of a South Korean-based religious cult, the Unification Church, known as the "Moonies." Moon was held responsible by thousands of American parents for brainwashing their children and transforming them into automatons who gave up their previous lives to devote nearly every waking hour in the service of Reverend Moon. These seemingly disembodied young people sold carnations at street corners or solicited donations with misleading claims about the money going to some worthy-sounding cause, without mentioning Moon or the Unification Church.

Gradually, however, Moon's Washington investments gained him access to many members of the nation's ruling elite and the worst of the negative press coverage subsided. Still, few Americans, even those who took his money, actually knew much about his life and his true allegiances. Recognizing the potential for negative publicity, his disciples had worked diligently to shroud Moon's biography in the fog of legend. Church publications were filled with inspirational Sunday-school-type tales of Moon's courage and beneficence. Critics were accused of religious or racial bias, supposedly disdaining Moon because he was a man of religion or because he was Korean. Conservative propagandists – many of whom had benefited from Moon's largesse – also tried to discredit attempts to investigate Moon's financial and political dealings.

Moon became to Washington – and especially to the conservative movement – something akin to the crazy aunt in the basement, who happens to control a large chunk of the family inheritance.

***

Moon was born on January 6, 1920, in a rural, northwestern corner of Korea, a rugged Asian peninsula then occupied by Japan, an occupation that would continue through the first 25 years of Moon's life. Allied forces liberated the peninsula from the Japanese in 1945 and then divided Korea into two sections, the south controlled by the United States and the north occupied by Soviet troops.

In this post-war period, Moon, who had been raised within a Christian sect, moved to southern Korea and joined a mystical religious group called Israel Suo-won. The group preached the imminent arrival of a Korean Messiah and practiced a strange sexual ritual called "pikarume," in which ministers purified women through sexual intercourse, the so-called "blessing of the womb." As he developed his own theology, Moon returned to the North, to communist-ruled North Korea, where he soon ran into legal troubles. North Korean authorities arrested him twice, apparently on morals charges connected to his sexual rites with young women. Moon's supporters, however, have tried to portray Moon as the victim of communist repression, claiming that he was arrested not for sex charges but for espionage.

Whatever the real story about his detention in North Korea, Moon's luck soon changed. On October 14, 1950, with war raging on the Korean peninsula, United Nations troops overran the prison where Moon was held, freeing Moon and all the other inmates. According to Unification Church histories, Moon then trekked south, carrying on his back an injured prisoner named Pak Chung Hwa. For years, church officials even published a photograph purportedly showing Pak piggy-backing on Moon across a river. But much of that story appears to be propaganda. Several church sources have since admitted that the photo was a hoax, that Moon is not the man in the picture and the location is not where Moon was.

Moon's southward journey ended in the South Korean port of Pusan, where he resumed his missionary work. He later moved to Seoul, South Korea's capital, where he founded his own church in May 1954. He called it T'ong-il Kyo, or Holy Spirit Association for the Unification of World Christianity. It became known as the Unification Church.

At the center of Moon's theology was a new twist to the Old Testament story about the Fall of Man. Instead of biting into a forbidden apple, Eve copulated with Satan and then passed on the sin by having sex with Adam. Thousands of years later, God sent Jesus to restore man to his original purity, Moon taught. But Jesus failed because he was betrayed by the Jews and died before he could father any sinless children. Sex, therefore, remained at the center of Moon's theology, the need for a Messiah to purify the human race through the reversal of the contamination caused by Satan's seduction of Eve.

Moon taught that the failure of Jesus to begin this purification process by fathering children forced God to send a second Messiah, who turned out to be Moon himself. Moon saw his task as starting this sexual purification process and thus establishing God's Kingdom on Earth. The ultimate goal would be a worldwide theocracy ruled by Moon and his followers cleansed of Satan's influence. Political power and religious authority went together, Moon lectured. "We cannot separate the political field from the religious," Moon said.

But in South Korea, Moon found that government continued to be an obstacle to his religious plans. When he began to concentrate his religious recruitment on young idealistic college students, especially from an all-girls Christian school, Moon landed in hot water again. The South Korean government arrested Moon in 1955 for allegedly conducting more sexual "purification" rites, according to U.S. intelligence reports. Moon was freed three months later because none of the young women would testify for fear of public humiliation, according to an undated FBI summary.[10] "During the next two years in the national news media of South Korea, Rev. Moon was the butt of scandalist humor," the FBI report said.

Church officials repeatedly have denied the reports of Moon's sexual rituals. But the charges received new attention in 1993 with the Japanese publication of *The Tragedy of the Six Marys* – a book by the early Moon disciple, Pak Chung Hwa, whom Moon supposedly carried to South Korea. According to Pak's book, Moon taught that Jesus was intended to save mankind by having sex with six already-married women who would then have sex with other men who would pass on the purification to other women until, eventually, all mankind would have pure blood.

Pak contended that Moon took on this personal duty as the second Messiah and began having sex with the "six Marys." But Pak alleged that Moon began to abuse the practice by turning the "six Marys" into a kind of rotating sex club. Pak wrote that Moon's first wife divorced him after catching him in a sex ritual. In all, Pak estimated that there were at least 60 "Marys," many of whom ended up destitute after Moon discarded them.

According to the testimony of one "Mary," named Yu Shin Hee, she met Moon in the early 1950s and became a follower along with her husband. Devoted to the church, her husband abandoned her and her five children, whom she then put into an orphanage. She, in turn, agreed to become one of Moon's "six Marys." But Yu Shin Hee claimed that Moon tired of her after just one "blood exchange," a phrase referring to sexual intercourse. Still, she was required to have sex with other men. Seven years later, a broken woman with no money, she tried to return to her children, but they also rejected her.

When Moon impregnated another one of the women, Moon sent her to Japan where she gave birth to a baby boy, according to Pak's account. Moon later admitted fathering the child, who died in a train crash at the age of 13. But Pak wrote that Moon refused to admit responsibility for other illegitimate children born to the women. "By forwarding this teaching, he violated mothers, their daughters, their sisters," Pak wrote. (After *The Tragedy of the Six Marys* was published, the Unification Church denounced the allegations as spurious. Under intense pressure, the aging Pak Chung Hwa agreed to recant. However, his book's accounts tracked closely with U.S. intelligence reports of the same period and interviews with former church leaders.)

Moon's history of sexual liaisons out of wedlock also was corroborated by Nansook Hong, one of Moon's daughters-in-law who broke with the so-called True Family in 1995 over abuse she suffered at the hands of Moon's eldest son, Hyo Jin Moon, during their 14-year marriage. Nansook Hong reported in her 1998 book, *In the Shadow of the Moons*, that family members, including Moon himself, acknowledged that he had "providential" sex with women in his role as the Messiah. Nansook Hong said she learned about Moon's sexual affairs when her husband, Hyo Jin, began justifying his affairs as mandated by God, as his father claimed his affairs were.

"I went directly to Mrs. Moon with Hyo Jin's claims," Nansook Hong wrote. "She was both furious and tearful. She had hoped that such pain would end with her, that it would not be passed on to the next generation, she told me. No one knows the pain of a straying husband like True Mother, she assured me. I was stunned. We had all heard rumors for years about Sun Myung Moon's affairs and the children he sired out of wedlock, but here was True Mother, confirming the truth of these stories. I told her that Hyo Jin said his sleeping around was 'providential' and inspired by God, just as Father's affairs were. 'No, Father is the Messiah, not Hyo Jin. What Father did was in God's plan.'" Later, in a discussion about the extramarital sex, Moon himself told Nansook Hong that "what happened in his past was 'providential,'" she wrote.[11]

As for the sexual purification rituals, Nansook Hong said the rumors had followed the church for decades, despite the official denials. "In the early days of the Unification Church, members met in a small house with two rooms," Nansook Hong wrote. "It was known as the House of the Three Doors. It was rumored that at the first door one was made to take off one's jacket, at the second door one's outer clothing, and at the third one's undergarments in preparation for sex." As for Chung Hwa Pak's *Tragedy of the Six Marys*, Nansook Hong said Moon succeeded in persuading his old associate to rejoin the church and then got him to disavow the memoirs. "I've always wondered what the price was of that retraction," Nansook Hong wrote.[12]

Madelene Pretorious, a Unification Church member from South Africa, also had worked closely with Moon's temperamental son, Hyo Jin, and had learned from him that the long-denied accounts of Moon's sexual rites with female initiates were true. "When Hyo Jin found out about his father's 'purification' rituals, that took a lot out of wind out of his sails," Pretorious told me in an interview after she left the church in the mid-1990s.

In late 1994, during conversations in Hyo Jin's suite at the New Yorker Hotel, "he confided a lot of things to me," Pretorious said. Hyo Jin also had discovered that the Reverend Moon fathered a child out of wedlock in the early 1970s. Moon arranged for the child to be raised by his longtime lieutenant Bo Hi Pak, Pretorious said. The boy – now a young man – had confronted Hyo Jin, seeking recognition as Hyo Jin's half-brother. Pretorious said she later corroborated the story with other church members.[13]

***

The alleged sexual rituals, which involved passing around women, would
become a point of embarrassment later, but the practices apparently helped
the Unification Church in recruiting men in the early days. By the late 1950s,
Moon had managed to build a small cadre of loyal followers and was
reaching out beyond Korea, sending his first missionaries to Japan and the
United States. By the early 1960s, the church was pulling in better educated
young men, including some with connections to South Korea's intelligence
agency, the KCIA.

Kim Jong-Pil and three other young English-speaking army officers
became closely associated with Moon's church during this transitional phase
as the institution evolved from an obscure Korean sect into a powerful
international organization. Beyond his association with Moon's sect, Kim
Jong-Pil was a rising star in South Korea's intelligence community. In 1961,
he founded the KCIA, which centralized Seoul's internal and external
intelligence activities. Another one of the promising young KCIA officers
was Colonel Bo Hi Pak, also a Moon disciple.

With these KCIA officers, however, it was never clear whether religion
was paramount or if they simply recognized the potential that an international
church held as a cover for intelligence operations. In many countries,
especially the United States, churches are granted broad protections against
government interference. With missionaries traveling around the world and
with church members attending international religious conferences, a church
also provided an effective cover for spying, money laundering or passing on
messages to agents.

In 1962, Kim Jong-Pil traveled to San Francisco where he met with
Unification Church members. According to an account later published by a
congressional investigation, the KCIA founder promised discreet support for
Moon's church. At the same time of his contacts with associates from the
Unification Church, Kim Jong-Pil was in charge of another sensitive
negotiation: talks to improve bilateral relations with Japan, Korea's historic
enemy. Those talks put Kim Jong-Pil in touch with two other important
figures in the Far East, Japanese rightists Yoshio Kodama and Ryoichi
Sasakawa, who once hailed Italian dictator Benito Mussolini as "the perfect
fascist."

Kodama and Sasakawa were jailed as fascist war criminals at the end of
World War II, but a few years later, both Kodama and Sasakawa were freed
by U.S. military intelligence officials. The U.S. government turned to
Kodama and Sasakawa for help in combating communist labor unions and
student strikes, much as the CIA protected German Nazi war criminals who
supplied intelligence and performed other services in the intensifying Cold
War battles with European communists. Kodama and Sasakawa obliged U.S.

intelligence by dispatching right-wing goon squads to break up demonstrations.

The pair also allegedly grew rich from their association with the *yakuza*, a shadowy organized crime syndicate that profited off drug smuggling, gambling and prostitution in Japan and Korea. Behind the scenes, Kodama and Sasakawa became power-brokers in Japan's ruling Liberal Democratic Party.[14]. Kim Jong-Pil's contacts with these right-wing leaders proved invaluable to the Unification Church, which had made only a few converts in Japan by the early 1960s. .

Immediately after Kim Jong-Pil opened the door to Kodama and Sasakawa in late 1962, 50 leaders of an ultra-nationalist Japanese Buddhist sect converted *en masse* to the Unification Church. According to David E. Kaplan and Alec Dubro in their authoritative book, *Yakuza*, "Sasakawa became an adviser to Reverend Sun Myung Moon's Japanese branch of the Unification Church" and collaborated with Moon in building far-right anti-communist organizations in Asia.[15]

The church's growth spurt did not escape the notice of U.S. intelligence officers in the field. One CIA report, dated February 26, 1963, stated that "Kim Jong-Pil organized the Unification Church while he was director of the ROK [Republic of Korea] Central Intelligence Agency, and has been using the church, which had a membership of 27,000, as a political tool."

***

With alliances in place in Tokyo and Seoul, the Unification Church next took aim at Washington. In 1964, Bo Hi Pak, who was emerging as one of Moon's most able lieutenants, moved to America and started the Korean Cultural and Freedom Foundation, a front that performed the dual purpose of helping Moon meet important Americans, while assisting the KCIA in its international operations. Bo Hi Pak named KCIA founder Kim Jong-Pil to be the foundation's "honorary chairman." The foundation also sponsored the KCIA's anti-communist propaganda outlets, such as Radio of Free Asia, according to the congressional report on the Koreagate scandal.

Moon's church also was active in the Asian People's Anti-Communist League, a fiercely right-wing group founded by the governments of South Korea and Taiwan. In 1966, the group expanded into the World Anti-Communist League, an international alliance that brought together traditional conservatives with former Nazis, overt racialists and Latin American "death squad" operatives. In an interview, retired U.S. Army General John K. Singlaub, a former WACL president, said "the Japanese [WACL] chapter was taken over almost entirely by Moonies."

By the 1970s, the U.S. public was aware of Moon and his church, but much of the attention was negative. The totalitarian nature of Moon's church stood out in his staging of mass marriages, or "blessings," in which he would pair up husbands and wives who had never met. Moon also regulated the sexual behavior of even his married followers, a practice that replaced the more personal method of "blessing the womb" that allegedly had prevailed in the church's early days.

In 1973, amid American reversals in Indochina, alarm began to spread within Seoul's right-wing dictatorship about the strength of the U.S. commitment to defend South Korea in case of aggression from the communist North. Those fears led the KCIA to begin plotting how to bolster its allies in the United States and undermine its critics. Lee Jai Hyon, the chief cultural and information attaché at the South Korean embassy in Washington, later testified before the U.S. Congress that he sat in on a series of meetings chaired by the KCIA's station chief, involving senior embassy officials. Lee Jai Hyon described six sessions over a five-week period in spring 1973 at which a conspiracy was outlined to "manipulate," "coerce," "threaten," "co-opt," "seduce," and "buy off" political and other leaders of the United States.[16]

Lee Jai Hyon said one of the South Koreans participating in the operation was Bo Hi Pak, a follower of Reverend Moon, whom Lee knew vaguely as a nutty evangelist. At the time, Moon was raising concerns among U.S. immigration authorities for bringing hundreds of foreign followers to the United States on tourist visas and then assigning them to mobile fund-raising teams. But Moon, who owned property outside New York City while maintaining a residence in South Korea, somehow managed to secure a "green card" from the Nixon administration on April 30, 1973. The permit making Moon a "lawful permanent resident" also granted him more legal rights than would be available to a foreign visitor.

"The advantages of using the First Amendment were seen early," wrote Robert Boettcher, the former staff director of the House Subcommittee on International Relations, in his 1980 book, *Gifts of Deceit*. "Before Moon moved to the United States in 1971, he and his small band of followers realized the operation would have the most flexibility if it was called a church. Businesses, political activities, and tax-exempt status could be protected."[17]

As Moon stepped up his activities, however, the FBI soon began to suspect that Moon's activities had a political motive. The FBI summary of its evidence about Moon's church was marked by a number indicating that the Unification Church was under a counter-intelligence investigation in the 1970s. The report's title, "Organizations and Individuals Associated with the Reverend Sun Myung Moon and/or the Unification Church," refers specifically to possible violation of the foreign agent registration law.[18]

Although blacked-out portions obscured who was stating some of the conclusions – an individual source or the FBI – the report described the church as "an absolutely totalitarian organization" which was part of an international "conspiracy" that functioned by its own rules. "One of the central doctrines of the Moon relig[i]ous aspects is what they call heavenly deception. ... It basically says that to take from Satan what rightfully belongs to God, you may do most anything. You may lie, cheat, steal or kill."

Despite the FBI's concerns, Moon began making friends in Washington the old fashioned way: by spreading around lots of money. Moon also had his followers cozy up to government officials. According to the FBI summary, Moon designated "300 pretty girls" to lobby members of Congress. "They were trying to influence United States senators and congressmen on behalf of South Korea," the FBI document read.[19]

"Moon had laid the foundation for political work in this country prior to 1973 [though] his followers became more openly involved in political activities in that and subsequent years," a congressional investigative report on the so-called "Koreagate" influence-buying scandal stated in 1978. The report added that Moon's organization used his followers' travels to smuggle large sums of money into the United States in apparent violation of federal currency laws.

Moon organized rallies in support of the Vietnam War and in defense of President Nixon during the Watergate scandal. Moon sponsored a National Prayer and Fast Committee, using the slogan: "forgive, love, unite." The public rallies earned Moon a face-to-face "thank you" from the embattled President on February 1, 1974.

***

In late 1975, the CIA intercepted a secret South Korean document entitled "1976 Plan for Operations in the United States." In the name of "strengthening the execution of the U.S. security commitment to the ROK [South Korea]," it called for influencing U.S. public opinion by penetrating American media, government and academia.

Thousands of dollars were earmarked for "special manipulation" of congressmen; their staffs were to be infiltrated with paid "collaborators"; an "intelligence network" was to be put into the White House; money was targeted for "manipulation" of officials at the Pentagon, State Department and CIA; some U.S. journalists were to be spied on, while others would be paid; a "black newspaper" would be started in New York; contacts with American scholars would be coordinated "with Psychological Warfare Bureau"; and "an organizational network of anti-communist fronts" would be created.

Several months later, in summer 1976, Moon returned to the United States and delivered a flattering pro-U.S. speech at a red-white-and-blue flag-draped rally at the Washington Monument. "The United States of America, transcending race and nationality, is already a model of the unified world," Moon declared on September 18, 1976. Calling America "the chosen nation of God," Moon said, "I not only respect America, but truly love this nation."

While professing his love for America in public, Moon shared with his followers a very different sentiment in private. He despised American concepts of individuality and democracy, believing that he was destined to rule through a one-world theocracy that would eradicate all personal freedoms. "Here's a man [Moon] who says he wants to take over the world, where all religions will be abolished except Unificationism, all languages will be abolished except Korean, all governments will be abolished except his one-world theocracy," said Steve Hassan, a former church leader, in an interview. "Yet he's wined and dined very powerful people and convinced them that he's benign."

In 1976, Moon's search for growing influence in the United States seemed to be following the KCIA script. Moon started a small-circulation newspaper in New York City that featured a column by civil rights leader Jesse Jackson. Moon promoted the anti-communist cause through front groups which held lavish conferences and paid speaking fees to academics, journalists and political leaders. In 1976, Moon, Bo Hi Pak and other church members deepened their investments in the U.S. capital, buying stock in the Washington-based Diplomat National Bank. Simultaneously, South Korean agent Tongsun Park was investing heavily in the same bank.

But the South Korean scheme backfired in the late 1970s with the explosion of the "Koreagate" scandal. Representative Donald Fraser, a Democrat from Minnesota, led a congressional probe which tracked Tongsun Park's influence-buying campaign and exposed the KCIA links to the Unification Church. The "Koreagate" investigation revealed a sophisticated intelligence project run out of Seoul, using the urbane Park and the mystical Moon to cultivate U.S. politicians as influential friends of South Korea – and to undermine politicians who were viewed as enemies.

The "Koreagate" investigation traced the church's chief sources of money to bank accounts in Japan, but could follow the cash no further. In the years since, the sources of Moon's money have remained cloaked in secrecy.

When I inquired about the vast fortune that the Unification Church has poured into its American operations, the church's chief spokesman refused to divulge dollar amounts for any of Moon's activities. "Each year the church retains an independent accounting firm to do a national audit and produce an annual financial statement," wrote the church's legal representative Peter D. Ross. "While this statement is used in routine financial transactions by the church, [it] is not my policy to make it otherwise available." Ross also refused to pass on interview requests to Moon and other church leaders.

In 1978, Fraser got a taste of the negative side of Moon's propaganda clout as the South Korean religious leader's new U.S. conservative allies mounted a strong defense against the "Koreagate" allegations. In pro-Moon publications, Fraser and his staff were pilloried as leftists. Anti-Moon witnesses were assailed as unstable liars. Minor bookkeeping problems inside the investigation, such as Fraser's salary advances to some staff members, were seized upon to justify demands for an ethics probe of the congressman.

One of those letters, dated June 30, 1978, was written by John T. "Terry" Dolan of the National Conservative Political Action Committee (NCPAC). Dolan's group was pioneering the strategy of "independent" TV attack ads against liberal Democrats. In turn, Moon's CAUSA International helped Dolan by contributing $500,000 to a Dolan group, known as the Conservative Alliance or CALL.[20] With support from Dolan and other conservatives, Moon weathered the Koreagate political storm. Facing questions about his patriotism, Fraser lost a Senate bid in 1978 and left Congress.

By the late 1970s, the conservative Counter-Establishment – with a growing capability of protecting its friends and destroying its enemies – was taking shape.

Chapter 6: The First Restoration

On March 23, 1979, late on a Friday afternoon, Chase Manhattan Bank Chairman David Rockefeller and his longtime aide Joseph Verner Reed arrived at a town house in the exclusive Beekham Place neighborhood on New York's East Side. They were met inside by a small, intense and deeply worried woman who had seen her life turned upside down in the last two months. Iran's Princess Ashraf, the strong-willed twin sister of the Iran's long-time ruler, had gone from wielding immense behind-the-scenes clout in the ancient nation of Persia to living in exile – albeit a luxurious one.

With hostile Islamic fundamentalists running her homeland, Ashraf also was troubled by the plight of her ailing brother, the ousted Shah of Iran, who had fled into exile, first to Egypt and then Morocco. Now, she was turning for help to the man who ran one of the leading U.S. banks, one which had made a fortune serving as the Shah's banker for a quarter century and handling billions of dollars in Iran's assets. Ashraf's message was straightforward. She wanted Rockefeller to intercede with Jimmy Carter and ask the President to relent on his decision against granting the Shah refuge in the United States. A distressed Ashraf said her brother had been given a one-week deadline to leave his current place of refuge, Morocco. "My brother has nowhere to go," Ashraf pleaded, "and no one else to turn to."[1]

Carter had been resisting appeals to let the Shah enter the United States, fearing that admitting him would endanger the personnel at the U.S. Embassy in Teheran and other U.S. interests. In mid-February 1979, Iranian radicals had overrun the embassy and briefly held the staff hostage before the Iranian government intervened to secure release of the Americans. Carter feared a repeat of the crisis. Already the United States was deeply unpopular with the Islamic revolution because of the CIA's history of meddling in Iranian affairs. The U.S. spy agency had helped organize the overthrow of an elected nationalist government in 1953 and the restoration of the Shah and the Pahlavi family to the Peacock Throne. In the quarter century that followed, the Shah kept his opponents at bay through the coercive powers of his secret police, known as the SAVAK.

As the Islamic Revolution gained strength in January 1979, however, the Shah's security forces could no longer keep order. The Shah – suffering from terminal cancer – scooped up a small pile of Iranian soil, boarded his jet, sat down at the controls and flew the plane out of Iran to Egypt. A few days later, Ayatollah Ruhollah Khomeini, an ascetic religious leader who had been forced into exile by the Shah, returned to a tumultuous welcome from crowds estimated at one million strong, shouting "Death to the Shah." The new Iranian government began demanding that the Shah be returned to stand trial for human rights crimes and that he surrender his fortune, salted away in overseas accounts. The new Iranian government also wanted Chase Manhattan to return Iranian assets, which Rockefeller put at more than $1 billion in 1978,[2] although some estimates ran much higher. The withdrawal might have created a liquidity crisis for the bank which already was coping with financial troubles.

Ashraf's personal appeal put Rockefeller in what he described, with understatement, as "an awkward position," according to his autobiography *Memoirs*. "There was nothing in my previous relationship with the Shah that made me feel a strong obligation to him," wrote the scion of the Rockefeller oil and banking fortune who had long prided himself in straddling the worlds of high finance and public policy. "He had never been a friend to whom I owed a personal debt, and neither was his relationship with the bank one that would justify my taking personal risks on his behalf. Indeed, there might be severe repercussions for Chase if the Iranian authorities determined that I was being too helpful to the Shah and his family."

Later on March 23, after leaving Ashraf's residence, Rockefeller attended a dinner with Happy Rockefeller, the widow of his brother Nelson who had died two months earlier. Also at the dinner was former Secretary of State Henry Kissinger, a long-time associate of the Rockefeller family. Discussing the Shah's plight, Happy Rockefeller described her late husband's close friendship with the Shah, which had included a weekend stay with the Shah and his wife in Teheran in 1977. Happy said that when Nelson learned that the Shah would be forced to leave Iran, Nelson offered to pick out a new home for the Shah in the United States. The dinner conversation also turned to the dangerous precedent that President Carter was setting by turning his back on a prominent U.S. ally. What message of American timidity was being sent to other pro-U.S. leaders in the Middle East?[3]

The dinner led to a public campaign by Rockefeller – along with Kissinger and former Chase Manhattan Bank Chairman John McCloy – to find a suitable home in exile for the Shah. Country after country closed their doors to the Shah as he began a humiliating odyssey as what Kissinger would call a modern-day "Flying Dutchman," wandering in search of a safe harbor. Rockefeller assigned his aide, Joseph Reed, "to help [the Shah] in any way he could," including serving as the Shah's liaison to the U.S. government.[4]

McCloy, one of the so-called Wise Men of the post-World War II era, was representing Chase Manhattan as an attorney with Milbank, Tweed, Hadley and McCloy. One of his duties was to devise a financial strategy for staving off Iran's withdrawal of assets from the bank.

Rockefeller also pressed the Shah's case personally with Carter when the opportunity presented itself. On April 9, 1979, at the end of an Oval Office meeting on another topic, Rockefeller handed Carter a one-page memo describing the views of many foreign leaders disturbed by recent U.S. foreign policy actions, including Carter's treatment of the Shah. "With virtually no exceptions, the heads of state and other government leaders I saw expressed concern about United States foreign policy which they perceived to be vacillating and lacking in an understandable global approach," Rockefeller's memo read. "They have questions about the dependability of the United States as a friend." An irritated Carter abruptly ended the meeting.[5]

Despite the mounting pressure from influential quarters, Carter continued to rebuff appeals to let the Shah into the United States. So the Shah's influential friends began looking for alternative locations, asking other nations to shelter the ex-Iranian ruler. Finally, arrangements were made for the Shah to fly to the Bahamas and – when the Bahamian government turned out to be more interested in money than humanitarianism – to Mexico.

"With the Shah safely settled in Mexico, I had hopes that the need for my direct involvement on his behalf had ended," Rockefeller wrote. "Therefore, while Henry [Kissinger] continued to publicly criticize the Carter administration for its overall management of the Iranian crisis and other aspects of its foreign policy, and Jack McCloy bombarded [Carter's Secretary of State] Cyrus Vance with letters demanding the Shah's admission to the United States, I did nothing else, publicly or privately, to influence the administration's thinking on this matter."[6]

When the Shah's medical condition took a turn for the worse in October, however, Carter relented and agreed to let the Shah fly to New York for emergency treatment. Celebrating Carter's reversal, Rockefeller's aide Joseph Reed wrote in a memo, "our 'mission impossible' is completed. ... My applause is like thunder."[7] When the Shah arrived in New York on October 23, 1976, Reed checked the Shah into New York Hospital under a pseudonym, "David Newsome," a play on the name of Carter's under-secretary of state for political affairs, David Newsom.[8]

* * *

The arrival of the Shah in New York led to renewed demands from Iran's new government that the Shah be returned to stand trial.

In Teheran, students and other radicals gathered at the university, called by their leaders to what was described as an important meeting, according to one of the participants whom I interviewed years later. The students gathered in a classroom which had three blackboards turned toward the wall. A speaker told the students that they were about to undertake a mission supported by Ayatollah Khomeini, Iran's spiritual leader and the *de facto* head of the government.

"They said it would be dangerous and that anyone who didn't want to take part could leave now," the Iranian told me. "But no one left. Then, they turned around the blackboards. There were three buildings drawn on the blackboards. They were the buildings of the U.S. embassy."[9]

The Iranian said the target of the raid was not the embassy personnel, but rather the embassy's intelligence documents. "We had believed that the U.S. government had been manipulating affairs inside Iran and we wanted to prove it," he said. "We thought if we could get into the embassy, we could get the documents that would prove this. We hadn't thought about the hostages. We all went to the embassy. We had wire cutters to cut through the fence. We started climbing over the fences. We had expected more resistance. When we got inside, we saw the Americans running and we chased them."[10]

Marine guards set off tear gas in a futile attempt to control the mob, but held their fire to avoid bloodshed. Other embassy personnel hastily shredded classified documents, although there wasn't time to destroy many of the secret papers. The militant students found themselves in control not only of the embassy and hundreds of sensitive U.S. cables, but dozens of American hostages as well. An international crisis had begun, a hinge that would swing open unexpected doors for both American and Iranian history.

David Rockefeller denied that his campaign to gain the Shah's admittance to the United States had provoked the crisis, arguing that he was simply filling a vacuum created when the Carter administration balked at doing the right thing. "Despite the insistence of journalists and revisionist historians, there was never a 'Rockefeller-Kissinger behind-the-scenes campaign' that placed 'relentless pressure' on the Carter administration to have the Shah admitted to the United States regardless of the consequences," Rockefeller wrote in *Memoirs*. "In fact, it would be more accurate to say that for many months we were the unwilling surrogates for a government that had failed to accept its full responsibilities."[11]

But within the Iranian hostage crisis, there would be hidden compartments within hidden compartments, as influential groups around the world acted in what they perceived to be their personal or their national interests. Rockefeller was just one of many powerful people who felt that Jimmy Carter had fallen down on the job and that a new direction was needed from Washington. With the hostage crisis started, a countdown of 365 days began toward the 1980 elections. Though he may have been only dimly aware of his predicament, Carter faced a remarkable coalition of enemies and adversaries both inside and outside the United States.

In the Persian Gulf, the Saudi royal family and other Arab oil sheiks blamed Carter for forsaking the Shah and feared their own playboy life styles might be next on the list for the Islamic fundamentalists. The Israeli government saw Carter as too cozy with the Palestinians and too eager to cut a peace deal that would force Israel to surrender land won in the 1967 war. European anti-communists believed Carter was too soft on the Soviet Union and was risking the security of Europe. Dictators in the Third World – from the Philippines and South Korea to Argentina and El Salvador – were bristling at Carter's human rights lectures.

Inside the United States, the Carter administration had made enemies at the CIA by purging many of the Old Boys who saw themselves as protectors of America's deepest national interests. Many CIA veterans, including some still within the government, were disgruntled. And, of course, the Republicans were determined to win back the White House, which many felt had been unjustly taken from their control after Nixon's landslide victory in 1972.

This subterranean struggle between Carter, trying desperately to free the hostages before the 1980 election, and those who stood to benefit by thwarting him became known popularly as the "October Surprise" controversy. The nickname referred to the possibility that Carter might have ensured his reelection by arranging the hostage return the month before the presidential election as an October Surprise, although it came ultimately to refer to clandestine efforts to stop Carter from pulling off his October Surprise.

But the question of whether George H.W. Bush and other Republicans, in fact, did conspire with Iranians and international operatives to block Carter's October Surprise would become not only a political mystery but a test of whether it is possible to determine the truth when many powerful interests are threatened by it. Given the complexity of the mystery and the questionable credibility of some witnesses, the October Surprise case also pressed the limits of how much the American people ever get to know about their nation's secret history.

***

Just as the trauma of Watergate and the CIA scandals may have instilled a temporary sense of caution among Republicans and other conservatives, the avoidance of serious political damage from incidents, such as the Letelier assassination in 1976 and the disclosure of Reverend Moon's influence-buying operations in 1978, emboldened them to take greater risks at the start of the 1980s.

In a similar way, Nixon may have undertaken his Watergate adventure in 1972, in part, because of his success in secretly sabotaging President Lyndon B. Johnson's last-ditch attempt to negotiate a Vietnam peace agreement at the end of the 1968 presidential campaign, when 500,000 U.S. troops were in Vietnam. Though Johnson got wind of Nixon's scheme, the Democratic President kept quiet, partly out of fear that the plot's exposure could devastate the international image of the United States, especially if Nixon still won. By staying silent, however, Johnson may have encouraged other Republican schemes, hatched out of a confidence that the Democrats were too ineffectual to discover the facts or too timid to blow the whistle.

Nixon's Vietnam gambit in 1968 was also the direct antecedent to the allegations of Reagan-Bush interference in Carter's hostage negotiations in 1980. Indeed, the evidence of Nixon's Vietnam scheming undercuts one of the strongest arguments against believing the allegations about the 1980 "October Surprise" case, that as bare-knuckled as U.S. politics can be, there are lines that no responsible political leader would cross, either out of patriotism or fear of getting caught. But the 1968 incident, as pieced together by journalists and historians in the three-and-a-half decades that followed, suggests that any such line might be fuzzier than believed or might not exist at all, that when the enormous power of the U.S. government is at stake, some politicians will do whatever it takes to win and worry about managing the consequences later.

The first major recounting of Nixon's sabotage of Johnson's Paris peace talks – by offering South Vietnam's President Nguyen van Thieu a better deal from Republicans than was available from the Democrats – came 15 years after the actual events, in Seymour Hersh's 1983 political biography of Henry Kissinger, *The Price of Power*. According to Hersh's book, Kissinger learned of Johnson's peace plans and warned Nixon's campaign. "It is certain," Hersh wrote, "that the Nixon campaign, alerted by Kissinger to the impending success of the peace talks, was able to get a series of messages to the Thieu government making it clear that a Nixon Presidency would have different views on the peace negotiations."[12]

Nixon's chief emissary was Anna Chennault, an anti-communist Chinese leader who was working with the Nixon campaign. Hersh quoted one former official in President Lyndon Johnson's Cabinet as stating that the U.S. intelligence "agencies had caught on that Chennault was the go-between between Nixon and his people, and President Thieu in Saigon. ... The idea was to bring things to a stop in Paris and prevent any show of progress."

In her memoirs, *The Education of Anna*, Chennault acknowledged that she was the courier. She quoted Nixon campaign manager John Mitchell as calling her a few days before the 1968 election and telling her: "I'm speaking on behalf of Mr. Nixon. It's very important that our Vietnamese friends understand our Republican position and I hope you have made that clear to them."[13]

On November 2, four days before the U.S. election, Thieu withdrew from his tentative agreement to sit down with the Viet Cong at the Paris peace talks, killing Johnson's last hope for a settlement of the war. A late Humphrey surge fell short and Nixon won a narrow election victory.

In *The Price of Power*, Hersh quoted Chennault as saying that after the election, in 1969, Mitchell and Nixon urged her to keep quiet about her mission, which could have implicated them in an act close to treason. [14] As the Vietnam War dragged on for another four years, tens of thousands of U.S. soldiers died, as did hundreds of thousands of Indochinese. When the allegations of the secret deal surfaced, survivors of the Nixon administration denied them, depicting Chennault as a freelance operative working on her own initiative.

Over the years, more historical pieces fell into place, however. In his 1991 memoirs, *Counsel to the President*, Clark Clifford, Johnson's Secretary of Defense, wrote that as the peace initiative advanced in October 1968, the Johnson administration was stunned by "our discovery, through intelligence channels, of a plot – there is no other word for it – to help Nixon win the election by a flagrant interference in the negotiations." [15]

Four years after Clifford's book, Daniel Schorr, the former CBS News correspondent, added more details to the story in a *Washington Post* article. Schorr cited decoded cables that U.S. intelligence had intercepted from the South Vietnamese embassy in Washington. On October 23, 1968, Ambassador Bui Diem cabled Saigon with the message that "many Republican friends have contacted me and encouraged me to stand firm," according to Schorr's article. On October 27, 1968, the Ambassador wrote, "The longer the present situation continues, the more favorable for us. ... I am regularly in touch with the Nixon entourage." [16]

Perhaps the fullest account of Nixon's 1968 gambit appeared in 2000 in Anthony Summers's *The Arrogance of Power*. "This is a story that has long hung between the shadows of Nixon's past and the disgrace of his Presidency, half reported on partial evidence, often exploited by partisan sources, yet never fully resolved," Summers wrote. "He escaped full opprobrium for his behavior while he was alive, yet the evidence implies a sin and a cynicism worse than any of the offenses that would later make headlines." [17]

Summers reported that Chennault brought South Vietnam's ambassador, Bui Diem, to Nixon's apartment in July 1968 for a secret meeting with Nixon. Chennault recalled Nixon saying that if he won the election, "I will have a meeting with your leader and find a solution to winning this war." Nixon designated Chennault his contact with Thieu's government, she said. Chennault said she met with Thieu, who expressed a preference for peace talks after the U.S. election and asked her to "convey this message to your candidate." [18]

At meetings with Nixon and Mitchell in New York, Chennault said she was told to tell Saigon that if Nixon won, South Vietnam would get "a better deal," a message that she then relayed. "They worked out this deal to win the campaign," Chennault said in an interview for the Summers book. Explaining why, she said, "Power overpowers all reason."

When President Johnson pressed ahead with his peace initiative in October 1968, Chennault said Mitchell repeatedly told her it was vital that she convince Thieu not to take part. A CIA bug planted in Thieu's office picked up the South Vietnamese president saying, "Johnson and Humphrey will be replaced and then Nixon could change the U.S. position."[19]

Then, on October 29, when Johnson announced a bombing halt to set the stage for the peace talks, he received fresh information from Wall Street banker Alexander Sachs that Nixon was "trying to frustrate the President, by inciting Saigon to step up its demands," Summers reported. "It all adds up," Johnson told his advisers. Johnson ordered Chennault placed under surveillance as he struggled to reverse the South Vietnamese position. Though Johnson grew angrier, he was reminded that he had no solid evidence tying Nixon directly to the peace-talks sabotage.

Author Summers said one FBI cable released in 1999 offered more evidence of Nixon's plot. From the wiretapping of Ambassador Bui Diem's phone, the FBI's Washington Field Office reported on November 2 that Chennault "contacted Vietnamese Ambassador Bui Diem, and advised him that she had received a message from her boss (not further identified), which her boss wanted her to give personally to the Ambassador. She said the message was that the Ambassador is to 'hold on, we are gonna win' and that her boss also said 'hold on, he understands all of it. ' She repeated that this is the only message[.] 'He said please tell your boss to hold on.' She advised that her boss had just called from New Mexico." Nixon's vice presidential running mate, Spiro Agnew, had been in Albuquerque, New Mexico, that day.[20]

Nixon learned of Johnson's fury over the Republican interference and called the President to deny the reports. Nixon insisted that Chennault was operating on her own. But Johnson didn't believe Nixon. "Johnson was certain in his own mind," aide Joe Califano said, "that Nixon had betrayed his country."

Though furious, Johnson kept quiet as did Humphrey, who doubted that the raw information available at the time could make a convincing case. Summers wrote, "Johnson's advisers decided it was too late and too potentially damaging to U.S. interests to expose what had been going on. If Nixon should emerge as the victor, what would the Chennault outrage do to his viability as an incoming President? And what effect would it have on American opinion about the war?"[21]

In 2002, former South Vietnamese Vice President Nguyen Cao Ky described the Republican initiative from the Saigon government's point of view in his memoirs *Buddha's Child*. Chennault, Ky wrote, "told us that Nixon was far more anticommunist than Humphrey and that if he was elected he would make sure that U.S. aid continued until the war was won. But,

Madame Chennault explained, first he needed *our* help. We could help by not going to the Paris peace conference until *after* the election. If we refused to participate in negotiations, she explained, Nixon would be able to condemn the Democratic Party and Humphrey as weaklings. There would be no light at the end of the tunnel, no hope for a quick peace. "[22]

Anna Chennault may have been right in her observation that "power overpowers all reason." But it is equally true that there is nothing irrational about the raw application of power if secrecy and privilege can protect you from exposure.

Chapter 7: The Pieces Arrayed

The October Surprise mystery in 1980 marked a new level of involvement in a scandal by George H.W. Bush.

After years of performing what might be called clean-up duty for Nixon and the CIA, Bush would emerge as a principal in the October Surprise case. Bush would serve as both a coordinator of a Republican intelligence operation about President Carter's Iranian initiatives and an alleged intermediary to the Iranians seeking their cooperation with the Reagan-Bush campaign.

What is not in doubt is that Bush – first as a Republican presidential candidate and then as the party's vice presidential nominee – served as a ringleader for a host of disgruntled former CIA officials, who had worked for Bush when he was CIA director. These ex-intelligence officers were so distraught over Carter's handling of the spy agency and his conduct of foreign policy that they cast off their traditional cloak of anonymity and joined the effort to oust the sitting President.

In Bush's campaign for the Republican nomination, ex-covert CIA officers volunteered as public foot soldiers. One joke making the rounds about Bush's announcement of his presidential candidacy on May 1, 1979, was that "half the audience was wearing raincoats." Bill Colby, Bush's predecessor as CIA director, said Bush "had a flood of people from the CIA who joined his supporters. They were retirees devoted to him for what he had done" at the spy agency.

All told, at least two dozen former CIA officials went to work for their former boss. Among them was the CIA's director of security, Robert Gambino, who left the CIA immediately before joining the Bush campaign, causing concern within the Carter administration because of Gambino's knowledge about security investigations of senior officials and the personal information that must be divulged in those inquiries.[1]

Beyond the ex-CIA personnel who joined the Bush campaign were other intelligence officers who remained in the CIA but still made clear their choice for President. "The seventh floor of Langley was plastered with 'Bush for President' signs,'" George Carver, a senior CIA analyst, told me.

Carter administration officials also worried about the personal relationships between some former CIA officers in Bush's campaign and active-duty CIA personnel who continued to hold sensitive jobs inside the

Democratic administration. For instance, Gambino, a 25-year CIA veteran, and CIA officer Donald Gregg, who served as a CIA representative on Carter's National Security Council, "are good friends who knew each other from the CIA," according to an unpublished section of a report by a House Task Force, which investigated the October Surprise issue in 1992.[*]

Still, Jimmy Carter never appreciated how much he was surrounded by enemies. He was the proverbial babe in the woods. Out of necessity or naivety, Carter and his administration also turned to people he believed might help resolve the hostage crisis while not knowing their full connections to some of his most dedicated adversaries.

***

Frantically looking for emissaries to Iran's revolutionary government in late 1979, the Carter administration accepted the assistance of an Iranian banker named Cyrus Hashemi, who presented himself as a conduit to the Iranian mullahs. A worldly businessman in his 40s with one foot in the West and the other back in Iran, Hashemi seemed a reasonable candidate. He was well-tailored, well-schooled and well-connected. Politically savvy, he could put together deals in a variety of commodities, especially oil and weapons. When he visited Europe, he stayed at the best hotels; when he crossed the Atlantic, he took the supersonic Concorde.

"When I first met Cyrus," former Attorney General Elliot Richardson said, "he was elegantly turned out by a Bond Street tailor. He was very personable, unassuming, soft-spoken, intelligent, gracious in manner. He seemed in every way consistent with being a well-educated Iranian with an advanced degree from Oxford that he was said to have, a person who would have moved comfortably in international banking circles. Everything about him was perfectly consistent with that image. He lived on a very opulent scale, not ostentatiously so, more Oxfordian than blatantly *nouveau riche*."[2]

Richardson had met Hashemi in 1979 and was one of the people who vouched for Hashemi with Carter administration officials who were overseeing the hostage negotiations. Richardson said Hashemi acted like the "kind of moderate, responsible, internationally oriented Iranian who would have been embarrassed by fundamentalism and would have been embarrassed by the seizure of the hostages." But Hashemi had a darker side. He was a high-rolling gambler, a womanizer and a man who hid his deepening financial troubles. When he died in London in 1986, Cyrus Hashemi owed casinos there three million pounds or about $5 million. His bank, Netherlands Antilles-based First Gulf Bank and Trust Company, was a shell. He left his family destitute.

---

[*] I found the deleted section – still marked "secret" – in unpublished task force files in 1994.

"He was by no means the urbane, civilized, decent banker/economist that he seemed to be when I met him," Richardson said. "Hashemi was a person capable of playing more than one role simultaneously and seeming quite convincing to his audience whoever it was. So what I know now is not wholly inconsistent to his having been playing a double or a triple game." In 1979, Cyrus Hashemi's principal audience was the Carter administration as he pitched himself as the missing link in reaching the hard-line mullahs around Khomeini.

Gary Sick, a Middle East expert on Carter's National Security Council, said Hashemi established himself in December 1979 as a well-informed Iranian who could help the administration sort out Iran's new ruling elite. "Cyrus Hashemi quickly demonstrated that he had access to a number of high-level officials in the Iranian revolutionary government, most notably the governor-general of Khuzistan [Ahmad Madani] but also individuals within Khomeini's own family," Sick wrote in his book, *October Surprise*. "He clearly understood the politics and internal decision-making within the still-mysterious Revolutionary Council, which had assumed supreme authority in the nation."[3]

Besides helping the Carter administration, however, Cyrus Hashemi was maintaining personal and business ties to key Republicans, most notably former U.S. intelligence officer John Shaheen, a Lebanese-born, New York-based businessman who was a close friend of William J. Casey, himself a former spy who had held senior positions in the Nixon administration, including chairman of the Securities and Exchange Commission. Shaheen and Casey had served together in the World War II-era Office of Strategic Services, the forerunner to the CIA. After the war, Shaheen and Casey remained friends and became business associates. Both men were known for cutting ethical corners in their checkered business dealings.

In the 1970s, Casey, a lawyer at the politically well-connected firm of Rogers and Wells, advised Shaheen on a troubled oil refinery that Shaheen built at the wind-swept coastal town of Come-by-Chance, Newfoundland. Casey traveled with Shaheen to Kuwait to negotiate a source of oil for the refinery, though the poorly engineered facility would ultimately fail, never having produced a drop of gasoline. Shaheen and Casey also kept their hands in the intelligence business and maintained close ties to the CIA.[4]

According to Cyrus's older brother, Jamshid Hashemi, the dealings between Cyrus and Shaheen dated back to the late 1970s when Cyrus was running his First Gulf and Trust out of offices in Manhattan and London. "For many years, he [Cyrus] had been cooperating with Mr. Shaheen," Jamshid told me. "I asked him [Cyrus] in 1979, at the end of 1979. He was very open about it. He knew that Mr. Shaheen had contacts with the government of the United States. At that time, I did not know which section or which organization."

The Shaheen connection led Cyrus Hashemi to William Casey, months before Casey would become officially associated with Ronald Reagan's presidential campaign, according to Jamshid Hashemi and a 1984 CIA memo that surfaced during a later investigation. According to the CIA memo, former Attorney General Richardson said in 1984 that Casey had recruited Shaheen and Cyrus in 1979 to sell off property in New York City belonging to the Shah's Pahlavi Foundation. At the time, the radical Islamic government in Teheran was claiming the property as its own and the Shah's family was desperate for the cash.

Shaheen also appears to have been the first person to put Cyrus Hashemi in touch with the CIA. A Shaheen friend whom I interviewed told me that Shaheen was the person who introduced Cyrus to the spy agency, helping to make him and his bank a conduit for funneling CIA funds to a variety of covert operations, a claim that was later backed up by Cyrus's brother Jamshid.[5]

***

In Iran, the Hashemi brothers already were known as politically dexterous businessmen. They managed to end up on the right side of the Iranian revolution by smartly throwing their support to the anti-Shah forces and exploiting family and personal connections. After the revolution, as Cyrus pursued his banking business outside Iran, older brother Jamshid Hashemi received an appointment from the new government to oversee the national radio network. That job, in turn, put him in touch with other influential Iranians, he said. One was a radical Islamic cleric, named Mehdi Karrubi. Another was Karrubi's brother, Hassan.

"As I was running the radio, Mr. Hassan Karrubi came as a representative of the Iman [Khomeini]," Jamshid Hashemi said. "From that day, I was sitting at one side of the table and he was sitting at the other side of the table, and we were running ... the different radios of Iran." Meanwhile, outside Iran, Cyrus Hashemi's First Gulf was emerging as a bank which handled clandestine money transfers for the new Iranian government. Jamshid Hashemi said that when Teheran feared that Iranian navy funds might be frozen at banks in the United States, the United Kingdom and West Germany, arrangements were made to shift the funds into First Gulf and then into newly created offshore banks.

"It was ordered that all these monies be transferred to an account of my brother, into his bank, which was done. The order of the transfer was from Admiral [Ahmad] Madani [who served as Iran's defense minister]. We went to the admiral with the telex and then we went to the war room of the navy in Teheran and we faxed it ... so he [Cyrus] could take over all the money, in late 1979, $30 to $35 million, to the account of the First Gulf."

Jamshid Hashemi said the attorney advising Cyrus Hashemi and John Shaheen about these transactions was William Casey. Casey "was the man who was actually putting all these things together for both of them in some foreign country at that time," Jamshid Hashemi said. "I didn't know which foreign country, but later on I found out that a bank had been physically opened in the Philippines and in Antigua. Casey was the adviser. ... On one occasion, Mr. Shaheen had come to [Cyrus's] house and they were discussing this matter of where to open the bank. Mr. Shaheen said that he was going to talk with and get advice from Mr. Casey whether the Philippines or this Caribbean city was the best place to open."

NSC official Gary Sick had a somewhat different take on the motive behind the Madani money transfer in late 1979. In his book *October Surprise*, Sick noted that Admiral Madani had emerged as a leading candidate for president of the new Iran, facing only one serious opponent, a popular academic, Abolhassan Bani-Sadr. Madani, who was widely respected as one of the few senior military officers who had the courage to criticize corruption in the Shah's government, had been close to both Cyrus and Jamshid Hashemi since childhood.

To beat Bani-Sadr, however, Madani needed money, and to arrange that money, Cyrus Hashemi persuaded military officers supporting the Madani candidacy to deposit defense ministry funds into First Gulf Trust in exchange for a five percent commission, Sick wrote. The commission money was then to be plowed into Madani's presidential campaign. But Cyrus Hashemi stiffed the military officers on the commission, according to Sick. They never got their five percent.[6]

When the pro-Madani officers started complaining, Cyrus began dangling the prospect of getting covert U.S. financing for the Madani campaign. Jamshid Hashemi said he received a call from his brother, summoning him from Iran to London. "I actually came for the purpose of getting funds for Admiral Madani's campaign to become president of the country," Jamshid said. "I did not plan to come to the United States at the time because we thought that through my brother we would get the necessary help. ... Once we came here [to London], my brother told me that the American government very much wanted to see and talk to me before I went back to Iran."

It was during that London stopover that Jamshid Hashemi said he met John Shaheen. "Mr. Shaheen was an elderly gentlemen of 60-62 at the time. I met him at the [London] office of my brother's bank, First Gulf and Trust. He had white hair and probably was an inch taller than me. ... He came and took my passport. I said if he wanted to get an American visa for me, he should not get it in my passport. He said he knows all about it, that I don't need to tell him. He knows what sort of visa I need on a piece of paper, and that is exactly what the next day I have, my passport with a piece of paper with a signature giving me a multiple entry visa into the United States. ... In those days for an Iranian to get a visa within a few hours, it would have been a miracle."

But after arriving in the United States on January 1, 1980, Jamshid soon figured out that Shaheen's links to the CIA explained the miracle. "At the first meeting which I had with Mr. [Harold] Saunders [a Carter administration diplomat], there was a man who was introduced to me as from the White House who I later learned was not from the White House by the way. ... He was a CIA man. I believe he is now at one of the universities."

"Harvard?" I asked. "You mean Charles Cogan?" Cogan had been chief of the CIA's Middle East operations at the time.

"Yes, Charles Cogan. He was introduced to me under another name as a man from the White House. He asked me if everything was okay with the visa and so on. I showed him this is what we have. ... He said, 'yes, we know Mr. Shaheen.' He spoke very highly of Mr. Shaheen."

The CIA gave the Hashemi brothers $500,000 to deliver to the struggling Madani campaign. But only a small amount reached Iran – about $100,000 – and Madani lost badly to Abolhassan Bani-Sadr in the election. After the CIA demanded an accounting of the money, the Hashemis returned $290,000 to the agency. Though the Madani campaign strategy had failed, it had opened – or at least widened – channels for the Hashemi brothers to the U.S. government and the CIA.

***

On January 21, 1980, George H.W. Bush stunned the Republican presidential field by beating Ronald Reagan in the Iowa caucuses. In the glow of victory, Bush saw his face on the cover of *Newsweek* and claimed to possess the "Big Mo," a preppyish phrase for momentum. Bush next took aim at New Hampshire, next door to Maine where his family vacationed in the summer.

But Bush's Big Mo would last only long enough to force one historic change in the Reagan campaign structure. Reagan and his close advisers decided to fire John Sears as head of the campaign. Foreign policy adviser Richard Allen was among the Reagan loyalists who recommended Bill Casey, a crafty old spymaster who had worked for Nixon and had bounced around the tough world of Long Island politics. On February 26, the day of the New Hampshire primary, which Reagan would win, the former California governor and movie star replaced John Sears with William Casey.

"I feel very strongly that this country is in trouble, that it needs to be turned around and I have felt for over a year that Governor Reagan is the only man in America who's ever turned a government around," Casey said in accepting the job.

Years later, Casey's widow, Sophia, gave me an unpublished paper containing Casey's personal reflections on the campaign. Though the report focused on campaign mechanics, it also revealed Casey's dread at the prospect of four more years of Jimmy Carter in the White House. "Everyone [in Reagan's camp] agreed that Jimmy Carter had to be removed from office in order to save the nation from economic ruin and international humiliation," Casey wrote. He also recognized the pivotal role played by the Iranian hostage crisis in highlighting Carter's shortcomings. "The Iranian hostage crisis was the focal point of the failure of Carter's foreign policy," Casey wrote.

After his appointment, Casey went to work building a staunchly conservative organization that soon was rolling up victories for Ronald Reagan. But Casey also didn't forget what he viewed as the single-most important variable of the campaign: the 52 hostages whose continuing plight was growing into a national obsession. Casey, the old OSS veteran, wanted to know all he could about Carter's progress toward resolving the crisis. "Over the ensuing months, Casey and the Republican campaign systematically constructed an elaborate and sophisticated intelligence organization targeted on their own government," wrote former NSC official Gary Sick.[7]

As the hostage crisis dragged on, the attention of many CIA Old Boys also turned toward the American humiliation in Iran, which they found doubly hard to take since it had been the site of the agency's first major victory, the restoration of the Shah to the Peacock Throne in 1953. A number of veterans from that operation were still alive in 1980. Archibald Roosevelt was one of the Old Boys from the Iranian operation. He had moved on to become an adviser to David Rockefeller at Chase Manhattan Bank. Another was Miles Copeland, who had served the CIA as an intermediary to Arab leaders, including Egyptian President Gamal Abdul Nasser. In his autobiography, *The Game Player*, Copeland claimed that he and his CIA chums prepared their own Iranian hostage rescue plan in March 1980.

When I interviewed Copeland in 1990 at his thatched-roofed cottage outside Oxford in the English countryside, he said he had been a strong supporter of George H.W. Bush in 1980. He even had founded an informal support group called "Spooks for Bush." Sitting among photos of his children who included the drummer for the rock group, The Police, and the manager for the rock star, Sting, Copeland explained that he and his CIA colleagues considered Carter a dangerous idealist.

"Let me say first that we liked President Carter," Copeland told me "He read, unlike President Reagan later, he read everything. He knew what he was about. He understood the situation throughout the Middle East, even these tenuous, difficult problems such as Arabs and Israel. But the way we saw Washington at that time was that the struggle was really not between the Left and the Right, the liberals and the conservatives, as between the Utopians and the realists, the pragmatists. Carter was a Utopian. He believed, honestly, that you must do the right thing and take your chance on the consequences. He told me that. He literally believed that."

Copeland's deep Southern accent spit out the words with a mixture of amazement and disgust. To Copeland and his CIA friends, Carter deserved respect for a first-rate intellect but contempt for his idealism.

"Most of the things that were done [by the United States] about Iran had been on a basis of stark realism, with possibly the exception of letting the Shah down," Copeland said. "There are plenty of forces in the country we could have marshaled. ... We could have sabotaged [the revolution]. I think in the long run we'd have had a hard time to do it because Islam is the march of the future. But, yes, we could have done something about it. But we had to do it early. We had to establish what the Quakers call 'the spirit of the meeting' in the country, where everybody was thinking just one way. The Iranians were really like sheep, as they are now."

But Carter, troubled by the Shah's human rights record, delayed taking decisive action and missed the moment of opportunity, Copeland said. Infuriating the CIA's Old Boys, Carter had sacrificed an ally on the altar of idealism. "Carter really believed in all the principles that we talk about in the West," Copeland said, shaking his mane of white hair. "As smart as Carter is, he did believe in Mom, apple pie and the corner drug store. And those things that are good in America are good everywhere else."

Veterans of the CIA and Republicans from the Nixon-Ford administrations judged that Carter simply didn't measure up to the demands of a harsh world. "There were many of us – myself along with Henry Kissinger, David Rockefeller, Archie Roosevelt in the CIA at the time – we believed very strongly that we were showing a kind of weakness, which people in Iran and elsewhere in the world hold in great contempt," Copeland said. "The fact that we're being pushed around, and being afraid of the Ayatollah Khomeini, so we were going to let a friend down, which was horrifying to us. That's the sort of thing that was frightening to our friends in Saudi Arabia, in Egypt and other places."

But Carter also was susceptible to bending to the moral suasions of the Shah's friends, who argued on humanitarian grounds that the ailing Shah deserved admission to the United States for medical treatment. "Carter, I say, was not a stupid man," Copeland said. Carter had even a greater flaw: "He was a principled man." So, Carter decided that the moral act was to allow the Shah to enter the United States for treatment, leading to the result Carter had feared: the seizure of the U.S. Embassy.

When the crisis wasn't quickly resolved, the Carter administration cranked up the pressure on the Iranians. Along with diplomatic initiatives, Iran's assets were frozen, a move that ironically helped David Rockefeller's Chase Manhattan Bank by preventing the Iranians from cleaning out their funds from the bank's vaults. In *Memoirs*, Rockefeller wrote that the Iranian "government did reduce the balances they maintained with us during the second half of 1979, but in reality they had simply returned to their historic level of about $500 million," Rockefeller wrote. "Carter's 'freeze' of official

Iranian assets protected our position, but no one at Chase played a role in convincing the administration to institute it."[8]

***

In the weeks that followed the embassy seizure, Copeland said he and his friends turned their attention to figuring a way out of the mess. "There was very little sympathy for the hostages," Copeland said. "We all have served abroad, served in embassies like that. We got additional pay for danger. I think, for Syria, I got fifty percent extra in salary. So it's a chance you take. When you join the army, you take a chance of getting in a war and getting shot. If you're in the diplomatic service, you take a chance on having some horror like this descend on you.

"But on the other hand, we did think that there were things we could do to get them out, other than simply letting the Iranians, the students, and the Iranian administration know that they were beating us," Copeland said. "We let them know what an advantage they had. That we could have gotten them out is something that all of us old professionals of the covert action school, we said from the beginning, 'Why don't they let us do it?'"

According to *The Game Player*, Copeland met his old friend, ex-CIA counter-intelligence chief James Angleton, for lunch. The famed spy hunter "brought to lunch a Mossad chap who confided that his service had identified at least half of the 'students,' even to the extent of having their home addresses in Teheran," Copeland wrote. "He gave me a rundown on what sort of kids they were. Most of them, he said, were just that, kids."[9]

The Israeli government was another deeply interested player in the Iran crisis. For decades, Israel had cultivated covert ties with the Shah's regime as part of a Periphery Strategy of forming alliances with non-Arab states in the region to prevent Israel's Arab enemies from focusing all their might against Israel. Though losing an ally when the Shah fell and offended by the anti-Israeli rhetoric from the Khomeini regime, Israel had gone about quietly rebuilding relations with the Iranian government. One of the young Israeli intelligence agents assigned to this task was an Iranian-born Jew named Ari Ben-Menashe, who had immigrated to Israel as a teen-ager and was valuable because he spoke fluent Farsi and still had friends in Iran, some of whom were rising within the new revolutionary bureaucracy.

In his own 1992 memoirs, *Profits of War*, Ben-Menashe said the view of Israel's Likud leaders, including Prime Minister Menachem Begin, was one of contempt for Jimmy Carter in the late 1970s. "Begin loathed Carter for the peace agreement forced upon him at Camp David," Ben-Menashe wrote. "As Begin saw it, the agreement took away Sinai from Israel, did not create a comprehensive peace, and left the Palestinian issue hanging on Israel's back."[10]

After the Shah fell, Begin grew even more dissatisfied with Carter's handling of the crisis and alarmed over the growing likelihood of an Iraqi attack on Iran's oil-rich Khuzistan province. Israel saw Iraq's Saddam Hussein as a far greater threat to Israel than Iran's Khomeini. Ben-Menashe wrote that Begin, recognizing the *realpolitik* needs of Israel, authorized shipments to Iran of small arms and some spare parts, via South Africa, as early as September 1979.

After the U.S. hostages were taken in November 1979, the Israelis came to agree with Copeland's hard-headed skepticism about Carter's approach to the hostage issue, Ben-Menashe wrote. Even though Copeland was generally regarded as a CIA "Arabist" who had opposed Israeli interests in the past, he was admired for his analytical skills, Ben-Menashe wrote.

"A meeting between Miles Copeland and Israeli intelligence officers was held at a Georgetown house in Washington, D.C.," Ben-Menashe wrote. "The Israelis were happy to deal with any initiative but Carter's. David Kimche, chief of Tevel, the foreign relations unit of Mossad, was the senior Israeli at the meeting. ... The Israelis and the Copeland group came up with a two-pronged plan to use quiet diplomacy with the Iranians and to draw up a scheme for military action against Iran that would not jeopardize the lives of the hostages."[11]

In late February 1980, Seyeed Mehdi Kashani, an Iranian emissary, arrived in Israel to discuss Iran's growing desperation for aircraft spare parts, Ben-Menashe wrote. Kashani, whom Ben-Menashe had known from their school days in Teheran, also revealed that approaches from some Republican emissaries had already been received, Ben-Menashe wrote.

"Kashani said that the secret ex-CIA-Miles-Copeland group was aware that any deal cut with the Iranians would have to include the Israelis because they would have to be used as a third party to sell military equipment to Iran," according to Ben-Menashe. In March, the Israelis made their first direct military shipment to Iran, 300 tires for Iran's F-4 fighter jets, Ben-Menashe wrote.[12]

Two Republican operatives favored by the Israelis – Earl Brian, who had been Governor Ronald Reagan's health secretary in California, and Robert McFarlane, an adviser to Texas Senator John Tower – met in Madrid in March with former Iranian leader Mehdi Bazargan, according to Ben-Menashe. Barzargan had resigned after the American hostages were seized but remained close to Khomeini and to another cleric, Mehdi Karrubi, who was in charge of foreign relations for Iran's Supreme Council. Ben-Menashe wrote that Reagan's campaign chief William Casey also attended a meeting with Karrubi in Madrid in March to explore possible future relations between the United States and Iran, although Ben-Menashe said that information was second-hand.[13]

In the 1990 interview at his house in the English countryside, Copeland told me that his hostage-rescue plan was developed at the request of a State

Department official scouting for a way to break the Iran stalemate. Copeland said the plan – which included developing political allies within Iran and using disinformation tactics to augment the military assault – was hammered out on March 22, 1980, in a meeting at his Georgetown apartment. Copeland said he was aided by Steven Meade, the ex-chief of the CIA's Escape and Evasion Unit; Kermit Roosevelt, who had overseen the 1953 coup in Iran; and Archibald Roosevelt, the adviser to David Rockefeller.

"Essentially, the idea was to have some Iranians dressed in Iranian military uniform and police uniform go to the embassy, address the students and say, 'Hey, you're doing a marvelous job here. But now we'll relieve you of it, because we understand that there's going to be a military force flown in from outside. And they're going to hit you, and we're going to scatter these [hostages] around town. Thanks very much." Copeland's Iranians would then move the hostages to the edge of Teheran where they would be loaded onto American helicopters to be flown out of the country.

To Copeland's chagrin, his plan fell on deaf ears in the Carter administration, which was developing its own rescue plan that would rely more on U.S. military force with only modest help from Iranian assets in Teheran. So, Copeland said he distributed his plan outside the administration, to leading Republicans, giving sharper focus to their contempt for Carter's bungled Iranian strategy.

"Officially, the plan went only to people in the government and was top secret and all that," Copeland said. "But as so often happens in government, one wants support, and when it was not being handled by the Carter administration as though it was top secret, it was handled as though it was nothing. ... Yes, I sent copies to everybody who I thought would be a good ally. ...

"Now I'm not at liberty to say what reaction, if any, ex-President Nixon took, but he certainly had a copy of this. We sent one to Henry Kissinger, and I had, at the time, a secretary who had just worked for Henry Kissinger, and Peter Rodman, who was still working for him and was a close personal friend of mine, and so we had these informal relationships where the little closed circle of people who were, a, looking forward to a Republican President within a short while and, b, who were absolutely trustworthy and who understood all these inner workings of the international game board."

***

By early spring, Reagan was rolling toward victory in the Republican race, though Bush hung on as the representative of the party's more moderate wing. In the background, the Iran-hostage stand-off continued to loom as a political wild card. The crisis threatened Carter's reelection chances if it lingered but offered hope for a rebound if the hostages returned home at a timely moment.

In the tradition of the best spy tradecraft, Casey wanted to have sources right in the middle of the action – and as it turned out, one of Casey's longtime friends, John Shaheen, was already in tight with Cyrus Hashemi, one of President Carter's intermediaries to the Iranian government. A Shaheen associate told me that Casey and Shaheen, the two old OSS guys, often discussed the hostage crisis in the context of their experience in the intelligence world. Sometimes their conversations turned to batting around their own ideas for how to resolve the standoff and how to show up Carter, the Shaheen associate said. Shaheen also was in touch with Arab leaders in Europe and sounded them out, too, about ways for ending the Iranian impasse, the associate said.

"Shaheen," the associate said, "loved this clandestine stuff. He ate it up. These guys [Casey and Shaheen] were real patriots. They would have been involved in it under the table, over the table and on the side of the table. But they would have done it."[14]

George Cave, a senior CIA officer then concentrating on Iran, told me that one reason for the Republican appetite for information about the hostage crisis was that "Democrats never briefed the Republicans" on sensitive developments, effectively causing the Republicans to seek out their own contacts. Cave, who was helping to coordinate the Carter administration's hostage-rescue plan, said Ted Shackley, a former senior CIA officer working then with the Bush campaign, held meetings with Iranians in London and in Hamburg, West Germany.

"Ted, I know, had a couple of contacts in Germany," Cave said. "I know he talked to them. I don't know how far it went. ... Ted was very active on that thing in the winter/spring of 1980."

Jamshid Hashemi said Casey's obsession with the hostage issue led the Reagan campaign chief to approach the Hashemi brothers directly. Jamshid Hashemi said that in March 1980, he was in his room at the Mayflower Hotel on Connecticut Avenue in Washington when Casey and another Shaheen associate, Roy Furmark, arrived. "The door was opened and Mr. Casey came in," Jamshid said. "He wanted to talk to me. I didn't know who he was or what he was. So I called my brother on the phone. I said, 'there's a gentleman here by the name of Mr. Casey who wants to talk to me.' I remember that my brother asked me to pass him the phone and he talked with Mr. Casey."

In spring 1980, Jamshid Hashemi also asserted that he met Donald Gregg, a CIA officer then serving on Carter's National Security Council staff and responsible for coordinating intelligence. Jamshid Hashemi said he encountered Gregg at Cyrus Hashemi's bank in Manhattan, and Cyrus introduced Gregg as "the man from the White House."[15]

The alleged involvement of Gregg is another highly controversial part of the October Surprise mystery. A tall man with a trim build and an easy-going manner, Gregg had known George H.W. Bush since 1967 when Bush was a first-term U.S. congressman. Gregg had briefed Bush when he was U.S. envoy to China. Gregg also served as the CIA's liaison to the ill-fated Pike Committee when Bush was CIA director.

"Although Gregg was uniformly regarded as a competent professional, there was a dimension to his background that was entirely unknown to his colleagues at the White House, and that was his acquaintance with one of the Republican frontrunners, George Bush," Sick wrote in *October Surprise*. As for why Gregg would meet with the Hashemi brothers, Sick wrote that "to the best of my knowledge, he had no responsibility for Iran policy."[16] (Gregg also had worked closely with Bush ally Ted Shackley since their days together as CIA officers in the Vietnam War.)

During later investigations, Gregg denied participation in any October Surprise operations. But Gregg was judged deceptive in that denial when he was questioned about the October Surprise by an FBI polygrapher working for Lawrence Walsh's Iran-Contra investigation in 1990. Gregg flunked the "lie detector" test when he gave a negative answer to the question: "Were you ever involved in a plan to delay the release of the hostages in Iran until after the 1980 Presidential election?"[17]

Meanwhile, less than two months after Casey had taken command of the Reagan campaign, Casey's own internal structure for monitoring Carter's progress in Iran was taking shape. On April 20, 1980, the Reagan campaign carved out from a larger body of Republican foreign policy experts a subgroup known as the Iran Working Group, congressional investigators later discovered. The foreign policy operation was run by Richard Allen, Fred Ikle and Laurence Silberman.

"A document listing these groups and their members makes mysterious reference to the Iran Working Group, noting, 'name of Advisors participating will remain *unlisted*,'" said an unpublished section of the House October Surprise Task Force report. "There is no other evidence of this particular group's existence, purpose or members, or the reason for the secrecy surrounding it."

***

In April 1980, Carter's patience was wearing thin, both with the Iranians and some U.S. allies. After discovering that the Israelis had made a secret shipment of 300 tires to Iran, Carter complained to Prime Minister Begin. "There had been a rather tense discussion between President Carter and Prime Minister Begin in the spring of 1980 in which the President made clear that the Israelis had to stop that, and that we knew that they were doing it, and that we would not allow it to continue, at least not allow it to continue privately and without the knowledge of the American people," Carter's press secretary Jody Powell told me. "And it stopped" – at least temporarily.

Questioned by congressional investigators a dozen years later, Carter said he felt that by April, "Israel cast their lot with Reagan," according to notes I found among the unpublished documents in the House Task Force files. Carter traced the Israeli opposition to his reelection to a "lingering concern [among] Jewish leaders that I was too friendly with Arabs." Carter's National Security Adviser Zbigniew Brzezinski also recognized the Israeli hostility. In an interview, Brzezinski told me that the Carter White House was well aware that the Begin government had "an obvious preference for a Reagan victory."

While encircled by growing legions of enemies, the Carter administration put the finishing touches on its own hostage-rescue operation. Code named "Eagle Claw," the assault involved a force of U.S. helicopters that would swoop down on Teheran, coordinate with some agents on the ground and extract the hostages.

Carter ordered the operation to proceed on April 24, but mechanical problems forced the helicopters to turn back. At a staging area called Desert One, one of the helicopters collided with a refueling plane, causing an explosion that killed eight American crewmen. Their charred bodies were then displayed by the Iranian government, adding to the fury and humiliation of the United States. After the Desert One fiasco, the Iranians dispersed the hostages to a variety of locations, effectively shutting the door on another rescue attempt, at least one that would have any chance of returning the hostages as a group.

***

Back on the campaign trail, Reagan's robust conservatism was helping him pile up delegates as he gained control of the Republican primaries. Bush pulled out some wins in Massachusetts, Connecticut, Pennsylvania and Michigan, but was dealt a crushing blow when he lost his home state of Texas on May 3. The path to the GOP nomination was now clear for Reagan.

As the Republican nominating battle drew to a close, Cyrus Hashemi and John Shaheen busied themselves more with business than politics as they tried to stave off Shaheen's financial ruin. Because of his failing Come-by-Chance refinery, Canadian courts had frozen Shaheen's bank accounts. In a bid to avert disaster, Shaheen sent a personal assistant to London with a power of attorney to arrange a desperately needed loan, according to a close Shaheen associate I interviewed. Shaheen told the assistant to contact Cyrus Hashemi, who took the assistant to the London offices of the Bank of Credit and Commerce International and Marine Midland Bank, seeking a $3 million bail-out.

Cyrus negotiated the loan for Shaheen on his second try, at Marine Midland. Since Canada had frozen Shaheen's accounts, the money apparently was funneled through a Bermuda-based front company called Mid

Ocean. FBI documents showed a $2.5 million deposit from "Mid Ocean" into Cyrus's First Gulf bank in summer 1980, possibly the Marine Midland loan minus $500,000 for expenses. Shaheen's reliance on Cyrus Hashemi for the infusion of cash also made clear that the two men were not just casual business associates. Shaheen counted on Hashemi to toss a $3 million life preserver that kept Shaheen's head above water. Yet even as their financial predicament worsened, the pair continued to plunge into the Iranian negotiations.

In July – four months after Jamshid Hashemi said William Casey approached the Iranian brothers in Washington – Cyrus Hashemi began a series of trips to Madrid on the hostage crisis. Ostensibly, the meetings were part of his initiative on behalf of the Carter administration, seeking inroads to the Iranian regime. But in Teheran, word spread that Cyrus Hashemi's real goal was to strike a deal on behalf of the Republicans.

Iranian President Abolhassan Bani-Sadr said he first learned of the Republican "secret deal" with the Iranian radicals in July after Reza Passendideh, a nephew of Ayatollah Ruhollah Khomeini, attended a meeting with Cyrus Hashemi and Republican lawyer Stanley Pottinger in Madrid on July 2, 1980. Though Passendideh was supposed to return with a proposal from the Carter administration, Bani-Sadr said Passendideh proffered instead a plan "from the Reagan camp," Bani-Sadr wrote in a letter to the House October Surprise Task Force on December 17, 1992.

"Passendideh told me that if I do not accept this proposal, they [the Republicans] would make the same offer to my [radical Iranian] rivals. He further said that they [the Republicans] have enormous influence in the CIA," Bani-Sadr wrote. "Lastly, he told me my refusal of their offer would result in my elimination." Bani-Sadr said he resisted the threats and sought an immediate release of the American hostages, but it was clear to him that the wily Khomeini was playing both sides of the U.S. political street.

Admiral Madani, the former defense minister who lost to Bani-Sadr despite covert CIA assistance funneled through Cyrus Hashemi, said he also learned about the Hashemi brothers double-dealing with the Republicans during this period. Madani said Cyrus brought up William Casey's name in connection with back-channel negotiations over the U.S. hostages and urged Madani to meet with the Reagan-Bush campaign director. "We are not here to play politics," Madani recalled chastising Cyrus.[18]

***

Palestinian leader Yasir Arafat is another Middle Eastern figure who claimed to have received a Republican overture in summer 1980. Arafat, who was then chairman of the Palestine Liberation Organization, said he was approached by a senior Republican who wanted to use Arafat's connections with the Iranian leadership to give the Reagan campaign an entrée to Iran over the hostage issue. Arafat disclosed this contact to Jimmy Carter in a face-to-face meeting in Gaza City 15 years after the end of the Carter Presidency.

"There is something I want to tell you," Arafat said, addressing Carter at a meeting in Arafat's bunker. "You should know that in 1980 the Republicans approached me with an arms deal [for the PLO] if I could arrange to keep the hostages in Iran until after the [U.S. presidential] election."

Arafat insisted that he rebuffed the offer, but he supplied Carter with few other details, no name of the Republican representative nor exactly when and where the approach was made. But the conversation was recounted by historian Douglas Brinkley who was present when Carter and Arafat spoke. Brinkley included the exchange in an article for the fall 1996 issue of *Diplomatic History*, a scholarly quarterly. Later, through a spokesman, Carter confirmed to me the conversation with Arafat had occurred as described by Brinkley.

Arafat's statement to Carter did not stand alone. Since the late 1980s, one of Arafat's senior aides, Bassam Abu Sharif, had given journalists a similar account of a Republican approach to the PLO in July 1980 when the PLO was maintaining close ties to the Islamic government in Iran. In 1990, during an interview in Tunisia, Bassam Abu Sharif told me that a senior figure in the Reagan campaign had contacted Arafat and the PLO in Beirut about engineering a delay in the hostage release.

"It was important for Reagan not to have any of the hostages released during the remaining days of President Carter," Bassam said. "The offer was, 'if you block the release of hostages, then the White House would be open for the PLO.' In spite of that, we turned that down. ...I guess the same offer was given to others, and I believe that some accepted to do it and managed to block the release of hostages." Other PLO sources said Arafat discovered during a September 1980 trip to Iran that his intervention was superfluous since the Republicans already had established other back channels to the radical Islamic mullahs.

***

On July 14, the Republican National Convention opened in Detroit. After a brief flirtation with the possibility of enlisting former President Ford as the vice presidential nominee, Reagan settled on George H.W. Bush.

After accepting the No. 2 spot, Bush began merging his CIA-heavy campaign apparatus with Reagan's. The united Reagan-Bush campaign created a strategy group, known as the "October Surprise Group," to prepare for "any last-minute foreign policy or defense-related event, including the release of the hostages, that might favorably impact President Carter in the

November election," according to a draft section of the House Task Force report.

"Originally referred to as the 'Gang of Ten,'" the draft report said the "October Surprise Group" consisted of Richard V. Allen, Charles M. Kupperman, Thomas H. Moorer, Eugene V. Rostow, William R. Van Cleave, Fred C. Ikle, John R. Lehman Jr., Robert G. Neumann, Laurence Silberman and Seymour Weiss. While that part of the draft made it into the Task Force's final report, another part was deleted, saying: "According to members of the 'October Surprise' group, the following individuals also participated in meetings although they were not considered 'members' of the group: Michael Ledeen, Richard Stillwell, William Middendorf, Richard Perle, General Louis Walt and Admiral James Holloway."

The draft report quoted members of the "October Surprise Group" as saying it "had no formal structure and only met approximately seven to eight times." The draft said Reagan foreign policy aide Allen described the "October Surprise Group" as 'a myth and a scam." Allen is quoted as saying, "the group sat and talked about everything including the release of hostages. But it was never designed, it didn't work or anything. We just sat in my office and talked about campaign strategy." According to the draft report, Allen "intended the press to pick up on his continued references to the 'October Surprise Group' and create the impression in the public's mind that any last-minute actions by President Carter were politically motivated."

The Task Force found evidence that Fred Ikle, a member of the group, "undoubtedly received information about the hostage situation from a variety of sources within the Washington Establishment," the draft chapter said. "William Van Cleave, who also worked with Allen and Ikle at Allen's office, says Ikle often received information on the hostages. Ikle, in his Task Force deposition, denies receiving information about the hostages from inside the [Carter] administration. Ikle likely had contact with Iranians who had information on the hostage situation. Ikle testified that he was approached by Iranian people in Washington who thought they could be 'helpful' and would claim, 'We can do something, find out what is happening, get the hostages out after Reagan is elected, whatever.'"

Deleted from the final report also was a section describing how the ex-CIA personnel who had worked for Bush's campaign became the nucleus of the Republican intelligence operation that monitored Carter's Iran-hostage negotiations for the Reagan-Bush team.

"The Reagan-Bush campaign maintained a 24-hour Operations Center, which monitored press wires and reports, gave daily press briefings and maintained telephone and telefax contact with the candidate's plane," the draft report read. "Many of the staff members were former CIA employees who had previously worked on the Bush campaign or were otherwise loyal to George Bush. The operation was set up by Stefan Halper, a former Bush campaign staff member, in late July when he joined the Reagan-Bush campaign. Ray Cline, a prominent former CIA employee, was Halper's father-in-law at the time of the campaign."

Reagan national security adviser Allen described the group from the Bush campaign as a "plane load of disgruntled former CIA" officers who were "playing cops and robbers."

***

Though post-convention polls showed Reagan leading Carter, Reagan's campaign chief Casey remained fixated on the Iran-hostage crisis. Since March, Jamshid Hashemi said he had given the Mayflower Hotel meeting little thought. But in summer 1980, Jamshid said his brother, Cyrus, confided that his role in the hostage negotiations had taken another turn.

"I was asked by my brother, since he thought the Republicans had the possibility of winning the election, that we should not play only in the hands of the Democrats," Jamshid Hashemi told me. He quoted his brother as saying "it was the wish of Mr. Casey to meet with someone from Iran."

"That's when I started getting on this work of inviting both Mehdi [Karrubi, a politically powerful Iranian cleric], to come directly, and Hassan [Karrubi, the cleric's brother], to come indirectly to Madrid," Jamshid Hashemi said. "I contacted them by telephone from here [London]. We had scramblers. He [Hassan] had a scrambler and I had a scrambler. Other times I used to fly to different cities in Europe [to contact him]. ... He came [to Europe] with a mission to purchase some commodities. I think it was Denmark."

Jamshid said he took a private plane to Hamburg, West Germany, where he picked up Hassan Karrubi and flew him to Madrid. "I explained everything [to Hassan Karrubi] aboard the plane," Jamshid recalled. "When we got to Madrid, we went to the Plaza Hotel. We registered there under different names. Mehdi Karrubi was [already in Madrid and staying] in the [Iranian] embassy. ... Casey came with another gentleman who was American." Jamshid Hashemi said Casey's companion was Donald Gregg, the CIA officer working on Carter's NSC who Jamshid said had lunched with the Hashemi brothers several months earlier.

Jamshid Hashemi said the Madrid meeting – with Mehdi Karrubi dressed in a turban and cloak – started at about 11 a.m. and extended into the afternoon. Jamshid said that when Casey put his cards on the table, his desire was clear. "What was specifically asked was when these hostages should be released, and it was the wish of Mr. Casey that they be released after the Inauguration," Jamshid said. "Then the Reagan administration would feel favorably towards Iran and release the FMS [foreign military sales] funds and the frozen assets and return to Iran what had already been purchased." The FMS sales referred to $150 million in military hardware that had been bought by the Shah but held back after Khomeini took power and the hostages were seized. Casey's offer also included F-14 spare parts, which were crucial to the maintenance of Iran's high-tech air force, Jamshid said.

In a separate interview with ABC News' *Nightline* program, Jamshid said the meetings spilled over into the morning of a second day, a detail that would become the focus of later attempts to disprove Jamshid's story.

After the July meeting with Casey, Jamshid Hashemi said, cleric Mehdi Karrubi returned to Teheran, where he consulted Khomeini and the ayatollah's senior advisers. Two to three weeks later, Karrubi called and asked Jamshid to arrange a second meeting with Casey, Jamshid said. New arrangements were made for a meeting in mid-August again in Madrid, he said. Karrubi "confirmed" that Khomeini's government had agreed to release the hostages only after Reagan gained power. "Karrubi expressed acceptance of the proposal by Mr. Casey," Jamshid said. "The hostages would be released after Carter's defeat."[19]

After the Madrid meetings, Jamshid said his brother, Cyrus, began organizing military shipments – mostly artillery shells and aircraft tires – from Eilat, in Israel, to Bandar Abbas, an Iranian port. To carry that materiel, Cyrus obtained a Greek ship, Jamshid said. "I do know for a fact the captain of the ship and the crew were all Greeks," Jamshid said. "They were told that each time [the ship] would go back and forth it would have a different name, so they would have a different name, documents, everything, delivered to them at each port that they would come in." Jamshid valued the military supplies in the tens of millions of dollars. Later, he said, the ship was scuttled in the Mediterranean Sea.

* * *

Three months after the Desert One fiasco, another prominent Republican – former President Nixon – was still fuming about Carter's ineptness and wondering about the feasibility of a second rescue attempt.

According to a 1989 article in the London *Sunday Telegraph*, Nixon consulted in late July 1980 with Alan Bristow, a helicopter specialist with close ties to the British Special Air Services, SAS, a clandestine military arm of British intelligence. When I contacted the reporter on the story in 1990, Simon O'Dwyer-Russell said Bristow had described an angry Nixon pacing the floor and denouncing Carter. But the idea of reviving the rogue rescue plan of Miles Copeland and his ex-CIA colleagues was no longer feasible with the hostages scattered to several locations.

By summer 1980, Copeland told me, the Republicans in his circle considered a second hostage-rescue attempt not only unfeasible, but unnecessary. They were talking confidently about the hostages being freed after a Republican victory in November, the old CIA man said.

"There was no discussion of a Kissinger or Nixon plan to rescue these people, because Nixon, like everybody else, knew that all we had to do was wait until the election came, and they were going to get out," Copeland said. "That was sort of an open secret among people in the intelligence community, that that would happen. ... The intelligence community certainly had some understanding with somebody in Iran in authority, in a way that they would hardly confide in me."

Copeland said his CIA friends had been told by contacts in Iran that the mullahs would do nothing to help Carter or his reelection. "At that time, we had word back, because you always have informed relations with the devil," Copeland said. "But we had word that, 'Don't worry. As long as Carter wouldn't get credit for getting these people out, as soon as Reagan came in, the Iranians would be happy enough to wash their hands of this and move into a new era of Iranian-American relations, whatever that turned out to be.'"

In the interview, Copeland declined to give more details, beyond his assurance that "the CIA within the CIA," his term for the true protectors of U.S. national security, had an understanding with the Iranians about the hostages. Copeland died on January 14, 1991, before I could interview him a second time.

Chapter 8: The Hostage Gambit

After Labor Day 1980, with the start of the general election campaign, Jimmy Carter began to show new signs of political life. Carter had survived a Democratic primary challenge from liberal Massachusetts Senator Edward Kennedy and was benefiting from a uniting of Democrats after their national convention.

There also were public doubts about Ronald Reagan, who was viewed by many as an extremist who might unnecessarily heat up the Cold War. Carter began to slowly close the gap on the former California governor. But the Iranian hostage crisis hovered over his campaign like an accursed spirit.

Though little noticed in Washington, political battles also were breaking out inside the Iranian leadership. Iran's acting Foreign Minister Sadegh Ghotbzadeh told Agence France Presse on September 6 that he had information that Reagan was "trying to block a solution" to the hostage impasse. The secret Republican plan to delay release of the hostages until after the U.S. elections had become a point of tension between Iranian President Bani-Sadr and Ayatollah Khomeini, according to Bani-Sadr's account sent to the House October Surprise Task Force. Bani-Sadr said his trump card was a threat to tell the Iranian people about the secret deal that the Khomeini forces had struck with the Republicans.

"On September 8, 1980, I invited the people of Teheran to gather in Martyrs Square so that I can tell them the truth," Bani-Sadr wrote in his 1992 letter to the House Task Force. "Khomeini insisted that I must not do so at this time. ... Two days later, again, I decided to expose everything. Ahmad Khomeini [the ayatollah's son] came to see me and told me, 'Imam [Khomeini] absolutely promises'" to reopen talks with Carter if Bani-Sadr would relent and not go public. Bani-Sadr said their dispute led Khomeini to pass on a new hostage proposal to Carter officials through his son-in-law, Sadegh Tabatabai.

Besides any threats of going public from Bani-Sadr, Iran's new flexibility may have been influenced by the rapidly forming war clouds along the Iraqi border. For months, tensions had been growing between Iran's fundamentalist Shia government and Iraq's secular regime led by Saddam Hussein and dominated by Sunni Muslims. Some of the Arab Gulf states also were viewing Iran's radical fundamentalism with alarm and were encouraging Hussein's powerful army to act as a buffer against Iran's radicals. With border skirmishes already presaging a wider war, Iran's U.S.-supplied military desperately needed spare parts, leverage that Carter was prepared to use to extract the hostages.

Sadegh Tabatabai, a handsome man fond of European-styled clothes, told me that he had approached Ayatollah Khomeini with a plan that focused on release of frozen Iranian funds and a commitment against future U.S. aggression. "The Imam [Khomeini] said that was what he pretty much had in mind," Tabatabai said. "The Imam suggested that we test this out with the Americans first."[1] After clearing the idea with several Iranian leaders, Tabatabai forwarded the plan to the Americans through the West Germans.

The Tabatabai message surprised the Carter negotiation team, which had pretty much given up hope that the Iranians would agree to any serious talks. Former NSC official Gary Sick described the proposal for settling the hostage impasse as "a set of conditions for ending the crisis that were really much gentler than anything Iran had offered before." The plan boiled down to unfreezing Iran's assets in the United States, giving Iran access to the Shah's overseas fortune, pledging no retaliation against Iran, and agreeing to refrain from future interference in Iran's internal affairs. The Iranians were no longer demanding the Shah's return – a moot point since he had died in July – nor a formal apology from the United States for past violations of Iran's sovereignty.

"The answer came fairly quickly," Tabatabai said. A meeting with an American delegation was arranged for Bonn, West Germany.

***

The sudden shift in the Iranian position coincided with a more intense interest among Republicans in the possibility that Carter might actually pull off his October Surprise. A flurry of meetings ensued involving purported Iranian emissaries and members of the Republican October Surprise monitoring operation.

On September 10, Reagan adviser Richard Allen said he was approached by Mike Butler, an aide to Senator John Tower, who asked for an appointment on "a confidential matter," according to Allen's memo to the file. "At about 12 o'clock, he and Bud McFarlane came to the office and we drove back down to [Capitol] Hill. On the way they told me about their meeting with a Mr. A.A. Mohammed, a Malaysian who operates from Singapore and who came to them via an old friend of Senator Tower's ... This afternoon, by mutual agreement, I met with Messrs. Mohammed, Butler and McFarlane. I also took Larry Silberman along to the meeting.

"As it turned out, Mr. Mohammed claims to have a scheme which has ostensibly received the approval of Ayatollah Khomeini to release the hostages once the son of the Shah is returned to Iran and installed as a figurehead monarch. Larry and I indicated our scepticism [sic] about the possibility of such an exercise, especially since it also involves the release of the hostages," Allen's memo read. "Both Larry and I indicated that we would be pleased to hear whatever additional news Mr. Mohammed might be able to turn up, and I suggested that that information be communicated via a secure channel."[2]When Allen presented this memo to the House Task Force in 1992, he claimed it recounted the facts surrounding a mysterious meeting that Allen, Silberman and McFarlane had acknowledged having with an Iranian emissary at the L'Enfant Plaza Hotel. When that L'Enfant Plaza meeting was disclosed in the late 1980s, it sparked the first press interest in what became known as the October Surprise issue.

But the L'Enfant Plaza meeting – believed to have occurred in late September or early October – was different in a number of respects from the meeting described in Allen's memo. According to Allen's previous descriptions of the L'Enfant Plaza session, McFarlane initiated the meeting and pestered Allen to go. Butler was not mentioned as a participant. The time of day also was off. Allen had said he knew about the meeting's purpose in the morning during a meeting of campaign foreign policy experts and asked Silberman to join him then. Allen also described the Iranian emissary as someone from the "Mediterranean littoral" – in Allen's colorful phrase – not from Southeast Asia.

The content of the meeting also was different. Allen had said the L'Enfant Plaza emissary offered to release the hostages to candidate Reagan, a proposal that Allen had said prompted an immediate rebuff of the proposal. The September 10 memo cited no such hostage offer and instead described a recommendation that Mr. Mohammed stay in touch "via a secure channel." A reasonable conclusion would be that the memo related to an entirely different meeting and that the Republican contacts with foreigners on the hostage issue were thus more frequent than the Reagan-Bush operatives wished to admit.

Other evidence from Reagan-Bush campaign files from this period pointed to contacts between the Rockefeller group and Casey during this pivotal period of Carter's hostage negotiations. According to a campaign visitor log dated September 11, David Rockefeller and several of his aides who were dealing with the Iranian issue signed in to see Casey at his campaign headquarters in Arlington, Virginia. With Rockefeller were Joseph Reed, whom Rockefeller had assigned to coordinate U.S. policy toward the Shah, and Archibald Roosevelt, the former CIA officer who was monitoring events in the Persian Gulf for Chase Manhattan and who had collaborated with Miles Copeland on the Iran hostage-rescue plan. The fourth member of the party was Owen Frisbie, Rockefeller's chief lobbyist in Washington.

In the early 1990s, all the surviving the participants – Rockefeller, Reed and Frisbie – declined to be interviewed about the Casey meeting. Rockefeller made no mention of the meeting in *Memoirs*. Casey is not even in the index for Rockefeller's 517-page autobiography.

Henry Kissinger, another Rockefeller associate, also was in discreet contact with campaign director Casey during this period, according to Casey's personal chauffeur whom I interviewed. The chauffeur, who asked not to be identified by name, said he was sent twice to Kissinger's Georgetown home to pick up the former Secretary of State and bring him to Arlington, Virginia, for private meetings with Casey, meetings that were not recorded on the official visitor logs.

On September 16, five days after the Rockefeller visit to Casey's office, Iran's acting foreign minister Ghotbzadeh again was quoted as citing Republican interference on the hostages. "Reagan, supported by Kissinger and others, has no intention of resolving the problem," Ghotbzadeh said. "They will do everything in their power to block it."[3]

That same day, Casey was focusing again on the crisis in the region. At 3 p.m., he met with senior Reagan-Bush campaign officials Edwin Meese, Bill Timmons and Richard Allen about the "Persian Gulf Project," according to a deleted section of the House Task Force report and Allen's notes. But the Task Force couldn't determine what the high-level meeting had been about. "The Task Force has found no other references to this project," the deleted chapter said. Two other participants at the meeting, according to Allen's notes, were Michael Ledeen and Noel Koch.

While the Republicans were busy meeting in Washington, Carter's emissaries in West Germany were hammering out the framework for a hostage-release settlement with Tabatabai.

"I was very optimistic at the time," Tabatabai said in an interview a decade later. "Mr. Carter had accepted the conditions set by the Iranians. I sent an encrypted message to the Imam [Khomeini], saying I would be back the next day." A settlement of the hostage crisis seemed to be in the offing. But Tabatabai's return was delayed by the outbreak of the Iran-Iraq War on September 22. "The airport in Teheran was being bombed by Iraqi forces," he said.

Tabatabai had to wait two weeks before he could return to Iran.

***

While Tabatabai was delayed, the Reagan-Bush campaign pondered what leverage the Iran-Iraq war might give the Carter administration and what effect that might have on the hostage crisis. Halper, the Bush aide who was running the campaign's Operations Center, pulled together some of the best available analysis in a memo sent to Bush.

"In late September, Halper wrote a memorandum directly to George Bush regarding information he [Halper] learned from General [Brent] Scowcroft and Dr. Al Cottrell of the Center for Strategic and International Studies about the Iran-Iraq War," the Task Force's draft chapter said. "The memorandum details the type of intelligence available and the location of the troops. The memorandum then reports that the 'Iranians have few spare parts. Even if U.S. provided them, no technicians to put them in. (218 tech. reps who serviced the 70 F-4s all gone). Spare parts could make little or no difference in force capacity at this time.' The memorandum further states, 'Hostages. Delay. Teheran one problem town. Khomeini & Bani-Sadr directly involved in war. Settlement soon viewed as unlikely. ...The fighting, now in its third day, forced Iran's Parliament to 'FREEZE INDEFINITELY' the debate on the fate of the 52 Americans who have been held for 326 days."

With little more than a month to go before the U.S. election, Republicans and Iranians allegedly met again in Washington. Indeed, one of the first public references to secret Republican-Iranian contacts was to the alleged meeting at the L'Enfant Plaza Hotel supposedly in late September or early October. Three Republicans – Allen, Silberman and McFarlane – have acknowledged a session with an Iranian emissary at the hotel, which is situated between the Washington Mall and the Potomac River. But none of them claimed to remember the person's name, his nationality or his position – not even McFarlane who purportedly arranged the meeting.

In a testy interview with me in 1990, Allen said the L'Enfant Plaza meeting occurred after McFarlane called Allen "several times in an attempt to get me to meet with someone about the Iranian problem." Allen said he was leery about such a meeting because he had been burnt by the controversy over the Nixon's Vietnam peace-talk interference in 1968. "Knowing what I'd been through in 1968 on this very problem, I was highly reluctant to do it," Allen said. "But McFarlane was working for John Tower; John Tower was a friend of mine. McFarlane is not a particular friend, an acquaintance, nothing more than that. He was quite insistent that I do this."

So Allen said he asked Silberman to join him at the meeting. "I want a witness in this meeting because I don't want it to turn into anything that could run against us. And I won't meet in this office. I will not have anybody say that he came to my office. I've said to McFarlane, 'I'll meet you in the L'Enfant Plaza Hotel, but only in the lobby where there's plenty of people out there. We're not going to have any meetings in a room.' So Larry Silberman and I got on the subway and we went down to the L'Enfant Plaza Hotel where I met McFarlane and there were many people milling about. We sat at a table in the lobby. It was around the lunch hour. I was introduced to this very obscure character whose name I cannot recall. ...

"The individual who was either an Egyptian or an Iranian or could have been an Iranian living in Egypt – and his idea was that he had the capacity to intervene, to deliver the hostages to the Reagan forces. Now, I took that at first to mean that he was able to deliver the hostages to Ronald Reagan, candidate for the Presidency of the United States, which was absolutely lunatic. And I said so. I believe I said, or Larry did, 'we have one President at a time. That's the way it is.' ...

"I was incredulous that McFarlane would have ever brought a guy like this or placed any credibility in a guy like this. Just absolutely incredulous, and so was Larry Silberman. This meeting lasted maybe 20 minutes, 25 minutes. So that's it. There's no need to continue this meeting. I'm not interested in this. I didn't even say I'll get back to you or anything of that nature. Silberman and I walked out."

Though not remembering the man's name or nationality, Allen said he was "stocky and swarthy, dark-complected." Allen then paused and said the man looked like a "person from somewhere on the Mediterranean littoral, how about that?" I asked Allen if he had asked McFarlane before the meeting "who is this guy?" Allen responded, "I don't recall having asked him, no."

I then said, "I guess I don't understand why you wouldn't say, 'Is this guy an Iranian, is he someone you've known for a while?" Allen snapped, "Well, gee, I'm sorry that you don't understand. I really feel badly for you. It's really too bad you don't understand, but that's your problem, not mine."

Allen said he had discussed the Iranian hostage crisis with "dozens and dozens of people. This was no different from anybody else I would meet on this subject."

"It obviously turned out to be different from most people you've met on the subject," I said.

Allen: "Oh, it turned out to be because this guy is the centerpiece of some sort of grand conspiracy web that has been spun."

"Well, were there many people who offered to deliver the hostages to Ronald Reagan?"

Allen: "No, this one was particularly different, but I didn't know that before I went to the meeting, you understand."

While Allen, Silberman and McFarlane were claiming fuzzy memories, two other figures in the October Surprise mystery – Iranian arms dealer Houshang Lavi and Israeli intelligence officer Ari Ben-Menashe – claimed that there was a reason the Republicans didn't want to say everything they knew: because the L'Enfant Plaza meeting fit into the larger scheme of secret arms shipments to Iran and Republican involvement in the back-channel negotiations with Iran.

Lavi, who had brokered the Shah's $2 billion purchase of F-14s years earlier, told me that he had arranged the meeting not with McFarlane, but with Silberman. "Silberman wanted me to go down to Washington and talk about the American hostage situation," Lavi said.

Lavi, a chunky man of modest height and dark complexion, described the meeting as occurring at a hotel that was near the Potomac River and had an expansive lobby, both of which fit with the L'Enfant Plaza Hotel. Lavi said the meeting occurred on October 2. To support his account, Lavi supplied a lined piece of paper that read: "Oct 2, 80. Eastern Shuttle to D.C. E.Plaza Hotel. ... To meet Silberman, Allen, Bob McFar. 40 page document

F14 parts already paid for in rtun of hostages. Swap in Karachi. Charter 707." But there was no way to know when Lavi's note was actually written.

After arriving at the hotel lobby, Lavi said, "I waited for Mr. Silberman to arrive. He arrived and he was accompanied by two other gentlemen." Lavi said one was identified as McFarlane, but Lavi didn't recall if Allen was the third American. According to Lavi's account, Silberman did most of the talking. "I believe he is the one who told me that 'Mr. Lavi, we have one government at a time.' I took it that they do not want to interfere, but it turned out to be, I found out later on, that that's not the case. The Reagan-Bush campaign made a deal with the Iranians together with the help of the Israelis for the supply of arms to Iran."[4]

I also interviewed Lavi's lawyer, Mitchell Rogovin, who was a former CIA counsel and then a senior adviser to the independent presidential campaign of Republican Congressman John Anderson. Rogovin said he was not aware of any Lavi meeting with Allen, Silberman and McFarlane. But Rogovin pulled out his calendar for that period and showed me that he had set up Lavi with a meeting on the morning of October 2 with a CIA officer. A partially declassified CIA memo has since confirmed that a CIA officer did meet with Lavi, starting at 10:30 a.m. The meeting lasted 55 minutes and involved Lavi proposing "delivery of $8 million to $10 million of F-14 spare parts" as part of a swap for the 52 American hostages, the memo said.

Though that proposal went no where, the CIA memo confirmed that Lavi was promoting a plan similar to the one he claimed to outline to the Reagan-Bush representatives later that same day. The House Task Force also obtained other Rogovin notes, including an entry for September 29, 1980, indicating that he had called senior CIA official John McMahon about Lavi's proposal and had arranged for the October 2 meeting. But the following entry after the McMahon phone call was stunning. It read: "Larry Silberman – still very nervous/will recommend … against us this P.M. I said $250,000 – he said why even bother."

When I called Rogovin back and asked what that entry meant, he said the Anderson campaign was seeking a loan from Crocker National Bank where Silberman coincidentally served as legal counsel. The note meant that Silberman was planning to advise the bank officers against the loan, Rogovin said. "Silberman was nervous about lending the money," Rogovin said.

I asked Rogovin if the Lavi hostage plan might have come up during the conversation with Silberman. "There was no discussion of the Lavi proposal," Rogovin said. But Rogovin acknowledged that Silberman was a friend from the Ford administration when both men had worked on intelligence issues – Rogovin as CIA counsel and Silberman as deputy attorney general.[5] So there was at least the plausibility of two friends interested in intelligence matters chatting about Iran, especially since Rogovin's client was busy promoting a hostage deal and Silberman was involved in the issue for the Reagan-Bush campaign.

After Reagan was elected, Silberman was named as a judge to the U.S. Court of Appeals in Washington and moved into a house next door to Rogovin. Their friendship flourished and the two men bought a boat together. So there also was a reason Rogovin might have played down the Lavi-Silberman connection when I talked with him in the early 1990s. He may have wanted to avoid embarrassing or implicating his friend, Silberman.

Israeli intelligence officer Ben-Menashe offered another account of the L'Enfant Plaza meeting. In Ben-Menashe's version, Lavi – an Iranian Jew living in the United States and working with the Israeli government – was involved as a coordinator for the meeting, but that Ben-Menashe and another Iranian, Ahmed Omshei, also participated. Ben-Menashe said the message to the three Republicans was that Israel's Begin government had changed course because of the Iran-Iraq War and now intended to move immediately toward resolving the hostage crisis. If the hostages could be freed in the first week of October, the way would be cleared for Israel to sell a wider array of military hardware to Iran, which was then under pressure from the Iraqi invasion, Ben-Menashe said.

Ben-Menashe said Omshei did most of the talking at the L'Enfant Plaza meeting, telling Allen, Silberman and McFarlane that the hostages would be delivered to a U.S. Air Force plane in Karachi, Pakistan, fitting with Lavi's' notation about "rtun of hostages. Swap in Karachi." Ben-Menashe said McFarlane nodded at the news and said, cryptically, "I'll report to my superiors."

By the time Ben-Menashe returned to Israel in a couple of days, he discovered that the planned release of the American hostages had fallen through because of Republican opposition, according to his book, *Profits of War*. The Republicans wanted a release of the hostages only after the November 4 election, Ben-Menashe wrote, with the final details to be arranged in Paris between a delegation of Republicans, led by George H.W. Bush, and a delegation of Iranians, led by cleric Mehdi Karrubi.[6]

In retrospect, some of Carter's negotiators felt they should have been much more attentive to the possibility of Republican sabotage. "Looking back, the Carter administration appears to have been far too trusting and particularly blind to the intrigue swirling around it," wrote former NSC official Gary Sick in *October Surprise*.[7]

Chapter 9: Hostage End Game

As the Carter administration's hopes soared briefly with the Tabatabai hostage initiative, the FBI also was learning more about the activities of Cyrus Hashemi. The FBI got court permission to bug Cyrus Hashemi's New York office at 9 West 57th Street under a federal counter-terrorism law because of suspicion that Cyrus might be helping to fund terrorist activities.

The wiretaps – installed in early September 1980 – failed to prove the suspicion about terrorist funding, but the FBI did discover a wide range of other curious activities being discussed over Hashemi's telephones. The wiretaps showed that Cyrus Hashemi was not only maintaining a business relationship with Casey's friend John Shaheen, but that Hashemi's activities intersected with financial dealings of Iran's Princess Ashraf, David Rockefeller's Geneva lawyer, the Bank of Credit and Commerce International, a Houston friend of George H.W. Bush, and Philippine dictator Ferdinand Marcos – a cast of characters who shared a host of reasons for getting Jimmy Carter out of the White House.

The millions of dollars sloshing around Cyrus Hashemi also suggested both motive and means to betray Carter's trust as one of the President's emissaries to the Iranians on the hostage crisis. The wiretaps also picked up discussions about Cyrus Hashemi's secret work arranging military shipments to Iran with Republican attorney Stanley Pottinger, a discovery that prompted a separate investigation into possible violations of the Arms Export Control Act.

Many of the FBI's notations have never been fully clarified beyond establishing a web of suspicious connections. On September 23, 1980, for instance, two men from Houston placed phone calls to Cyrus Hashemi with a cryptic message that "a Greek ship captain" would be delivering a $3 million deposit from Beirut to Hashemi's Netherlands Antilles-registered bank. Hashemi was told the "Greek ship captain" would use the name "Fibolous."

One of the Houston callers, a former Texas judge named Harrel Tillman, considered himself a longtime friend of George H.W. Bush and was supporting the Reagan-Bush ticket in 1980. In a 1995 interview, Tillman also said he was working at the time as a consultant to Iran's radical Islamic government. But, asked about the contents of the phone call to Cyrus Hashemi, Tillman said he had no recollection of the $3 million deposit.

"I don't remember having that conversation," Tillman told me. "I'm not trying to be evasive."

Cyrus Hashemi and John Shaheen also were continuing their business scheming, having obtained apparent new sources of capital. An FBI intercept revealed that Mid Ocean, the Bermuda-based front company that had helped Shaheen circumvent the Canadian freeze on his assets, and Hashemi's First Gulf, "as partners, intend to open a bank in the United Kingdom with capital investment of $10 million with $5 million each partner."

By mid-October, Cyrus Hashemi also was claiming to have plenty of money to save Shaheen's bankrupt Come-by-Chance refinery. Cyrus was proposing a $45 million bail-out that would have continued the Shaheen family control of the refinery. Explaining the offer, Cyrus said he wanted to expand his oil investments and "other satisfactory financing relationships" with Shaheen, according to an article in *The Wall Street Journal*.[1]

Cyrus Hashemi also boasted of interlocking relationships between two of his companies, First Gulf Trust and Yorkhouse Trading Company, and two high-flying Middle Eastern financial institutions, the Arabian Overseas Corporation and the Bank of Credit and Commerce International. In 1980, with strong backing from the Persian Gulf royal families and the chiefs of Saudi intelligence, BCCI was emerging as a leading bank in the Islamic world. BCCI also was expanding into Great Britain and the United States, with a *modus operandi* of buying influence and assisting sensitive Western intelligence operations with financial transfers.

The FBI wiretaps picked up other evidence that Hashemi and Shaheen were trying to establish a bank with Philippine interests in either the Caribbean or in Hong Kong. In mid-October 1980, Hashemi deposited "a large sum of money" in a Philippine bank and planned to meet with Philippine representatives in Europe, an FBI intercept discovered. The negotiations led Shaheen to an agreement with Herminio Disini, an in-law of Philippine First Lady Imelda Marcos, to establish the Hong Kong Deposit and Guaranty Company. Disini also was a top moneyman for Philippine President Ferdinand Marcos.

The $20 million used as starting capital for the bank came through Jean A. Patry, David Rockefeller's lawyer in Geneva, Switzerland. But the original source of the money, according to two Shaheen associates I interviewed, was Princess Ashraf, the Shah's twin sister. Why, I asked one of the associates, would Ashraf have invested $20 million in a bank with these dubious characters? "It was funny money," the associate answered. He believed it was money that the Islamic revolutionary government was claiming as its own. The other Shaheen associate said Shaheen was particularly secretive when asked about his relationship with the deposed princess. "When it comes to Ashraf, I'm a cemetery," Shaheen once said.

(Hashemi's bail-out plan for Shaheen's oil refinery ultimately failed when it was rejected by a Newfoundland bankruptcy court unwilling to gamble again on Shaheen. The poorly designed plant never produced any gasoline and led to Canada's largest bankruptcy, leaving behind $600 million in debts. An angry Newfoundland government launched an investigation into possible fraud in Shaheen's construction of the refinery.)

***

By October 1980, Carter was clawing his way back into the presidential race, with the possibility that an Iranian hostage settlement finally could change the dynamic of the race. Sensing the political danger, the Republicans opened the final full month of the campaign by trying to make Carter's hostage negotiations look like a cynical ploy to influence the election's outcome.

On October 2, Republican vice-presidential candidate George H.W. Bush brought up the issue with a group of reporters: "One thing that's at the back of everybody's mind is, 'What can Carter do that is so sensational and so flamboyant, if you will, on his side to pull off an October Surprise?' And everybody kind of speculates about it, but there's not a darn thing we can do about it, nor is there any strategy we can do except possibly have it discounted."

With Bush's comments, Carter's supposed "October Surprise" was publicly injected into the campaign. But there was "a darn thing" or two that the Republicans could do – and were doing – to prepare themselves for the possibility of a last-minute hostage release, including gathering their own intelligence about the Iranian developments.

"Of course, we watched for the possibility of some dramatic impact," Richard Allen told me. "We're not foolish. Of course, it was incumbent on us as running an election, to be aware of what might happen to derail or to dent in any way the kind of juggernaut victory that we expected to turn in."

Even scraps of news about the hostages were rushed to the campaign hierarchy. Allen recalled one urgent memo he wrote when he was told by a journalist that Secretary of State Edmund Muskie had floated the possibility of a swap of military spare parts for the hostages. Like a scene in a spy novel, Allen coded the journalist as "ABC" and Muskie as "XYZ" and compiled a quick memo on the hot news. "I breathlessly sent this out to the campaign, to [campaign director William] Casey, to [pollster Richard] Wirthlin, to [senior adviser Edwin] Meese, I think [to] the President and maybe [to] George Bush."[2]

Allen took notes, too, about a call on October 13, 1980, from Angelo Codevilla, a Republican staffer on the Senate Intelligence Committee. Allen scribbled down that Codevilla had obtained "admin. embargoed intelligence" showing that the hostages purportedly were being returned to the U.S. Embassy. When I asked Allen about the note, he responded that it meant "nothing more than the fact that my logs were filled with volunteered information of that type."[3]

***

The big October Surprise question, however, has always been whether the Reagan-Bush campaign sealed the deal for a post-election hostage release with direct meetings in Paris between senior Iranians and senior Republicans, including vice presidential candidate George H.W. Bush.

The idea of Bush slipping away during the final weeks of the campaign for a secret trip to Paris has always been the most explosive part of the October Surprise story and, for many, the most implausible. The secret trip would have required the cooperation of at least a few Secret Service agents who would have had to file inaccurate reports on the candidate's whereabouts and activities. The trip also would have carried a high political risk if exposed, though the senior George Bush's experience at the CIA had taught him a lot about how to contain embarrassing disclosures especially when a national security claim could be asserted. If a flat denial didn't work, perhaps he could have tried a patriotic cover story about trying to get the hostages home when Carter couldn't. But often the most effective tactic is simply to deny, deny, deny.

My own resistance to the October Surprise tales came, in part, from my middle-American background. I simply had trouble picturing the various players taking secret, night-time flights across the Atlantic to meet with foreign leaders in luxury hotels surrounded by security agents. The "James Bond factor" made the story seem more like a pulp novel or an escapist movie than a real historic event. But in covering intelligence operations since the early 1980s, I also had come to grips with the fact that people who have made themselves part of that clandestine world thrive on risks that the average person – or politician – would aver.

It's also clear that lies are told to protect the secrecy of all kinds of missions, even something trivial like George W. Bush's surprise flight to Iraq for Thanksgiving dinner in 2003. To give Bush's flight additional security – and extra drama – phony flight plans were filed, a false call sign was employed and Air Force One was identified as a "Gulfstream 5" in response to a question from a British Airways pilot.

"A senior administration official told reporters that even some members of Bush's Secret Service detail believed he was still in Crawford, Texas, getting ready to have his parents over for Thanksgiving," *Washington Post* reporter Mike Allen wrote. "It was just one reflection of the extraordinary preparation – and secrecy – that went into this most unusual presidential trip."[4]

Besides falsely telling reporters that George W. Bush planned to spend Thanksgiving at his Texas ranch and would call a few soldiers in Iraq by phone, Bush's handlers spirited Bush to Air Force One in an unmarked vehicle, with only a tiny Secret Service contingent, the *Post* reported. Bush later relished describing the scene to reporters. "They pulled up in a plain-looking vehicle with tinted windows. I slipped on a baseball cap, pulled 'er down – as did Condi. We looked like a normal couple," he said, referring to national security adviser Condoleezza Rice.

"The shades in the press cabin on Air Force One had been pulled down," the *Post*'s Allen reported, "and both doors were closed, so the reporters could not see Bush arrive or what personnel and firepower accompanied him. The reporters knew he was aboard only when they heard the engines rev."

Though the melodramatic deception surrounding Bush's flight to Baghdad soon became public – since it was in essence a publicity stunt – it did prove the ability of high-ranking officials to conduct their movements in secrecy and the readiness of security personnel to file false reports as part of these operations.

Plus, the notion that Secret Service agents wouldn't doctor an activity report fails to take into account their primary role of protecting leaders who otherwise might choose to go it alone, either for a romantic tryst or a questionable political meeting. As was made clear during the investigation of President Bill Clinton's sex life, Secret Service agents are loathe to report on what they see because they understand that they wouldn't be able to do their jobs – whether protecting U.S. leaders or foreign dignitaries – if they were seen as potential snitches. They get to be close to a person being protected because the person trusts that the Secret Service agents won't squeal. Discretion is as vital a trait for Secret Service agents as skill in handling a weapon.

Still, many critics of the October Surprise story insist that it is impossible to conceive of George H.W. Bush, the former CIA director, arranging for a secret flight to Paris while under Secret Service protection in mid-October 1980. These critics have argued that this story must have been concocted for political reasons after the Iran-Contra scandal broke in late 1986 when a "conspiracy fever" gripped Washington. But whatever the larger truth, the suspicion that the October Surprise allegations were invented *after* the Iran-Contra scandal has turned out to be wrong. The story of George H.W. Bush's alleged trip to Paris was circulating among Republicans by mid-October 1980.

***

David Henderson, then a State Department Foreign Service officer, recalled the date as October 18, 1980, when *Chicago Tribune* correspondent John Maclean arrived at Henderson's house in Washington. The purpose of the interview was to discuss Henderson's criticism of the Carter administration's handling of Cuban refugees who had been arriving in the Mariel boat lift. But Maclean, the son of author Norman Maclean who wrote *A River Runs Through It*, had something else on his mind, Henderson recalled. Maclean had just been told by a well-placed Republican source that vice presidential candidate George H.W. Bush was flying to Paris for a clandestine meeting with a delegation of Iranians about the 52 American hostages.

Henderson wasn't sure whether Maclean was looking for some confirmation or whether he was simply sharing an interesting tidbit of news. Henderson had not previously heard of the Bush trip and wondered out loud if it might be part of a bipartisan effort to finally resolve the long-running hostage crisis. Unable to offer any independent knowledge of his own, the Foreign Service officer turned to the topic of the Cuban refugees.

For his part, Maclean never wrote about the leak he had received from his well-placed Republican source because, he said, a campaign spokesman subsequently denied it. As the years passed, the memory of that Bush-to-Paris leak faded for both Henderson and Maclean, until October Surprise allegations bubbled to the surface again in the early 1990s. Several intelligence operatives were claiming that Bush had undertaken a secret mission to Paris in mid-October 1980 to give the Iranian government an assurance from one of the two Republicans on the presidential ticket that the promises of future military and other assistance would be kept.

Henderson mentioned his conversation with the journalist in a 1991 letter to a U.S. senator. I obtained a copy while working on a follow-up to a documentary that the Public Broadcasting Service's *Frontline* program had done that April on the October Surprise issue. In the letter, Henderson recalled the comments about Bush's trip to Paris but not the name of the *Chicago Tribune* reporter. A producer at *Frontline* searched some newspaper archives to find the story about Henderson and the Mariel boat lift as a way to identify Maclean as the journalist who had interviewed Henderson.

Though not eager to become part of the October Surprise story in 1991, Maclean confirmed that he had received the Republican leak. He also agreed with Henderson's recollection that their conversation occurred on or about October 18, 1980. But Maclean still declined to identify his source.

The significance of the Maclean-Henderson conversation was that it was a piece of information locked in a kind of historical amber, untainted by subsequent claims by intelligence operatives whose credibility had been challenged. One could not accuse Maclean of concocting the Bush-to-Paris allegation for some ulterior motive, since he hadn't used it in 1980, nor had he volunteered it a decade later. He only confirmed it when approached by *Frontline* and even then wasn't particularly eager to talk about it.

Though inconclusive on its own, the Maclean-Henderson conversation provided important corroboration for the claims by the intelligence operatives, including Israeli intelligence officer Ari Ben-Menashe who said he saw Bush attend a final round of meetings with Iranians in Paris. Ben-

Menashe said he was in Paris as part of a six-member Israeli delegation that was coordinating the arms deliveries to Iran. He said the key meeting occurred at the Ritz Hotel in Paris.

"We walked past the vigilant eyes of the French security men to be confronted by two U.S. Secret Service types," Ben-Menashe wrote in *Profits of War*. "After checking off our names on their list, they directed us to a guarded elevator at the side of the lobby. Stepping out of the elevator, we found ourselves in a small foyer where soft drinks and fruits had been laid out." Ben-Menashe said he recognized several Americans already there, including Robert Gates, Robert McFarlane, Donald Gregg and George Cave, the CIA expert on Iran.

"Ten minutes later, [cleric Mehdi] Karrubi, in a Western suit and collarless white shirt with no tie, walked with an aide through the assembled group, bade everyone a good day, and went straight into the conference room," Ben-Menashe wrote. "A few minutes later George Bush, with the wispy-haired William Casey in front of him, stepped out of the elevator. He smiled, said hello to everyone, and, like Karrubi, hurried into the conference room. It was a very well-staged entrance. My last view of George Bush was of his back as he walked deeper into the room – and then the doors were closed."[5]

Ben-Menashe said the Paris meetings served to finalize a previously outlined agreement calling for release of the 52 hostages in exchange for $52 million, guarantees of arms sales for Iran, and unfreezing of Iranian monies in U.S. banks. The timing, however, was changed, he said, to coincide with Reagan's expected Inauguration on January 20, 1981. Then the participants dispersed, the Israeli said.

"It was such a secret arrangement that all hotel records of the Americans' and the Israelis' visits to Paris – I cannot speak for the Iranians – were swept away two days after we left town," Ben-Menashe wrote.[6] Though uncertain about the precise dates of these October meetings, Ben-Menashe testified under oath before Congress about seeing Bush and other Republicans in Paris in October 1980. Gates, McFarlane, Gregg and Cave all denied participating in the meeting.

But Ben-Menashe's testimony received support from several sources, including pilot Heinrich Rupp, who said he flew Casey from Washington's National Airport to Paris on a flight that left very late on a rainy night in mid-October. Rupp said that after arriving at LeBourget airport outside Paris, he saw a man resembling Bush on the tarmac. The night of October 18 indeed was rainy in the Washington area. Also, sign-in sheets at the Reagan-Bush headquarters in Arlington, Virginia, placed Casey within a five-minute drive of National Airport late that evening. The sign-in sheets showed Casey stopping in at the campaign headquarters at about 11:30 p.m. for a ten-minute visit to the Operations Center, which was staffed by CIA veterans monitoring developments in Iran.

There were other bits and pieces of corroboration about the Paris meetings. As early as 1987, Iran's ex-President Bani-Sadr had made similar claims about a Paris meeting. A French arms dealer, Nicholas Ignatiew, told me in 1990 that he had checked with his government contacts and was told that Republicans did meet with Iranians in Paris in mid-October 1980. A well-connected French investigative reporter Claude Angeli said his sources inside the French secret service confirmed that the service provided "cover" for a meeting between Republicans and Iranians in France on the weekend of October 18-19. German journalist Martin Kilian had received a similar account from a top aide to the fiercely anti-communist chief of French intelligence, Alexandre deMarenches.[7]

During the final weeks of the House Task Force investigation in 1992, another witness came forward: the biographer for deMarenches, David Andelman, an ex-*New York Times* and CBS News correspondent. Andelman testified that while working with deMarenches on the biography, the spymaster said he had helped the Reagan-Bush campaign arrange meetings with Iranians about the hostage issue in the summer and fall of 1980, with one meeting held in Paris in October. Andelman said deMarenches ordered that the secret meetings be kept out of his memoirs because the story could otherwise damage the reputation of his friends, William Casey and George H.W. Bush.[8]

"I'm quite confident that the count [deMarenches] will deny it because that is what he does," Andelman told me in an interview. "He thought the world of Casey and Bush, and never wanted anything to come out that would hurt Bush's chances for reelection [in 1992] or Casey's legacy." Andelman said that when he again raised the issue of Bush's alleged participation in the Paris meetings during a 1992 book promotion tour, deMarenches refused to discuss it, responding: "I don't want to hurt my friend, George Bush."

***

While the Republicans have long denied the claims of a Paris meeting, there is no doubt that military hardware was soon heading to Iran and that some of the principals in the hostage intrigue were active in the shipments.

Back in New York, with the FBI listening in, Cyrus Hashemi began work with Republicans lining up military shipments to Iran, including parts for helicopter gun ships and night-vision goggles for pilots. The FBI wiretap summary also contained references to Hashemi facing accusations at home that he had been duplicitous about the hostage issue. On October 22, the FBI bugs caught Hashemi's wife, Houma, scolding her husband for his denials that he had discussed the hostages with a prominent Iranian. "It is not possible to be a double agent and have two faces," Houma warned Cyrus.

On October 23, the FBI listened in on John Shaheen using one of the bugged phones in Hashemi's Manhattan office to brief a European associate,

Dick Gaedecke, on the latest hostage developments. On October 24, an FBI agent wrote down another cryptic note from the wiretaps indicating that Hashemi may have had ties to Ronald Reagan himself. Using Cyrus Hashemi's initials, the FBI's notation read: "CH-banking business about Reagan overseas corp." (The possibility of a Reagan-Hashemi link also was raised in a 1992 Reuters news story which quoted FBI sources in New York as saying that agents heard Ronald Reagan on one Hashemi tape. But the House Task Force said Reagan was not recorded speaking on the 548 tapes made available to Congress, except for some television background noise.)

Meanwhile, back in Europe, a French-Israeli arms shipment to Iran was under way. Iranian arms merchant Ahmed Heidari said he had approached deMarenches in September 1980 to seek help getting weapons for the Iranian military, which was then battling the Iraqi army in Khuzistan province. Heidari said deMarenches put him in touch with a French middleman, Yves deLoreilhe, who facilitated the arms shipment. The flight left France on October 23, stopped in Tel Aviv to load 250 tires for U.S.-built F-4 fighters, returned to France to add spare parts for M-60 tanks, before going to Teheran on October 24. When Carter learned of the shipment, he again protested to Israeli Prime Minister Menachem Begin.[9]

***

With little more than a week left in the 1980 campaign, the Republicans were getting nervous about Reagan's slippage in the polls. New surveys put Ronald Reagan and Jimmy Carter in a virtual dead heat. There were also continued rumblings that Carter might finally be successful in winning the freedom of the 52 hostages.

While heading off to campaign in Pittsburgh, George H.W. Bush got an unsettling message from former Texas Governor John Connally, the ex-Democrat who had switched to the Republican Party during the Nixon administration. Connally said his oil contacts in the Middle East were buzzing with rumors that Carter had achieved the long-elusive breakthrough on the hostages.

So, at 2:12 p.m., October 27, George Bush called Richard Allen, who was still keeping tabs on Carter's hostage progress. Bush ordered Allen to find out what he could about Connally's tip. Allen's notes, which I discovered many years later in an obscure Capitol Hill storage room, made clear that Bush was the man in charge of the intelligence-gathering operation.

"Geo Bush," Allen's notes began, "JBC [Connally] – already made deal. Israelis delivered last wk spare pts. via Amsterdam. Hostages out this wk. Moderate Arabs upset. French have given spares to Iraq and know of JC [Carter] deal w/Iran. JBC [Connally] unsure what we should do. RVA [Allen] to act if true or not."

In a "secret" 1992 deposition to the House October Surprise Task Force, Allen explained the cryptic notes as meaning Connally had heard that President Carter had ransomed the hostages' freedom with an Israeli shipment of military spare parts to Iran. Allen said Bush then instructed him, Allen, to query Connally, who was at the influential Vinson & Elkins law firm in Houston. Allen was then to pass on any new details to two of Bush's aides.

According to the notes, Allen was to relay the information to "Ted Shacklee [sic] via Jennifer." Allen said the Jennifer was Jennifer Fitzgerald, Bush's longtime assistant including during his year at the CIA. Allen testified that "Shacklee" was Theodore Shackley, the legendary CIA covert operations specialist known inside the spy agency as the "blond ghost." During the Cold War, Shackley had run many of the CIA's most controversial paramilitary operations, from Vietnam and Laos to the JMWAVE operations against Fidel Castro's Cuba. When Bush was CIA director in 1976, he appointed Shackley to a top clandestine job, associate deputy director for operations.

But Shackley's CIA career ended in 1979, after three years of battling Carter's CIA director, Stansfield Turner. Shackley believed that Turner, by cleaning out hundreds of covert officers was destroying the agency – as well as Shackley's career. After retiring, Shackley went into business with another ex-CIA man, Thomas Clines, a partner with Edwin Wilson, the rogue spy who later would go to prison over shipments of terrorist materials to Libya. Clines himself would be convicted of tax fraud in the Iran-Contra scandal, another controversy in which Shackley's pale specter would hover in the background.

But in 1980, Shackley was working to put his former boss, George Bush, into the White House and possibly securing the CIA directorship for himself. Biographer David Corn said Shackley approached Bush for a position in the campaign in August 1980, after Reagan had picked Bush as his vice presidential nominee. But other sources have said Shackley's informal assistance to Bush's campaign dates back earlier and was more frequent. "Within the spook world the belief spread that Shackley was close to Bush," Corn wrote in *Blond Ghost*. "Rafael Quintero [an anti-Castro Cuban with close ties to the CIA] was saying that Shackley met with Bush every week. He told one associate that should Reagan and Bush triumph, Shackley was considered a potential DCI," director of the Central Intelligence Agency.[10]

The Allen notation, however, was the first piece of documentary evidence that Bush and Shackley were working together on the Iranian hostage crisis, a relationship that makes more credible other claims of involvement by CIA personnel who had were close to Shackley during his long CIA career. For instance, Donald Gregg, a CIA officer alleged to have participated in Republican meetings with Iranians, served under Shackley's command in Vietnam.

In 1980, Shackley also was working with conservative "journalist" Michael Ledeen, another participant in the Reagan-Bush campaign's October Surprise monitoring effort, according to an unpublished section of the House Task Force report. Shackley had teamed up with Ledeen as paid consultants to a "war game" for SISMI, the right-wing Italian intelligence service. In late October, Ledeen co-wrote a damaging story for *The New Republic* alleging that President Carter's brother Billy accepted $50,000 in unreported payments from Libya and held meetings with Palestinian leaders George Habash and Yasir Arafat.

The story, whose accuracy was disputed by Billy Carter and a special Senate subcommittee that had investigated the President's brother,[11] was leaked by SISMI in an apparent move to undermine Jimmy Carter's campaign. Ledeen's article appeared in *The New Republic* without mentioning that Ledeen was working for SISMI and was secretly assisting the Reagan-Bush campaign.[12]

While writing for *The New Republic*, Ledeen also was writing memos to the Reagan-Bush campaign urging more aggressive attacks on Carter over the hostage crisis. Ledeen sent Halper, the chief of the Operations Center, a two-page memo entitled "Notes on Iran," which was discovered by the House Task Force.

"Election Day is the first anniversary of the seizure of the American hostages in Teheran," Ledeen wrote. "The voters of this country are entitled to answers to the basic questions surrounding this act of national humiliation. Why were our men and women in Tehran not protected? After all, the American Embassy had been repeatedly attacked and threatened by Iranian mobs during the preceeding [sic] months ... These are not the only questions. The seizure of the hostages, terrible though it is, was just one act in a terrible drama that humiliated this country throughout the world."

***

There were other loose ends to the October Surprise suspicions in the days before the November 4 election. Later evidence, for instance, suggested that Casey may have obtained funding for some of his off-the-books Republican operations from Philippine dictator Ferdinand Marcos.

According to a letter revealed in the Philippines after Marcos's overthrow in 1986, President Reagan wanted Marcos to hand over files about the campaign payments before Marcos would be allowed to flee to Hawaii. The letter, purportedly written by Marcos's executive assistant, Victor Nituda, said Senator Paul Laxalt, a Nevada Republican who had served as chairman of Reagan's 1980 campaign, "expects all documents checklisted during his last visit or the deal is off." One of the files was marked "1980

SEC-014, Funds to Casey." Another file was slugged "1980 SEC-015, Reagan Funds Not Used."

In a follow-up letter three days later, Nituda added, "we urgently need to fly the last batch to Clark [Air Force base] soonest. [National Security Adviser William] Clark and [Reagan chief of staff Michael] Deaver are not happy with what we've sent them so far." Laxalt wanted files from 1984, too, including papers on bank loans and Marcos's "donations to Gen. [John] Singlaub," who was raising money for the Nicaraguan contra rebels, the letter said.

While in exile in Hawaii, Marcos reportedly boasted to a visitor that he gave $4 million to Ronald Reagan's 1980 campaign and $8 million in 1984. He made the admission to a Republican lawyer named Richard Hirschfeld, who secretly tape-recorded the conversation. Hirschfeld turned part of the tape over to Congress, but no serious investigation was ever undertaken. For years, Laxalt's spokesmen have denied that the senator had any discussions with Marcos about the information referenced in the Nituda letter. In an interview, Deaver also told me that he has no idea what Nituda meant.

In his 1996 book, *Bare Knuckles and Back Rooms*, Republican campaign strategist Ed Rollins added another piece to the puzzle, recounting a dinner he had with a top Filipino politician in 1991. Over drinks, the man casually asserted that he had delivered an illegal $10 million cash payment in a suitcase from Marcos to Reagan's 1984 reelection campaign.

"I was the guy who gave the ten million from Marcos to your campaign," the Filipino told Rollins, who was Reagan's 1984 campaign manager. "I was the guy who made the arrangements and delivered the cash personally. ...It was a personal gift from Marcos to Reagan." The first thought that raced through his head, Rollins wrote, was "Cash? Holy shit."

Rollins withheld the names of both the Filipino and the Republican lobbyist who allegedly received the cash for Reagan. As for the larger significance of the information, Rollins shrugged it off, noting that the statute of limitations for illegal campaign contributions had probably expired.[13]

Despite lacking details, the Rollins book provides important corroboration that Marcos did make sizable illicit payments to Reagan. Rollins wrote, too, that he asked Laxalt about the $10 million payment when the two men were alone at cabins they own in Front Royal, Virginia. "Christ, now it all makes sense," Laxalt exclaimed. "When I was over there cutting off Marcos's nuts, he gave me a hard time. 'How can you do this?' he kept saying to me. 'I gave Reagan ten million dollars. How can he do this to me?' I didn't know what the hell he was talking about. Now I get it."

Though Laxalt's comment seems self-serving if not disingenuous, it does confirm that he and Marcos discussed the alleged payoffs to Reagan, a point that Laxalt's aides consistently denied. But it's also possible that Laxalt, who had been chairman of the 1980 Reagan-Bush campaign and was one of Reagan's closest advisers, understood exactly what Marcos meant.

Certainly in 1980, Marcos was hoping that by defeating Jimmy Carter, Reagan would put an end to the nagging about human rights violations. Marcos wanted to be treated as an important Asian ally, not simply a despot. As Marcos had hoped, Reagan did drop the human rights lectures, looked the other way on Marcos's corruption, and sent Vice President George Bush to toast Marcos for his "adherence to democratic principles."

***

On November 4, 1980, one year to the day after the Iranian militants seized the U.S. Embassy in Teheran, Ronald Reagan routed Jimmy Carter in the U.S. presidential elections, receiving about 44 million votes to Carter's 35 million and Anderson's 5.5 million. Reagan carried 44 states for a total of 489 electoral votes, with Carter claiming only six states and the District of Columbia for 49 electoral votes.

In the transition period after Ronald Reagan's victory, the Iran-hostage negotiations sputtered ahead and the participants in the alleged October Surprise gambit kept busy.

On November 20, Tillman, the Houston friend of George H.W. Bush, was back on the phone with Cyrus Hashemi, this time talking about the "purchase of [a] refinery," according to the "secret" FBI wiretap summary. Tillman said he had been in touch with Vice President-elect Bush and had consulted with "the 'Bush' people" about the troubles that Hashemi and his business associate, John Shaheen, were having with the bankrupt oil refinery in Newfoundland. "Bush people would be cooperative with this matter and make it a showcase," Tillman said, according to the summary. "But the 'Bush' people would not act on it until after the Inauguration" in January 1981.

Also on November 20, Hashemi boasted to fellow Iranian Mahmood Moini about ties to Casey, who was then running President-elect Reagan's transition office. "I have been, well, close friends ... with Casey for several years," Hashemi told Moini.

Although the Carter administration had finally frozen Cyrus Hashemi out of the hostage talks after the FBI picked up evidence of his arms dealing with Iran, the shrewd Iranian banker kept his hand in. On January 15, 1981, Hashemi met with Iranian Revolutionary Guard officials in London and opened an account for them with 1.87 million pounds (roughly equal to $3 million), according to the FBI wiretaps. The money apparently was to finance more arms sales, but also had the look of a possible payoff to Khomeini's hard-line military backers.

On January 19, 1981, the last day of the Carter Presidency, Hashemi was back on one of the bugged phones, describing to a cohort "the banking arrangements being made to free the American hostages in Iran." Hashemi was also moving ahead with military shipments to Iran, amid concern that there might be more competition ahead.

"How should we proceed with our friend over there?" the associate asked Hashemi. "I'm just a little bit nervous that everyone is trying to move in on the action here."

As the Inauguration neared, Republicans talked tough, making clear that Ronald Reagan wouldn't stand for the humiliation that the nation endured for 444 days under Jimmy Carter. The Reagan-Bush team intimated that Reagan would deal harshly with Iran if it didn't surrender the hostages. A joke making the rounds of Washington went: "What's three feet deep and glows in the dark? Teheran ten minutes after Ronald Reagan becomes President."

On Inauguration Day, January 20, 1981, just as Reagan was beginning his inaugural address, word came from Iran that the hostages were freed. The American people were overjoyed. The coincidence in timing between the hostage release and Reagan's taking office immediately boosted the new President's image as a tough guy who wouldn't let the United States be pushed around.

On another level, however, the participants in the October Surprise mystery went about what looked like collecting payments for their services, arranging more secret military deliveries to Iran, and taking advantage of their cozy relationship with the new American government.

The bank deal that Cyrus Hashemi and John Shaheen had discussed for months took final shape two days after Reagan's Inauguration. On January 22, 1981, Shaheen opened the Hong Kong Deposit and Guaranty Bank with $20 million that had been funneled to him through Jean Patry, the Rockefeller lawyer in Geneva who was fronting for the Shah's twin sister, Princess Ashraf. The bank sported on its board other powerful world players, including Herminio Disini, known as Philippine President Marcos's personal bag man. Indeed, a Shaheen lawyer told me that Shaheen flew to Manila in early 1981 to meet face-to-face with Marcos, the man whom Shaheen considered really "in charge" of the bank. The lawyer said the Hong Kong bank was a way for Marcos "to get his hands on some of the Arabs' Euro-petrodollars."

From 1981 to 1984, Hong Kong Deposit and Guaranty did pull in hundreds of millions of petrodollars, just as Marcos had hoped. The bank also attracted high-flying Arabs to its board of directors. Two directors were Ghanim Al-Mazrouie, the Abu Dhabi official who controlled 10 percent of the corrupt Bank of Credit and Commerce International, and Hassan Yassin, a cousin of Saudi financier Adnan Khashoggi and an adviser to BCCI principal Kamal Adham, the former chief of Saudi intelligence.

Though Cyrus Hashemi's name was not formally listed on the roster of the Hong Kong bank, he did receive cash from BCCI, al-Mazrouie's bank. An FBI wiretap of Hashemi's office in early February 1981 picked up an advisory that "money from BCCI [is] to come in tomorrow from London on Concorde."

In 1984, the Hong Kong Deposit and Guaranty collapsed and an estimated $100 million disappeared. The crash put Shaheen in hot water again, but he died of liver cancer on November 1, 1985, so the bank's loss was buried with him, in his estate. The biggest loser in the deal – Princess Ashraf – told the House Task Force that she considered her $20 million investment just a routine business investment, though it might have looked to more suspicious investigators like a payoff to Shaheen and Hashemi. The curious BCCI money flight on the Concorde has never been explained.

***

Early in the Reagan-Bush administration, Joseph Reed, the aide to David Rockefeller, was appointed and confirmed as the new U.S. ambassador to Morocco. Before leaving for his posting, he visited the CIA and its new director, William Casey. As Reed arrived, CIA official Charles Cogan was getting up and preparing to leave Casey's office at CIA headquarters in Langley, Virginia.

Knowing Reed, Cogan lingered at the door – and later recounted the incident to the House Task Force. Cogan said he had a "definite memory" of a comment Reed made about disrupting Carter's "October Surprise" of a pre-election release of the 52 American hostages in Iran. But Cogan said he couldn't recall the precise verb that Reed had used. "Joseph Reed said, 'we' and then the verb [and then] something about Carter's October Surprise," Cogan testified. "The implication was we did something about Carter's October Surprise, but I don't have the exact wording."

One congressional investigator, who discussed the recollection with Cogan in a less formal setting, concluded that the verb that Cogan chose not to repeat was "fucked" – as in "we fucked Carter's October Surprise."

During Cogan's deposition, David Laufman, a Republican lawyer on the Task Force and a former CIA official, asked Cogan if he had since "had occasion to ask him [Reed] about this" recollection? Yes, Cogan replied, he recently had asked Reed about it, after Reed moved to a protocol job at the United Nations. "I called him up," Cogan said. "He was at his farm in Connecticut, as I recall, and I just told him that, look, this is what sticks in my mind and what I am going to say [to Congress], and he didn't have any comment on it and continued on to other matters."

"He didn't offer any explanation to you of what he meant?" asked Laufman.

"No," answered Cogan.

"Nor did he deny that he had said it?" asked another Task Force lawyer Mark L. Shaffer.

"He didn't say anything," Cogan responded. "We just continued on talking about other things."

And so did the Task Force lawyers at this remarkable deposition on December 21, 1992. The lawyers even failed to ask Cogan the obvious follow-up: What did Casey say and how did Casey react when Reed allegedly told Reagan's ex-campaign chief that "we fucked Carter's October Surprise."

***

In unpublished Task Force files, I also discovered the notes of an FBI agent who tried to interview Joseph Reed about his October Surprise knowledge. The FBI man, Harry A. Penich, had scribbled down that "numerous telephone calls were placed to him [Reed]. He failed to answer any of them. I conservatively place the number over 10."

Finally, Penich, armed with a subpoena, cornered Reed arriving home at his 50-acre estate in Greenwich, Connecticut. "He was surprised and absolutely livid at being served at home," Penich wrote. "His responses could best be characterized as lashing out." Reed threatened to go over Penich's head. In hand-written "talking points" that Penich apparently used to brief an unnamed superior, the FBI agent wrote: "He [Reed] did it in such a way as to lead a reasonable person to believe he had influence w/you. The man's remarks were both inappropriate and improper."

But the hard-ball tactics worked. When Reed finally consented to an interview, Task Force lawyers just went through the motions. Penich took the interview notes and wrote that Reed "recalls no contact with Casey in 1980," though Reed added that "their paths crossed many times because of Reed's position at Chase." As for the 1981 CIA visit, Reed added that as the newly appointed U.S. ambassador to Morocco, he "would have stopped in to see Casey and pay respect." But on whether Reed made any remark about obstructing Carter's October Surprise, Reed claimed he "does not specifically know what October Surprise refers to," Penich scribbled down.

The Task Force lawyers didn't press hard. Most strikingly, the lawyers failed to confront Reed with evidence that would have impeached his contention that he had "no contact with Casey in 1980." According to the sign-in sheets at the Reagan-Bush campaign headquarters in Arlington, Virginia, which the Task Force had obtained, Reed saw Casey on September 11, 1980, less than two months before the election.

***

Within days of the FBI picking up word of Cyrus Hashemi's BCCI-Concorde money flight in February 1981, the Reagan-Bush Justice Department ordered the wiretaps pulled from Hashemi's office. Though the FBI and field prosecutors wanted to use the wiretap information immediately to mount an arms-trafficking case against Hashemi, the proposed indictment languished for more than three years. Even then, in May 1984, when the evidence finally went to a grand jury, the Justice Department insisted on tipping off Hashemi, allowing him to cancel a flight from London to New York and avoid arrest. His brother, Jamshid, also avoided arrest for his alleged involvement in the weapons deals.

In a cable to FBI headquarters, FBI agents in New York noted sarcastically that other targets of the probe "will also receive the above DOJ-sponsored courtesy. ... Obviously the arrests will not be announced if they do not occur which in the final analysis is not likely. This case began on July 18, 1980, and because of above, results of a positive nature do not appear forthcoming despite the mammoth investigative effort put forth thus far."[14]

Only a few days before the indictments were scheduled, the FBI's terrorism section also discovered that two wiretap tape recordings had disappeared. The loss of the tapes weakened the case and prevented the possible indictment of Hashemi's Republican lawyer, Stanley Pottinger, a former Justice Department official during the Nixon and Ford administrations who had collaborated with Cyrus on his Iran activities.[15]

Despite the 1984 indictment, Cyrus Hashemi would keep wheeling and dealing from his base in London, continuing to offer his services to U.S. intelligence. Less than a year later, in early spring 1985, Israeli arms dealers, Albert Schwimmer and Ya'acov Nimrodi, arrived at a luxury London hotel to meet with Cyrus Hashemi, Saudi financier Adnan Khashoggi and an Iranian intelligence man named Manucher Ghorbanifar. Hashemi was proposing more weapons sales for Iran. He was working again with John Shaheen and William Casey.

A year later, still in London, Cyrus Hashemi fell suddenly ill with what was diagnosed as acute leukemia. He died on July 21, 1986. But what Hashemi started in that London hotel room in 1985 would become known a few months after Hashemi's death as the Iran-Contra Affair.

Chapter 10: 'Debunked?'

The October Surprise case of 1980 merged almost seamlessly with the Iran-Contra scandal of 1985-86. Or at least that is one way to read the available evidence, the two scandals really just the first and last chapters of the same narrative.

Indeed, some of us who investigated the Iran-Contra events in the latter half of the 1980s and then looked back to the scandal's possible 1980 precursor were surprised to discover how much the two cases intertwined. Many of the relationships that existed before Jimmy Carter's ouster from the White House extended well into Ronald Reagan's occupancy.

Three of these common players from October Surprise who showed up in Iran-Contra were the trio of wheeler-dealers: Cyrus Hashemi, John Shaheen and William Casey. In the mid-1980s, they were pushing the idea that arms shipments to Iran could be currency for helping to free a new set of U.S. hostages held by Islamic fundamentalists in Lebanon, extremists supposedly influenced by Iran. The Iranian Karrubi brothers were back, too, smoothing the deals with Teheran's mullahs. Other returning players included Robert McFarlane, Robert Gates, Donald Gregg and George H.W. Bush.

Some of the alleged October Surprise arms dealers and intelligence operatives would keep their hands in the later transactions as well. On the shadowy fringes of the scandal could be found former CIA clandestine specialist Ted Shackley, who got the Iran-Contra ball rolling with a meeting with Hassan Karrubi and other Iranians in Hamburg in 1984. Also, playing an early role was Shackley's associate, Michael Ledeen, who promoted the Iranian contacts in 1985 as a part-time consultant to Reagan's National Security Council.

The Israelis were there, though their internal rivalries – between Likud and Labor – added some new twists and turns. Israeli intelligence officer Ari Ben-Menashe first met some American journalists in early-to-mid-1986 as he tried to leak secrets about the U.S. arms sales to Iran to *Time* magazine and *Newsday*. The reason, Ben-Menashe said, was that his allies in Likud were being squeezed out by rivals in the Labor Party.

Ben-Menashe's account of U.S. arms to Iran had faced Reagan-Bush denials in mid-1986, too. The White House told U.S. journalists that there was nothing to those crazy allegations, causing the journalists to set aside Ben-Menashe's story, though his claims were confirmed a few months later in the Beirut weekly, *Al-Shiraa*. (In 1990 during Ben-Menashe's trial in New York, *Time* magazine correspondent Raji Samghabadi, one of the journalists who received Ben-Menashe's early tip, testified about the Israeli's knowledge of the scandal, helping to convince the jury that Ben-Menashe was telling the truth about his intelligence work for Israel. The jury acquitted Ben-Menashe of federal charges that he had illegally sold military equipment to Iran.[1])

Looked at from the view of the sizable mountain of evidence that connected October Surprise and Iran-Contra, the two scandals appeared in many ways to be one, a continuous network of corrupt relationships arising from an act of political treachery in 1980 and extending through years of secret deals, arms shipments and money laundering only partly exposed in 1986. When one cover-up crumbled, another was put into place; one set of lies followed another; a sordid history of entangling alliances relentlessly hidden from the American people.

But that is not how Official Washington saw the issue. Washington's conventional wisdom held that the October Surprise was a mythical conspiracy theory, a hoax perpetrated by a cast of delusional characters who – for whatever their reasons – besmirched the honor of honest leaders, including Ronald Reagan and George H.W. Bush. Most of the major news media – both conservative and mainstream – viewed the conspiracy as one perpetrated against Reagan and Bush, not by Reagan and Bush against Jimmy Carter and the hostages.

Even the Iran-Contra arms-for-hostage affair, which popped out in 1986, was just a small blemish on Ronald Reagan's Presidency, according to this prevailing view. Iran-Contra had been a foreign-policy initiative that briefly spun out of control, an anomalous event driven by Reagan's sympathy for new U.S. hostages in Beirut and by his unrelated pressure on subordinates to get money to the contra rebels fighting in Nicaragua. Then, some "men of zeal," including White House aide Oliver North, exceeded their mandate by funneling profits from the Iran arms sales to the contras, while Reagan paid too little attention to his subordinates.

It wasn't that Reagan, Bush and other administration officials consciously lied about the secret operations, this version of events went. They were just kept in the dark by North's little cabal. When they learned the facts, they cooperated fully with investigators to get to the bottom of the affair. Only some out-of-step recalcitrants like Iran-Contra prosecutor Lawrence Walsh saw a more sinister cover-up.

So what's the truth? Is the conventional wisdom right? Was the October Surprise case nothing and Iran-Contra much ado about almost nothing? Or is this official version of history another indication of how powerful the conservative infrastructure had grown in its ability to prevent "another Watergate," even to the point of rewriting important historical events of the recent past?

Getting at the truth in such cases is never easy, especially given the lapse of time and the proficiency of many principal players in covering their tracks. Our October Surprise investigation at PBS *Frontline* produced two one-hour-long documentaries, in 1991 and 1992, but didn't reach any firm conclusions about whether the Republicans had struck a hostage deal with the Iranians behind Carter's back. My 1993 book, *Trick or Treason*, was a narrative of that investigation, adding many details that couldn't fit into the documentaries and challenging the often irrational judgments of the official investigations, but it, too, left open the ultimate question of whether the core October Surprise events were fact or fiction, trick or treason.

In the decade since, more evidence floated to the surface or was dug out of secret government files. That evidence pointed increasingly to the conclusion that the Reagan-Bush campaign not only succeeded in negotiating with the Iranians behind Carter's back in 1980 but managed to protect those secrets from any serious examination when Congress half-heartedly undertook an investigation in 1992.

But if the October Surprise and Iran-Contra scandals were really two peaks at the end of the same mountain range, one of the first points that needed to be established was whether there was a continuation of the Iran weapons shipments that had begun in 1980, some sign of a payoff for the alleged October Surprise deal. That was a principal question addressed by the *Frontline* investigation in 1991. And having covered the Iran-Contra scandal closely in the mid-to-late 1980s, I was among those who were amazed to learn that the Iranian arms shipments continued during the early years of the Reagan-Bush administration.

***

In a PBS interview aired in the first documentary, Nicholas Veliotes, the Reagan-Bush administration's assistant secretary of state for the Middle East, traced the "germs" of the Iran-Contra scandal to the start of the 1980s. Veliotes said he first discovered the secret arms pipeline to Iran when an Israeli weapons flight was shot down over the Soviet Union on July 18, 1981, after straying off course on its third mission to deliver U.S. military supplies from Israel to Iran via Larnaca, Cyprus.

"We received a press report from Tass [the official Soviet news agency] that an Argentinian plane had crashed," Veliotes said. "According to the documents ... this was chartered by Israel and it was carrying American military equipment to Iran. Obviously, I was interested in that because we had a very firm policy [against trading arms with Iran]. I don't need to tell you that Ronald Reagan was no friend of the ayatollah, and we [were] all still scarred by the hostage crisis. ...

"So I did what you usually do under those circumstances, I tried to get to the bottom of it. And it was clear to me after my conversations with people on high that indeed we had agreed that the Israelis could transship to Iran some American-origin military equipment. Now this was not a covert operation in the classic sense, for which probably you could get a legal justification for it. As it stood, I believe it was the initiative of a few people [who] gave the Israelis the go-ahead. The net result was a violation of American law."[2]

The reason that the Israeli flights violated U.S. law was that no formal notification had been given to Congress about the transshipment of U.S. military equipment as required by the Arms Export Control Act. After his discovery of the U.S. acquiescence, Veliotes said he objected to deceptive wording that was put in the official State Department "press guidance" about the Tass report. But no one in the Washington press corps at the time caught on to the larger scandal.

In checking out the circumstances surrounding the Israeli flight, Veliotes also concluded that the Reagan-Bush camp's dealings with the Iranian government may have gone back to before the 1980 election. "The actual timing on when the Americans got involved with the Israelis in an effort to reach out to the post-Shah government, different people date it at different times," he said. "But it seems to have started in earnest in the period probably prior to the election of 1980, as the Israelis had identified who would become the new players in the national security area in the Reagan administration. And I understand some contacts were made at that time."

Q: "Between?"

Veliotes: "Between Israelis and these new players."[3]

In my work on the Iran-Contra scandal, I also had obtained a classified summary of testimony from a mid-level State Department official, David Satterfield, who saw the early shipments as a continuum of Israeli policy toward Iran. "Satterfield believed that Israel maintained a persistent military relationship with Iran, based on the Israeli assumption that Iran was a non-Arab state which always constituted a potential ally in the Middle East," the summary read. "There was evidence that Israel resumed providing arms to Iran in 1980."

A Mideast counter-terrorism expert, Satterfield described one overture from then-Israeli Defense Minister Ariel Sharon in December 1981. "Sharon approached Secretary [of State Alexander] Haig and stated that Israel was in contact with key Iranian officials and wanted to engage in some arms transactions involving United States weapons in order to develop these contacts," the Satterfield summary said. "Haig told Israel that 'in principle' this was okay, but only for limited F-4 spare parts. Haig told Israel that these had to be commercial, rather than FMS [foreign military sales], transactions."[4]

Over the years, senior Israeli officials claimed that those early shipments had the discreet blessing of top Reagan-Bush officials. In May 1982, Sharon told *The Washington Post* that U.S. officials had approved the Iranian arms transfers. "We said that notwithstanding the tyranny of Khomeini, which we all hate, we have to leave a small window open to this country, a tiny small bridge to this country," Sharon said.

A decade later, in 1993, I took part in an interview with former Israeli Prime Minister Yitzhak Shamir in Tel Aviv during which he said he had read Gary Sick's 1991 book, *October Surprise*, which made the case for believing that the Republicans had intervened in the hostage negotiations. With the topic raised, one interviewer asked, "What do you think? Was there an October Surprise?"

"Of course, it was," Shamir responded without hesitation. "It was." Later in the interview, Shamir seemed to regret his frankness and tried to backpedal on his answer.

At the time of the Shamir interview, the Israelis were determined to discredit their rogue intelligence officer Ari Ben-Menashe, who had not only alleged the secret arms shipments to Iran but had described some of Israel's top-secret nuclear weapons projects to investigative reporter Seymour Hersh for his book about Israeli nuclear strategy, *The Samson Option*. American journalists, who had close ties to Israel's Likud Party, then led the attacks against Ben-Menashe's credibility and against anyone who treated his accounts seriously. Shamir seemed to understand that by corroborating the October Surprise charges, he would have raised Ben-Menashe's standing.

***

Just as Jimmy Carter found himself confronting an array of powerful interests during the Iranian hostage crisis in 1980, so too did those trying to uncover the truth years later encounter row after row of defenders representing many of those same interests.

In 1991, when *Frontline* broadcast its first documentary on the topic and when Gary Sick went public with his conclusion that the Republicans had pulled off an October Surprise conspiracy, George H.W. Bush was U.S. President, He was still wrapped in the glow of victory from the Persian Gulf War and looking forward to continued control of the White House. Busy tamping down the embers of the Iran-Contra scandal fires, the Republicans surely didn't want a new scandal to rage out of control.

On the international front, the Saudi royal family was indebted to the senior Bush for his defense of their interests in the face of Iraq's Saddam Hussein. They had no reason to expose their good friend and ally. The Europeans, known for their discreet intelligence services, also had no incentive to blow the whistle. Neither did the Iranian mullahs, who had built their political standing by denouncing the Great Satan and might face domestic political retribution for having secretly collaborated with the Americans. And the Israelis feared that their secret arms shipments to Iran during the painful hostage crisis of 1980 could be used by their enemies in the United States to harm Israel's reputation with the American people.

One might think that the Democrats would have an obvious political motive for pursuing the October Surprise investigation, but they had already bent under Republican pressure to curtail the Iran-Contra inquiry and were looking at poll figures in spring 1991 showing George H.W. Bush with approval ratings of 80 and 90 percent. A few months later, the Senate Intelligence Committee would pull its punches on Bush's nomination of Robert Gates to be CIA director, an appointment that put one of the principal figures from the Iran-Contra and October Surprise controversies into control of the spy agency that held many of the secrets.

The steady growth of the U.S. conservative news media also was putting pressure on Washington journalists who might be inclined to be skeptical of the Reagan-Bush administrations. Given the growing political imbalance in Washington – between sharp-elbowed conservatives and weak-kneed liberals – an investigation of an issue as complex as the October Surprise realistically had little hope of success, even if all the witnesses were playing it straight, which wasn't the case with the October Surprise issue. A couple of "witnesses," who had insinuated themselves into the story by demonstrating some real knowledge of events, then mixed in enough misinformation to discredit the larger story.

One of these "witnesses" – Oswald LeWinter – admitted to me in an interview that he had added bogus information to his story. He made the admission after being caught lying about Richard Allen's supposed presence at one of the European meetings in 1980. When I confronted him with proof of his lie, LeWinter began asserting that he had been hired by elements in U.S. intelligence to perform just that function. "I was asked by some people to mount a disinformation campaign," LeWinter said in an interview in Dusseldorf, Germany. LeWinter – a once promising poet with a fondness for classical music and cowboy boots – said he was paid $100,000 to salt the October Surprise story with enough bogus information so it could then be discredited.

"The people who asked me to intervene felt that the country could not stand another Watergate, another major political scandal and upheaval, and also worried that the Democratic Party's candidate might have hurt the intelligence community, which was just in the process of recovering from the damage that had been done on it during the Carter administration," LeWinter said.[5]

Though LeWinter's new story could be given no more credence than his earlier one – he was after all an admitted liar – intelligence experts do say that it is common practice to plant disinformation within real operations to confuse anyone trying to ascertain the truth, whether a rival intelligence service or a curious journalist. Inserting a disinformationist, especially one who can be "exploded" at an auspicious moment, is a classic technique. Whether LeWinter was a paid disinformationist or simply a freelance fabricator, his lies and those of a couple of other "witnesses" did give ammunition to October Surprise critics trying to shoot down the broader investigation.[6]

***

Beyond weeding out disinformationists like LeWinter, the October Surprise investigation required digging back more than a decade in time, when even honest witnesses might have memory lapses, when other participants were dead, and when some key players still held positions of great power and influence. So the October Surprise case was a challenging target to investigate, but it was an easy story to attack. And the attacks began in earnest in fall 1991.

Leading the pack were the trending-neoconservative *New Republic* and the consciously trendy *Newsweek*. In their denunciations of the October Surprise story, both magazines employed a combination of ridicule against the witnesses, disdain for anyone who took the witnesses seriously, and a complex set of alibis for William Casey and George H.W. Bush that supposedly disproved the October Surprise allegations.

Yet, while extremely important in setting a hostile tone toward the October Surprise story, the twin "debunkings" were built like a house of cards, with the alibis forming a foundation that then allowed the key witnesses to be discredited as liars, thus justifying the ridicule of investigators who wanted to examine the issue more deeply. If the magazines' alibis fell apart, the rest of the construction should logically follow.

So the fundamental question became the alibis, particularly one featured by *The New Republic* and *Newsweek* for Casey's whereabouts in late July 1980. Both magazines concluded that Casey could not have attended two days of meetings in Madrid in late July – as described by Jamshid Hashemi – because Casey's schedule supposedly didn't have a two-day "window."

The reasoning went as follows: Jamshid Hashemi recalled that the Madrid meetings took place on two consecutive mornings. ABC News' *Nightline* reported that a Hashemi alias was registered at Madrid's Plaza Hotel starting Friday, July 25. Casey's secretary, Barbara Hayward, told *Nightline* that her calendar put Casey in Washington on Saturday, July 26. Casey also gave a speech at a historical conference in London on the morning of July 29, a Tuesday, and he had returned to Washington by July 30, a Wednesday. So, the logic went, the Madrid meetings must have occurred on Sunday, July 27, and Monday, July 28.

But *The New Republic* and *Newsweek* argued that Casey could not have been in Madrid for meetings that covered those two mornings because he arrived in London on Sunday night, July 27, and was at the historical conference on the morning of July 28. "Casey is ... accounted for ... the night of July 27 and all day except for a brief absence, on July 28," said *The New Republic* article by Steven Emerson and Jesse Furman. "This makes Jamshid's story of two consecutive days of meetings impossible."

The New Republic faulted *Nightline* for failing "to find out that Casey was not in Madrid, but in London." The magazine also mocked anchor Ted Koppel for a *Nightline* update, which was the first story to note that Casey had made the unannounced trip to London, despite his campaign duties. Koppel had observed that Madrid was only a 90-minute flight from London, making Jamshid Hashemi's story possible. "*Nightline* was wrong again," Emerson and Furman gloated.[7]

I was ridiculed, too, as one of the "entrepreneurial journalists" who had investigated the October Surprise story, presumably for financial gain. I also was assigned the role of Jamshid Hashemi's "supporter" and a believer that Cyrus Hashemi "was murdered to shut him up" and that "the U.S. government has covered up the murder." All that was news to me. I had never believed or written that Cyrus Hashemi was murdered, nor that the motive for this supposed murder would have been the October Surprise, nor that the U.S. government was covering it up. After all, Cyrus Hashemi had died in London.

But the point of *The New Republic* article was not a fair exposition of the October Surprise facts. Rather, the article's ugly tone seemed calibrated to put the October Surprise investigation outside the realm of acceptable discussion and to protect the interests of both the Republicans and the Israeli Likud Party, which had a close relationship with the principal author, Steven

Emerson. (Investigative reporter Robert I. Friedman later disclosed that Likud Party leaders stayed at Emerson's apartment during their frequent trips to Washington.)[8]

To match *The New Republic* on the newsstands the first weekend in November 1991, *Newsweek* slapped together its own October Surprise debunking that also accepted the supposed impossibility of a Casey side trip to Madrid. "Casey's whereabouts are convincingly established by contemporary records at the Imperial War Museum in London," *Newsweek* wrote. "Casey, it turns out, took a three-day breather from the campaign to participate in the Anglo-American Conference on the History of the Second World War."[9]

The New Republic and *Newsweek* both splashed their findings on their covers – and the articles left no doubt about the conclusions: There had been no October Surprise contacts between Casey and the Iranians. The allegations were a "myth." The witnesses were liars. The October Surprise story was "a conspiracy theory run wild." Republicans in Congress quickly seized on the findings to argue that no official investigation was needed.

One cannot overstate the significance of these two articles in eviscerating chances for any serious investigation of the October Surprise case. The two articles were classics of the period: smug, omniscient, mocking. Anyone who didn't agree with the two influential opinion magazines was a dupe or worse. From that point on, anyone who tried to deal with the October Surprise investigation did so under a steady barrage of ridicule. The only acceptable tone to take toward the story was derision.

***

But how good were the debunkings? Did the crucial records in London prove categorically that Jamshid Hashemi lied about the meeting between William Casey and Mehdi Karrubi?

Inside *Newsweek,* reporter Craig Unger had disagreed with the magazine's October Surprise conclusions, specifically with the decision to frame the late July 1980 "window" for the Madrid meeting by using the dates July 27 to 29. Unger complained that the magazine did not check how reliable the calendar entry of Casey's secretary was, supposedly showing Casey in Washington on July 26. "They knew the window was not real," Unger said in an interview.

The same calendar, for example, had failed to show any Casey trip to Europe at all or the London conference that Casey had attended. So why should one presume that the secretary's notation was correct for July 26, Unger reasoned. "It was the most dishonest thing that I've been through in my life in journalism," Unger said in 1992, when he had been in journalism for 20 years. After the "myth" cover story, Unger left *Newsweek* and was denigrated by *Newsweek* editors as an "October Surprise true-believer."[10] (Unger's suspicions about the reliability of the secretary's calendar would be borne out when the House Task Force uncovered documentary evidence that Casey had left Washington a day earlier, on July 25.)

But even accepting the "window" as framed by the two magazines, how reliable was their interpretation of the key records at the World War II historical conference? *The New Republic* and *Newsweek* debunkings rested on attendance records maintained by Jonathan Chadwick, the Imperial War Museum's director. When a *Frontline* producer had first contacted Chadwick in the summer of 1991, he had no recollection when Casey had arrived. But as he spoke to more reporters, Chadwick began insisting that Casey had arrived on Monday morning, July 28, which presumably would have precluded the two-day meeting in Madrid.

Chadwick started interpreting his complex system for recording attendance – with checks and x's in pencil and ink – as showing that Casey attended the morning session that Monday, left for several hours over lunch and then returned late in the afternoon. There was a notation in the afternoon box for Casey that read: "came at 4 p.m." *Newsweek* and *The New Republic* concluded that the several hours for the long lunch would not give Casey enough time to fly to Madrid and return. So it was the certainty that Casey had attended the morning session that was crucial to the October Surprise debunkings.

But as much as the debunkings made fun of journalists, such as Koppel, who supposedly hadn't done their homework, it was really *Newsweek* and *The New Republic* that had fallen down on the job. At *Frontline*, producer Jim Gilmore interviewed 23 of the conference participants and discovered an uncertainty about when Casey arrived. For instance, Sir William Deacon, the British chairman of the conference, recalled Casey arriving for the first time on late Monday afternoon, July 28. The head of the American delegation, Arthur Funk, also told Gilmore that he believed Casey first arrived late in the day on Monday. So did three other members of the U.S. delegation.

When I interviewed Chadwick, he repeated his belief that his checks and x's indicated that Casey had arrived by Monday morning. But he acknowledged that his memory was not as precise as he was leading people to believe. "My recollection – and all recollections – are inherently unreliable eleven years later," he said. "But my recollection is that on that morning of 28th of July, Casey arrived with the other Americans, in a sort of bunch."[11] But Americans in the "bunch" were saying Casey wasn't among them. There was also that peculiar notation – "came at 4 p.m." – to explain. Could that have been when Casey arrived for the first time?

What was clear from Chadwick's muddled presentation to me was that the certitude of the *New Republic-Newsweek* debunking was based on a fragile foundation, a foundation then crumbled when *Frontline* producer Gilmore located one American conference participant who had a particularly clear memory of that Monday morning – renowned historian Robert Dallek.

"I was on the program the first morning, that Monday morning," Dallek said in an interview. "And I have a very strong memory of not seeing Mr. Casey at the conference that morning, because I was giving my talk at 11:30 in the morning and I looked for him in the room. I remember looking for him in the room. I knew he was a prominent figure. I was interested to know whether he was going to be there or not. And the room wasn't that crowded. And it wasn't as if it were an audience that you looked out at, but there was a long table and people sitting around the table and people sitting on the sides of the room."

Dallek said Casey did not arrive until late that first day. "I remember meeting him late that afternoon, because we walked around the Imperial War Museum together," Dallek said. The next morning Casey joined Dallek for breakfast at the Royal Army Medical College before going to the second day of the conference. Casey gave his own talk that morning and then left, Dallek said. Dallek's memory, which conformed to the recollections of the other Americans, also fit with Chadwick's curious note: "came at 4 p.m." In Dallek's version, that's when Casey first arrived.

As for Chadwick's check mark for the morning of the first day, Dallek had another recollection that could help explain that. There had been an announcement in the morning that Casey was on his way to the conference, but had been delayed because "he had to see people or something to that effect," Dallek said. When I checked back with Chadwick, he acknowledged that it would have been "very feasible" that he would have put check marks down for Casey the whole day if he was expected to arrive. That would explain both the checks and the reason for the notation "came at 4 p.m.," the time Casey actually reached the conference.

In other words, the alibi at the center of the *New Republic-Newsweek* debunkings had collapsed. But it had only collapsed in reality, not in the context of Washington's potent conventional wisdom. Despite their serious error, the two magazines never ran a correction and their phony alibi remained a powerful taboo within the perceptions of the Washington Establishment. Since very few people in Washington knew that the alibi that underpinned the double debunkings had proven false, the October Surprise case remained a nearly untouchable subject.

The lack of attention on the *New Republic-Newsweek* error was an example of how the distorted media environment of Washington shaped how the American people end up perceiving events. If such a major journalistic error had been harmful to the Republicans, it would have become a *cause celebre* to the conservative news media, which would have pounded the two magazines for shoddy journalism and demanded corrections, even dismissals of the offending journalists. But no comparable liberal media existed in Washington that could force *The New Republic* and *Newsweek* to admit their mistakes. None of the writers responsible for the two debunking articles faced any punishment, except for Craig Unger who was dumped by *Newsweek* after he objected to the magazine's rush to its erroneous judgment.

***

The poisonous atmosphere created by *The New Republic* and *Newsweek* helps explain why the congressional October Surprise inquiries concentrated more on disproving the allegations than seriously examining them. Republicans cited the magazines' findings as reason to look no further and rhetorically pummeled journalists and government officials who didn't heed the new conventional wisdom.

In the Senate, Republicans mounted a filibuster against a bill that would have authorized and funded an official investigation. The GOP filibuster prevailed when the Democrats could muster only 51 votes, nine short of what was needed to force an up-or-down vote. Despite the Republican victory, an informal investigation was undertaken by the Senate Foreign Relations subcommittee on the Middle East, headed by Senators Terry Sanford, a North Carolina Democrat, and Jim Jeffords, a Vermont Republican. But the lack of funds sharply curtailed the probe.

When the House took up the issue on February 5, 1992, strident Republicans under the leadership of Congressman Newt Gingrich of Georgia came armed with poster-board displays of *The New Republic* and *Newsweek* covers declaring the October Surprise story a "myth." The Republicans accused the Democrats of ginning up a phony scandal as a way to hurt George H.W. Bush's reelection campaign.

"This select committee," said Republican Congressman Bob McEwen of Ohio, "is a platform established for the partisan purpose: to smear George Bush so they can take every incompetent impostor and fraud, and let me quote *The New Republic*, the key sources, on whose word their story rests, are documented frauds and impostors representing themselves as intelligence operatives."

The Republicans also took aim at one of the congressional staffers who had pushed for the October Surprise investigation, R. Spencer Oliver, who two decades earlier had been the Democratic official whose telephone was bugged by the Watergate burglars.

Since the Watergate scandal, when he resisted pressure to back off the Democrats' lawsuit, Oliver had been a thorn in the Republicans' side and an annoyance to Democrats who favored accommodation to confrontation. As chief counsel to the House International Affairs Committee in the 1980s, he spurred an investigation of CIA Director William Casey's domestic propaganda operations, which had involved placing a top CIA propagandist, Walter Raymond Jr., on the staff of the National Security Council. From there, Raymond managed what became known as a "perception management" project for influencing how Americans viewed foreign policy issues, such as the contra war in Nicaragua.[12] In 1992, Oliver also was demanding a thorough review of the secret Reagan-Bush policies of supporting Saddam Hussein's government in Iraq, another investigation the Republicans were denigrating as a wild goose chase.

In connection with the October Surprise case, Oliver had written a letter of appreciation for testimony given by arms trafficker Dirk Stoffberg, a minor October Surprise witness who was in prison facing a court sentencing. The Republicans wanted Oliver censured for sending the letter. "This isn't an arms-for-hostage scandal," McEwen declared. "It's an arms-dealers-for-hogwash scandal. And this action has put the House of Representatives right in the middle of this slop."[13]

Reacting to the harsh Republican attack on Oliver, his boss, Congressman Dante Fascell of Florida, chairman of the House International Affairs Committee, took to the floor. "I authorized what was done" with the Stoffberg letter, Fascell said. "It was my staff member who did it under my direction." The confrontation over the Republican bid to censure Oliver energized the Democrats who defeated the Republican censure motion against Oliver on a party-line vote. Then, by a 217-192 margin, the House agreed to create a special Task Force to examine the October Surprise issue.

***

Though the House Task Force had been established, it was clear from the start that the Republicans would do all they could to prevent any damage to George H.W. Bush's reelection campaign or to Ronald Reagan's legacy.

The Republicans picked Congressman Henry Hyde of Illinois to head their side. Hyde, a blustery conservative, had been one of the most determined loyalists for the Reagan-Bush administration during the Iran-Contra investigation in 1987. Hyde selected as the Task Force's Republican staff director, attorney Dick Leon, who had been another staunch Reagan-Bush defender as a staffer on the Iran-Contra panel. Leon had helped draft the Republican minority report, which found no wrongdoing in the Iran-Contra scandal.

On the other side, the Democrats opted for a more bipartisan approach, tapping Congressman Lee Hamilton of Indiana as the chairman. Renowned for his commitment to congressional comity, the mild-mannered Hamilton had never pressed too hard when faced with evidence of Republican wrongdoing. Indeed, he had become the favorite choice of Republicans when they were under investigation because he would always give them the benefit of the doubt. As a reward, Hamilton rose in stature as a new Wise Man who resisted the trend toward harsh partisanship.

***

Hamilton went about staffing the Democratic side of the October Surprise Task Force with lawyers and investigators who often seemed more eager to disprove the October Surprise allegations than to search for evidence that might support the charges.

One of the first applicants in line for the job of chief counsel was Lawrence Barcella, a federal prosecutor who had made his name by helping to capture and convict renegade CIA agent Edwin Wilson during the early years of the Reagan administration. On the surface, Barcella appeared to be a reasonable choice. He had shown imagination in laying a complex trap for Wilson who was lured to the Dominican Republic with false promises before being hustled into U.S. custody.

But even that victory has lost its shine over the years because of a belated admission that Wilson's conviction was aided by a U.S. government decision to lie about Wilson's secret work for the CIA and to withhold exculpatory information from Wilson's defense. The discovery of this prosecutorial abuse – after Wilson had been imprisoned for two decades – led U.S. District Judge Lynn N. Hughes in 2003 to vacate Wilson's conviction for selling military items to Libya.

Judge Hughes said overturning the conviction was justified because the prosecutors submitted a false affidavit that had denied Wilson's claims that he was in frequent contact with the CIA. "There were, in fact, over 80 contacts, including actions parallel to those in the charges," Judge Hughes wrote in the decision.

There were other troubling aspects of Barcella's career, including a tolerance for the back-scratching ways of Washington. That attitude was revealed in some of his personal ties to alleged participants in the October Surprise case. For instance, according to author Peter Maas in *Manhunt*, a book on the Wilson case, Barcella had entertained a nighttime visit in 1982 from Michael Ledeen, the neoconservative writer who then was working as a State Department consultant on terrorism. Ledeen and Barcella were personal friends who socialized together. Barcella also had sold Ledeen a house and the two aspiring Washington professionals shared a housekeeper.

That evening, Ledeen was concerned that two of his associates, Ted Shackley and Erich von Marbod, had come under suspicion in the Wilson case.[14] "I told Larry that I can't imagine that Shackley [or von Marbod] would be involved in what you are investigating," Ledeen told me. "I wasn't trying to influence what he [Barcella] was doing. This is a community in which people help friends understand things."

Barcella also saw nothing wrong with the out-of-channel approach. "He wasn't telling me to back off," Barcella told me. "He just wanted to add his two-cents worth." Barcella said the approach was appropriate because Ledeen "wasn't asking me to do something or not do something." Later, Shackley and von Marbod were dropped from the Wilson investigation.[15]

In the context of the October Surprise case, however, the Ledeen connection raised other questions about Barcella's objectivity. The Task Force staff would discover that Ledeen was considered an informal member of the Reagan-Bush campaign's "October Surprise Group" and had other connections to the October Surprise case, including the work that Ledeen and Shackley had done for the Italian intelligence service SISMI in 1980 at a time Shackley was working for George H.W. Bush on the Iran hostage issue.

Barcella himself had played a small role in the Iran-Contra scandal. In 1985, as an assistant U.S. Attorney in Washington, Barcella was contacted by a Pentagon official who wanted to get legal advice so retired Major General John Singlaub could ship weapons to the Nicaraguan contras. At the time, the Pentagon and the CIA were legally barred from "directly or indirectly" assisting the contras militarily. The call from the Pentagon also should have raised questions in a prosecutor's mind about possible violations of the Neutrality Act, which prohibits plotting unauthorized acts of war against foreign nations.

Instead of objecting to the potential crimes, Barcella gave advice on how Singlaub could skirt the Arms Export Control Act by buying the weapons overseas. Following Barcella's suggestion, Singlaub obtained light assault weapons from Poland that were shipped to Honduras for the contras in July 1985. Singlaub, however, was not acting on his own. He was a front man for the secret White House contra-support operation run by Oliver North and overseen by William Casey. So Barcella had gotten an early look into the Iran-Contra criminal conspiracy, but instead of acting to thwart it as a government prosecutor, he chose to offer legal advice to the conspirators.

Barcella told me the Pentagon official "asked me a hypothetical" about the potential illegality of an arms shipment to Central America. "But it was clear to both of us that it was not a hypothetical," Barcella said. Though he admitted the facts of the Pentagon approach, which had been first disclosed in a news article in the *Hartford Courant* in Connecticut, Barcella refused to identify the Pentagon official who had contacted him.[16]

After leaving the U.S. Attorney's Office and going into private practice, Barcella represented Barbara Studley, the president of GMT, the Washington-based company that Singlaub had used to arrange contra arms shipments to Central America. The shadowy firm, which employed a number of former intelligence officials, was closely linked to William Casey's rogue CIA operations and to the clandestine activities of Oliver North.

Barcella also went to work for the scandal-plagued Bank of Credit and Commerce International in the late 1980s as it was trying to frustrate press and government investigations into its worldwide fraudulent activities, including money laundering for drug traffickers. Barcella's law firm – Laxalt, Washington, Perito & Dubuc – collected $2.16 million in legal fees from BCCI from October 1988 to August 1990, according to a Senate Foreign Relations Committee report on the BCCI scandal. As part of his work for BCCI, Barcella tried to discourage journalists who were sniffing out BCCI's secret ownership of First American Bank in Washington.

BCCI also had popped up on the October Surprise radar scopes through its dealings with Cyrus Hashemi and John Shaheen. Shortly after Ronald Reagan's Inauguration in 1981, the FBI intercepted a message to Hashemi about BCCI delivering a payment from London via the Concorde. When Shaheen set up his mysterious Hong Kong bank, one of the directors was Ghanim Al-Mazrouie, who owned ten percent of BCCI's shares.

The identity of the lead partner in Barcella's law firm also represented a potential conflict of interest. Paul Laxalt, the former senator, was one of Reagan's closest political allies and was chairman of the 1980 Reagan-Bush campaign, the principal subject of the October Surprise investigation. The Senate BCCI report said Barcella worked directly with Laxalt on the BCCI account.[17] Barcella told me that he didn't believe that his work for BCCI created a conflict of interest.

At lower staff levels, the Task Force had almost no aggressive investigators inclined to prove the October Surprise allegations. In filling those slots, Barcella and the Republicans repeatedly turned to veterans of the Reagan-Bush Justice Department and other Executive Branch agencies. Three Task Force lawyers on the Democratic side had worked for the Reagan-Bush Justice Department, including Barcella's chief aide, Michael Zeldin. Democratic deputy counsel Zeldin also described himself as a close friend of *New Republic* writer Steven Emerson.[18]

Less surprisingly, ranking Republican Henry Hyde also recruited senior Reagan-Bush lawyers from main Justice and U.S. Attorney's offices. Minority staff director John P. Mackey had been associate deputy attorney general before joining the Task Force. Deputy chief minority counsel

Gregory W. Kehoe had handled the BCCI drug-money-laundering case for the U.S. Attorney's office in the middle district of Florida. That case ended in a controversial plea bargain that outraged some members of Congress as too lenient. Kehoe had negotiated that plea bargain with BCCI lawyer Lawrence Barcella.

The Republicans' senior associate counsel, David H. Laufman, was brought over from the minority staff of the House International Affairs Committee. But from 1980 to 1984, Laufman had worked as an analyst at the CIA, a position that meant his bosses included William Casey and Robert Gates.[19]

***

While the Task Force staff was stacked with Reagan-Bush veterans, experienced Democratic congressional staff investigators found themselves out in the cold. Even Democratic congressmen on the Task Force complained about being kept in the dark by the Task Force staff that Hamilton and Hyde had assembled.

When Congressman Sam Gejdenson of Connecticut tried to fill his Task Force slot with House International Affairs Committee chief counsel Spencer Oliver, Barcella and the Republicans objected. Though Oliver may have been the most knowledgeable investigator in Congress on the international maneuverings of the Republicans in the 1980s, he was a *bete noire* to the Republicans because he had recommended the October Surprise investigation in the first place.

Chairman Hamilton asked ranking Republican Hyde if he objected to Gejdenson's choice. After consulting with the other Republicans, Hyde said his side adamantly opposed allowing Oliver on the Task Force. Oliver "raised a red flag with the minority," Hamilton told me. "It was our judgment that it would not be a good idea to put him on as a Task Force staffer." When I asked Hamilton whether it wasn't unusual for the Democrats to give Republicans a veto power over Democratic staff selections, he responded that "it was a decision that I take responsibility for. I don't think he [Oliver] was the right man for the job."

So, with the Task Force stacked with Reagan-Bush defenders and almost no investigators inclined to prove that the Republicans did strike an October Surprise deal, witnesses encountered an odd phenomenon. Those alleging wrongdoing were treated like the targets of the investigation and those accused of wrongdoing were handled with kid gloves, almost apologetically. Though the key October Surprise witnesses stuck to their allegations under oath, all were treated as liars and often faced blunt warnings that they would face perjury charges if they didn't back off their testimony.

A senior House investigator told me that throughout the process, the Republican lawyers acted openly as "defense attorneys" for the Reagan-Bush campaign officials, assuring that the Republican witnesses were never pressed too hard even when their stories were implausible or contradicted by documentary evidence, as in the case of the strange L'Enfant Plaza meeting. By contrast, both the majority and minority investigators hammered the "allegators," treating those making allegations of wrongdoing as common criminals and pounding them over minor inconsistencies in their testimony.

The treatment led Jamshid Hashemi to conclude that Republican chief counsel Dick Leon was effectively running the investigation. "I found this Mr. Leon – who I knew as the 'fat man' – every time we had a break and my lawyer would go to the washroom, he would rush into my room where I was sitting and say, 'come on, change the story,'" Jamshid told me in an interview several years later. "I said I would not change my story at all. The last time he opened the door, I said, 'Get out of my office. If you have anything to say, say it in front of my lawyer.'"*

Jamshid Hashemi told me it made no sense for him to have invented his October Surprise account, which he then repeated under oath to Congress. He had nothing to gain by making the public charges and a great deal to lose, he said. "Who has ever paid me a single dime?" Jamshid asked. "I had to pay all my lawyer's fees. What did I gain here?"

Israeli intelligence officer Ben-Menashe also repeated his October Surprise allegations under oath, in the face of threatened perjury charges. When the Task Force tried to check out Ben-Menashe's allegations in Israel, the Israeli government first stalled – citing scheduling conflicts from a religious holiday – and then barred the U.S. investigators altogether. Instead, the ever-accommodating Hamilton let the Israelis conduct the investigation themselves.

When the Israeli report arrived, it denied any collusion with the Republicans in 1980 and dismissed Ben-Menashe as just a low-level translator without access to sensitive secrets. The Israeli report was received with little skepticism from the House Task Force, even though Tel Aviv's claims about Ben-Menashe had been riddled with inconsistencies since the intelligence officer first surfaced in 1990.

After Ben-Menashe's arrest in the United States on charges of selling planes to Iran, the Israeli government had completely disowned him as an impostor who never had worked for Israeli intelligence. However, in 1990,

---

*In 2002, President George W. Bush named Leon to the federal bench as a U.S. District Court judge in Washington.

after interviewing Ben-Menashe in federal prison in New York, I was able to obtain documentary evidence written by several of Ben-Menashe's superiors describing his responsible role in an office of Israeli military intelligence. In these letters of reference, dated September 1987, his superiors had commended him for handling "a task which demanded considerable analytical and executive skill" and holding "key positions."

When I confronted the Israeli government with this evidence, it reversed itself, admitting that Ben-Menashe had worked for military intelligence but then dismissing him as only a "low-level translator." The "low-level translator" claim was soon picked up by journalists friendly to the Likud Party, including *The New Republic*'s Emerson. But the claim was clearly untrue, since Ben-Menashe had operated as an intelligence officer on behalf of the Israeli government in locations as varied as Poland, the United States and Latin America – and had verifiably been trying to leak details about the Reagan-Bush arms sales to Iran in 1986. The Israeli government wouldn't have permitted these activities by a "low-level translator."

Indeed, while trashing Ben-Menashe in general, the Israeli report to the House Task Force shifted Tel Aviv's account of his career again. The report said he had been assigned to a military signals intelligence unit in the mid-1970s, had worked for the External Relations Department of Israeli Military Intelligence [ERD] from 1977 to 1987, and had spent three of those years as a "staff officer in the means of war [armaments] unit" of ERD.

The Israeli report to the House Task Force did cite some senior Israeli officials attacking Ben-Menashe's credibility, but didn't include an interview with Moshe Hebroni, the former chief of staff to the military intelligence director. Any independent investigation would have insisted on getting Hebroni's views, since he had been quoted publicly by Israeli and American journalists as saying that Ben-Menashe indeed did have access to highly sensitive Israeli intelligence secrets and had met with the military intelligence chief, Yehoshua Saguy.[20]

Though the evidence suggested that the Israeli government was still hiding a great deal, the House Task Force accepted the Israeli report at face value.

* * *

Like the *New Republic-Newsweek* debunking articles, the House Task Force repudiation of the October Surprise case was built like a house of cards, albeit a more elaborate structure. Beyond heaping similar insults on the witnesses and similarly accepting denials from those implicated, the House Task Force's findings rested primarily on two alibis, a new one for William

Casey's whereabouts in late July 1980 and another for George H.W. Bush's activities over the weekend of October 18-19, 1980.

As with the *New Republic-Newsweek* articles, these alibis were crucial because, if correct, they would prove that the October Surprise witnesses were liars, again. If, for instance, Jamshid Hashemi claimed to see Casey in Madrid on a specific day when Casey was verifiably elsewhere, Jamshid could be reasonably discredited.

But that's where the House Task Force ran into trouble. Because of *Frontline*'s destruction of the *New Republic-Newsweek*'s London alibi for Casey in late July 1980, the Task Force had to find a new alibi for those days – and set out with some determination to construct one. But the new alibi, which became known as the "Bohemian Grove alibi," was even more factually challenged than the discredited London alibi promoted by *The New Republic* and *Newsweek*.

Here's how the Task Force did it: The Bohemian Grove alibi was based on the testimony of two Grove members – Darrell Trent, who was Casey's host at the Grove on one of two possible weekends in summer 1980, and Bernard Smith, a Casey associate from New York. Trent told the Task Force that he traveled with Casey from Los Angeles to San Francisco and then to the Bohemian Grove in northern California either the last weekend of July or the first weekend of August. In 1980, Trent attended only those two weekends of the three-weekend-a-summer getaway for rich and powerful men.

Bernard Smith testified that he attended the Grove only on the last weekend of July 1980 and had a recollection of seeing Casey with Trent at the Grove's Parsonage camp. That meant, the Task Force concluded, that Casey was at the Grove on the last weekend of July, which, in turn, would have precluded Casey from attending the two-day meeting in Madrid as described by Jamshid Hashemi.

While agreeing that *The New Republic* and *Newsweek* were wrong in claiming that Casey was in London on that Monday morning, July 28, the Task Force maintained that Casey's attendance at the Grove that weekend would have prevented him from going to Madrid on Sunday, July 27, or Monday, July 28. The Task Force postulated that Casey must have flown overnight from San Francisco to London, arriving on Monday afternoon. So, the new Bohemian Grove alibi was slipped in to replace the old discredited London alibi. Case closed, again.

The only problem with the House Task Force's Bohemian Grove alibi was that it collapsed under any careful inspection. It was not only a selective reading of the evidence; it was flatly disproved by the documentary record that the Task Force itself had assembled. But the Task Force assumed – correctly as it turned out – that almost no one would be looking closely at the logic or checking the documentary record of Casey's movements. Again, the October Surprise debunkers would benefit from the complexity of the evidence and the lack of any attention span by the Washington news media.

Here's why the Bohemian Grove alibi was false: First, it was Trent's recollection that he left for the Grove from Los Angeles at around noon on Thursday, July 24, and indeed there are three dated-and-signed bar receipts showing that Trent was at the Grove that Thursday. However, Casey was filmed collecting a matching-fund check at the Federal Election Commission in Washington on July 24. The same day, other records show that Casey was charged for using the telephone at the Metropolitan Club, also in Washington. Even the House Task Force agreed that the evidence showed that Casey could not have flown to Los Angeles until Friday at the earliest.

In other words, Casey could not have left Los Angeles with Trent on Thursday, as Trent described. Alone, that documentary evidence should have exploded the Bohemian Grove alibi, but there was much more that disproved this core element in the Task Force's case.

On Friday, July 25, Trent stayed at the Grove, according to the club's financial records. He signed two more Grove bar tabs and was charged for skeet shooting, a daytime activity. Trent never claimed that he made another round-trip to Los Angeles and the documents show that he didn't.

But a theoretical return trip by Trent to Los Angeles was irrelevant because the documentary record shows that Casey didn't go to the West Coast that Friday. His personal calendars list two meetings in the GOP campaign headquarters in Arlington, Virginia, on Friday morning. And while the Task Force found no documentary evidence showing Casey flew to Los Angeles, it did find a ticket that Casey bought for the Eastern Airlines Washington-to-New York shuttle on Friday, July 25. It was the type of ticket that was purchased and signed at the airport before a person gets on the plane. So instead of flying to Los Angeles and then San Francisco, the documentary record shows Casey going to New York City.

Two days into Casey's imaginary July trip to the Bohemian Grove, his calendar for Saturday, July 26, shows a meeting with a "Mrs. Tobin." The investigators identified the woman as Mary Jane Tobin, a New York-based right-to-life advocate. She confirmed meeting with Casey at his estate at Roslyn Harbor, Long Island, but could not remember the precise date. When I called her, Mrs. Tobin did say that she recalled the weather was very hot. The temperature on July 26 in New York was in the 90s. So her memory matched the documentary record of Casey going to New York for this meeting.

The House Task Force also located a group photo of guests and members at the Parsonage camp on Sunday, July 27. Casey was not in the photo, though Trent was.

But as consistent as the documentary evidence was that Casey stayed on the East Coast from July 24 through the morning of July 26 – and was not at the Bohemian Grove – the evidence was even stronger that Casey traveled to Los Angeles and to the Grove on the following weekend, the first weekend of August.

For starters, Casey's calendar showed that he was in Los Angeles on Friday, August 1. Meeting notes taken by Reagan foreign policy adviser Richard Allen put Casey at a campaign strategy session in Los Angeles on that date. Allen's diagram of the seating arrangement also revealed that Darrell Trent sat across the table from Casey. So while Trent could not have left with Casey for the Grove on July 24 because Casey was in Washington, the two men were together on August 1 in Los Angeles before Trent left for the Grove that weekend.

Trent's Bohemian Grove bill showed him with three more bar tabs at the resort on August 1. Also, on that date, both Trent and Casey were charged $9 apiece for the Grove "play book," which commemorates the annual play put on by Bohemian Club members that last weekend of the encampment.

At *Frontline*, producer Jim Gilmore had interviewed two Grove members who had attended the Grove only on the last weekend of July 1980 and neither had any memory of Casey being there, a recollection that matched with the group photograph with Casey not present. Gilmore also found a Bohemian Club member, San Francisco businessman Matthew McGowan, who attended the Grove each weekend in 1980 and kept a diary. For August 3, the last Sunday of the Grove encampment, McGowan wrote: "1980 Bohemian Grove encampment closed this date. A very good encampment for me. We had Bill Casey, Gov. Reagan's campaign mgr., as our guest this last weekend."

Even the Task Force investigators acknowledged that "on its face" McGowan's diary entry would prove that Casey attended the Bohemian Grove on the first weekend of August 1980, not the last weekend of July. So, of course, did all the other meaningful documentary evidence.

But the House Task Force wouldn't let go. To counter all the evidence showing that Casey went to the Grove the first weekend of August, not the last weekend of July, the Task Force embraced a piece of paper that Barcella's team claimed overcame the other documents. That "proof" was a handwritten sheet of phone calls made by Richard Allen on August 2, 1980. At the bottom of the page was scribbled a Long Island phone number for Casey. That meant, the investigators concluded, that Casey must have been on Long Island for the first weekend in August, thus nixing it as the Bohemian Grove weekend and thereby proving finally that Casey must have gone to the Grove the last weekend of July (and thus not to Madrid).

But the Allen phone-call sheet didn't support that Task Force conclusion at all. Other phone calls on the page showed times for the conversations and included notations about what was said. The Casey number is accompanied by neither a time for the presumed call nor any notation of a conversation. Indeed, when questioned, Allen had no recollection of talking to Casey on that date. "I can't tell you whether or not I got through," Allen testified. The Reagan foreign policy adviser said only that he believed he asked his secretary for Casey's home number and wrote it down. He presumed he called it, but has no memory of the call being answered. Allen also had no telephone bill showing a completed call and no notes of a conversation.

In other words, experienced investigators were contending that because someone wrote down a person's home phone number and may have gotten no answer when a call was made, the person was, therefore, at home. Having sidelined any investigators who might have challenged such silliness, the House Task Force was disappearing down Alice's rabbit hole of irrational arguments.

As for the last pillar of the Task Force's Bohemian Grove alibi – Bernard Smith's recollection of seeing Casey and Trent together at the Parsonage camp – there was an obvious explanation for that, too. Smith, Trent and Casey were all at the Bohemian Grove in the summer of 1981, the following year. That year, Casey stayed at the Mandalay, a neighboring camp to the Parsonage, so Casey easily could have visited Trent at the Parsonage as Smith recalled.

But in defiance of the overwhelming documentary evidence and the most obvious logic, the Task Force concluded that "the great weight of the evidence" put Casey at the Bohemian Grove from July 25 to 27. That, in turn, proved Casey did not attend the meeting in Madrid and that Jamshid Hashemi again was made out to be a liar.

In the mid-1990s, when I asked Jamshid Hashemi for his reaction to the Task Force's report, he responded, "Rubbish, that's what I think, just a whitewash of the whole situation. It's a cover-up."

As for his reasons for testifying in the first place, Jamshid, who had become an American citizen, said, "I thought it was my duty that the people in the United States should know. They should know. They should be the judge of it." On whether he would speak out again, he answered, "I certainly would do it again because the moment I swore to the flag of the United States, from that moment onward, my commitment toward the people of the United States was 10 times what it was before."

***

Yet, in its determined tilting of the evidence, the House Task Force made the Bohemian Grove alibi a classic example of how any investigation – or even the history of the United States – can be distorted by a consistent slanting in favor of one political side.

If every piece of evidence from that side, no matter how flawed, is accepted as true, and every piece of evidence on the other side is challenged or thrown out, the result is virtually predetermined. Indeed, in the October Surprise "debunking," it was obvious that the outcome *was* predetermined.

In that sense, the bogus Bohemian Grove alibi can be viewed as an archetype of how the accumulation of conservative ideological pressure – in the political and media worlds – has misshapen the information that reaches the American people. It's not simply that evidence is made up; it's that evidence is filtered through a process that removes solid facts and lets through only the dross that favors the preferred conclusions.

Chapter 11: Where Was George?

By late spring 1992, President George H.W. Bush's reelection prospects were sliding from near certainty to doubtful. Weighed down by a leaden economy, Bush also was facing three intersecting investigations: the Iran-Contra probe was continuing as special prosecutor Lawrence Walsh broke through the long-running White House cover-up; a few Democrats were clamoring for a thorough examination of secret U.S. aid to Iraq's Saddam Hussein in the 1980s; and the House Task Force was puttering around on the October Surprise case.

While the Washington press corps had little interest in any of the three investigations. The common wisdom on the Iran-Contra Affair was that it had gone on too long and was too boring. The Iraqgate inquiry, driven by Texas Congressman Henry Gonzalez, was viewed as inconclusive and a touch flaky. But the most intense disdain was reserved for the October Surprise case, partly because almost no journalist in Washington was aware that the alibi at the center of the *New Republic-Newsweek* debunkings had itself been debunked.

So some eyebrows were raised when President Bush began ranting against the October Surprise case at a news conference on June 4, 1992. Asked by a reporter if the President felt that an independent counsel was needed to investigate the Iraqgate allegations, Bush snapped, "I wonder whether they're going to use the same prosecutors that are trying out there to see whether I was in Paris in 1980."

As a surprised hush fell over the press corps, Bush continued, "I mean, where are we going with the taxpayers' money in this political year?" Bush then asserted, "I was not in Paris, and we did nothing illegal or wrong here" on Iraq.

At another news conference at the world environmental summit in Brazil, Bush also brought up the October Surprise probe in reaction to an unrelated question. He called the probe "a witch hunt" and insisted that the Congress clear him of having traveled to Paris for the alleged meeting with Iranians. Responding to Bush's demand, House Republicans warned Hamilton and the Democrats that funding for the October Surprise Task Force – which needed reauthorization by July 1 – would be blocked if Bush wasn't absolved by June 30, 1992.

Though normally investigations are completed before results are announced, the ever-accommodating Hamilton was willing to comply. The difficulty was that the Bush administration was blocking the Task Force's access to Secret Service records containing details that supposedly would have given the President an iron-clad alibi. In response to previous Freedom of Information Act requests, the Secret Service had released partially censored reports about Bush's movements for the days around October 18 and 19 which were the most likely days for his alleged secret trip to Paris.

On the surface, the Secret Service records appeared to indicate that Bush had taken the weekend off from campaigning and was spending the two days at his Washington home. The records for the key day of Sunday, October 19, purported to show Bush going to the Chevy Chase Country Club in the morning and to visit someone's private residence in the afternoon. If Bush indeed had been on those side trips, it would close the window on any possible flight to Paris and back.

Investigators of the October Surprise mystery – including those of us at *Frontline* – put great weight on the Secret Service records. But little is really known about the Secret Service's standards for recording the movements of protectees, who can include foreign dignitaries as well as candidates for national office, top Executive Branch officers and their families. Since the cooperation of the protectee is essential to the Secret Service staying in position to thwart any attacker, the agents presumably must show flexibility in what details they report. Reasonably, the agents might have to fudge or leave out some of the facts.

So, just to be sure about the Secret Service daily reports on Bush's movements, the congressional investigators asked for uncensored versions, including the names of the agents and anyone who could corroborate Bush's presence in the Washington area. Just one credible witness who could place Bush at the Chevy Chase Country Club in the morning or at the personal home in the afternoon could wrap matters up. But finding that credible witness proved harder than the Task Force expected.

When congressional investigators questioned the Secret Service agents on the Bush detail, only one – supervisor Leonard Tanis – claimed a clear recollection of the trip to the Chevy Chase Country Club that Sunday. Tanis recalled Mr. and Mrs. Bush going to the Chevy Chase club for brunch with Justice and Mrs. Potter Stewart.

But at *Frontline*, we had already gone down that path and found it to be a dead end. We had obtained Mrs. Bush's protective records for that day and they showed her going to the C&O Canal jogging path in Washington, not to the Chevy Chase club. We also had reached Justice Stewart's widow, who had no recollection of any Chevy Chase brunch. So it appeared that Tanis was wrong, a conclusion the Task Force also reached, though it judged Tanis's false statement to be an honest mistake.

House International Affairs Committee counsel Spencer Oliver was more suspicious, however. In a six-page memo urging a closer look at the Bush question, Oliver argued that the Secret Service had withheld the uncensored daily report for no justifiable reason not just from the Task Force but from the congressional General Accounting Office, which had been trying to settle the question of Bush's whereabouts for two years.

"Why did the Secret Service refuse to cooperate on a matter which could have conclusively cleared George Bush of these serious allegations?" Oliver asked. "Was the White House involved in this refusal? Did they order it?"

Oliver also noted Bush's strange behavior in raising the October Surprise issue in the two news conferences. "It can be fairly said that President Bush's recent outbursts about the October Surprise inquiries and [about] his whereabouts in mid-October of 1980 are disingenuous at best," wrote Oliver, "since the administration has refused to make available the documents and the witnesses that could finally and conclusively clear Mr. Bush ... of these serious allegations."

Oliver wrote that "the administration has refused – for nearly two years – to turn over to Congress the complete Secret Service records for that weekend" and "at least one of the two Secret Service supervisors who has been made available has lied to investigators in an interview."

Oliver urged that all relevant documents and witnesses be subpoenaed. "Until these steps are taken, this matter can never be finally resolved," he wrote. "The Republicans have been against this investigation from the outset, they have condemned it and criticized it at every opportunity. They have sought to block, limit, restrict and discredit the investigation in every possible way and have even employed the President of the United States to lead the attack on this investigation. ... They have attempted to button up the investigation and to cover up the evidence. The public has a right to know these things."

While Oliver's suggestions were not followed, the collapse of Tanis's testimony did mean that the Task Force had no credible eyewitness who could corroborate the sketchy information included in the Secret Service report for October 19. President and Mrs. Bush were spared questioning, and the Secret Service was continuing to keep secret the location of the afternoon trip and the identity of the person visited.

Though there was some speculation that the Secret Service might have been concealing a romantic tryst, that didn't seem likely since Mrs. Bush's daily report showed that she went on the same side trip to the private residence. The real question was whether the Secret Service supervisors, as a favor to former CIA Director Bush, had inserted some manufactured details, such as his accompanying Mrs. Bush on her afternoon visit to a friend's house when that never happened. The Secret Service refused to budge on filling in the report's blanks.

Finally, on June 29, 1992, two days before the Republican deadline, the House Task Force reached a compromise of sorts with the Secret Service. Task Force chief counsel Lawrence Barcella was allowed to see the name of the person supposedly visited on that Sunday afternoon if he agreed not to interview the alibi witness or to ever divulge the name. The House Task Force accepted this strange condition. Barcella was allowed to look at the name, but not to ask the witness any questions.

In other words, possibly for the first time in investigative history, a suspect (Bush) was allowed to supply an alibi witness who supposedly could vouch for his innocence as long as the investigators agreed not to check out the alibi or question the witness. It is hard to believe that any serious investigator would accept these terms, since the information is effectively worthless. It's also never been explained why Bush wouldn't let the alibi witness be questioned, although one possibility must remain that he feared the alibi witness would tell investigators that Bush wasn't there when Barbara Bush came to call.

Nevertheless, the House Task Force issued an interim report on July 1, 1992, doing as Bush had demanded, clearing him of any suspicion that he made a secret trip to Paris in October 1980 to meet with Iranian emissaries and to assure them that the future Republican administration would keep its word on an arms-for-hostage exchange. "All credible evidence leads to the conclusion that President Bush was in the United States continuously during the October 18-22 [1980] time period, and not attending secret meetings in Paris, France," Task Force chairman Hamilton said.

When I asked Barcella what good it did to know the name of the supposed alibi witness without questioning the person, the Task Force chief counsel stammered defensively, "Well, we got the name."

* * *

The House Task Force displayed the same debunking bias when it came to the question of William Casey flying to Paris on the weekend of October 18-19, 1980.

For Casey, the alibi went this way: Casey's nephew Larry told the Task Force that he remembered his late father calling Casey on that Sunday, October 19, and finding Casey hard at work at the campaign office in Arlington, Virginia. Larry Casey said his recollection of the phone call was clear, though he had no phone records because it was a local call. Since Larry's father and William Casey were both dead by 1992, they couldn't provide any corroboration either.

Despite the implausibility of someone remembering the date of a phone call from a dozen years earlier, the House Task Force accepted Larry Casey's testimony as proof that William Casey could not have gone to Paris. But besides the implausibility of the phone call recollection, there was another problem with Larry Casey's account: he had given an entirely different alibi when we had interviewed him at *Frontline*.

In the *Frontline* interview, Larry Casey had said his mother and father had gone to dinner with William Casey on October 19 at the Jockey Club restaurant in Washington. "It was very clear in my mind even though it was 11 years ago, my uncle actually taking them to dinner at the Jockey Club," Larry Casey said in a videotaped interview. Then, with the camera rolling, I handed Larry Casey the visitor logs for the Reagan-Bush headquarters. The logs showed Larry's parents arriving at William Casey's office on October 15, not October 19. An American Express receipt also showed the Jockey Club dinner on October 15. Larry Casey's recollection was four days off.

A year later, Larry Casey had jettisoned the Jockey Club alibi and replaced it with the phone call. Although I informed both Republican and Democratic investigators on the House Task Force about this problem in Larry Casey's account, they didn't care.

To pound in other nails, the Task Force simply embroidered what some of the witnesses had claimed so the supposed assertions could be knocked down. In dismissing, Iranian arms dealer Lavi and Israeli intelligence officer Ben-Menashe, the Task Force cited their supposed claims that Cyrus Hashemi had been in Paris over the weekend of October 18-19, 1980. Based on the FBI wiretaps of Cyrus's home office, there was no doubt that Cyrus was in the New York area that weekend. So, the reasoning went, Lavi and Ben-Menashe were lying.

But in reality, neither Lavi nor Ben-Menashe had specifically put Cyrus Hashemi in Paris that weekend. Ben-Menashe testified that he understood that Cyrus wanted to join these meetings but had been barred. The Israeli said he was told that Cyrus did travel to Paris several days after the main meetings, but Ben-Menashe claimed no first-hand information about Cyrus's whereabouts.

Lavi had told me that he wasn't sure when Cyrus had traveled to Paris in October 1980, but that it might have been "around October 20." Lavi did say that he met Cyrus in London on the trip and they flew together to Paris. Lavi claimed that Cyrus then talked with a variety of foreigners about Iranian arms deals, but Lavi did not say he saw any of the alleged American principals. FBI documents reported that Cyrus traveled to London and then Paris on a trip beginning October 28.

***

Other strange alibis appeared in the House Task Force report. For instance, the Task Force claimed that Cyrus Hashemi couldn't have attended the alleged Madrid meeting in late July 1980, as Jamshid Hashemi said, because phone records showed a one-minute phone calls from Republican lawyer

Stanley Pottinger to Hashemi's house on Sunday night, July 27, and a one-minute phone call back 49 minutes later.

While the Task Force considered those calls proof that Cyrus Hashemi was in the United States and not in Madrid, the timing and length of the calls would more likely suggest a call from Pottinger to Cyrus's family about when Cyrus was due back and then a return call to give Pottinger an answer.[1] (The FBI wiretaps were not installed until September, so only the phone billing records were available for July.)

CIA officer Donald Gregg supplied photos of himself and his family at the beach in bathing suits to prove he wasn't at the alleged Paris meeting on the weekend of October 18-19, 1980. But there was no way to determine when the photos were taken. A stamp on the back showed they had been processed in October 1980, but that didn't mean they had necessarily been taken in October or that they were taken that weekend.[2]

Possibly the most curious part of the various strained alibis was how unconvincing they were given the prominence of the individuals and the narrow time "windows" that needed to be closed. In normal police investigations, any group of suspects who provided the authorities such a string of curious or failed alibis would almost certainly be suspected of guilt, not hailed for their innocence.

The Task Force also encountered strange gaps in the documentary evidence. Though the House investigators had subpoena power, they were unable to get key documents. The investigators learned that William Casey's calendars, passports and travel records had been catalogued by the CIA and were turned over to his family after his death in 1987. When the investigators searched Casey's two homes, they found all the catalogued records, except Casey's passport for 1980, a "hostages" file, two personal calendars and loose pages from a third calendar which covered the period of July 24, 1980, to December 18, 1980. Checked against the CIA's index, the only folders missing were the ones relevant to the October Surprise issue.

House investigator Richard Pedersen, a veteran of the Bureau of Alcohol, Tobacco and Firearms, informed Mrs. Casey and her daughter, Bernadette Smith, that "we have a problem." But the two women said they had no idea where the missing documents were. Later, Bernadette Smith turned in the "hostages" file, but it was filled with general campaign documents, not papers pertinent to the hostage crisis. Under further prodding from Pedersen, more documents from the file were delivered.

On September 8, 1992, Smith showed up at the Task Force offices with some other missing material: the "Standard Diary-1980," the "Monthly Minder-1980" and most of the loose calendar pages. The family said the missing documents had been found under a box on a basement hearth in the McLean, Virginia, house, an explanation that Pedersen termed "incredible" in light of the earlier searches.

But there was a bigger problem with the belatedly delivered documents. The loose calendar pages for the weekend of July 26-27, 1980, the days before the alleged Madrid meeting, were missing as were pages for October 21, October 29, November 3 to 11, and November 13. Casey's 1980 passport, conceivably the most important single document for the investigation, had not reappeared.[3]

The Task Force ran into similar troubles trying to get relevant business papers and a detailed calendar for Casey associate John Shaheen. Those documents were missing for 1980 though found for years earlier and later.[4] There were also gaps in the FBI's wiretaps of Cyrus Hashemi's office, including one tape that jumped eight days without explanation. The FBI men who handled the bugging recalled no period that long when the tape recorders were shut down.[5]

Ronald Reagan's lawyers balked at delivering some documents from his presidential library, according to a letter by chief counsel Barcella that I found in the Task Force's unpublished files. In the September 22, 1992, letter to Reagan's personal attorney Theodore Olson, Barcella wagged a finger at the Republicans for not producing the requested information, but immediately threw up his hands in surrender.

"Your letter indicates that the library was unable to locate and, therefore, did not send, some of the documents requested by the Task Force staff," Barcella wrote. "In addition, some of the documents they did send do not appear to correspond to the request noted on the list of requested documents, e.g. the date, title or number of pages do not correspond."

But then Barcella added, "Although we are disappointed that we have not received every document we tabbed for copying, time constraints do not permit us to pursue this issue further at this time." In other words, Barcella was surrendering on a document request with more than three months to go in the investigation.

***

After George H.W. Bush lost his reelection bid on November 3, 1992, the House Task Force turned to finishing up work on its October Surprise report about another pivotal election a dozen years earlier. Though there were more interviews to do and documents to read, the conclusion was set: the October Surprise allegations would be declared a myth, fabricated on virtually all counts.

But new evidence kept intruding, leaving chief counsel Barcella not entirely confident in that definitive conclusion. On December 8, he instructed his deputies "to put some language in, as a trap door" in case later disclosures disproved parts of the report or if complaints arose about selective omission of evidence. "This report does not and could not reflect every single lead that was investigated, every single phone call that was made, every single contact that was established," Barcella suggested as "trap door" wording. "Similarly, the Task Force did not resolve every single one of the scores of 'curiosities,' 'coincidences,' sub-allegations or question marks that have been raised over the years and become part of the October Surprise story."

But some of the information that would arrive during the investigation's final month would deal not just with "curiosities," but with central questions of the mystery.

On December 17, 1992, former Iranian President Bani-Sadr sent a letter describing the internal battles of the Iranian government over the Republican intervention in 1980. Bani-Sadr recounted his threats to expose the secret deal between Reagan-Bush campaign officials and Islamic radicals around Ayatollah Khomeini. But the Task Force simply dismissed Bani-Sadr's account as "hearsay."[6]

On December 18, biographer David Andelman testified that French intelligence chief Alexandre deMarenches admitted arranging meetings for Republicans with Iranians in Paris in October 1980. After Andelman's testimony, the Task Force called deMarenches, but the imperious French spymaster failed to return the call.

The Task Force concluded, paradoxically, that Andelman's testimony was "credible" but was "insufficiently probative." The reasoning went that Andelman could not "rule out the possibility that deMarenches had told him he was aware of and involved in the Casey meetings because he, deMarenches, could not risk telling his biographer he had no knowledge of these allegations."[7]

On December 21, former CIA officer Charles Cogan recounted the remark by David Rockefeller's aide Joseph Reed to then-CIA Director William Casey in the early days of the Reagan-Bush administration. "Joseph Reed said, 'we' and then the verb [and then] something about Carter's October Surprise," Cogan testified in a "secret" deposition. Task Force investigators understood the full quote to have been, "We fucked Carter's October Surprise," a claim that was at the heart of what the Task Force was assigned to investigate, but the Task Force left out the information altogether.

The pattern of the Task Force's selective judgments began to grate on some of the Democratic members. Though the October Surprise allegations supposedly were a myth, the information developed by the Task Force staff was kept under tight security. Congressmen were only allowed to review the evidence in a secure room under guard. The restrictions meant that many members were forced to rely on the staff that had been assembled largely by excluding anyone who thought the allegations might actually be true, investigators who could pass muster from the Republicans.

On January 3, 1993, Congressman Mervyn Dymally, a California Democrat and Task Force member, submitted a dissent to the impending Task Force debunking of the allegations. Dymally's dissent complained about selective handling of evidence to clear the Reagan-Bush campaign.

Dymally, who was retiring from Congress, cited the investigation's reliance on shaky circumstantial data for exonerating the Republicans and the uncritical acceptance of accounts from Casey's associates.

In reviewing the Task Force report, Dymally's staff aide, Marwan Burgan, quickly spotted some of the report's absurd alibis, including the claim that because someone wrote down Casey's home phone number on one day that proved Casey was home, or that because a plane flew from San Francisco directly to London on another important date that Casey must have been onboard.

According to sources who saw Dymally's dissent, it argued that "just because phones ring and planes fly doesn't mean that someone is there to answer the phone or is on the plane." But Dymally's reasonable observations were fiercely opposed by Barcella, who enlisted Task Force chairman, Lee Hamilton, to pressure Dymally into withdrawing the dissent. Dymally told me that the day his dissent was submitted, he received a call from Hamilton warning him that if the dissent was not withdrawn, "I will have to come down hard on you."

The next day, Hamilton, who was becoming chairman of the House International Affairs Committee, fired the staff of the Africa subcommittee that Dymally had headed. The firings were billed as routine, and Hamilton told me that "the two things came along at the same time, but they were not connected in my mind." Hamilton said his warning to Dymally referred to a toughly worded response that Hamilton would have fired off at Dymally if the dissent had stood. However, hoping to salvage the jobs of some of his staff, Dymally agreed to withdraw the dissent.[8]

So the House Task Force's report was shipped off to the printers with its conclusion that there was "no credible evidence" of Republican double-dealing with Iran over the 52 U.S. hostages in 1980. The report was scheduled for release on January 13, 1993, just one week before George H.W. Bush's Presidency would come to an end. But there was still one more surprise for the October Surprise Task Force.

On January 11, Chairman Hamilton received a response to a query he had sent to the Russian government on October 21, 1992, requesting any information that Moscow might have about the October Surprise case.

Chapter 12: The Russian Report

The nation's capital was readying itself for the Inauguration of President Bill Clinton, the first Democrat to sit in the Oval Office in a dozen years. Temporary grandstands were going up along Pennsylvania Avenue. The city brimmed with a celebratory air that fills the capital whenever a grand event like an Inauguration takes place. Workmen were rushing to complete the preparations.

But in an obscure set of offices near the U.S. Capitol, congressional investigators were coping with another problem. The House October Surprise Task Force was concluding a year-long investigation into claims that Ronald Reagan's 1980 presidential campaign had interfered with President Jimmy Carter's negotiations to free 52 Americans held hostage in Iran, a scheme that may have helped end the last Democratic Presidency.

The possibility that this turning point in modern American history had resulted from a nearly treasonous dirty trick had drawn angry denials from Reagan-Bush loyalists – and even from Democrats who feared that the public might lose faith in politics if the charges proved true. So, with a collective sigh of relief, the House Task Force had decided to debunk the charges. The 968-page report then was shipped off to the printers.

But two days before the news conference, a cable arrived from the U.S. Embassy in Moscow containing a report prepared by Sergey V. Stepashin, chairman of the Supreme Soviet's Committee on Defense and Security Issues, a job roughly equivalent to chairman of the Senate Intelligence Committee. Responding to a request for information from Task Force chairman Lee Hamilton, Stepashin had provided a summary of what Russian intelligence files showed about the October Surprise charges and other secret U.S. dealings with Iran.

In the 1980s, after all, the Soviet KGB was not without its own sources on a topic as important to Moscow as developments in neighboring Iran. The KGB also had penetrated or maintained close relations with many of the intelligence services linked to the October Surprise allegations, including those of France, Spain, Germany, Iran and Israel. History had shown, too, that the KGB had spies inside the CIA and other U.S. intelligence agencies. So, Soviet intelligence certainly was in a position to know a great deal about what had or had not happened in 1980.

The Supreme Soviet's response was delivered to the U.S. Embassy by Nikolay Kuznetsov, secretary of the subcommittee on state security. Kuznetsov apologized for the "lengthy preparation of the response." It was quickly translated by the U.S. embassy and forwarded to Hamilton.

To the shock of the Task Force, the six-page Russian report stated, as fact, that Casey, Bush, CIA officials and other Republicans had met secretly with Iranian officials in Europe during the 1980 presidential campaign. The Russians depicted the hostage negotiations that year as a two-way competition between the Carter White House and the Reagan-Bush campaign to outbid one another for Iran's cooperation on the hostages. The Russians asserted that the Reagan-Bush team had disrupted Carter's hostage negotiations, the exact opposite of the Task Force conclusion.

As described by the Russians, the Carter administration had offered the Iranians supplies of arms and unfreezing of assets for a pre-election release of the hostages. One important meeting occurred in Athens in July 1980 with Pentagon representatives agreeing "in principle" to deliver "a significant quantity of spare parts for F-4 and F-5 aircraft and also M-60 tanks ... via Turkey," the Russian report said. The Iranians "discussed a possible step-by-step normalization of Iranian-American relations [and] the provision of support for President Carter in the election campaign via the release of American hostages."

But the Republicans were making their own overtures to the Iranians, also in Europe, the Russian report said. "William Casey, in 1980, met three times with representatives of the Iranian leadership," the report said. "The meetings took place in Madrid and Paris."

At the Paris meeting in October 1980, "R[obert] Gates, at that time a staffer of the National Security Council in the administration of Jimmy Carter,* and former CIA Director George Bush also took part," the Russian report said. "In Madrid and Paris, the representatives of Ronald Reagan and the Iranian leadership discussed the question of possibly delaying the release of 52 hostages from the staff of the U.S. Embassy in Teheran."

Both the Reagan-Bush Republicans and the Carter Democrats "started from the proposition that Imam Khomeini, having announced a policy of 'neither the West nor the East,' and cursing the 'American devil,' imperialism and Zionism, was forced to acquire American weapons, spares and military supplies by any and all possible means," the Russian report said. The Republicans just won the bidding war.

"After the victory of R. Reagan in the election, in early 1981, a secret agreement was reached in London in accord with which Iran released the American hostages, and the U.S. continued to supply arms, spares and military supplies for the Iranian army," the Russian report continued. The

---

* Actually, by October 1980, Gates had moved from the NSC staff to a new job as executive assistant to then-CIA Director Stansfield Turner.

deliveries were carried out by Israel, often through private arms dealers, the Russian report said. Spares for F-14 fighters and other military equipment went to Iran from Israel in March-April 1981 and the arms pipeline kept flowing into the mid-1980s.

"Through the Israeli conduit, Iran in 1983 bought surface-to-surface missiles of the 'Lance' class plus artillery of a total value of $135 million," the Russian report said. "In July 1983, a group of specialists from the firm, Lockheed, went to Iran on English passports to repair the navigation systems and other electronic components on American-produced planes." In 1985, the weapons tap opened wider, into the Iran-Contra shipments.

The matter-of-fact Russian report was stunning. It also matched other information the Task Force had. The Task Force had discovered that the Israelis, for example, had shipped U.S. military spares to Iran in the early 1980s, with the acquiescence of senior Reagan-Bush administration officials.

After receiving the Russian report, a U.S. Embassy political officer went back to the Russians seeking more details. But the Russians would state only that the data came from the Committee on Defense and Security Issues. The embassy political officer then speculated that Moscow's report might have been "based largely on material that has previously appeared in the Western media."

But there was no serious follow-up by the House Task Force or the U.S. government – even though Moscow, the communist enemy in the 1980s, claimed to possess incriminating evidence about two CIA directors (Casey and Gates) and two U.S. Presidents (Reagan and Bush). Though the Russian claims about Carter's negotiations with Iran might cause embarrassment, Carter, as President, possessed the constitutional authority to negotiate with a foreign power. The Republicans did not.

"We got the stuff from the Russians just a few days before" the Task Force's own report was set for release, Task Force chief counsel Lawrence Barcella told me. Since the Task Force's official mandate had expired on January 3, 1993, about a week earlier, Barcella said the Task Force felt there was nothing that could be done with the Russian material. "We weren't going to be able to look into it, whether it was new information, disinformation or whatever it was," he said.

When I asked why the Task Force simply didn't release the Russian report along with the Task Force report, Barcella responded that the Russian report was classified, precluding its disclosure to the public. He also told me that several months earlier, he had urged Congressman Hamilton to extend the life of the Task Force a few more months to consider the surge of new material that had begun arriving near the end of the investigation, but that Hamilton had rejected the idea because it would have required getting renewed authorization from the new Congress.

So the extraordinary Russian report was simply boxed up and filed away with other unpublished information that the Task Force had obtained.

Barcella said he envisioned the Task Force material ending up in some vast warehouse, "like in the movie 'Raiders of the Lost Ark.'" Actually, it found an even less elegant resting place.

***

On January 13, 1993, two days after the Russian report arrived, the House Task Force went ahead with its scheduled press conference to release its report debunking the October Surprise allegations. Some selected reporters had received early briefings which guaranteed dismissive stories about the October Surprise "hoax" in the morning newspapers, but the Task Force wouldn't allow journalists to look at the report until the press conference was over. Copies of the report, wrapped in plastic, sat on the desks of the House International Affairs Committee hearing room as the press conference proceeded.

Task Force Chairman Lee Hamilton and ranking Republican Henry Hyde took questions, but the queries could not make specific references to what was in or out of the Task Force report because the copies had not been distributed. Though an unusual process – normally copies are distributed on an embargoed basis so reporters *can* ask informed questions – most of the reporters didn't seem to mind. The conventional wisdom against the October Surprise case was so strong that one right-wing "journalist" at the press conference suggested that some sort of legal action might be in order to punish reporters who had spread the October Surprise "myth." Congressman Hyde demurred that such punishment might be going a bit too far.

In a *New York Times* opinion article, Hamilton wrote that one of the keys to debunking the October Surprise suspicions was proving where Casey was on days when the meetings in Madrid and Paris were alleged to have happened. Having established solid Casey alibis for the last weekend of July 1980 (the "Bohemian Grove alibi") and on October 19, 1980 (the phone call remembered by nephew Larry Casey), Hamilton wrote, the Task Force's findings "should put the controversy to rest once and for all."[1]

The dismissive October Surprise findings further enhanced Hamilton's reputation as a politician above partisanship. Columnist David Broder, viewed as the dean of Washington pundits, cited Hamilton's repudiation of the October Surprise allegations as more evidence that Hamilton had become the "conscience of Congress."

On February 3, 1993, Republican congressmen took turns rubbing the October Surprise findings in. During a "special order" speech delivered on the House floor, Congressman Hyde, a white-haired rotund Republican from Illinois, acknowledged some weaknesses in the House Task Force findings. William Casey's 1980 passport had disappeared, for instance, as had key pages of his calendar, Hyde said. He noted, too, that French intelligence chief deMarenches had told his biographer that Casey did hold hostage talks with the Iranians in Paris in October 1980, a claim corroborated by several French intelligence officials.

But Hyde insisted that two solid blocks of evidence proved that the October Surprise allegations were a "myth." Hyde said the first cornerstone was hard-rock alibis for Casey and other suspects. "We were able to locate [Casey's] whereabouts with virtual certainty" on the dates when he allegedly met with Iranians in Europe to discuss the hostages, Hyde said. For instance, Casey had been in California on the late July 1980 weekend of a purported meeting with Iranians in Madrid, Hyde said, referring to the "Bohemian Grove alibi." There was an alibi, too, that weekend for the late Cyrus Hashemi. Hyde placed Hashemi in Connecticut. That was a reference to the two one-minute phone calls from and to lawyer Pottinger.

The second debunking cornerstone, Hyde said, was the absence of anything incriminating on FBI wiretaps of Cyrus Hashemi over five months in late 1980 and early 1981. Hyde noted that according to the Task Force report, "there is not a single indication that William Casey had contact with Cyrus or Jamshid Hashemi. ... Indeed, there is no indication on the tapes that Casey or any other individuals associated with the Reagan campaign had contact with any persons representing or associated with the Iranian government."

But under any examination, Hyde's two cornerstones turned to dust. The "Bohemian Grove alibi" flew in the face of the clear documentary record. Plus, the "proof" of Hashemi's presence in Connecticut consisted of phone records showing two one-minute calls. There was no evidence that Hashemi received or made the calls.

Hyde was wrong, too, about the absence of incriminating evidence on the Hashemi wiretaps. But since those wiretaps were secret in 1993, that argument was impossible to assess at the time. Later, when I accessed the raw House documents, I found a classified summary of the FBI bugging. According to that summary, the bugs actually revealed Cyrus Hashemi enmeshed in business schemes with Bill Casey's close friend, John Shaheen.

Contrary to the Task Force's claim of "not a single indication" of contact between Casey and Cyrus Hashemi, the Iranian banker was recorded as boasting that he and Casey had been "close friends" for years. That claim was supported by a CIA memo which stated that Casey recruited Cyrus Hashemi into a sensitive business arrangement in 1979 involving sale of Pahlavi Foundation property.

The secret FBI summary also showed Hashemi receiving a $3 million offshore deposit, arranged by Houston lawyer Harrel Tillman, who said he was a longtime friend of then-vice presidential candidate George Bush and was representing the Iranian government in 1980. After Reagan defeated Carter in November 1980, Tillman was back on Cyrus Hashemi's line promising help from the "Bush people" for one of Hashemi's floundering business deals.

**

As for me, I wanted to put the October Surprise issue in the past, too. Even two years earlier, when I took on the investigative project, I had done so with hesitation. Though the conclusions of the *Frontline* investigation had been measured, that didn't protect me from the counterattack that I had anticipated from the start. Like the few other reporters and scholars who tried to examine the issue, I was pummeled.

The intensity of the attacks might have suggested to some observers that there was more to the allegations than the Republicans were willing to admit. But in the early 1990s, Washington was increasingly falling under the sway of a potent conservative media infrastructure, which prided itself in ripping into anyone who threatened the Republican hold on the White House. With their tone and 'tude, *The Wall Street Journal* editorial page, *The Washington Times*, magazines like the *American Spectator*, and conservative talk radio already were reshaping the media power relationships at the national level.

Plus, many of the publications that weren't actively supporting the Reagan-Bush administration were actively trying to prove they weren't "liberal." Given that Washington *Zeitgeist,* it wasn't surprising that the attacks on the October Surprise allegations also came from more mainstream publications, such as my old employer, *Newsweek.* While part of me had hoped that my colleagues in the Washington news media would realize what we were trying to do in exploring a challenging historic topic, I had always expected to be smeared for our efforts. In that assumption, I was not wrong.

So, after the House Task Force's debunking, I finished work on *Trick or Treason*, a narrative recounting the difficult investigation that *Frontline* had recruited me to undertake. Though noting shortcomings in the evidence, I also pointed out weaknesses in the official investigations. I tried to put the story in a more objective context than the House Task Force had done. I dedicated the book "to those I have met who care more about truth than their reputations." Then I tried to put the whole issue behind me.

I worked on a couple of other projects for *Frontline*, including a documentary about the political violence in Haiti. I also did some reporting in early 1994 on the growing campaign by the American Right to destroy Bill Clinton and his Presidency. The conservative media infrastructure that Richard Nixon and William Simon had envisioned in the 1970s was taking shape in the 1990s as possibly the most potent – and intimidating – political force in the United States.

The conservative news media was setting the journalistic agenda for Washington, with the mainstream press now eager to tag along. From suspicions about "mysterious deaths" attributed to the Clintons to endless investigations into the minutiae of their Whitewater real estate investment,

Washington journalism passed "through-the-looking-glass" into a world where ideological conservatives got to define what was news.

Having poured billions of dollars into magazines, newspapers, radio talk shows and television, the conservatives also were riding a rising tide of popular support. In November 1994, the tough-guy Republicans – led by Newt Gingrich – ripped control of both the House and Senate from the wimpy Democrats. House Speaker Thomas Foley was turned out of office by the voters, and Lee Hamilton was set to lose his chairmanship of the House International Affairs Committee.

The change of party control, however, meant that I would have to move quickly if I wanted to examine the records of the October Surprise House Task Force. The chances of getting access would likely decline after the Republicans got control of the House International Affairs Committee, which had jurisdiction over the records.

I also had heard from sources close to the Clinton administration that some Iranians had expressed bemusement over how wrong the October Surprise findings had been and that Iran might finally be willing to confirm the contacts with the Republicans in 1980. According to these sources, the Iranian offer had gone to the highest levels of the Clinton administration where the decision was made not to reopen the old controversy.

Still, I thought it was time to see what the Task Force might have left out of its final report. When I called in December 1994 to ask about examining the Task Force's records, the staff of the House International Affairs Committee told me there had not been a single prior request. The records had simply been collecting dust in an obscure office off the Rayburn House Office Building's parking garage, situated across from the U.S. Capitol. I was told that I would be allowed to examine the unclassified documents and make a limited number of copies.

***

On December 20, 1994, two years after the House Task Force had been finishing up its final report, I parked my car on Capitol Hill, walked along the horseshoe drive of the Rayburn House Office Building and passed through the metal detectors into the building. Although I'd spent many years covering Congress, I had to read carefully the notes giving me directions to find the storage place for the Task Force records. The office, where the records were stored, was one I had never heard of before.

I had been told to take an elevator to the garage level. From there, I was to pass through the parking area, turn left and walk almost to the south exit of the garage. I was to look to my right for an interior office near the guard's kiosk. After wandering among the parked cars for several minutes, I finally spotted the office on my right. Its windows looking out onto the garage were

covered with narrow Venetian blinds. I knocked on the locked metal door
and a young tall blond man opened it.

"I'm here to look at the October Surprise files," I said.

"Oh, yes, you're the reporter," he responded politely, having been
alerted to my arrival earlier. "They're in here, in the back."

I followed him into the cramped office, which had cloth-covered
partitions creating compartments for three or four staffers. A large, old
copying machine sat against the left wall.

"How long do you expect to be?" the young man asked.

"I really don't know," I answered.

"Well, I'm supposed to stay while you're here and I still have some
Christmas shopping to finish. I'd like to get out early."

"Yes, so would I."

We turned left into a small hallway and passed through a door into a
room with a hard concrete floor, a mirror on one wall and two bathroom
stalls. Dozens of boxes were piled in mounds along the walls. Some boxes
were brown cardboard, others gray. The fluorescent lighting shone off the
salmon-colored wall tiles. A metal contraption with a crank was hanging at
eye level on one wall above the boxes. It was an empty tampon dispenser.
The records from the October Surprise investigation had ended up in a
former Ladies Room.

"Well, I'll be out here if you need anything," the young man said,
retreating toward his cubicle.

"They told me I could make some copies."

"Yes, but they don't want you making too many."

"Right, they said a dozen pages or so."

The young man disappeared. I stared down at the boxes. With a sigh, I
began pulling the tape off the first box.

As I pored through the files, I soon realized that not only did they
contain unclassified notes and documents about the Task Force's work, but
also "secret" and even "top secret" papers that had been left behind,
apparently in the haste to wrap up the investigation. One of the "secret"
depositions included former CIA officer Charles Cogan's recollection of
Joseph Reed's quote about disrupting Carter's October Surprise.

Another box contained a "secret" summary of FBI wiretaps placed on
phones belonging to Cyrus Hashemi, the Iranian financier who allegedly was
double-dealing the Carter administration in 1980. There were previously
undisclosed notes, too, describing George Bush's active involvement in
monitoring Carter's Iran hostage negotiations. According to one set of notes,
dated October 27, 1980, Bush instructed foreign policy adviser Richard Allen
to funnel last-minute information about the negotiations back to him via
former CIA officer Theodore Shackley.

Another file contained a summary of all "secret" and "top secret" State
Department records on arms sales to Iran in the 1980s. One "top

secret/sensitive" document recounted private meetings that Secretary of State
Alexander Haig had with Middle Eastern leaders during a trip in May 1981.
Haig wrote that Egyptian President Anwar Sadat and Saudi Prince Fahd told
him that "Iran is receiving military spares for U.S. equipment from Israel."
Haig added that, "It was also interesting to confirm that President Carter gave
the Iraqis a green light to launch the war against Iran through Fahd."

I found a "secret" draft chapter on the monitoring of Carter's hostage
negotiations that contained sections, such as references to former CIA
officers close to George Bush, that had been deleted from the final report.
The hidden documents also shed more light on the interlocking relationships
of David Rockefeller, Joseph Reed, Princess Ashraf, John Shaheen, Cyrus
Hashemi, the Marcos family and BCCI.

When the Task Force final report was issued, there was nothing
mentioned about BCCI's Concorde flight; nor was there reference to Princess
Ashraf's $20 million and the Hong Kong Deposit and Guaranty slush fund;
nor the information about Reed's boast and his evasive reaction to questions
from the FBI agent; nor a word about Paul Laxalt and the alleged Philippine
contributions to the 1980 Reagan-Bush campaign.

In every area where Task Force chief counsel Barcella faced a potential
conflict of interest from his law work for Laxalt and BCCI, the information
didn't make it into the final report. Other deletions corresponded to areas
where Barcella's associates might have faced embarrassment. For instance,
the final report did note the existence of the ten-member "October Surprise
Group" and said that "additional people may have participated in other
meetings." What was deleted was the list of those "additional people," who
included Barcella's friend Michael Ledeen.

On the key question of whether Casey knew Cyrus Hashemi before the
1980 election, the Task Force brushed aside a CIA memo that recounted a
statement by former Attorney General Eliot Richardson who said in 1984
that Casey and Hashemi had cooperated on a plan to sell property for a
foundation in 1979. The memo was briefly mentioned, but the Task Force
still concluded that there was "no evidence" that Casey had met Cyrus
Hashemi before the 1980 election. The Task Force also deleted the identity
of the foundation. The word "Pahlavi" was excised, thus obscuring the fact
that the memo indicated that Casey and Cyrus Hashemi were not only
working together in 1979, but collaborating on a project relating to Iran.[2]

I also found the "confidential" October Surprise report that had been
sent by Russia's Supreme Soviet informing the Task Force that Moscow's
national security files contained evidence that Casey, Bush and other
Republicans had negotiated secretly with Iranians in Europe in 1980.

Limited in how many pages I was allowed to copy and concerned that
the staffer would notice the bright-red "secret" stamps on the pages, I first
read some of the documents into a tape recorder and scribbled down notes on
others. Then, I volunteered to do the copying myself, making sure that the

words "secret" and "top secret" couldn't be seen from across the room. There were some tense moments when the old copier jammed. But I made the quick fixes so as not to require the assistance of my minder.

Since I couldn't get through all the boxes the first day, I told the committee that I would have to return – and did so several times retracing my steps through the Rayburn parking garage to the little office and to the abandoned Ladies Room. Whenever I found a document that seemed newsworthy, I tried to copy at least a few pages, staying within my dozen-or-so-page limit, partly so I wouldn't attract too much attention.

After extracting some of this hidden history, I began to follow up on key parts of it. I contacted one well-placed official in Europe who checked with the Russian government for me. "This was real information based on their own sources and methods," the official told me when he called back. As for the possibility that the Russian report was simply blowback from the U.S. media, the official insisted that the Russians "would not send something like this to the U.S. Congress at that time, if it was bullshit."

Instead, the Russians considered their report "a bomb" and "couldn't believe it was ignored," the official said. Only later did the Russians learn that their "bomb" had ended up in a cardboard box among hundreds of other documents piled, ingloriously, on the floor of a Ladies Room.

In early 1995, my next step was to prepare a summary of the unreleased October Surprise documents. I then sent the proposed article to several magazine editors. But I was rebuffed. No editors seemed interested in the old "discredited" October Surprise case. I began to refer to the papers as "the October Surprise X-Files," after the "X-Files" science fiction series then popular on television. In late 1995, I took the advice of my oldest son, Sam, and started something called a "Web site" on the Internet, a concept with which I had little familiarity.

With Sam providing the technical skills and learning as we went, we launched *Consortiumnews.com* as a site for well-researched investigative articles that couldn't find a home in the national U.S. news media.

Chapter 13: Analyst Obstacles

Like a Civil War victory at a major train junction, the election of Ronald Reagan and George H.W. Bush in 1980 put conservatives in control of key switching points in Washington for the transportation of ideas throughout the U.S. political system. By regaining the Executive Branch and winning the Senate, Republicans had their hands on many of the levers that could expedite the movement of favorable information to the American public and sidetrack news that might cause trouble.

Having learned how dangerous it was when critical scandals like Watergate or the CIA abuses started rolling down the tracks and building up steam, the conservatives took pains to keep hold of this advantage over what information sped through to the public and what didn't. Though often disparaged for being behind the times, conservatives – far better than liberals – grasped the strategic advantage that came with controlling these logistics of information. With the ability to rush public relations shock troops and media artillery to political battle fronts, conservatives recognized that they could alter the tactics and the strategies of what they called "the war of ideas."

Not losing any time, Republicans began devising new ways to manage, manufacture and deliver their message in the weeks and months after the Reagan-Bush victory. Some would call the concept "public diplomacy"; others would use the phrase "perception management." But the idea was to control how the public would perceive an issue, a person or an event. The concept was to define the political battlefield at key moments – especially when a story was just breaking – and thus enhance the chances of victory.

The Republican approach would be helped immeasurably by President Reagan's communication skills and by the image wizardry of White House aide Michael Deaver. But the administration's capability was given an important boost, too, by the intelligence backgrounds of two key figures, former campaign chief William Casey, who was named Reagan's CIA director, and Vice President George H.W. Bush, a former CIA director and a veteran of previous battles fought to contain political scandals. From their experiences in the intelligence fields, they understood what the CIA Old Boys, like Miles Copeland, meant when they talked about setting the "the spirit of the meeting" as a crucial element in managing political events.

***

While many of the "perception management" battles would be fought against the Washington press corps in the early 1980s, the incoming administration mounted an important offensive, too, against the CIA's Directorate of Intelligence – or DI – the analytical division. Given the traditional respect granted the U.S. intelligence community's assessments, the incoming administration knew that the DI represented a strategic high ground that either could help pin down ideological adversaries or, if in enemy hands, could threaten Reagan-Bush policies from the rear. While the CIA's Directorate of Operations – which runs paramilitary wars, propaganda operations and spying – encountered its share of controversies, the DI's analysts maintained a good, though far from perfect, reputation for professionalism.

The immediate problem for the Reagan-Bush team was that many of the CIA's academically oriented analysts didn't share the new administration's conviction about the Soviet Union as a ten-foot-tall ogre wreaking virtually all the world's havoc. The analysts didn't buy into the theory that Moscow was directing world terrorism, planning a first-strike nuclear attack and provoking conflict in Central America and the Third World to isolate and ultimately defeat the United States. The CIA's view of the Soviet Union was of a difficult enemy, but one with weaknesses, vulnerabilities and limited ambitions – a nuanced view that would not entirely fit with the new era's "Evil Empire" rhetoric.

Between the Reagan-Bush victory and the Inauguration, the task of softening up the CIA analytical division fell to a transition team of conservatives and neoconservatives under the leadership of Laurence Silberman – the abrasive lawyer who had attended the mysterious L'Enfant Plaza meeting several weeks earlier. The Reagan-Bush intelligence transition team, in effect, was resuming the assault on the CIA's analytical division that had begun with Team B during George H.W. Bush's tenure as CIA director in 1976.

"That the Reaganites saw their arrival as a hostile takeover was apparent in the most extraordinary transition period of my career," recalled CIA officer Robert Gates, himself an anti-Soviet hardliner and another alleged participant in the October Surprise case.

"For the first time in decades, an incoming President orchestrated a comprehensive battle plan to seize control of a city long believed to be in enemy hands," Gates wrote in his memoirs, *From the Shadows*. "Main force political units, flanking maneuvers, feints, sappers, and psychological warfare all played their part as Reagan and company between November and January deployed their forces for a political blitzkrieg. During the transition, every department and agency became a political and ideological battlefield."[1]

That was especially true of the CIA's analytical division. In a scalding assessment of the CIA's Soviet analysis, the Reagan-Bush transition team accused the DI of "an abject failure" to foresee a supposedly massive Soviet buildup of strategic weapons and "the wholesale failure" to comprehend the sophistication of Soviet propaganda. The transition team even questioned the patriotism of the career analysts who supposedly had underestimated the Soviet commitment to world domination. "These failures are of such enormity," the transition report said, "that they cannot help but suggest to any objective observer that the agency itself is compromised to an unprecedented extent and that its paralysis is attributable to causes more sinister than incompetence."[2]

This head-on assault against the CIA's analytical division set the stage for its later retreats. "The reaction inside the Agency to this litany of failure and incompetence" from the transition team, Gates wrote, "was a mix of resentment and anger, dread and personal insecurity."[3] Amid rumors that the transition team wanted to purge several hundred top analysts, career officials feared for their jobs, especially those considered responsible for assessing the Soviet Union as a struggling power often seeking to avoid confrontation and eager for détente with the United States.

Once Reagan and Bush took office and Casey arrived at the CIA, the war over intelligence broke out in earnest. The first pitched battle came over an analysis of the Soviet Union's support for international terrorism. It had become an article of faith among the Reagan-Bush newcomers that Moscow was supporting international terror groups as a way to destabilize the West in general and the United States in particular. Conservative author Claire Sterling was making this case in her book, *The Terror Network* – and the foreign policy principals of the Reagan-Bush administration were fans of Sterling's hypothesis.

"The day after Reagan's Inauguration, Secretary of State Alexander Haig, believing that Moscow had tried to assassinate him in Europe where he served as Supreme Allied Commander [of NATO], linked the Soviet Union to all acts of international terrorism," wrote Melvin Goodman, then-chief of the CIA's office for Soviet analysis. "There was no evidence to support such a charge but Casey had read ... Claire Sterling's *The Terror Network* and, like Haig, was convinced that a Soviet conspiracy was behind global terrorism."[4]

CIA analysts had a secret reason for doubting Sterling's theories, however. "Specialists at CIA dismissed the book, knowing that much of it was based on CIA 'black propaganda,' anticommunist allegations planted in the European press," Goodman wrote. "But Casey contemptuously told CIA analysts that he had learned more from Sterling than from all of them."

Another believer in Sterling's conspiracy view was State Department consultant Michael Ledeen, who saw international terrorism as a "sort of Wurlitzer being played by people in the basement of the Kremlin." Other backers included two newly minted State Department officials Robert McFarlane and Paul Wolfowitz, Goodman wrote.[5] Like Casey and Gates,

McFarlane and Ledeen were two other figures who had popped up in the October Surprise case. Wolfowitz had been a member of Team B.

Carolyn McGiffert Ekedahl of the CIA's Soviet office was the unfortunate analyst who was handed the assignment to prepare the analysis on Soviet support for terrorism. The request had arrived from the State Department in late January after the State Department's intelligence office had disputed, internally, Secretary Haig's view that the Soviets were instigating terrorism across Europe.

"Because of the importance of the request and the volatility of the issue, exceedingly high priority was given to collecting and evaluating *all* available information dealing with Soviet involvement, direct and indirect, to *any* group dealing in terrorist activities," Ekedahl testified later before the Senate Intelligence Committee. "I worked extremely closely with the Directorate of Operations to make sure it provided every piece of information it had, as well as with the State Department and the Defense Intelligence Agency; we discarded no piece of evidence and, when I wrote the draft, I included an annex with *all* the evidence, good and bad, carefully described and explained."[6]

Contrary to Sterling's allegations, Ekedahl said the consensus of the intelligence community was that the Soviets discouraged acts of terrorism by groups getting support from Moscow for practical, not moral, reasons. "We agreed that the Soviets consistently stated, publicly and privately, that they considered international terrorist activities counterproductive and advised groups they supported not to use such tactics," Ekedahl said. "We had hard evidence to support this conclusion."

Still, the CIA analysis noted that the Soviets did provide assistance to revolutionary or resistance groups, such as the Yasir Arafat's Palestine Liberation Organization and Nelson Mandela's African National Congress. The PLO was challenging Israel's occupation of the West Bank and Gaza, while the ANC was resisting the white supremacist government of South Africa. Both the PLO and the ANC were accused of employing terrorist tactics in their struggles, though their organizations also represented the aspirations of broader popular movements.

"We reported that we had found no persuasive evidence of Soviet support for those European terrorist groups (the IRA, the Red Brigades and the Red Army Faction) about which Secretary Haig had specifically asked," Ekedahl said about the analytical division's draft of its intelligence estimate.

Ekedahl also denied that the CIA analytical division was just being obstreperous in its conclusions. "There was *no* effort to 'stick our finger in the policy maker's eye,'" a complaint from then-Casey assistant Robert Gates, Ekedahl said. "On the contrary, we had expanded the scope of the paper to include groups in which Haig had expressed no interest so that we could point out that the Soviets *did* support militant groups and *did* pursue destabilizing policies."

Ekedahl said Gates, dissatisfied with the analysis, joined in rewriting the draft "to suggest greater Soviet support for terrorism and the text was altered by pulling up from the annex reports that overstated Soviet involvement." In his memoirs, Gates denied politicizing the CIA's intelligence product while acknowledging that he was aware of Casey's hostile reaction to the analysts' disagreement with Sterling's theory.

"The first draft by the analysts proved beyond a shadow of a doubt that Haig had exaggerated the Soviet role – that the Soviets did not organize or direct international terrorism," Gates wrote.[7] But Casey was mad, telling the division chiefs that he was "greatly disappointed" with the report and vowing not to pass the analysis on to senior officials, Gates wrote.

Casey believed the CIA analysts were too wedded to solid evidence while the director felt "the practical judgments on which policy is based in the real world do not require that standard of proof, which is frequently just not available," Gates wrote. Casey denigrated the Soviet analysts as "deficient in intellectual and semantic rigor" and too reliant on Soviet statements. Casey then assigned the terrorism project to a new group of analysts at the Defense Intelligence Agency.[8]

"All the DIA analysts who had been involved originally had been replaced by people new to the subject who insisted on language emphasizing Soviet control of international terrorist activities," Ekedahl said. "Director Casey read the estimate on March 24 and rejected it; he asked DIA to prepare a new draft. The second draft, completed on April 8, asserted that the Soviet Union was directly supporting and controlling most international terrorist activity. Casey liked the draft."[9]

A donnybrook ensued inside the U.S. intelligence community. Some senior officials responsible for analysis fought back against Casey's dictates, warning that the revised draft would undermine the integrity of the process that had been used for decades to analyze intelligence. Casey agreed to permit some modifications of his favored analysis, but senior CIA officials accepted the bureaucratic reality that the revision was being done "under constraints," Ekedahl said.[10]

"I was the only one of the original group of analysts ... who attended the coordination meetings on the third draft," Ekedahl said. "I was told that I could not speak unless I were asked a direct question," a restriction that Ekedahl said she violated a few times when she observed "serious misuse of operational material."[11]

***

Working with Gates, Casey undertook a series of institutional changes that gave him fuller control of the analytical process. He required that drafts needed clearance from his office before they could go out to other intelligence agencies. Casey also appointed Gates to be director of the DI and consolidated Gates's control over analysis by also making him chairman of the National Intelligence Council, another key analytical body.

"Casey and Gates used various management tactics to get the line of intelligence they desired and to suppress unwanted intelligence," Ekedahl said. "The latter is relatively simple because a given report or estimate can be dismissed on a variety of grounds (insufficient evidence, irrelevance, poor analysis, etc.) not clearly traceable to politicization."

The tradition of expressing opposition in footnotes also suffered. "During the period of Gates's tenure, the DI was effectively prevented from dissenting when its analysts disagreed with estimates of interest to Casey/Gates," Ekedahl said.[12]

With Gates using top-down management techniques, CIA analysts sensitive to their career paths intuitively grasped that they could rarely go wrong by backing the "company line" and presenting the worst-case scenario about Soviet capabilities and intentions, Ekedahl and other CIA analysts said.

"Replacing experts with people willing to cooperate became a central element in the Casey-Gates approach to intelligence management," Ekedahl said. "Whereas the pre-Gates ethic emphasized analytic independence and objectivity, the new culture is that of the 'hired pen,' loyal to the current leadership and its views. Whereas intelligence production should be based on informed and objective analysis of the available evidence, in the Gates's culture it is based on the anticipated reaction of senior managers and officials."[13] (Ekedahl left the Office of Soviet Analysis in September 1985 because of "issues involving politicization," she said.)[14]

Mel Goodman, the chief of the Soviet analysis office in the early 1980s, said the clash over Soviet support for terrorism began a period of career retribution against out-of-step analysts. "Junior analysts became responsible for analysis on Soviet domestic and foreign policy as senior analysts sought other positions inside the intelligence community and elsewhere," Goodman told the Senate Intelligence Committee a decade later.

Largely outside public view, the CIA's proud Soviet analytical office underwent a purge of its most senior people. "Nearly every senior analyst on Soviet foreign policy eventually left the Office of Soviet Analysis," Goodman said. "The picture for Soviet domestic policy is similar, with the departure of most senior analysts and the introduction of managers with virtually no experience in Soviet domestic politics."[15]

Another management strategy used to assert control was a restructuring of the analytical division, which had traditionally functioned along disciplinary lines – economics, politics, military and technical analysis – rather than within geographical areas. That changed in September 1981 when the old subject-area offices were abolished and were replaced with new ones structured along geographic lines, a change that allowed wholesale removal of senior management personnel.

"The ripping off of the mask of the plan was when all the Directorate of Intelligence office chiefs were invited to go to an off-site conference over the weekend," recalled Peter Dickson, an analyst who concentrated on proliferation issues. "When they came back the offices didn't exist anymore. The offices were abolished out from under them."

Dickson told me that the significance of the structural change became apparent at the start of 1982 when Casey promoted the boyish-looking Gates to run the analytical division. "The structure was changed to give Bobby Gates a blank slate to create his own DI," Dickson said. "He was able to pick a whole new set of cadre, chiefs, and they were beholden to him. You had an awesome regime change in the Directorate of Intelligence with that act."

Gates's rise under Casey was considered meteoric. Though entering the CIA as an analyst, Gates spent a relatively short time at the Langley-based spy agency. He followed an unusual career path that involved two stints on the National Security Council staff where he operated within a more political environment than most CIA professionals experienced. Gates would say that his White House tours helped him understand the shortcomings of the CIA product because he had viewed the process through the eyes of the "consumers" of intelligence, not just the producers.

Gates made clear he intended to shake up the DI's culture, demanding greater responsiveness to the needs of the White House and other policymakers. In a speech to the DI's analysts and managers on January 7, 1982, Gates berated the division for producing shoddy analysis that administration officials didn't find helpful. Gates went through a litany of complaints.

Gates said the DI's weaknesses included "analysis that was irrelevant or untimely or unfocused or all three; ... close-minded, smug, arrogant responses to legitimate questions and constructive criticisms; ...flabby, complacent thinking and questionable assumptions combined with an intolerance of others' views, both in and out of the CIA; ... poor, verbose writing; ...a pronounced tendency to confuse 'objectivity' and 'independence' with avoidance of issues germane to the U.S. government and policymakers."

Gates also endorsed some of the criticisms of the CIA that conservatives had raised in the Team B experiment in 1976 and in other forums. "We significantly misjudged the percentage of Soviet GNP allocated to defense," Gates said. "We ignored Soviet interest in terrorism."

Gates unveiled an 11-point management plan to whip the DI into shape. His plan included rotating division chiefs through one-year stints in policy agencies and requiring CIA analysts to "refresh their substantive knowledge and broaden their perspective" by taking courses at Washington-area think tanks and universities. He declared that a new Production Evaluation Staff would aggressively review their analytical products and serve as his "junkyard dog."[16]

Gates's message was that the DI, which had operated as an "ivory tower" for academically oriented analysts committed to an ethos of objectivity, would take on a more corporate culture with a product designed to fit the needs of those up the ladder both inside and outside the CIA.

"It was a kind of chilling speech," recalled Dickson. "I remember people coming back from it who were more senior than I who went down to listen to it. One of the things he wanted to do, he was going to shake up the DI. He was going to read every paper that came out. What that did was that everybody between the analyst and him had to get involved in the paper to a greater extent because their careers were going to be at stake. He was saying he didn't trust anyone. He's the top guy and he's going to review all the papers. And he made an effort to do that. It had a chilling effect."

A chief Casey-Gates tactic for exerting tighter control over the analysis was to express concern about "the editorial process," Dickson said.

"You can jerk people around in the editorial process and hide behind your editorial mandate to intimidate people," Dickson said. Gates "created an increasingly layered process which wore down people. The effect of that was a gradual process of intimidation. It got very nasty, very Darwinian. ... There was a weeding out process of people who could stand up and defend positions. There was a grinding down of the independent mind of the analysts."

In describing this corporate-style takeover of the CIA's analytical division, Dickson compared Casey to the corporate raider, Gordon Gecko, in the movie "Wall Street," with Gates serving as his protégé, Bud Fox. "People who don't know this history don't understand what happened to people who work inside the business and why the culture changed," Dickson said.

Gates soon was salting the analytical division with his allies, a group of managers who became known as the "Gates clones." Some of those who rose with Gates were David Cohen, David Carey, George Kolt, Jim Lynch, Winston Wiley, John Gannon and John McLaughlin (who would become acting CIA director in July 2004 after George Tenet's resignation).

Though Dickson's area of expertise – nuclear proliferation – was on the fringes of the Reagan-Bush primary concerns, it ended up getting him into trouble, anyway. In 1983, he clashed with his superiors over his conclusion that the Soviet Union was more committed to controlling proliferation of nuclear weapons than the administration wanted to hear. His CIA superiors didn't want to give the Soviets any credit for demonstrating caution on the nuclear technology front. When Dickson stood by his evidence, he soon found himself facing accusations about his psychological fitness and other pressures that eventually led him to leave the CIA.

Dickson also was among the analysts who raised alarms about Pakistan's development of nuclear weapons, another sore point because the Reagan-Bush administration wanted Pakistan's assistance in funneling weapons to Islamic fundamentalists fighting the Soviets in Afghanistan. One of the effects from the exaggerated intelligence about Soviet power and intentions was to make other potential risks – such as allowing development of a nuclear bomb in the Islamic world or training Islamic fundamentalists in techniques of sabotage – pale in comparison.

While worst-case scenarios were in order for the Soviet Union and other communist enemies, best-case scenarios were the order of the day for Reagan-Bush allies, including Osama bin Laden and other Arab extremists rushing to Afghanistan to wage a holy war against European invaders, in this case, the Russians. As for the Pakistani drive to get a nuclear bomb, the Reagan-Bush administration turned to word games to avoid triggering anti-proliferation penalties that otherwise would be imposed on Pakistan.

"There was a distinction made to say that the possession of the device is not the same as developing it," Dickson told me. "They got into the argument that they don't quite possess it yet because they haven't turned the last screw into the warhead. As long as they haven't done that, they don't possess it yet. So the aid could continue. No matter how you look at that there was a subordination of intelligence to a policy to aid the Afghan rebels no matter what."

Finally, the intelligence on the Pakistan Bomb grew too strong to continue denying the reality. But the delay in confronting Pakistan ultimately allowed the Muslim government in Islamabad to produce nuclear weapons. Pakistani scientists also shared their know-how with "rogue" states, such as North Korea and Libya.

After years of battles with the Casey-Gates bureaucracy, Dickson left the CIA, taking with him the kind of quirky but creative intellect that was once prized at Langley. Like other purged analysts, Dickson enjoyed the intellectual experience of getting to the bottom of complex questions. In his spare time, Dickson puzzled over historical mysteries, such as the real identity of William Shakespeare and the behind-the-scenes story of Christopher Columbus's political connections that got him his three-boat Spanish fleet for sailing to the New World.

***

In one of the tragic-comic moments of the early Reagan-Bush period, Secretary of State Haig promoted suspicions that mysterious "yellow rain" that had been reported in Indochina was an example of a deadly Soviet chemical warfare agent being deployed against anticommunist insurgents. However, independent scientists eventually concluded that the "yellow rain" was bee feces.

In another case, the Reagan administration pressed the CIA to accept right-wing allegations that the Soviet KGB was behind the May 13, 1981, assassination attempt against Pope John-Paul II. The attack had been carried out by Turkish neo-Nazi Mehmet Ali Agca, but Sterling and other conservatives built a case against the KGB, in part, because Agca traveled through Bulgaria and because the Soviets supposedly had a motive: the Pope's symbolic value to the Polish Solidarity movement. But CIA analysts knew that the Soviets saw the Pope as a stabilizing influence in Poland.

Standing up against the KGB-Pope-assassination conspiracy theory brought the CIA analysts in for another round of pummeling from the Right for supposedly going soft again on the Soviet Union. Even hardliner Gates marveled at the intensity of the criticism. "Some accused us of trying to cover up the Soviet role, though why we – and especially Casey – would do such a thing I never grasped," Gates wrote in his memoirs.

When conservatives continued to complain about the CIA's supposed failure to pin the 1981 papal assassination plot on Moscow, Casey and his team decided to cook the intelligence books with a special review of the issue in 1985, Goodman said.

"Earlier CIA assessments – and Gates's testimony to the Senate Select Committee on Intelligence in 1983 – had concluded that Moscow had no role in the papal plot, and senior officials of the Directorate of Operations informed both Casey and Gates that Moscow had stopped political assassination and that strong evidence indicated neither the Soviets nor the Bulgarians were involved," Goodman wrote in *Foreign Policy* magazine.[17]

But Casey was determined to undermine Secretary of State George Shultz's diplomatic overtures to Moscow and thus commissioned a special paper alleging a connection to the shooting of the Pope. "Gates made sure that CIA analysts worked *in camera* to prevent proper vetting and coordination of the assessment," Goodman recalled. "Indeed, 'Agca's Attempt to Kill the Pope: The Case for Soviet Involvement' read like a novelist's fantasy of communist conspiracy, but Gates's covering note to the President and the Vice President described the report as a 'comprehensive examination' that 'we feel able to present . . . with some confidence.' ...

"Casey was not going to let the facts stand in his way and Gates, who previously had told the SSCI [Senate Select Committee on Intelligence] that the Soviets were not involved, again pandered to the Casey agenda, making sure that the draft document was reviewed in less than twenty-four hours and not seen by senior officials familiar with the issue."

With the 1985 report on the papal assassination plot, Goodman wrote that the CIA's politicization of intelligence on the Soviet Union hit "rock bottom." But he said the broader consequence of the hyped intelligence was to prime the pump for an expensive U.S. military expansion.

"The CIA caricature of a Soviet military octopus whose tentacles reached the world over supported the administration's view of the 'Evil Empire,'" Goodman wrote. "Gates used worst-case analysis to portray a Soviet capability to neutralize the strategic capabilities of the United States. Moscow, in fact, had no capability to target dispersed mobile ICBMs and lacked an air defense system that could counter strategic bombers. Moscow had no confidence that its efforts to destroy warheads on land-based missiles would actually find missiles still tethered to their launchers, and CIA's emphasis on Moscow's 'launch on warning' capability was nothing more than a doomsday scenario."

Though Gates has consistently denied "politicizing" the CIA's analysis, he acknowledged that Casey did put pressure on analysts, especially when they were working on a subject dear to his heart, such as the Soviet threat.

"Casey complained bitterly and often graphically when the analysis he got seemed fuzzy-minded, lacked concreteness, missed the point, or in his view was naïve about the real world, when it lacked 'ground truth,'" Gates wrote. "An analyst had to be tough and have the courage of his or her convictions to challenge Casey on something he cared about and knew about. He argued, he fought, he yelled, he grumped with the analysts in person and on paper. He pulled no punches. Some thrived on it. Many were put off by his abrasiveness, his occasional bullying manner. ...

"For a cadre of analysts accustomed to 'gentlemanly discourse' and even more to a hands-off approach to their work from their own senior managers in the analysis directorate, such intrusiveness and assertiveness on the part of the DCI was unprecedented, and unwelcome."[18]

In the trenches at the CIA, however, Casey's bluster often was amplified by the new senior managers who had risen to power under Casey and Gates, according to several CIA analysts whom I interviewed. Some analysts were verbally berated until they agreed to change their findings; some faced job threats; others experienced confrontations with supervisors who threw papers around the office and sometimes into the analysts' faces. The scars left on the CIA's tradition of objective analysis ran deep and affected later intelligence failures, the analysts said.

"The politicization that took place during the Casey-Gates era is directly responsible for the CIA's loss of its ethical compass and the erosion of its credibility," said Mel Goodman, the former chief of the Soviet analysis office. "The fact that the CIA missed the most important historical development in its history – the collapse of the Soviet Empire and the Soviet Union itself – is due in large measure to the culture and process that Gates established in his directorate."[19]

In Goodman's view, the failure to notice the decline and the disintegration of the Soviet Union can be traced directly to the Gates-Casey intervention in the analytical process. "They systematically created an agency view of the Soviet Union that overemphasized the Soviet threat, ignored Soviet vulnerabilities and weaknesses," said Goodman, who served as a senior CIA analyst on Soviet policy from 1966 to 1986.[20]

By the mid-1980s, more practical conservatives, such as Secretary of State Shultz, were finding the CIA's Soviet analysis increasingly divergent from the reality that he encountered as the reformist forces around Mikhail Gorbachev consolidated their power in the Kremlin. In his memoirs, *Turmoil and Triumph,* Shultz described a frank foreign policy discussion he had with National Security Adviser Frank Carlucci on January 4, 1987.

"I told him that I had no confidence in the intelligence community, that I had been misled, lied to, cut out," Shultz wrote. "I felt that CIA analysis was distorted by strong views about policy. ... The CIA, I told Carlucci, had been unable to perceive that change was coming in the Soviet Union. When Gorbachev first appeared at the helm, the CIA said he was 'just talk,' just another Soviet attempt to deceive us. As that line became increasingly untenable, the CIA changed its tune: Gorbachev was serious about change, but the Soviet Union had a powerfully entrenched and largely successful system that was incapable of being changed; so Gorbachev would fail in his attempt to change it. When it became evident that the Soviet Union was, in fact, changing, the CIA line was that the changes wouldn't really make a difference."[21]

But the CIA's exaggerated intelligence on Soviet military power did make a difference in Washington by loosening the budgetary purse strings. Congress – fearing criticism for being soft on Moscow – authorized hundreds of billions of dollars in new weapons systems often to face down imaginary threats.

"The CIA in the 1980s overstated every aspect of the Soviet military (army, navy, air force, air defense, and strategic weaponry), thus contributing to increased defense spending and reduced interest in arms control," Goodman wrote. "Some of these errors were acknowledged, but only after Gates left the CIA in 1989 to join the National Security Council. Meanwhile, these errors appeared in the unclassified DIA publication, 'Soviet Military Power,' which served as a propaganda vehicle for the Department of Defense until 1991. ...

"Two years later, the General Accounting Office concluded that the DOD deliberately exaggerated Soviet capabilities and misrepresented the cost and performance of U.S. systems in order to gain congressional authorization for desired military programs. The CIA, created as an independent agency in 1947, had failed in its role as 'honest broker' with respect to intelligence and policy."[22]

The CIA also turned its back on evidence of the accelerating pace of Moscow's economic decline. Those signs were emerging by the mid-1970s and were cited in the work of economists, such as Sweden's Anders Aslund.[23] Academic analysts and businessmen who visited the Soviet Union also observed its backwardness, especially in crucial areas of technological development and production of consumer goods, but the CIA was mostly blind to these historic developments.

"CIA estimates on the Soviet Union were dead wrong on the size and performance of the economy and the military burden," Goodman wrote. "CIA economists continued to compare the Soviet and American economies in dollar values that exaggerated the size of the Soviet economy," putting it at about 60 percent of the size of the U.S. economy when Aslund was calculating a number closer to 40 percent.[24] By the mid-1980s when the CIA began to accept the reality of lower Soviet economic growth rates, some European economists were seeing no growth at all for the first half of the decade.

Former CIA analyst Dickson said he believed that the pattern of politicization at the DI could be traced back even earlier than Casey's arrival at the CIA in 1981 – to George H.W. Bush's year at the agency's helm when he acquiesced to the conservative Team B counter-analysis in 1976.

"Did not something happen here with Bush coming back as the V.P. that the Republicans came to see the agency as malleable?" Dickson wondered, adding that perhaps "Bush senior had learned the lessons of what you could do with the intelligence business."

Ironically, however, one historic result of the faulty CIA analysis overestimating Soviet strength in the early 1980s was to exaggerate the impact of Reagan-Bush policies in supposedly "winning the Cold War." Having presided over a politicized intelligence process that made the tottering Soviet empire look invincible, Ronald Reagan then got the principal credit for its collapse in the late 1980s and early 1990s, a popular assessment that was cemented as conventional wisdom with the week-long ceremonies after Reagan's death on June 5, 2004.

***

The question of "politicization" at the CIA cropped up briefly as a national issue in 1991 when President George H.W. Bush appointed Robert Gates to be CIA director. In a break with tradition, CIA analysts stepped out of the shadows and testified openly before the Senate Intelligence Committee against Bush's choice.

Led by Soviet specialist Goodman, the CIA dissidents fingered Gates as the key "politicization" culprit. Their testimony added to doubts about Gates, who was already under a cloud for dubious testimony he had given on the Iran-Contra scandal, allegations that he had participated in a covert scheme to arm Saddam Hussein's Iraq, and claims that he played a role in the October Surprise operation of fall 1980. But the elder George Bush lined up solid Republican backing for Gates and enough accommodating Democrats – particularly Senator David Boren of Oklahoma, the Senate Intelligence Committee chairman – to push Gates through. In his memoirs, Gates denied all the charges against him, but credited his friend, David Boren, for clearing away any obstacles. "David took it as a personal challenge to get me confirmed," Gates wrote in *From the Shadows*.

Part of running interference for Gates included rejecting the testimony of witnesses who implicated Gates in scandals beginning with the alleged back-channel negotiations with Iran in 1980 through the arming of Iraq's

Saddam Hussein in the middle of the 1980s. Boren's Intelligence Committee brushed aside two witnesses connecting Gates to the alleged schemes, former Israeli intelligence official Ari Ben-Menashe and Iranian businessman Richard Babayan. Both offered detailed accounts about Gates's alleged connections to the schemes.

Ben-Menashe, who worked for Israeli military intelligence from 1977-87, first fingered Gates as an operative in the secret Iraq arms pipeline in August 1990 during an interview that I conducted with him for PBS *Frontline*. Ben-Menashe was still in jail in New York on charges of trying to sell cargo planes to Iran (charges which were later dismissed). At the time, Gates was in an obscure position, as deputy national security adviser to President George H.W. Bush and not yet a candidate for the top CIA job.

In that prison interview and later under oath to Congress, Ben-Menashe put Gates in a 1986 meeting with Chilean arms manufacturer Carlos Cardoen, who allegedly was supplying cluster bombs and chemical weapons to Saddam Hussein's army. Babayan, an Iranian exile working with Iraq, also connected Gates to the Iraqi supply lines and to Cardoen. Ben-Menashe insisted, too, that Gates joined in meetings between Republicans and senior Iranians in Paris in October 1980. Ben-Menashe said he also arranged Gates's personal help in bringing a suitcase full of cash into Miami in early 1981 to pay off some of the participants in the hostage gambit.

Gates has steadfastly denied involvement in either the October Surprise caper or the Iraqgate arms deals. "I was accused on television and in the print media by people I had never spoken to or met of selling weapons to Iraq, or walking through Miami airport with suitcases full of cash, of being with Bush in Paris in October 1980 to meet with Iranians, and on and on," Gates wrote in his memoirs. "The allegations of meetings with me around the world were easily disproved for the committee by my travel records, calendars, and countless witnesses."

Gates blamed the Ben-Menashe/Babayan charges on "the magnetic attraction of media attention in drawing out all manner of very strange people." But none of Gates's supposedly supportive evidence was ever made public by either the Senate Intelligence Committee or the later inquiries into either the October Surprise case or Iraqgate. Not one of Gates's "countless witnesses" who could vouch for Gates's whereabouts was identified. Though Boren pledged publicly to have his investigators question Babayan, they never did.

Perhaps most galling for those of us who had struggled with the question of Ben-Menashe's credibility was the Intelligence Committee's failure to test Ben-Menashe's claim that he met with Gates in Paramus, New Jersey, on the afternoon of April 20, 1989. The date was pinned down by the fact that Ben-Menashe had been under Customs surveillance in the morning. So it was a perfect test for whether Ben-Menashe – or Gates – was lying. When I first asked about this claim, congressional investigators told me that

Gates had a perfect alibi for that day. They said Gates had been with Senator Boren at a speech in Oklahoma. But when *Frontline* checked that out, we discovered that Gates's Oklahoma speech had been on April 19, a day earlier. Gates also had not been with Boren and had returned to Washington by that evening.

So where was Gates the next day? Could he have taken a quick trip to northern New Jersey? Since senior White House national security advisers keep detailed notes on their daily meetings, it should have been easy for Boren's investigators to interview someone who could vouch for Gates's whereabouts on the afternoon of April 20. But the committee chose not to nail down an alibi for Gates. The committee said further investigation wasn't needed because Gates denied going to New Jersey and his personal calendar made no reference to the trip. But the investigators couldn't tell me where Gates was that afternoon or with whom he may have met. Essentially, the alibi came down to Gates's word.

Gates's denials about a role in the Iraqgate controversy pretty much held until January 1995 when a new witness linked Gates to arms shipments to Iraq. Howard Teicher, a staffer on Ronald Reagan's National Security Council, submitted a sworn affidavit in an arms-to-Iraq case in Miami. "Under CIA Director Casey and Deputy Director Gates, the CIA authorized, approved and assisted [Carlos] Cardoen in the manufacture and sale of cluster bombs and other munitions to Iraq," Teicher wrote. In other words, an insider on Reagan's NSC staff was leveling the same Iraqgate charge against Gates that Ben-Menashe and Babayan had made earlier.

(Boren's key staff aide who helped limit the investigation of Gates was George Tenet, whose behind-the-scenes maneuvering on Gates's behalf won the personal appreciation of the senior George Bush. Those political chits would serve Tenet well a decade later when the younger George Bush protected Tenet as his own CIA director, even after the intelligence failure of September 11, 2001, and later embarrassing revelations about faulty intelligence on Iraq's weapons of mass destruction. Tenet finally resigned in July 2004 amid a growing scandal over the faulty intelligence that led the United States to war in Iraq. Gates did not respond to a requested interview for this book.)

***

U.S. policymakers weren't inclined to demand major reforms of the CIA, despite its failure to give policymakers much warning about the Soviet Union's collapse in the early 1990s. With the Soviet Union gone, neither leading Democrats nor Republicans grasped the potential danger of allowing a corrupted U.S. intelligence process to remain in place – or perhaps some politicians didn't mind the idea of a politically accommodating CIA.

There was a brief window for reform with Bill Clinton's election in 1992. Former CIA analyst Peter Dickson was among the CIA veterans to put the "politicization" issue before Clinton's incoming national security team. Dickson sent a two-page memo, dated December 10, 1992, to Samuel "Sandy" Berger, a top Clinton national security aide. Dickson urged Clinton to appoint a new CIA director who understood "the deeper internal problems relating to the politicization of intelligence and the festering morale problem within the CIA."

In urging a housecleaning, Dickson wrote, "This problem of intellectual corruption will not disappear overnight, even with vigorous remedial action. However, the new CIA director will be wise if he realizes from the start the dangers in relying on advice of senior CIA office managers who during the past 12 years advanced and prospered in their careers precisely because they had no qualms about suppressing intelligence or slanting analysis to suit the interest of Casey and Gates. This is a deep systemic problem. ...

"The lack of accountability also became a systemic problem in the 1980s. ... A recent CIA inspector general investigation confirms the near total breakdown in confidence among employee[s] that management is willing to deal honestly and objectively with their complaints. Many of them concern the lack of professional ethics and in some cases personal abuse at the hands of senior officer managers – a group of individuals beholden and therefore loyal to Gates."

But the appeals from Dickson and other CIA veterans were largely ignored by Clinton and his top aides, who were more interested in turning around the U.S. economy and enacting some modest social programs. The Clinton administration didn't want to "refight the battles of the 1980s," a senior Democrat told me. Although Gates was removed as CIA director, Clinton appointed James Woolsey, a neoconservative Democrat who had worked closely with the Reagan-Bush administrations.

One well-placed Democratic source said the incoming Clinton team defended the choice of Woolsey as a reward to some neoconservative Democrats at *The New Republic* and elsewhere who had split from George H.W. Bush and lent their support to Clinton. Under Woolsey and Clinton's subsequent CIA directors, the Gates team *sans* Gates remained in top management positions and consolidated its bureaucratic power. The old ideal of intelligence analysis free from political taint was never restored.

***

Clinton's last CIA director, George Tenet, earned more gratitude from the Bush family when he presided over a ceremony in 1999 to rename the CIA's headquarters the George Bush Center for Intelligence.

"This is a great day at the Central Intelligence Agency and a great day for our CIA Family," Tenet gushed. "We are deeply proud that you are part

of our CIA Family. As you know, the sense of family here is very strong."
(Some old-time CIA analysts, however, were troubled by the decision to put
such a partisan name on the CIA, which had been created by President Harry
Truman to provide impartial intelligence without political taint.)

Kept on by George W. Bush in 2001, Tenet continued to prove himself
a loyal bureaucrat to the second Bush administration. On February 5, 2003,
when Secretary of State Colin Powell addressed the U.N. Security Council
about Iraq's alleged WMD program, Tenet was prominently seated behind
Powell, giving the CIA's imprimatur to Powell's assertions that turned out to
be a mixture of unproved assertions, exaggerations and lies.

"If one goes back to that very long presentation [by Powell], point by
point, one finds that this was not a very honest explanation," said Greg
Thielmann, a former senior official in the State Department's Bureau of
Intelligence and Research, in an interview with PBS *Frontline*. "I have to
conclude Secretary Powell was being a loyal secretary of state, a 'good
soldier' as it were, building the administration's case before the international
community."[25]

In one telling example of how malleable the CIA's analysis had
become, a Defense Intelligence Agency employee, assigned to CIA
headquarters, was rebuffed when he objected to Powell's citation of "first-
hand" evidence from an Iraqi defector about Iraq's possession of mobile
bioweapons labs. After reviewing a draft of Powell's testimony a few days
before the secretary's U.N. speech, the DIA employee questioned the
"validity of the information" and doubted that it should be used "as the
backbone of one of our major findings for the existence of a continuing BW
[bioweapons] program!"

Inside the U.S. intelligence community, there had been concern about
the reliability of the defector, an Iraqi engineer code-named "Curve Ball,"
who was initially debriefed by the German Federal Intelligence Service in
2000. When questioned by the DIA official in May 2000, the defector arrived
suffering from a hangover. Subsequently, the Germans told the DIA official
that they had misgivings about the defector and couldn't make him available
for additional questioning.

When the DIA official restated his doubts about including the defector's
information in Powell's U.N. speech, the deputy chief of the CIA's Iraq task
force e-mailed back: "Let's keep in mind the fact that this war's going to
happen regardless of what Curve Ball said or didn't say, and that the Powers
That Be probably aren't terribly interested in whether Curve Ball knows what
he's talking about. However, in the interest of Truth, we owe somebody a
sentence or two of warning, if you honestly have reservations." The e-mail
exchange was included in the Senate Intelligence Committee's July 9, 2004,
report on the Iraqi intelligence failures.[26]

The Senate Intelligence Committee broadly condemned the CIA's
analysis on the military threat posed by Iraq, blaming analytical "groupthink"

that led the CIA and other U.S. intelligence agencies into a pattern of errors on Iraq's WMD program and other issues. "A series of failures, particularly in analytic trade craft, led to the mischaracterization of intelligence," the committee said in a 511-page report. "Most of the major key judgments [in a pivotal October 2002 National Intelligence Estimate were] either overstated, or were not supported by, the underlying intelligence reporting."[27]

Even as CIA Director Tenet put up little fight for the CIA's tattered integrity, the Bush administration didn't want to chance having its Iraqi WMD allegations vetted by any serious intelligence professionals. At the State Department, Pentagon and White House, senior political officials created their own channels for accessing raw or untested intelligence that was then used to buttress the charges against Iraq.

In a *New Yorker* article about CIA analysts on the defensive, journalist Seymour Hersh described this "stovepiping" process of sending raw intelligence to the top. Intelligence agencies have historically objected to this technique because policy makers will tend to select unvetted information that serves their purposes. "The analysts at the CIA were beaten down defending their assessments," a former CIA official told Hersh. "And they blame Tenet for not protecting them. I've never seen a government like this."[28]

***

Beyond beating down the remaining intelligence professionals unwilling to play along, Bush loyalists rhetorically beat up almost anyone who gained a public platform to question the rush to war. As George W. Bush's invasion order of March 19, 2003, neared, his administration did whatever it took to silence meaningful opposition.

To constrain the debate, Bush's backers ostracized virtually all major critics of the administration's WMD claims, including the U.N.'s chief weapons inspector Hans Blix and former U.N. weapons inspector Scott Ritter. Blacklisting campaigns were mounted against celebrities, such as actor Sean Penn and the music group Dixie Chicks, for criticizing Bush's policies. When France urged more time for U.N. weapons inspections, Bush's supporters organized boycotts of French products, poured French wine in gutters and renamed "French fries" as "Freedom Fries."

Even when U.S. inspectors failed to find the supposed WMD stockpiles, Bush's supporters continued the drumbeat of vilification against the critics. On June 12, 2003, for instance, Fox News anchor Bill O'Reilly teamed up with Representative Mike Pence, a Republican of Indiana, to air suspicions that Ritter had been bribed by the Iraqis to help them cover up their illegal weapons. Neither O'Reilly nor Pence had any evidence that Ritter accepted a bribe, so they framed the segment as a demand that the FBI investigate Ritter with the purported goal of clearing him of any suspicion of treason.

The segment noted that a London newspaper reporter had found Iraqi documents showing that Ritter had been offered some gold as gifts for his family. "I turned down the gifts and reported it to the FBI when I came back," Ritter said in an interview with Fox News. Though Ritter's statement stood unchallenged, O'Reilly and Pence demanded that the FBI disclose what it knew about Ritter's denial.

"Now, we want to know whether that was true," said O'Reilly about whether Ritter had reported the alleged bribe. "The FBI wouldn't tell us."

O'Reilly then asked Pence what he had done to get the FBI to investigate Ritter. "After that report in the British newspaper, many of us on Capitol Hill were very concerned," Pence said. "Candidly, Bill, there's no one who's done more damage to the argument of the United States that Iraq was in possession of large stores of weapons of mass destruction leading up to Operation Iraqi Freedom other than Scott Ritter, and so the very suggestion that … there's evidence of treasonous activity or even bribery, I believe, merits an investigation. I contacted the Attorney General about that directly."

While Pence's point was clear – that Ritter's role as a skeptic about Bush's WMD claims made him an appropriate target for a treason investigation – O'Reilly tried to present the case as simply a desire to corroborate Ritter's on-air statements.

"I mean Ritter came on here. He said, hey, yes, they made the offer, I declined it, I turned it over to the FBI," O'Reilly said. "All we want to do is confirm Ritter's story."[29]

**

A similar pattern of sly denigration confronted former Ambassador Joseph Wilson when he went public with the fact that he had been assigned by the CIA in 2002 to investigate suspicions that Iraq had been trying to obtain "yellowcake," a form of processed uranium from the African country of Niger. Wilson had found the claims bogus and reported his findings to the CIA in March 2002.

So Wilson was surprised when George W. Bush declared in his 2003 State of the Union address that "the British government has learned that Saddam Hussein recently sought significant quantities of uranium from Africa." As it turned out, the British government's information was based on a forgery. After being allowed to inspect the documentation, the International Atomic Energy Agency pronounced the papers "not authentic" and the Bush administration quickly backed away from the claim.[30]

Still, Wilson wrote in his memoirs, *The Politics of Truth*, that White House officials "continued to dissemble what they had actually known at the time of the President's speech. In fact, they had chosen to ignore three reports that had been in their files for nearly a year: mine as well as two others – one submitted by the American ambassador to Niger, Barbro Owens-Kirkpatrick, and the other by four-star Marine Corps General Carleton Fulford, who had also traveled there. Instead, the administration chose to give credence to forgeries so crude that even *Panorama*, the Italian weekly magazine that first received them, had declined to publish."[31]

Wilson wrote that over the next four months, he tried to convince Bush administration officials to set the record straight before he finally penned an Op-Ed for *The New York Times* on July 6, 2003. Entitled "What I Didn't Find in Africa," the article revealed that the administration had examined the Niger-yellowcake issue more than a year before Bush's State of the Union and had received intelligence debunking the claim.

Wilson's article touched off a controversy about Bush using discredited intelligence to make his case for war. As that dispute swirled through Washington, conservative pundit Robert Novak gave voice to the administration's anger about Wilson. In a July 14, 2003, column, Novak identified Wilson's wife, Valerie Plame, as a CIA employee and suggested that Wilson had gotten the Niger assignment out of nepotism.

"His wife, Valerie Plame, is an Agency operative on weapons of mass destruction," Novak wrote. "Two senior administration officials told me Wilson's wife suggested sending him to Niger to investigate the Italian report."

Wilson saw the Novak column as a crude attempt by the Bush administration to silence a whistleblower by putting his wife's career and safety in jeopardy. A week later, Wilson said he received a phone call from MSNBC's Chris Matthews, who stated that "I just got off the phone with [Bush's political adviser] Karl Rove. He says, and I quote, 'Wilson's wife is fair game.'" Stunned by the bluntness of the threat, Wilson called Rove's action "tantamount to declaring war on two U.S. citizens, both of them with years of government service."[32]

In the case of Novak's column, the disclosure of Plames's identity also could be construed as a felony under a federal law prohibiting the willful exposure of undercover CIA personnel. Several months later, the Novak story did spark a federal investigation into the possible violation of the law. George W. Bush told reporters that he hoped the leaker would be identified and "taken care of," but he also stated that he doubted the culprit would ever be caught. Meanwhile, Bush allies continued to attack Wilson.

An unnamed Republican aide on Capitol Hill told *The New York Times* that the underlying White House strategy was to "slime and defend," that is to "slime" Wilson and "defend" Bush.[33] The "slime and defend" strategy was soon obvious at conservative news outlets such as *The Wall Street Journal* editorial page and Reverend Sun Myung Moon's *Washington Times*.

"Joseph C. Wilson IV, the man accusing the White House of a vendetta against his wife, is an ex-diplomat turned Democratic partisan," declared a front-page article in *The Washington Times*. "Mr. Wilson told *The*

Washington Post he and his wife are already discussing who will play them in the movie."[34]

The Washington Times returned to its anti-Wilson campaign several days later. "As for Mr. Wilson himself, his hatred of Mr. Bush's policies borders on the pathological," wrote *Washington Times* columnist Donald Lambro. "This is a far-left Democrat who has been relentlessly bashing the President's Iraq war policies. ... The mystery behind this dubious investigation is why this Bush-hater was chosen for so sensitive a mission."[35]

The Wall Street Journal also raised questions about Wilson's motives. "Joe Wilson (Ms. Plame's husband) has made no secret of his broad disagreement with Bush policy since outing himself with an Op-Ed," the *Journal* wrote in a lead editorial on October 3, 2003.

The attacks on Wilson's alleged bias (which he denied) continued even as Bush's hand-picked Iraqi weapons inspector David Kay was confirming Wilson's findings about the falsity of the Niger allegations. In a report to the CIA and Congress, Kay said no evidence has been found to support allegations about Iraq acquiring African uranium. "To date we have not uncovered evidence that Iraq undertook significant post-1998 steps to actually build nuclear weapons or produce fissile material," Kay said.

As the Iraq-WMD examples showed, the Republican strategy for managing how the American people got to perceive a set of facts was a tag-team approach: first make sure any independent-minded intelligence analysts are cowering in one corner; then use cohorts in the news media to body-slam anyone who might wander into the ring and cause trouble. It was a pattern for controlling the flow of information that dated back to the early days of the Reagan-Bush administration – and to the curious concept of "perception management."

Chapter 14: The Magic Words

Just as the Reagan-Bush administration sought control over the CIA's intelligence analysis, the victors in the 1980 election wanted a handle on what the American people were hearing from the national news media. Still blaming the press corps for the Watergate scandal and the American defeat in Vietnam, the Reagan-Bush team was determined to put journalists back in their place. The goal was to make sure that the news media could never again threaten Republican political power or – in the view of conservatives – never again undermine U.S. national interests.

The process for building this conservative Counter-Establishment had begun in the 1970s, following Richard Nixon's recognition of this Republican vulnerability and William Simon's coordination of conservative foundations to inject money into right-wing media outlets and think tanks. With this money priming the conservative pump, policy papers and opinion articles began to flow out of right-wing institutions, most notably the Heritage Foundation. New conservative magazines began to fill the news racks. Conservative editorial pages, such as *The Wall Street Journal*'s, staked out aggressive pro-Reagan-Bush positions. An expanding network of conservative activists, from groups like Reed Irvine's Accuracy in Media, scoured mainstream news articles looking for evidence of "liberal bias."

Many working-level journalists bent over backwards not to be tagged as "liberal" because they knew that most senior editors and network executives tilted conservative. At the Associated Press, for instance, AP's general manager Keith Fuller, the company's top news executive, was known to share many of the Reagan-Bush political views. Although AP took pride in its reputation for impartiality, Fuller eventually began speaking openly about his opinion that the arrival of the Reagan-Bush administration was a positive turning point for the nation.

"As we look back on the turbulent Sixties, we shudder with the memory of a time that seemed to tear at the very sinews of this country," Fuller said in a speech on January 28, 1982, in Worcester, Massachusetts. "While our soldiers were dying in old Indochina, our young people, at least some of them, were chanting familiar communist slogans on the campuses around this nation. … Popular entertainers of that day were openly supporting a communist regime, denouncing the American position and a propaganda barrage against America was loosed in places like France and Britain and Scandinavia, Italy, Greece, all carefully financed and orchestrated by the USSR."

According to Fuller, America continued to decline through the 1970s before Ronald Reagan's election put the country back on the right track. "I think it changed at the ballot box in November. And I'm not speaking here of Democrats or Republicans at all. Totally apolitical. I think a nation is crying, 'Enough.' A nation is saying, 'We don't really believe that criminal rights should take precedence over the rights of victims. We don't believe that the union of Adam and Bruce is really the same as Adam and Eve in the eyes of Creation. We don't believe that people should cash welfare checks and spend them on booze and narcotics. We don't really believe that a simple prayer or a pledge of allegiance is against the national interest in the classroom. We're sick of your social engineering. We're fed up with your tolerance of crime, drugs and pornography. But most of all, we're sick of your self-perpetuating, burdening bureaucracy weighing ever more heavily on our backs."

Though Fuller presented his commentary as analysis, rank-and-file AP journalists understood that his litany of complaints represented his personal opinions. While that did not mean that all AP reporters would bend their journalism to the right to please the boss, it did mean that there was an additional burden on reporters who uncovered information that would upset the Reagan-Bush administration. Like the analysts who were under pressure at the CIA, reporters knew that in the murky world of mixed or uncertain evidence, they couldn't expect much support if the White House lodged a complaint or if conservative pressure groups went on the attack.

So, in the weeks after the Reagan-Bush election, just as the CIA's analysts were getting softened up by accusations of being soft on the Soviets, the Washington press corps was confronting a new and more hostile environment, too. The Reagan-Bush victory, in effect, merged the Right's fledgling operations – designed to "controversialize" wayward reporters – with the immense power of the federal government, an ideological public-private partnership that would change the face of American politics. As this collaborative infrastructure expanded, it let the Reagan-Bush administration inject intelligence-style operations into the American body politic, much as the CIA inserted propaganda into the politics of other countries.

The intelligence world's phrase for manipulating how a population understood events and viewed politicians was "perception management," the magic words of the professional propagandist. To counter an adversary or promote an ally, the CIA cared less about truth than consequence. Reality became less important than how people perceived reality. If a target population thought that an honest leader was corrupt, he might as well have been corrupt. If a population saw a new government as representing the nation's interests, it mattered little that the regime actually might be standing in for American interests. Controlling the flow of information through the news media was crucial to this process.

In the early 1980s, this concept of "perception management" came home to roost. With the arrival of the new administration, intelligence veterans – including Vice President George H.W. Bush – held down key jobs in the Executive Branch. Hardliners William Casey and Robert Gates were in charge of the CIA. Plus, some intelligence right-wingers, still fuming about the Vietnam War protests and Watergate, saw some of their fellow Americans as a kind of "enemy within." It only made sense, therefore, that these intelligence experts would turn their propaganda skills onto the most important target population of all: the American people. The key would be building an infrastructure and applying the techniques for managing how Americans perceived the world.

The overriding motive behind the strategy was summed up by J. Michael Kelly, a deputy assistant secretary of the Air Force for force support, in an address to a National Defense University on "low-intensity conflict," more commonly known as guerrilla wars. "The most critical special operations we have ... today is to persuade the American people that the communists are out to get us," Kelly told the conference. "If we win the war of ideas, we will win everywhere else."[1]

***

Despite Ronald Reagan's decisive victory in 1980, the administration still had a hard sell in promoting its counterinsurgency plans for Central America. Reagan-Bush hardliners saw the region as a crucial front in an escalating Cold War. But many Americans remained doubtful. The pain of the Vietnam War, which had ended only six years earlier, had not been forgotten.

The Reagan-Bush hardliners also stumbled out of the starting blocks, seeming to side too forcefully with unsavory right-wing military regimes in countries, such as El Salvador and Guatemala. While most Americans weren't fans of the leftist Sandinistas who had seized power from the Somoza military dictatorship in Nicaragua, the idea of supporting the remnants of that ousted government wasn't very appealing either.

Clumsily, the Reagan-Bush team sought to defend the Salvadoran military from allegations that its soldiers had participated in the rape-murder of four American churchwomen on December 2, 1980. On that night, two of the women, Ursuline nun Dorothy Kazel and lay missionary Jean Donovan, drove a white mini-van to the international airport outside San Salvador to pick up Maryknoll nuns Ita Ford and Maura Clarke, who had attended a conference in Nicaragua. The four women then headed back to the city.

After leaving the airport, the van encountered a roadblock manned by a squad of Salvadoran soldiers who took the four churchwomen into custody.

After a phone call apparently to a superior officer, the sergeant in charge said the orders were to kill the women. The soldiers raped them first and then executed the women with high-powered rifles at close range.

The atrocity was just one of hundreds committed by the right-wing Salvadoran security forces each month in a grotesque counterinsurgency campaign that was less a war against guerrillas than the systematic torture and murder of suspected leftists who were unlucky enough to be caught up in military sweeps in the cities and the countryside. All told, some 70,000 people would die in the violence, the vast majority slaughtered by government security forces.

But the rape-murder of the four churchwomen stood out because they were Americans and because the U.S. public had yet to grow accustomed to the brutal logic of anti-communist counter-insurgencies that made few distinctions between armed fighters and their unarmed political sympathizers. Many of the Reagan-Bush hardliners, however, already had crossed that line. They had supported similar ruthless operations in Argentina and Chile – and their world view of an ascendant Soviet Union poised to enslave the United States made even the most extreme measures seem palatable.

So, instead of joining U.S. Ambassador Robert White in denouncing the Salvadoran military's apparent role in raping and murdering four U.S. citizens, the incoming Reagan-Bush hardliners acted like defense lawyers for the Salvadoran government.

Jeane Kirkpatrick, Reagan's nominee to be U.S. ambassador to the United Nations, said, "I don't think the government [of El Salvador] was responsible. The nuns were not just nuns; the nuns were political activists. We ought to be a little more clear-cut about this than we usually are. They were political activists on behalf of the [leftist opposition] Frente and somebody who is using violence to oppose the Frente killed them."[2]

Later, Reagan's first Secretary of State, Al Haig, told the House Foreign Affairs Committee that "I would like to suggest to you that some of the investigations would lead one to believe that perhaps the vehicle that the nuns were riding in may have tried to run a roadblock or may have accidentally been perceived to have been doing so, and there may have been an exchange of fire." State Department officials responsible for the investigation were stunned at Haig's comments. All the evidence pointed to a cold-blooded murder: the women had been taken to a remote location; they had been sexually assaulted and executed. There was no evidence of attempted evasion ending in a shoot-out.

While one might have expected liberals to be furious over the churchwomen case, the fury often seemed stronger on the Right, over alleged exaggeration of crimes blamed on the Salvadoran security forces. At one Washington press conference I attended, families of the churchwomen described what they had learned about the murders and criticized the Reagan-Bush administration's foot-dragging. A small group of right-wing journalists began asking hostile questions. "They weren't raped," one man yelled at the stunned family members. Even after Ronald Reagan's victory, there was a chip-on-the-shoulder attitude among these conservatives, which would become possibly their most enduring trait over the next quarter century.

In the early days of the Reagan-Bush administration, that anger often was directed at mainstream journalists who reported about the ongoing slaughter in Central America. One of the conservatives' favorite targets became Raymond Bonner, who reported on the Salvadoran violence for *The New York Times* and traced much of the killing to government security forces. The fury against Bonner reached a peak in late January 1982 after he and *Washington Post* reporter Alma Guillermoprieto reported on an alleged massacre by the Salvadoran army of civilians in and around the remote village of El Mozote in the northeastern Morazan province of El Salvador.

In a front-page article on January 27, 1982, Bonner reported that the Atlacatl Battalion, the first U.S.-trained Salvadoran army unit, had killed about 800 men, women and children after seizing the village in December 1981. A similar story by Guillermoprieto appeared the same day in *The Washington Post*, as President Reagan was preparing the next day to certify that the Salvadoran security forces were making a "concerted" effort to respect human rights and the government was "achieving substantial control over all elements of its own armed forces," a prerequisite for continuing military aid.

As pieced together a dozen years later by *The New Yorker*'s Mark Danner – after forensic investigations of the site and interviews with survivors – the Salvadoran soldiers began the massacre on December 11. The soldiers bound the hands of the men, executing them by using machetes for decapitations and automatic rifles fired at their heads. The women were the next to die, with younger ones including girls as young as 10, first being taken to the hills to be gang-raped before being killed. The older women were dragged into a house and were shot to death.

The screaming children were locked in another house. Soldiers entered and began hacking the children with machetes or using rifle butts to smash the children's skulls. Other children were herded into the church sacristy and were shot by soldiers using U.S.-supplied M-16s. Still other children were burned alive when the soldiers set the buildings on fire. The massacre extended to other populated areas outside the village of El Mozote.

Though the articles by Bonner and Guillermoprieto lacked some of those details, they described a major massacre occurring in El Mozote, causing serious embarrassment for President Reagan, who issued the required human rights certification anyway. To check on the reports, the U.S. Embassy in San Salvador sent two officials, Todd Greentree and John McKay, to Morazan province. They interviewed terrified refugees and concluded that "there had been a massacre," but could not reach the site of the massacre because of ongoing military activity.

Greentree and McKay reported the results of their trip to senior embassy officials who then massaged the information into a cable for transmission to Washington. The cable minimized evidence of Salvadoran military guilt. One diplomat who worked on the cable said the embassy knew that the White House didn't want confirmation of the massacre, so the report was drafted "intentionally devoid of judgment."[3]

In Washington, the watered-down cable gave the administration an opening to delete even the mixed results of the Greentree-McKay mission and simply challenge the newspaper stories as unfounded. Assistant secretaries of state Thomas Enders and Elliott Abrams went up to Capitol Hill where they denounced the El Mozote massacre stories as false or at least wildly exaggerated.

"There is no evidence to confirm that government forces systematically massacred civilians in the operations zone, or that the number of civilians even remotely approached the 733 or 926 victims cited in the press," Enders testified. He dismissed the two newspaper articles with the observation that "there were probably not more than 300" people living in El Mozote at the time, a clever sleight of hand since Enders referred to the village's normal population – not including the surrounding areas and not taking into account refugees who had fled into the village during the military sweep. International aid workers estimated the area's population at about 1,000 in December 1981.

The Enders-Abrams testimony signaled open season on Bonner and *The New York Times*. Accuracy in Media, the right-wing press watchdog group, and *The Wall Street Journal*'s editorial page led the attacks, accusing Bonner of alleged leftist sympathies and gullibility for accepting a supposedly bogus story from Marxist guerrillas. A lead *Wall Street Journal* editorial called Bonner "overly credulous." The combined attacks from the administration and the conservative press, singling out an individual *New York Times* journalist, sent chills down the spines of reporters and editors at leading news outlets throughout Washington and New York.

As the pressure built, *Times* executive editor Abe Rosenthal flew to Central America to assess the complaints first-hand. Considered by many to be politically neoconservative with strong sympathies for Reagan-Bush foreign policies, Rosenthal soon limited Bonner's role in the *Times*' bureau and word spread that Bonner would be recalled.

When I was in El Salvador on an Associated Press reporting assignment in fall 1982, I spent some time with two senior U.S. officials in the region who claimed credit for orchestrating Bonner's ouster. "We finally got rid of that son of a bitch," a ranking U.S. military officer told me. In early 1983, Rosenthal did recall Bonner from Central America and stuck him in an obscure job on the business desk in New York. Bonner soon resigned from the *Times.**

***

The Reagan-Bush administration had similar public relations problems with Guatemala, another Central American country dominated by a right-wing oligarchy and kept in line by a repressive security service long renowned for torture and assassination. Despite that reputation, the Reagan-Bush administration sought to overturn or circumvent human rights embargoes that the Carter administration had imposed on Guatemala. The Reagan-Bush hardliners saw Guatemala as another important front in America's battle to hold off the ascendant Soviet superpower. In that view, virtually anything was justified, a position shared by the Guatemalan military.

"Believing that the ends justified everything, the military and the state security forces blindly pursued the anticommunist struggle, without respect for any legal principles or the most elemental ethical and religious values, and in this way, completely lost any semblance of human morals," stated Christian Tomuschat, a German jurist who was chairman of Guatemala's official Historical Clarification Commission, which issued a report in 1999 on decades of human rights abuses. "Within the framework of the counterinsurgency operations carried out between 1981 and 1983, in certain regions of the country agents of the Guatemalan state committed acts of genocide against groups of the Mayan people."[4]

The commission's report documented that in the 1980s, the Guatemalan army committed 626 massacres against Mayan villages. The army "completely exterminated Mayan communities, destroyed their livestock and crops," the report said. In the north, the report termed the slaughter a "genocide." The report concluded that the U.S. government also gave money and training to a Guatemalan military that committed "acts of genocide" against the Mayans.[5]

"The massacres that eliminated entire Mayan villages ... are neither perfidious allegations nor figments of the imagination, but an authentic chapter in Guatemala's history," the commission said. Besides carrying out murder and "disappearances," the army routinely engaged in torture and rape. "The rape of women, during torture or before being murdered, was a

---

* The truth about El Mozote would not be clarified until the civil war ended in 1992 and a United Nations forensic team excavated the area, finding hundreds of skeletons including many tiny ones of children. Bonner was subsequently rehired by the *Times*, but no one in El Salvador or in Washington was ever punished in connection with the El Mozote massacre, either for the killings or the cover-up.

common practice" by the military and paramilitary forces, the report said. The commission also found that the "government of the United States, through various agencies including the CIA, provided direct and indirect support for some [of these] state operations."

The commission estimated that the Guatemalan conflict claimed some 200,000 lives with the worst of the bloodletting occurring in the 1980s. Based on a review of about 20 percent of the dead, the panel blamed the army for 93 percent of the killings and leftist guerrillas for three percent. Four percent were listed as unresolved. The report did not single out culpable individuals either in Guatemala or the United States.

So, in the early 1980s – as this bloodbath was underway – the new Reagan-Bush administration faced a challenge cleaning up the image of the Guatemalan government. As in El Salvador, a favored administration technique was to discredit anyone presenting information about Guatemala's human rights abuses. That strategy was pursued even though the U.S. government was aware that the Guatemalan security forces were guilty of widespread abuses, as revealed in the administration's own internal documents. According to "secret" cables, the CIA was confirming Guatemalan government massacres in 1981-82 even as the administration was deflecting questions about Guatemala's record and moving to loosen a military aid ban.

In April 1981, for instance, a secret CIA cable described a massacre at Cocob, near Nebaj in the Ixil Indian territory. According to the cable, government troops on April 17, 1981, attacked the area believed to support leftist guerrillas. The cable cited a CIA source saying "the social population appeared to fully support the guerrillas" and "the soldiers were forced to fire at anything that moved." The CIA cable added that "the Guatemalan authorities admitted that 'many civilians' were killed in Cocob, many of whom undoubtedly were non-combatants."

Despite the CIA account and other similar reports, Reagan permitted Guatemala's army to buy $3.2 million in military trucks and jeeps in June 1981. To permit the sale, Reagan removed the vehicles from a list of military equipment that was covered by the human rights embargo. Apparently confident of the Reagan-Bush administration's support, the Guatemalan government continued its political repression without apology.

According to a State Department cable on October 5, 1981, Guatemalan leaders left no doubt about their plans when they met with retired General Vernon Walters, Reagan's roving ambassador and Bush's former deputy at the CIA. Guatemala's military leader, General Fernando Romeo Lucas Garcia, "made clear that his government will continue as before – that the repression will continue. He reiterated his belief that the repression is working and that the guerrilla threat will be successfully routed."

Human rights groups saw the same picture of continued repression. The Inter-American Human Rights Commission released a report on October 15,

1981, blaming the Guatemalan government for "thousands of illegal executions."[6] But the Reagan administration was set on justifying the ugly scene. A State Department "white paper," released in December 1981, blamed the violence on leftist "extremist groups" and their "terrorist methods" prompted and supported by Cuba's Fidel Castro.

In March 1982, General Efrain Rios Montt seized power in Guatemala in a military coup. An avowed fundamentalist Christian, he immediately impressed Washington where President Reagan hailed Rios Montt as "a man of great personal integrity." But under Rios Montt, the slaughter in the countryside and selective assassinations in the cities only grew worse.

By July 1982, Rios Montt had begun a new scorched-earth campaign called his "rifles and beans" policy. The slogan meant that pacified Indians would get "beans," while all others could expect to be the target of army "rifles." In October, he secretly gave *carte blanche* to the feared "Archivos" intelligence unit to expand "death squad" operations. Based at the Presidential Palace, the "Archivos" masterminded many of Guatemala's most notorious assassinations.

The U.S. embassy was soon hearing more accounts of the army conducting Indian massacres. However, during a swing through Latin America, Reagan discounted the mounting reports of hundreds of Mayan villages being eradicated. On December 4, 1982, after meeting with dictator Rios Montt, Reagan hailed the general as "totally dedicated to democracy" and asserted that Rios Montt's government was "getting a bum rap."

On January 7, 1983, Reagan lifted the ban on military aid to Guatemala and authorized the sale of $6 million in military hardware. Approval covered spare parts for UH-1H helicopters and A-37 aircraft used in counterinsurgency operations. Radios, batteries and battery chargers were also in the package. State Department spokesman John Hughes said political violence in the cities had "declined dramatically" and that rural conditions had improved, too.

In February 1983, however, a secret CIA cable noted a rise in "suspect right-wing violence" with kidnappings of students and teachers. Bodies of victims were appearing in ditches and gullies. CIA sources traced these political murders to Rios Montt's order to the "Archivos" in October to "apprehend, hold, interrogate and dispose of suspected guerrillas as they saw fit."

Despite these grisly facts on the ground, the annual State Department human rights survey praised the supposedly improved human rights situation in Guatemala. "The overall conduct of the armed forces had improved by late in the year" 1982, the report stated.

***

The Nicaraguan contras – short for counterrevolutionaries – presented the Reagan-Bush administration with another public-relations problem that needed managing. Taking shape from the remnants of dictator Anastasio Somoza's notorious National Guard, the contras represented an unruly lot who operated along Nicaragua's northern border with Honduras. The administration saw the contras as a weapon to stop the spread of revolution in Central America and eventually to drive the Sandinistas from power. But the contras soon gained their own reputation for brutality, rape and drug trafficking – a reality that needed shielding from the American people.

By 1981, the contras were under the tutelage of Argentine intelligence officers, fresh from their own "dirty war" that had killed thousands of Argentines, many after arrest and torture and many without acknowledgement of a victim's fate. That practice of "disappearing" political dissidents was already being called the "Argentine method" as it spread through Central America and was adopted by the Salvadoran and Guatemalan security forces.

The dispatch of Argentine trainers to Central America to work with the contras was also not out of character. As a member of the Chilean-led cross-border assassination program, known as Condor, Argentina's security services were already active in an international crusade against communists and leftists. Plus, the Sandinistas had given refuge to a number of hunted South American leftists. So training the contras, in many ways, was a logical extension of Argentina's duties within the Condor operation.

Argentina's contingent of contra trainers was headed by Colonel Osvaldo Ribeiro, considered an expert in the tactics of "disappearances."[7] Ribeiro helped the initial contra force coalesce as "the Fifteenth of September Legion" behind a former Somoza National Guard officer, Colonel Enrique Bermudez. The initial contra force was soon engaging in acts of terrorism, including an assault on a Costa Rican radio station that was broadcasting news critical of the Argentine "dirty war." Three Costa Ricans died in the attack.

Inside Honduras, the Argentines also organized the contras into roving "death squads" that helped the Honduran military "disappear" almost 200 labor leaders, students and other political activists during the 1980s, according to an official report issued by Honduran human rights ombudsman Leo Valladares in 1993. The report, entitled "The Facts Speak for Themselves," identified for blame a dozen of the contras' Argentine advisers, including Ribeiro, and the group's money-launderer Leonardo Sanchez-Reisse.

Valladares said "systematic, clandestine and organized" disappearances in Honduras started in 1979, coinciding with the arrival of the Argentine military advisers who began training the contras. As in Argentina's "dirty war," many Honduran victims were kidnapped, taken to clandestine jails, and tortured before secret execution, the human rights report said.

Another secret tactic passed on to the contras was how to finance operations through drug trafficking and drug money laundering. According to Argentine money-launderer and contra trainer Sanchez-Reisse, Argentine intelligence arranged an early flow of drug money into the contras' coffers. In closed testimony to Senator John Kerry's contra-drug investigation in 1987, Sanchez-Reisse said Bolivian drug kingpin Roberto Suarez earmarked more than $30 million to support right-wing paramilitary operations in Central and South America, including the contra war.

Sanchez-Reisse, who oversaw the operation's money laundering, said the drug money first helped finance a 1980 military coup in Bolivia that ousted a democratically elected left-of-center government. Argentine intelligence officers – and a cadre of European neo-Nazis – assisted in the putsch, which became known as the Cocaine Coup because it gave the drug lords free run of the country.

Sanchez-Reisse said he and an Argentine neo-fascist "death squad" leader named Raul Guglielminetti oversaw the Miami-based money-laundering front that shared some profits with the contras. Sanchez-Reisse said the Miami money laundry used two front companies – Argenshow, a promoter of U.S. entertainment acts in Argentina, and the Silver Dollar, a pawn shop that was licensed to sell guns. Sanchez-Reisse said the real work of the companies was the transfer of Roberto Suarez's $30 million into political and paramilitary operations that had the blessings of the CIA.

The money for the Bolivian Cocaine Coup "was shipped from Bahamas to United States," Sanchez-Reisse said. "It was money [that] belonged to people connected with drug traffic in Bolivia at the time, specifically Mr. Roberto Suarez in Bolivia."

The Cocaine Coup had its own extraordinary history. One organizer of the Bolivian coup was World War II Nazi fugitive Klaus Barbie, the notorious "Butcher of Lyon" who was working as a Bolivian intelligence officer under the name Klaus Altmann. Barbie drew up plans modeled after the 1976 Argentine coup and contacted hardliners in the Argentine security services for help. One of the first Argentine officers to arrive, Lieutenant Alfred Mario Mingolla, later described Barbie's role to German journalist Kai Hermann. "Before our departure, we received a dossier on [Barbie]," Mingolla said. "There it stated that he was of great use to Argentina because he played an important role in all of Latin America in the fight against communism."

Beyond the routine planning, Barbie enlisted a younger generation of Italian neo-fascists, including Stefano della Chiaie, who was already working with the Argentine "death squads." Barbie established a secret lodge called "Thule," where he lectured his followers underneath swastikas by candlelight.[8] The Bolivian military coup leader was Colonel Luis Arce-Gomez, the cousin of drug lord Roberto Suarez. Dr. Alfred Candia, the

Bolivian leader of the World Anti-Communist League, coordinated the arrival of the paramilitary operatives.

Planning for the coup proceeded almost in the open. There were reports about a June 17, 1980, meeting between six of Bolivia's largest drug traffickers and the Bolivian military conspirators to hammer out financial arrangements for the future protection of the cocaine trade. The plotting was so brazen that one La Paz businessman dubbed the operation the Cocaine Coup, a name that stuck.[9]

On July 17, 1980, the Cocaine Coup unfolded, spearheaded by Barbie and his neo-fascist acolytes who went by the name Fiancés of Death. "The masked thugs were not Bolivian; they spoke Spanish with German, French and Italian accents," wrote Michael Levine, an undercover Drug Enforcement Administration agent operating in South America. "Their uniforms bore neither national identification nor any markings, although many of them wore Nazi swastika armbands and insignias."[10]

The slaughter was fierce. When the putschists stormed the national labor headquarters, they wounded labor leader Marcelo Quiroga, who had led the battle to indict former military dictator Hugo Banzer on drug and corruption charges. Quiroga "was dragged off to police headquarters to be the object of a game played by some of the torture experts imported from Argentina's dreaded Mechanic School of the Navy," Levine wrote. "These experts applied their 'science' to Quiroga as a lesson to the Bolivians, who were a little backward in such matters. They kept Quiroga alive and suffering for hours. His castrated, tortured body was found days later in a place called 'The Valley of the Moon' in southern La Paz."[11]

To DEA agent Levine back in Buenos Aires, it was soon clear "that the primary goal of the revolution was the protection and control of Bolivia's cocaine industry. All major drug traffickers in prison were released, after which they joined the neo-Nazis in their rampage. Government buildings were invaded and trafficker files were either carried off or burned. Government employees were tortured and shot, the women tied and repeatedly raped by the paramilitaries and the freed traffickers."

Colonel Arce-Gomez, the pot-bellied cousin of drug lord Roberto Suarez, grabbed broad powers as Interior Minister. General Luis Garcia Meza became Bolivia's new president. After the coup, Arce-Gomez went into partnership with big narco-traffickers, including Mafia-connected Cuban-American smugglers based in Miami. According to DEA agent Levine, Arce-Gomez bragged to one trafficker, "we will flood America's borders with cocaine," a boast that proved prescient.

"Bolivia soon became the principal supplier of cocaine base to the then fledgling Colombian cartels, making themselves the main suppliers of cocaine to the United States," Levine said. Cartel money-launderer Ramon Milian Rodriguez corroborated the importance of the Bolivian supply line for the Colombian cartels in the early days. "Bolivia was much more significant than the other countries," Milian Rodriguez said in testimony to Senator Kerry's contra-drug investigation on April 6, 1988.

***

Another significant aspect of the Cocaine Coup was that it was the point of contamination for the Nicaraguan contra operation, another secret that would have to be protected by the Reagan-Bush administration. Though both President Reagan and Vice President Bush were sympathetic to the harsh anticommunism practiced by the Argentines and their Latin American allies, the disclosure of cocaine trafficking that implicated the contra movement would have devastated the fragile public support for the operation.

Still, the Argentine training and support for the contras proceeded. The Argentine intelligence officers who had assisted in the Cocaine Coup simply moved their base of operation from Bolivia to Honduras, where the ragtag force of former Nicaraguan national guardsmen was taking shape. Argentine money-launderer Sanchez-Reisse said the money from the Argenshow-Silver Dollar laundry was soon flowing into the contras' coffers. Sanchez-Reisse said his partner, Guglielminetti, befriended American farmer John Hull, who let the contras use his ranch in Costa Rica near the Nicaraguan border.

In the months after the Cocaine Coup, the Bolivian drug lords also strengthened their ties to Cuban-American drug dealers in Miami, U.S. government records showed. On December 16, 1980, Cuban-American Ricardo Morales told a Florida prosecutor that he had become an informer in Operation Tick-Talks, a Miami-based investigation that implicated Cuban-American Frank Castro and other Cuban exiles in a conspiracy to import cocaine from the new military rulers of Bolivia.

By 1981, Argentine-trained contra operatives also were opening their own drug-trafficking channels, U.S. intelligence officers reported internally. According to a draft CIA field report in June 1981, the Fifteenth of September Legion, also known as ARDREN, chose early on "to stoop to criminal activities in order to feed and clothe their cadre." A September 1981 cable to CIA headquarters stated that the group had started using drug trafficking. Two ARDREN members made the first delivery of drugs to Miami in July 1981, the CIA cable reported.

Other contra-connected drug traffickers also dealt with the Bolivian drug lords. Norwin Meneses, a notorious Nicaraguan drug smuggler, went to work as a fund-raiser for the contras, a relationship that helped him conduct his drug business. One of his lieutenants, Oscar Danilo Blandon, said he and Meneses were *en route* to Bolivia to complete a drug transaction in 1982 when they stopped in Honduras for meetings with contra commander Enrique Bermudez, who didn't seem troubled by their means of raising money for the contra cause. "The ends justify the means," Bermudez told the drug smugglers, according to Blandon's later statements to U.S. government investigators.

After the Bermudez meeting, Meneses and Blandon headed to the airport in Tegucigalpa to complete their journey to Bolivia, but Blandon was stopped by Honduran authorities who suspected correctly that the $100,000 in his possession was for an illicit drug deal. At that touchy moment, Nicaraguan contras intervened and assured the Hondurans that the $100,000 belonged to the contra movement, enabling the drug dealers to fly to Bolivia and complete their deal, Blandon said.

In early 1982, with knowledge of contra drug activity spreading throughout the U.S. law enforcement community, CIA Director William Casey came up with a plan that effectively shut off the legal requirement that CIA officers in the field share with the Justice Department information about criminal activities by operatives. Casey lobbied Attorney General William French Smith to exempt the CIA from a duty to report drug crimes by its foreign assets, a waiver Smith granted on February 11, 1982, in a secret memorandum of understanding.

Chapter 15: War at Home

The combination of gross human rights violations by Guatemalan and Salvadoran security forces and drug connections within the fledging Nicaraguan contra movement presented the Reagan-Bush administration with a dilemma. If the conservatives' assessment of a growing Soviet menace was correct and if Moscow's plan was to attack the United States from beachheads in Central America, then drastic action would be required, even if that meant tolerating unsavory behavior by some allies.

But that was a hard sell to the American people, who – polls showed – didn't share the administration's alarm about leftist guerrillas in El Salvador and Guatemala or the Sandinista government in Nicaragua. So what to do?

Inside the new Reagan-Bush administration, political advisers bemoaned the lack of adequate media resources to make their case. Despite some progress in building a rudimentary conservative media, the machinery still wasn't there to carry out a sustained "political action" campaign that would turn around the perceptions of the press corps, the Congress and the American people.

Some Reagan-Bush officials bristled at restrictions on government propaganda that exist in a democratic society compared with totalitarian systems. "The totalitarian states whose intelligence and propaganda apparatus we face have no internal problem in denying their citizens access to information or even flagrantly lying to them," wrote Kate Semerad, an external-relations official at the Agency for International Development, in a summary of the internal administration debate in the early 1980s. "We have neither the apparatus nor the legal mechanism which would allow the success of an effort to emulate that of Moscow, Habana [sic] and Managua."

But the Semerad memo envisioned the creation of a U.S. propaganda apparatus that would level the supposedly tilted playing field. "We can and must go over the heads of our Marxist opponents directly to the American people," Semerad wrote. "Our targets would be: within the United States, the Congress, specifically the Foreign Affairs Committees and their staffs, ... the general public [and] the media."

The original name for the Reagan-Bush administration's plan to mount its own propaganda campaign within the United States was "Project Truth." It later merged with a broader program that combined domestic and international propaganda under the umbrella of "Project Democracy." The central figure in the administration's media operations was Walter Raymond Jr., a 30-year veteran of the CIA's propaganda office who was assigned to the National Security Council staff in 1982.

President Reagan took the first formal step to create the propaganda bureaucracy on January 14, 1983, by signing National Security Decision Directive 77, entitled "Management of Public Diplomacy Relative to National Security." The secret directive deemed it "necessary to strengthen the organization, planning and coordination of the various aspects of public diplomacy of the United States Government." Reagan defined public diplomacy broadly as "those actions of the U.S. Government designed to generate support for our national security objectives."

To direct these "public diplomacy" campaigns, Reagan ordered the creation of a Special Planning Group – or SPG – within the National Security Council. "The SPG ... shall ensure that a wide-ranging program of effective initiatives is developed and implemented to support national security policy, objectives and decisions."

Reagan turned to Raymond to manage the public diplomacy operations at home and abroad. The veteran CIA propagandist was a slight, soft-spoken New Yorker who reminded some of a character from a John leCarré spy novel, an intelligence officer who "easily fades into the woodwork," according to one acquaintance. Associates said Raymond's CIA career stayed close to headquarters because of special care required for a sick child. Still, he rose to senior levels of the CIA's Directorate of Operations – the DO which is responsible for spying, paramilitary actions and propaganda – where his last job title was considered so revealing about the CIA's disinformation capabilities that it remained a highly classified secret.

Critics would later question the assignment of a career CIA propagandist to carry out an information program that had both domestic and foreign components. After all, in CIA propaganda operations, the goal is not to inform a target population, but rather to manipulate it. The trick is to achieve a specific intelligence objective, not foster a full-and-open democratic debate. In such cases, CIA tactics include disinformation to spread confusion or psychological operations to exploit cultural weaknesses. A skillful CIA operation will first carefully analyze what "themes" can work with a specific culture and then select – and if necessary distort – information that advances those "themes." The CIA also looks for media outlets to disseminate the propaganda. Some are created; others are compromised with bribes to editors, reporters or owners.

Raymond naturally carried his professional experiences with him to his new job, which he defined as engaging in the "war of ideas," a phrase that is meant less metaphorically than some outsiders read it. To national security experts in the Reagan-Bush administration, the "war of ideas" was, in many ways, an extension of the life-and-death struggle between the United States and its enemies. Within the then-trendy concept of "low-intensity conflict," enemy propaganda and political activities were placed on the lower end of the spectrum that extended to include guerrilla conflicts, regional war and even nuclear conflagration.

In later testimony to the congressional Iran-Contra committees, Raymond said his first concern in confronting his new responsibilities was the administration's lack of an infrastructure to carry out a domestic "public diplomacy" campaign. "We were not configured effectively to deal with the war of ideas," he said.

In early 1983, less than two weeks after Reagan signed NSDD-77, Raymond volunteered his professional advice for creating what he called this "new art form" in foreign policy. "It is essential that a serious and deep commitment of talent and time be dedicated to this," Raymond wrote in a January 25, 1983, memo to then NSC adviser William Clark. "Programs such as Central America, European strategic debate, Yellow Rain [the later-debunked allegations that the Soviets were using a yellow chemical warfare agent], and even Afghanistan have foundered by a failure to orchestrate sufficient resources and forces [for] these efforts."

Raymond advocated a "public diplomacy" apparatus that would "provide central focus for insuring greater commitment of resources, greater concentration of effort in support of our foreign policies; call it political action, if you will." At the CIA, "political action" is a term of art encompassing a wide range of activities, both overt and covert, to achieve a desired political result.

But federal law was an obstacle on the domestic side of the proposed operation. Under presidential executive orders, the CIA was barred from influencing U.S. politics and policies, a safeguard designed to prevent the spy agency from corrupting U.S. democratic institutions. Federal law also prohibited the Executive Branch from spending money to lobby Congress, except for the traditional practices of giving testimony, making speeches and talking one-on-one with members. Beyond the "bully pulpit," Presidents weren't allowed to spend taxpayers' money to disseminate propaganda or to organize grassroots lobbying campaigns to pressure Congress.

Sensitive to the CIA restriction, Raymond formally resigned from the CIA in April 1983 so "there would be no question whatsoever of any contamination of this," he said in his Iran-Contra testimony. But the larger question remained whether Raymond's "new art form" amounted to a CIA-style propaganda campaign directed at the American people.

Raymond cracked the whip within the newly formed Central American Public Diplomacy Task Force, an interagency committee that met every Thursday morning. In that job, he coordinated the public diplomacy work of the State Department, the United States Information Agency, the Agency for International Development, the Defense Department, the CIA and the NSC staff. The minutes of those Thursday morning meetings showed Raymond as the bureaucratic taskmaster, making sure documents were released on time, checking the budgets and ensuring adequate staffing.

Given the Reagan-Bush emphasis on stressing the positive and containing the negative about its Central American policies, Raymond's team made that region its top focus. On May 5, 1983, a classified "public diplomacy strategy paper" noted that "Our Central American policy is facing an essentially apathetic and in some particulars hostile U.S. public. There is serious opposition in Congress ... As far as our Central American policy is concerned, the press perceives that: the USG [U.S. government] is placing too much emphasis on a military solution, as well as being allied with inept, right-wing governments or groups. ...

"The focus on Nicaragua has not been the repression of pluralism by the Sandinistas but on the alleged U.S.-backed 'covert' war against the Sandinistas. Moreover, the opposition to the Sandinistas is widely perceived as being led by former Somozistas rather than being broad-based and including many who initially supported the Sandinista revolution. Further areas of press concentration have been the USG is exaggerating the communist threat; the USG is supporting 'covert' efforts to overthrow the Sandinistas in Nicaragua; the USG is not supporting a political solution of the Salvadoran 'civil war'; the USG is opposed to negotiation with Nicaragua to solve outstanding issues."

The internal strategy paper accurately outlined the challenges facing the Reagan-Bush administration, while inadvertently pointing out why the domestic "public diplomacy" campaign would prove so threatening to a healthy democratic process. If the administration's goal was to purge these impressions held by the American public and much of the news media, it would have to suppress many facts that were demonstrably true. The administration *was* stressing a military solution; it *was* allied with some unsavory right-wing groups; it *was* sponsoring a covert war in Nicaragua; it *was* relying heavily on former Somoza national guardsmen as the nucleus of the contra army; it *was* seeking to oust the Sandinistas; it *was* showing little interest in serious talks to settle the wars in El Salvador and Nicaragua.

To a great degree, the Reagan-Bush administration's attitude toward Nicaragua was colored by the theory espoused by U.N. Ambassador Jeane Kirkpatrick, who justified U.S. support for right-wing authoritarian governments as preferable to tolerating left-wing totalitarian regimes on the grounds that authoritarian government could evolve into democracies while totalitarian governments couldn't. Only a military victory could be expected to alter the status quo. In the early 1980s, the Kirkpatrick Doctrine was another fixture of conservative orthodoxy, though it would be proven false in less than a decade as Soviet bloc governments changed into democracies and the Sandinistas surrendered power after losing an election, not because the contras marched into Managua.

Nevertheless, Raymond and his "public diplomacy" crew saw their daunting task as forcing changes in the public perceptions about Central America, essentially berating anyone who presented evidence in support of the accurate impressions that had been cited in the May 5 strategy paper.

The strategy paper recommended a "public diplomacy effort" that would "foster a climate of editorial and public opinion that will encourage congressional support of administration policy." As for the press, "a comprehensive and responsive strategy, which would take timely advantage of favorable developments in the region, could at least neutralize the prevailing climate and perhaps, eventually overcome it," the paper said. It also urged the use of "opinion leaders in the mass media" to convey the administration's message to the American people.

The strategy recognized, too, the need to target specific American interest groups defined by geography, religion and ethnic backgrounds. "Themes will obviously have to be tailored to the target audience," the paper said. An addendum matched up key members of Congress with their hometown newspapers that would get special attention from the "public diplomacy" operatives. By influencing the local newspapers' editorial boards, the administration would bring pressure on its congressional critics.

Pollster Richard Wirthlin defined one "hot button" that might work for Americans living in the Southwest: the fear of refugees. Using focus groups, Wirthlin found that anticommunist pitches didn't score well because many Americans didn't take the threat that seriously. But when he asked about the prospect of millions of Central American refugees flooding into the United States, he discovered that eight out of ten respondents expressed a "great deal of concern."

The public diplomacy team quickly translated Wirthlin's findings into the "feet people" theme, arguing that ten percent of each Central American country would flee if a "Marxist dictatorship" took power. Reagan personally deployed the new theme in a June 1983 speech, declaring that "a string of anti-American Marxist dictatorships" in Central America could lead to "a tidal wave of refugees, and this time, they'll be 'feet people' and not 'boat people' swarming into our country."

While effective in rallying support for the administration's policies, the "feet people" theme also demonstrated how fear and emotionalism could be used to overwhelm rational debate in a public diplomacy campaign. Like CIA propaganda – seeking to exploit cultural weaknesses – the "feet people" theme played on American fears of an influx of dark-skinned foreigners.

The argument also lacked factual support. The administration never supplied any documentation to back up its ten percent estimate, and the reality was that in the early 1980s, the bulk of the Central American refugees were streaming north from El Salvador and Guatemala, not from Nicaragua.

In other words, they were fleeing violence in rightist-ruled countries, not in leftist Nicaragua. The obvious reason is that people try to escape danger whatever its political ideology.

People also migrate when jobs are scarce or when they see little opportunity for a better future. U.S. intelligence officials told me at the time that they were surprised that the Sandinistas had been able to maintain a fairly stable economy through the first half of the 1980s. Ironically, the flow of Nicaraguan refugees to the United States increased in the latter half of the decade when the contra war and a U.S. economic embargo succeeded in devastating Nicaragua's economy.

***

Besides hyping evidence to make the Sandinistas look bad, the Reagan-Bush administration struggled to keep under wraps the brutality committed by some of the Argentine-trained-and-CIA-backed contra units.

Contra director Edgar Chamorro was one of the leaders recruited by the CIA to a new contra umbrella group, the Nicaraguan Democratic Force – or FDN – because he was free of any taint from the Somoza dictatorship. But Chamorro, a university professor in pre-revolutionary Nicaragua, gradually grew deeply disillusioned by what he witnessed and the lies he was forced to tell as a chief contra spokesman.

Chamorro told me later that his first personal crisis came in late 1982 when the contras kidnapped an elderly Nicaraguan couple, Felipe and Maria Barreda. Chamorro had known the family before the revolution in Esteli and tried to intervene to protect them. But witnesses said the contras tortured the couple into confessing that they were Sandinista intelligence agents and then executed them. The Sandinistas later denied that the Barredas were intelligence agents.

At times, Chamorro recognized that the contra violence was tinged with madness, a kind of blood lust that often surfaced in the Nazi-like excesses of South American political repression. While the Reagan-Bush administration played down reports of contra atrocities as either Sandinista propaganda or the acts of renegades, Chamorro knew that human rights crimes were committed even by "model" contra commanders who were showcased when American reporters were doing fact-finding trips in the region.

One of these top commanders went by the *nom de guerre* Suicida and stood out as an aggressive field commander. In June 1983, one of Suicida's campaigns in northern Nicaragua brought ghastly reports of executions and torture. Members of Congress began asking questions about atrocities being reported in the international press.

But no one could control Suicida, who raped many of his women captives and slept with women under his command. He complained to journalists about the far-to-the-rear general staff. "It's me who's burning his balls down here fighting the communists," Suicida told *Washington Post* reporter Christopher Dickey.

When one of his favorite contra lovers, La Negra, was killed in an ambush in spring 1983, Suicida took his revenge out on Nicaraguan border towns. When the grief-stricken Suicida threw his forces onto the hapless tobacco village of El Porvenir, Suicida had no plan other than fighting and killing. The Sandinistas launched a devastating counterattack with heavy artillery and mortars, decimating Suicida's troops, driving Suicida and his surviving contras back to Honduras.

As Dickey described in his book, *With the Contras*, Suicida was court-martialed on charges of insubordination, rape and murder. The contra high command then had Suicida and three subordinates taken to the border where the three underlings were immediately executed. But Dickey received reports that Suicida was first stripped naked and tortured for several days, before he too was executed apparently sometime in October 1983.[1] (For the next year, Suicida's fate remained a secret until his execution was reported by Brian Barger for *The Washington Post* on October 31, 1984)

But Suicida was not alone as a "model" contra commander who committed atrocities. One night when I was interviewing Chamorro at his home in Key Biscayne, Florida, he choked up as he described a visit he and a doctor made to a hospital in a contra base camp in Honduras. They encountered two hysterical contra women soldiers who were undergoing treatment. Amid screams and tears, they told Chamorro and the doctor how their contra field commander, known as Tigrillo, had raped them at knifepoint. Tigrillo was another prominent contra commander who was touted to American journalists. In 1987, however, he was found guilty of murdering one of his contra subordinates.

*   *   *

The Reagan-Bush public diplomacy team had its work cut out for it, with the ongoing genocide in Guatemala, the "death squads" in El Salvador and a contra problem in Nicaragua that involved both atrocities and cocaine smuggling. If the American people had a clear picture of what their tax dollars were funding, they might not stand for it. So, the task of regulating what the American people would get to see became a job for Walter Raymond's "public diplomacy" operation.

Later, one National Security Council official told me, the "perception management" campaign was modeled after CIA psychological operations abroad where information is manipulated to bring a population into line with a desired political position. "They were trying to manipulate [U.S.] public opinion – using the tools of Walt Raymond's trade craft which he learned from his career in the CIA covert operations shop," the official said.

Another administration official offered a similar description to *The Miami Herald*'s Alfonso Chardy. "If you look at it as a whole, the Office of Public Diplomacy was carrying out a huge psychological operation, the kind the military conduct to influence the population in denied or enemy territory," the official said.

In memos to the public diplomacy staff, Raymond made clear that the goal was to create a simplistic image in the minds of the American people. "In the specific case of Nica[ragua], concentrate on gluing black hats on the Sandinistas and white hats on UNO," the United Nicaraguan Opposition, the contras' political arm, Raymond wrote. There was no room for the gray hats that were more appropriate for both sides.

Dutifully, Reagan's speechwriters penned descriptions of Sandinista-ruled Nicaragua as a "totalitarian dungeon" and the contras as the "moral equals of our Founding Fathers." Neither description was accurate. Both were hyperbole. But Reagan and his team were putting down markers and daring their critics to take the challenge. Few did.

Another part of the administration's strategy was to target journalistic "enemies" – the likes of Raymond Bonner – while rewarding ideological allies. According to one National Security Council memo dated May 20, 1983, U.S. Information Agency director Charles Z. Wick brought together private donors to the White House Situation Room for a fund-raiser that collected $400,000 for Accuracy in Media, Freedom House and other groups assisting the public diplomacy operations. Raymond told me that the $400,000 went to support a public diplomacy campaign in Europe, although Accuracy in Media's principal activity was attacking reporters in the United States for alleged liberal bias.

In early August 1983, CIA Director Casey personally participated in a day of public relations planning on Central America. Hunched over a desk at the Old Executive Office Building – next to the White House – Casey took notes as ad executives and P.R. experts spun out ideas for selling the administration's Central America policies to the American people.

"Casey was kind of spearheading a recommendation" for better public relations, recalled William I. Greener Jr., one of the advertising executives at the session. Greener said the ad men sketched out two main proposals: creation of a high-powered communications operation inside the White House and the raising of private money to finance an outreach program to build support for U.S. intervention in the region.

Raymond was soon implementing the recommendations, including a scheme to have Australian media mogul Rupert Murdoch chip in money for ostensibly private groups that would back Reagan-Bush policies. According to a memo dated August 9, 1983, Raymond reported to USIA director Wick that "via Murdock [sic], may be able to draw down added funds" to support public diplomacy initiatives.

The public diplomacy chief suggested routing the "funding via Freedom House or some other structure that has credibility in the political center." With Raymond's support, Freedom House – a prominent critic of the Sandinistas – also would become a major recipient of U.S. government largesse. The government-funded National Endowment for Democracy awarded Freedom House $200,000 in 1984 to build "a network of democratic opinion-makers." By 1988, the endowment would give Freedom House $2.6 million, which would total more than one-third of Freedom House's budget.

Besides avoiding congressional oversight, private money had the benefit of creating the impression that an independent group was embracing the administration's policies on their merits. Without knowing that the money had been arranged by the government, the public would be inclined to believe that the position was more objective than the word of a government spokesman. In foreign countries, the CIA often used similar techniques to create what intelligence operatives called "the Mighty Wurlitzer," a propaganda organ playing the desired notes in a carefully scripted harmony.

To be most effective, the U.S. government's fingerprints had to be kept off the ostensibly independent groups. "The work done within the administration has to, by definition, be at arms length," Raymond wrote in an August 29, 1983, memo.

* * *

Besides planting favorable stories, the Reagan-Bush "public diplomacy" operatives took note when U.S. reporters insisted on revealing unfavorable facts. While Raymond oversaw the broader program from the National Security Council staff, a new organization within the State Department, the Office of Public Diplomacy for Latin America [S/LPD] challenged individual journalists and appealed to their editors when troublesome stories made it into the public domain.

To run the office, the administration picked Cuban exile Otto Reich, a former Miami businessman and city official known as a fierce anticommunist. For Reich – a blustery, zealous and combative man – the "war of ideas" was all about winning. One public diplomacy official told me that Reich acted like a coach of a sports team. If a "favorable" story about the Sandinistas appeared in the U.S. media, Reich would exhort his "players" to get those points back by scoring with the placement of some anti-Sandinista articles, the official said.

Reich also seemed to be keeping score when he confronted National Public Radio in 1984 with complaints that the network had run more "anti-contra" minutes versus "pro-contra" minutes. "We said, 'how could you decide what was anti-contra?" asked NPR's foreign editor Paul Allen. "But the point was, 'we're monitoring you – holding a stop watch on you.' The point was, someone was listening and they were doing it with a very critical view."[2]

Bill Buzenberg, NPR's foreign affairs correspondent, later described the meeting with Reich in a speech in Seattle. Buzenberg said Reich informed the NPR editors that he had "a special consultant service listening to all NPR programs" on Central America, analyzing them for possible bias against U.S. policy. Reich also referred to his larger campaign to force changes in U.S. press coverage, saying he had "made similar visits to other unnamed newspapers and major television networks [and] had gotten others to change some of their reporters in the field because of perceived bias," Buzenberg said.

For Allen, who oversaw NPR's coverage worldwide, the intervention by a government official to pressure the radio network to alter its coverage of an important public topic was extraordinary. "Never in our coverage of Poland, South Africa, Lebanon, Afghanistan had they chosen to come in and remonstrate with us," Allen told me. "We understood what Otto Reich's job was. He was engaged in an effort to alter coverage. It was a special effort."

Given NPR's sensitivity to government strings on its public funding, the intervention also worked. At Allen's next job evaluation, NPR executives upbraided him for one of the stories singled out by Reich. A year later, Allen resigned from NPR and left journalism.

As Reich indicated to the NPR staff, he was busy with other news outlets, too. In April 1984, Reich visited the Washington office of CBS News after President Reagan got mad at the network's coverage of El Salvador and Nicaragua. After Reich's trip, Secretary of State George Shultz sent Reagan a memo describing how Reich had spent one hour complaining to the correspondent involved and two more hours with his Washington bureau chief "to point out the flaws in the information." Shultz wrote that the CBS trip was just one example of "what the Office of Public Diplomacy has been doing to help improve the quality of information the American people are receiving. ... It has been repeated dozens of times over the past few months."

Beyond hectoring wayward journalists and going over their heads to news executives, the Office of Public Diplomacy also disseminated the administration's propaganda messages through as many outlets as possible. In its first year alone, Reich's office booked more than 1,500 speaking engagements from radio appearances to editorial-board interviews; published three booklets on Nicaragua; and distributed material to 1,600 libraries, 520 political science faculties, 122 editorial writers and 107 religious organizations.

While the Reagan-Bush "public diplomacy" campaign racked up victories in getting some reporters reassigned and some editors relieved of their duties, the more permanent solution to the information problem was to have reliable conservative news outlets that would join the administration's chorus willingly, not only after visits from Otto Reich. By the early 1980s, that list was growing.

But the biggest splash in the Washington media pond in the first half of the 1980s came from the chunky figure of Sun Myung Moon. The self-proclaimed Messiah from South Korea had managed to fend off most of the negative consequences from the congressional Koreagate investigation into his covert activities on behalf of the KCIA. Still, the revelations of his mysterious money flows led to a federal prosecution of Moon for violating U.S. tax laws and a 13-month prison term.

Nevertheless, by 1982, Moon was in position to make one of his boldest bids for political influence. With the blessings of the Reagan-Bush administration, Moon launched *The Washington Times* newspaper and related publications, including *Insight* magazine. *The Washington Times* was just what the administration had wanted, a reliable voice for its version of events that could inject that message into the public debate. Though Moon would have to subsidize his publications with hundreds of millions of dollars from his seemingly bottomless pool of cash, *The Washington Times* would – over the next two decades – change the parameters of how the national press corps works and affect the course of U.S. presidential campaigns.

Ronald Reagan would soon hail Moon's publication as his "favorite newspaper." But the greatest beneficiaries of Moon's propaganda sheet would turn out to be George H.W. and George W. Bush.

Chapter 16: Moon Rising

Authors Scott Anderson and Jon Lee Anderson wrote in their 1986 book, *Inside the League*, that Sun Myung Moon was one of five indispensable Asian leaders who made the World Anti-Communist League possible. The five were Taiwan's dictator Chiang Kai-shek, South Korea's dictator Park Chung Hee, *yakuza* gangsters Ryoichi Sasakawa and Yoshio Kodama, and Moon, "an evangelist who planned to take over the world through the doctrine of 'Heavenly Deception,'" the Andersons wrote.[1]

WACL became a well-financed worldwide organization after a secret meeting between Sasakawa and Moon, along with two Kodama representatives, on a lake in Yamanashi Prefecture, Japan. The purpose of the meeting was to create an anti-communist organization that "would further Moon's global crusade and lend the Japanese *yakuza* leaders a respectable new façade," the Andersons wrote.[2]

Mixing organized crime and political extremism, of course, has a long tradition throughout the world. Violent political movements often have blended with criminal operations as a way to arrange covert funding, move operatives or acquire weapons. Drug smuggling has proven to be a particularly effective way to fill the coffers of extremist movements, especially those that find ways to insinuate themselves within more legitimate operations of sympathetic governments or intelligence services.

In the quarter century after World War II, remnants of fascist movements managed to do just that. Shattered by the Allies – the United States, Great Britain and the Soviet Union – the surviving fascists got a new lease on political life with the start of the Cold War, helping both Western democracies and right-wing dictatorships battle international communism. Following a global "lesser evil" strategy, the United States and other Western democracies found justification in allying with fascists to defeat the Soviet Union, much as the democracies had allied with the Soviet Union during World War II to defeat the fascists.

Some Nazi leaders faced war-crimes tribunals after World War II, but others managed to make their escapes along "rat lines" to Spain or South America or they finagled intelligence relationships with the victorious powers, especially the United States. Argentina became a natural haven given the pre-war alliance that existed between the European fascists and prominent Argentine military leaders, such as Juan Peron. The fleeing Nazis also found a home with like-minded right-wing politicians and military officers across Latin America who already used repression to keep down the indigenous populations and the legions of the poor.

In the post-World War II years, some Nazi war criminals chose reclusive lives, but others, such as former SS officer Klaus Barbie, sold their intelligence skills to less-sophisticated security services in countries like Bolivia or Paraguay. Other Nazis on the lam trafficked in narcotics. Often the lines crossed between intelligence operations and criminal conspiracies. Auguste Ricord, a French war criminal who had collaborated with the Gestapo, set up shop in Paraguay and opened up the French Connection heroin channels to American Mafia drug kingpin Santo Trafficante Jr., who controlled much of the heroin traffic into the United States. Columns by Jack Anderson identified Ricord's accomplices as some of Paraguay's highest-ranking military officers.

Another French Connection mobster, Christian David, relied on protection of Argentine authorities. While trafficking in heroin, David also "took on assignments for Argentina's terrorist organization, the Argentine Anti-Communist Alliance," Henrik Kruger wrote in *The Great Heroin Coup*. During President Nixon's "war on drugs," U.S. authorities smashed the famous French Connection and won extraditions of Ricord and David in 1972 to face justice in the United States.[3]

By the time the French Connection was severed, however, powerful Mafia drug lords had forged strong ties to South America's military leaders. An infrastructure for the multi-billion-dollar drug trade, servicing the insatiable U.S. market, was in place. Trafficante-connected groups also recruited displaced anti-Castro Cubans, who had ended up in Miami, needed work, and possessed some useful intelligence skills gained from the CIA's training for the Bay of Pigs and other clandestine operations. Heroin from the Golden Triangle of Southeast Asia soon filled the void left by the broken French Connection and its mostly Middle Eastern heroin supply routes.

***

During this time of transition, Sun Myung Moon brought his evangelical message to South America. His first visit to Argentina had occurred in 1965 when he blessed a square behind the presidential Pink House in Buenos Aires. But he returned a decade later to make more lasting friendships. Moon first sank down roots in Uruguay during the 12-year reign of right-wing military dictators who seized power in 1973. He also cultivated close relations with military dictators in Argentina, Paraguay and Chile, reportedly ingratiating himself with the juntas by helping the military regimes arrange arms purchases and by channeling money to allied right-wing organizations.[4]

"Relationships nurtured with right-wing Latin Americans in the [World Anti-Communist] League led to acceptance of the [Unification] Church's political and propaganda operations throughout Latin America," the Andersons wrote in *Inside the League*. "As an international money laundry, ... the Church tapped into the capital flight havens of Latin America. Escaping the scrutiny of American and European investigators, the Church could now funnel money into banks in Honduras, Uruguay and Brazil, where official oversight was lax or nonexistent."[5]

***

In 1980, Moon made more friends in South America when Bolivia's Cocaine Coup plotters seized power. Before the coup, WACL associates, such as Alfred Candia, allegedly had coordinated the arrival of some of the paramilitary operatives who assisted in the violent coup. Afterwards, one of the first well-wishers arriving in La Paz to congratulate the new government was Moon's top lieutenant, Bo Hi Pak. The Moon organization published a photo of Pak meeting with the new strongman, General Garcia Meza. After the visit to the mountainous capital, Pak declared, "I have erected a throne for Father Moon in the world's highest city."

According to later Bolivian government and newspaper reports, a Moon representative invested about $4 million in preparations for the coup. Bolivia's WACL representatives also played key roles, and CAUSA, one of Moon's anti-communist organizations, listed as members nearly all the leading Bolivian coup-makers.[6]

Soon, Colonel Luis Arce-Gomez, a coup organizer and the cousin of cocaine kingpin Roberto Suarez, went into partnership with big narco-traffickers, including Trafficante's Cuban-American smugglers. Nazi war criminal Klaus Barbie and his young neo-fascist followers found new work protecting Bolivia's major cocaine barons and transporting drugs to the border.[7] "The paramilitary units – conceived by Barbie as a new type of SS – sold themselves to the cocaine barons," German journalist Kai Hermann wrote. "The attraction of fast money in the cocaine trade was stronger than the idea of a national socialist revolution in Latin America."[8]

A month after the coup, General Garcia Meza participated in the Fourth Congress of the Latin American Anti-Communist Confederation, an arm of the World Anti-Communist League. Also attending that Fourth Congress was WACL president Woo Jae Sung, a leading Moon disciple.[9] Moon claimed to have split with WACL as of 1975, calling the group "fascist," but his followers remained active in the organization.[10]

As the drug lords consolidated their power in Bolivia, the Moon organization expanded its presence, too. Hermann reported that in early

1981, war criminal Barbie and Moon leader Thomas Ward were often seen together in apparent prayer. Mingolla, the Argentine intelligence officer, described Ward as his CIA paymaster, with the $1,500 monthly salary coming from the CAUSA office of Ward's representative.[11]

On May 31, 1981, Moon representatives sponsored a CAUSA reception at the Sheraton Hotel's Hall of Freedom in La Paz. Moon's lieutenant Bo Hi Pak and Bolivian strongman Garcia Meza led a prayer for President Reagan's recovery from an assassination attempt. In his speech, Bo Hi Pak declared, "God had chosen the Bolivian people in the heart of South America as the ones to conquer communism." According to a later Bolivian intelligence report, the Moon organization sought to recruit an "armed church" of Bolivians, with about 7,000 Bolivians receiving some paramilitary training.

But by late 1981, the cocaine taint of Bolivia's military junta was so deep and the corruption so staggering that U.S.-Bolivian relations were stretched to the breaking point. "The Moon sect disappeared overnight from Bolivia as clandestinely as they had arrived," Hermann reported. Only Ward and a couple of others stayed on with the Bolivian information agency as it worked on a transition back to civilian rule.

According to Hermann's account, Mingolla had a talk with Ward in the cafeteria Fontana of La Paz's Hotel Plaza in March 1982. Ward was discouraged about the Bolivian operation. "The whole affair with Altmann [Barbie], with the whole fascism and Nazism bit, that was a dead-end street," Ward complained. "It was stupid having Moon and CAUSA here."[12]

The Cocaine Coup leaders soon found themselves on the run, too. Interior Minister Arce-Gomez was eventually extradited to Miami and was sentenced to 30 years in prison for drug trafficking. Drug lord Roberto Suarez got a 15-year prison term. General Garcia Meza became a fugitive from a 30-year sentence imposed on him in Bolivia for abuse of power, corruption and murder. Barbie was returned to France to face a life sentence for war crimes. He died in 1992.

But Moon's organization suffered few negative repercussions from its association with the Cocaine Coup. By the early 1980s, flushed with seemingly unlimited funds, Moon had moved on to promoting himself with the new Republican administration in Washington. An invited guest to the Reagan-Bush Inauguration, Moon made his organization useful to President Reagan, Vice President Bush and other leading Republicans.

***

An early concern of the Reagan-Bush administration was the possibility that a popular movement – similar to the anti-Vietnam War protests – would undermine the hard-line policies that the new U.S. government considered indispensable for stopping the spread of Soviet influence in Central America. Some staunch anticommunists in the administration also suspected that some groups opposed to U.S. intervention in the region could be discredited for holding suspect political loyalties. Though Moon's organization itself had been exposed by the Koreagate investigation as a foreign intelligence operation, the administration still turned to it to help probe the loyalty of American citizens.

Starting in 1981, the FBI cooperated with one of Moon's front groups during a five-year nationwide investigation of the Committee in Solidarity with the People of El Salvador (CISPES), a domestic organization critical of Reagan's policies in Central America. According to FBI documents obtained by *Boston Globe* reporter Ross Gelbspan, the FBI collected reports from Moon's Collegiate Association for the Research of Principles (CARP), which was spying on CISPES supporters. The reports came from CARP members at ten university campuses around the United States and included commentaries on the purported political beliefs of Reagan's critics.[13]

One CARP report called a CISPES supporter "well-educated in Marxism" while other CARP reports attached "clippings culled from communist-inspired front groups." The *Globe* investigation reported that Frank Varelli, who worked for the FBI from 1981 to 1984 coordinating the CISPES probe, said an FBI agent paid members of the Moon organization at Southern Methodist University while the Moon activists were raiding and disrupting CISPES rallies. "Every week, an agent I worked with used to go to SMU to pay the Moonies," Varelli said in an interview. Because of the CARP harassment, CISPES closed its SMU chapter.

While Moon's organization was helping spy on American citizens, the Reagan-Bush administration dropped the investigation of Moon as a suspected intelligence agent for South Korea. It's still not clear why.

"I don't think there was any doubt that the Moon newspaper took a virulently pro-South Korea position," Oliver "Buck" Revell, then a senior FBI official in the national security area, told me. "But whether there was something illegal about it..." His voice trailed off. As for the internal security investigation of Moon, Revell added only: "It led its full life."

***

From its start in 1982, *The Washington Times,* asserted that it would be independent of Moon and the Unification Church, even though senior Moon lieutenants were assigned as top executives. Often, *Washington Times* defenders argued that the newspapers didn't proselytize for the church nor did Moon operatives dictate the newspaper's daily content. They compared *The Washington Times* with other newspapers sponsored by religious groups, such as the *Christian Science Monitor*.

The arguments, however, missed the point about how *The Washington Times* has functioned and its political significance. Though it's true that the newspaper doesn't openly promote the Unification Church's religious views,

The Washington Times does something far more important: it promotes politicians who then find themselves in position to protect Moon's interests. If *The Washington Times* can help assure the election of a U.S. President, for instance, his administration may feel indebted enough not to examine the financial workings of Moon's operations too closely.

So, while Moon can count on his mid-level editors to assure that the daily content of the newspaper is tilted to the right, Moon's hand-picked moneymen and top editors need only guarantee that a few politically strategic stories are spun aggressively. Those articles can be planted to embarrass a political adversary at key a moment in an election campaign or to discredit an investigation that is getting too close to Moon's core interests. Indeed, this is how effective propaganda has always worked. Good propaganda depends on some measure of public trust based on the fact that most of the articles in a news outlet are reliable. That way, the readers' defenses are down when encountering the occasional piece of disinformation or propaganda.

In one telling case, Edmund Jacoby, a former *Washington Times* national security writer, described how in 1988 he was assigned to interview Soviet dissident Mikhail Makarenko who told an apparently fabricated first-person account about Soviet slave labor camps. Jacoby reported that the *Times* editors pushed him to write a favorable article about Makarenko and were annoyed when he debunked much of the dissident's tale. Jacoby discovered later that the Unification Church was secretly supporting Makarenko through CAUSA International.

"Why would any newspaper work so hard to get one of its own reporters to tell an apparently false story?" Jacoby asked. "The answer lies in the nature of Moon's enterprises in the United States. ... In a world in which the perception of power is power, the purpose of everything that's done at the *Times* is to give Moon the appearance of having power. For Moon to gain cachet in the eyes of offshore anticommunists who might extend privileges or cash to his operations, it's necessary to demonstrate from time to time that he has the capacity to influence decisions in Washington."[14]

Often, the beneficiaries of dubious stories in *The Washington Times* have been members of the Bush family. For example, when Vice President George H.W. Bush was struggling in his 1988 presidential campaign against Democratic nominee, Massachusetts Governor Michael Dukakis, *The Washington Times* published a slanted story about Dukakis's mental health.

Times reporter Gene Grabowski interviewed a Dukakis relative and asked whether Dukakis had ever sought psychiatric help during a low period in his life. "It's possible, but I doubt it," the relative responded. Grabowski's editors, however, snipped out the phrase "but I doubt it" while keeping the phrase "it's possible" and then spotlighting the story under a headline, "Dukakis Kin Hints at Sessions." Dukakis's supposedly questionable mental health became an important theme for the Republicans. President Reagan personally underscored the message by referring to Dukakis as a "cripple," which forced more mainstream publications to reprise the suspicions about the suspected psychiatric treatment. The story spread doubts among the electorate about Dukakis's fitness for office. For his part, Grabowski, a former Associated Press reporter, resigned in protest of the distortion, but by then the damage to Dukakis was done.

As the conservative news media has expanded, other *Washington Times* "hit pieces" have gained greater currency within American politics. A *Times* story will go quickly to Rush Limbaugh and other radio talk shows; it can buzz around the Internet; it can show up on the Fox News cable network, putting pressure on more mainstream cable networks, like CNN, to run the story as well. *The Washington Times'* front page is regularly hoisted by C-SPAN talk show hosts who discuss its articles with the same neutral tone that they would use in referring to articles in *The New York Times* or the *Los Angeles Times*.

***

Where Moon gets his cash has been a long-running mystery that few American conservatives have been eager to solve. "Some Moonie-watchers even believe that some of the business enterprises are actually covers for drug trafficking," wrote Scott and Jon Lee Anderson. "Others feel that, despite the disclosures of Koreagate, the Church has simply continued to do the Korean government's international bidding and is receiving official funds to do so."[15]

While Moon's representatives have refused to detail how they've sustained their far-flung activities – including many businesses that insiders say lose money – Moon's spokesmen have denied recurring allegations about profiteering off illegal trafficking in weapons and drugs. In a typical response to a gun-running question by the Argentine newspaper, *Clarin*, Moon's representative Ricardo DeSena responded, "I deny categorically these accusations and also the barbarities that are said about drugs and brainwashing. Our movement responds to the harmony of the races, nations and religions and proclaims that the family is the school of love."[16]

Without doubt, however, Moon's organization has had a long record of association with organized crime figures, including ones implicated in the drug trade. Besides collaborating with Sasakawa and other leaders of the Japanese *yakuza* and the Cocaine Coup government of Bolivia, Moon's organization developed close ties with the Honduran military and with Nicaraguan contras units tied to drug smuggling. Moon's organization also used its political clout in Washington to intimidate or discredit government officials and journalists who tried to investigate those criminal activities.

In the mid-1980s, for instance, when journalists and congressional investigators began probing the evidence of contra-connected drug trafficking, they came under attacks from Moon's *Washington Times*. An

Associated Press story that I co-wrote with Brian Barger about a Miami-based federal probe into gun- and drug-running by the contras was denigrated in a front-page *Washington Times* article with the headline: "Story on [contra] drug smuggling denounced as political ploy."[17]

When Senator John Kerry of Massachusetts conducted a Senate probe and uncovered additional evidence of contra drug trafficking, *The Washington Times* denounced him, too. The newspaper first published articles depicting Kerry's probe as a wasteful political witch hunt. "Kerry's anti-contra efforts extensive, expensive, in vain," announced the headline of one *Times* article.[18]

But when Kerry exposed more contra wrongdoing, *The Washington Times* shifted tactics. In 1987 in front-page articles, it began accusing Kerry's staff of obstructing justice because their investigation was supposedly interfering with Reagan-Bush administration efforts to get at the truth. "Kerry staffers damaged FBI probe," said one *Times* article that opened with the assertion: "Congressional investigators for Sen. John Kerry severely damaged a federal drug investigation last summer by interfering with a witness while pursuing allegations of drug smuggling by the Nicaraguan resistance, federal law enforcement officials said."[19]

Despite the attacks from *The Washington Times* and pressure from the Reagan-Bush administration to back off, Kerry's contra-drug investigation eventually concluded that a number of contra units – both in Costa Rica and Honduras – were implicated in the cocaine trade. "It is clear that individuals who provided support for the contras were involved in drug trafficking, the supply network of the contras was used by drug trafficking organizations, and elements of the contras themselves knowingly received financial and material assistance from drug traffickers," Kerry's investigation stated in a report issued April 13, 1989. "In each case, one or another agency of the U.S. government had information regarding the involvement either while it was occurring or immediately thereafter."

Kerry's probe also found that Honduras had become an important way station for cocaine shipments heading north during the contra war. "Elements of the Honduran military were involved ... in the protection of drug traffickers from 1980 on," the report said. "These activities were reported to appropriate U.S. government officials throughout the period. Instead of moving decisively to close down the drug trafficking by stepping up the DEA presence in the country and using the foreign assistance the United States was extending to the Hondurans as a lever, the United States closed the DEA office in Tegucigalpa and appears to have ignored the issue."[20]

The Kerry investigation represented an indirect challenge to Vice President George H.W. Bush, who had been named by President Reagan to head the South Florida Task Force for interdicting the flow of drugs into the United States and was later put in charge of the National Narcotics Border Interdiction System. In short, Bush was the lead official in the U.S.

government to counter the drug trade, which he himself had dubbed a national security threat.

If the American voters came to believe that Bush had compromised his anti-drug responsibilities to protect the image of the Nicaraguan contras and other rightists in Central America, that judgment could have threatened the political future of Bush and his politically ambitious family. By publicly challenging press and congressional investigations of this touchy subject, *The Washington Times* helped keep an unfavorable media spotlight from swinging in the direction of the Vice President.

The available evidence now shows that there was much more to the contra drug issue than either the Reagan-Bush administration or Moon's organization wanted the American people to know in the 1980s. The evidence – assembled over the years by inspectors general at the CIA, the Justice Department and other federal agencies – indicates that Bolivia's Cocaine Coup government was only the first in a line of drug enterprises that tried to squeeze under the protective umbrella of Ronald Reagan's favorite covert operation, the contra war.[21]

Other cocaine smugglers soon followed, cozying up to the contras and sharing some of the profits as a way to minimize investigative interest by the Reagan-Bush law enforcement agencies. The contra-connected smugglers included the Medellin cartel, the Panamanian government of Manuel Noriega, the Honduran military, the Honduran-Mexican smuggling ring of Ramon Matta Ballesteros, and the Miami-based anti-Castro Cubans with their connections to Mafia operations throughout the United States.

The drug traffickers' strategy also worked. In some cases, U.S. intelligence officials bent over backwards not to take timely notice of contra-connected drug trafficking out of fear that fuller investigations would embarrass the contras and their patrons in the Reagan-Bush administration. For instance, on October 22, 1982, a cable written by the CIA's Directorate of Operations stated, "There are indications of links between [a U.S. religious organization] and two Nicaraguan counter-revolutionary groups. These links involve an exchange in [the United States] of narcotics for arms." The cable added that the participants were planning a meeting in Costa Rica for such a deal. (Even years later when the document was released, the CIA excised the identity of the "U.S. religious organization" and the location of the meeting.)

When the cable arrived, senior CIA officials were concerned. On October 27, 1982, CIA headquarters asked for more information. The law enforcement agency expanded on its report by telling the CIA that representatives of the contra FDN and another contra force, the UDN, would be meeting with several unidentified U.S. citizens. But then, the CIA reversed itself, deciding that it wanted no more information on the grounds that U.S. citizens were involved. "In light of the apparent participation of

U.S. persons throughout, agree you should not pursue the matter further," CIA headquarters wrote on November 3, 1982.

Two weeks later, after discouraging additional investigation, CIA headquarters suggested it might be necessary to knock down the allegations of a guns-for-drugs deal as "misinformation." The CIA's Latin American Division, however, responded on November 18, 1982, that several contra officials had gone to San Francisco for meetings with supporters, presumably as part of the same guns-for-drugs deal. But no additional information about that deal was found in CIA files. By keeping the names censored, when the documents were released in 1998, the CIA prevented outside investigators from examining whether the "U.S. religious organization" had any affiliation with Moon's network of quasi-religious groups, which were assisting the contras at that time.[22]

Justice Department Inspector General Michael Bromwich cited other irregularities when he reviewed the handling of the contra-drug issue in 1998. In one instance, in 1983, fifty drug traffickers – many Nicaraguan exiles – were nabbed in what became known as the Frogman Case, so called because some smugglers were caught in wet suits as they carried cocaine ashore near San Francisco. By summer 1984, contras in Costa Rica had claimed in a letter to the federal court that $36,800 seized from Frogman Case drug defendant Julio Zavala actually belonged to them. As word spread inside the administration, an alarmed CIA headquarters protested prosecution plans to depose contra figures in Costa Rica. Assistant U.S. Attorney Mark Zanides said that in mid-1984, he was approached by CIA counsel Lee Strickland. In an "opaque conversation," Zanides recalled, Strickland said the CIA would be "immensely grateful" if the depositions were dropped – and they were. The money also was returned to Zavala.

Word of the deal soon reached Central America. On August 17, 1984, the CIA's station in Costa Rica messaged CIA headquarters with news that the U.S. consul was saying that the Frogman trip was "cancelled by 'the funny farm,'" which the consul meant as "a reference to the CIA." On August 22, CIA counsel Strickland wrote internally that "I believe the station must be made aware of the potential for disaster. While the [contra-drug] allegations might be entirely false, there are sufficient factual details which would cause certain damage to our image and program in Central America." Two days later, CIA headquarters sent a cable to the Costa Rica station acknowledging the CIA's role in derailing the depositions. "We can only guess as to what other testimony may have been forthcoming," the cable explained.

Recalling these maneuvers, a retired CIA official, identified as "Ms. Jones," told Bromwich's investigators that in 1984, the "burning issue" in the Zavala case was the "explosive" potential for bad publicity if the drug case implicated the contras. "What would make better headlines?" she asked.

Though both the CIA and Justice Department continued downplaying the significance of the contra-drug evidence in 1998, their findings confirmed that the Reagan-Bush administration repeatedly interfered with drug investigations that presented the danger of exposing the contras to public condemnation and possible prosecution.[23]

This official pattern of obstruction of justice occurred while Vice President Bush was a principal figure in the administration's national security hierarchy and was in charge of stanching the flow of drugs to the United States. At the same time, Moon's organization, which had its own relationships with some of the same drug traffickers, was aggressively promoting the contra cause and making the lives of critics more difficult.

***

As Moon continued to expand his influence in American politics, some Republicans began to raise red flags. In 1983, the GOP's moderate Ripon Society charged that the New Right had entered "an alliance of expediency" with Moon's church. Ripon's chairman, Representative Jim Leach of Iowa, released a study which alleged that the College Republican National Committee "solicited and received" money from Moon's Unification Church in 1981. The study also accused Reed Irvine's Accuracy in Media of benefiting from low-cost or volunteer workers supplied by Moon.

Leach said the Unification Church has "infiltrated the New Right and the party it wants to control, the Republican Party, and infiltrated the media as well." Leach's news conference was disrupted when then-college GOP leader Grover Norquist accused Leach of lying. (Norquist is now a prominent conservative leader in Washington with close ties to the highest levels of George W. Bush's administration.) *The Washington Times* dismissed Leach's charges as "flummeries" and mocked the Ripon Society as a "discredited and insignificant left-wing offshoot of the Republican Party."[24]

Despite periodic fretting over Moon's influence, conservatives continued to accept his deep-pocket assistance. When White House aide Oliver North was scratching for support for the Nicaraguan contras, for instance, *The Washington Times* established a contra fund-raising operation. By the mid-1980s, Moon's Unification Church had carved out a niche as an acceptable part of the American Right. In one speech to his followers, Moon boasted that "without knowing it, even President Reagan is being guided by Father [Moon]."

Yet, Moon also made clear that his longer-range goal was destroying the U.S. Constitution and America's democratic form of government. "History will make the position of Reverend Moon clear, and his enemies, the American population and government will bow down to him," Moon said, speaking of himself in the third person. "That is Father's tactic, the natural subjugation of the American government and population."

In a 1987 article in the *American Spectator*, conservative columnist Andrew Ferguson wrote that Moon's church had attracted U.S. conservatives by advocating a muscular anticommunism. But Ferguson added: "There is little else in Unificationism that American conservatives will find compelling," except, of course, the money. "They're the best in town as far as putting their money with their mouth is," Ferguson quoted one Washington-based conservative as saying.[25]

Though Moon's money sources remained shrouded in secrecy, his cash undeniably gave the Right an edge over its political adversaries. After the Iran-Contra scandal exploded in fall 1986, *The Washington Times* and other Moon-related organizations rushed to the battlements to defend Reagan's White House and Oliver North. Ronald S. Godwin, who was a link between Reverend Jerry Falwell's Moral Majority and Moon's *Washington Times*, raised funds for North through a group called the Interamerican Partnership, which was a forerunner to North's own Freedom Alliance.[26]

Another Moon-connected group, the American Freedom Coalition, went to bat for North. According to Andrew Leigh, who worked for a Moon front called Global Image Associates, AFC broadcast a pro-North video, "Ollie North: Fight for Freedom," more than 600 times on more than 100 TV stations. Leigh quoted one AFC official as saying that AFC received $5 million to $6 million from business interests associated with Moon. AFC also bragged that it helped put George Bush into the White House in 1988 by distributing 30 million pieces of political literature.[27]

But even as Moon consolidated his influence in Washington during the 12-year Reagan-Bush reign, Moon's weird behavior was splitting the church leadership and making some American conservatives nervous. In 1989, published reports disclosed that Moon had declared that one of his sons, Heung Jin Moon who died in a car crash in 1984, had come back to life in the body of a church member from Zimbabwe. The muscular African – known inside the church as the "black Heung Jin" – then compelled church leaders to stand before him and engage in humiliating self-criticisms, sometimes making them sing songs.

During one of these rituals in December 1988, the Zimbabwean severely beat longtime Moon lieutenant Bo Hi Pak, who was then publisher of *The Washington Times*. Pak reportedly suffered brain damage and impaired speech from the assault, which church sources told me had been sanctioned by Moon after Pak had fallen out of favor. Afterwards, Pak was transferred back to Asia.

Commenting on the beating of Pak, former *Washington Times* editor William P. Cheshire wrote, "Where the Moonies are concerned, it seems clear, we are dealing with something besides just an exotic cult. The Pak beating smacks strongly of Jonestown [the site of a mass murder-suicide by a religious cult]. And with Moon lavishing hundreds of millions of dollars a year on newspapers, magazines and political-action groups in this country and abroad, such occult and aggressive practices give rise to secular apprehensions. If the 'reincarnation' doesn't rock those conservative shops that have been taking money from Moon, not even fire-breathing dragons would disturb them."[28]

***

But Moon's organization had proved itself too valuable to be cast aside, regardless of the strange behavior and the questionable sources of money. By the late 1980s and early 1990s, *The Washington Times* was the daily billboard where conservatives placed their messages to each other and to the outside world.

In 1991, when conservative commentator Wesley Pruden was named the new editor of *The Washington Times*, President George H.W. Bush invited Pruden to a private White House lunch. The purpose, Bush explained, was "just to tell you how valuable the *Times* has become in Washington, where we read it every day."[29]

While the Moon organization was promoting the interests of the Reagan-Bush team, the administration was shielding Moon's operations from federal probes into its finances and possible intelligence role, U.S. government documents show. According to Justice Department documents released under the Freedom of Information Act, administration officials were rebuffing hundreds of requests – many from common U.S. citizens – for examination of Moon's foreign ties and money sources.

Typical of the responses was a May 18, 1989, letter from Assistant Attorney General Carol T. Crawford rejecting the possibility that Moon's organization be required to divulge its foreign-funded propaganda under the Foreign Agent Registration Act (FARA). "With respect to FARA, the Department is faced with First Amendment considerations involving the free exercise of religion," Crawford said. "As you know, the First Amendment's protection of religious freedom is not limited to the traditional, well-established religions."

A 1992 PBS documentary about Moon's political empire and its free-spending habits started another flurry of citizen demands for an investigation, according to the Justice Department files. One letter from a private citizen to the Justice Department stated, "I write in consternation and disgust at the apparent support, or at least the sheltering, of the Reverend Sun Myung Moon, a foreign agent ... who has subverted the American political system for the past 20 years. ... Did Reagan and/or Bush receive financial support from Moon or his agents during any of their election campaigns in violation of federal law?"

Another letter complained that "apparently Moon gave the Bush and Reagan campaigns millions of dollars in support and helped fund the

[Nicaraguan] contras as well as sponsoring rallys [sic] in 50 states to support the Persian Gulf War. No wonder the Justice Department turns a blind eye?"

"I feel it is necessary to find out who is financing the operation and why other countries are trying to direct the policies of the United States," wrote another citizen. "If even one-half of the allegations are true, Moon and his assistants belong in jail rather than being welcomed and supported at the highest level of Washington."

As public demands mounted for Moon and his front groups to register as foreign agents, the Justice Department added a new argument to its reasons to say no. In an August 19, 1992, letter, Assistant Attorney General Robert S. Mueller rebuffed a demand that the Moon-backed American Freedom Council register under FARA by noting that Moon, a South Korean citizen, had obtained U.S. resident-alien status – or a "green card."

Mueller, who is now FBI director, wrote that "in the absence of a foreign principal, there is no requirement for registration. ... The Reverend Sun Myung Moon enjoys the status of permanent resident alien in the United States and therefore does not fall within FARA's definition of foreign principal. It follows that the Act is not applicable to the [American Freedom] Council because of its association with Reverend Moon."

Although Moon relocated from the United States to Uruguay in the 1990s, the federal government has declined to say whether Moon renounced his "green card." Moon's spokesmen also did not respond to questions about Moon's immigration status. As of the mid-1990s, a consular official at Uruguay's embassy in Washington told me that Moon does not have residency status in Uruguay and traveled to Uruguay with a multiple-entry visa on his South Korean passport.[*]

---

[*] Mueller, who went out of his way to find reasons not to investigate Moon, touts in his official FBI biography his background investigating and prosecuting "major financial fraud, terrorist and public corruption cases, as well as narcotics conspiracies and international money launderers."

Chapter 17: Untouchables

George H.W. Bush often was underestimated by Washington political analysts. Many viewed him as a pleasant, ineffectual preppy, someone who dashed off gushy notes to congratulate colleagues but didn't have a grand vision for running the country, a man who knew the etiquette of politics but lacked the charisma of leadership, the guy who coasted to the White House on the coattails of Ronald Reagan. Many Washington journalists snickered at Bush as a guy who left "light footprints" during his years as Vice President – an assessment some of my *Newsweek* colleagues had in 1988.

In this view, Bush's one great accomplishment was lining up a coalition of foreign leaders – many of whom he had rubbed shoulders with for decades – to bounce Saddam Hussein's Iraqi army from Kuwait. Even then Bush fell short in constructing the larger New World Order that was supposed to bring international cooperation to problems of disorder and violence.

This conventional view of this one-term President, however, ignored the more complicated and compelling characteristics of Bush as a politician and leader. While not a talented orator or a dynamic personality, the senior George Bush was a master at the secret machinations of government power. From his privileged background and his intelligence experience, he understood how to exploit the best connections, how to pull the right strings – and how to make sure the public didn't see too much. There was a calculated ruthlessness behind the fractured syntax.

Behind the curtains of secrecy, Bush was a clever operative. Some of the savviest investigators who examined the Iran-Contra Affair concluded that Bush – possibly more than any other U.S. government official – was instrumental in the clandestine operations in Central America and Iran in the 1980s. The same was true of the secret overtures toward Saddam Hussein's Iraq.

At a turning point in the Iran-Iraq War, Bush traveled to the Middle East on a trip that many journalists dismissed as one long photo op, but behind the scenes, Bush was conveying secret tactical military advice to Saddam Hussein's regime through Arab intermediaries. Years later, an article by Murray Waas and Craig Unger in *The New Yorker* described the senior Bush conveying messages to Saddam on how to conduct a more aggressive bombing campaign. Waas and Unger said the advice was a kind of diplomatic billiard shot. By getting Iraq to expand use of its air force, the Iranians would be made more desperate for U.S.-made HAWK anti-aircraft missile parts, giving Washington more leverage with the Iranians over U.S. hostages then held in Lebanon.[1]

Indeed, if Bush did leave "light footprints," it was more like those of a cat burglar who gains surreptitious entry and cracks the safe before anyone knows what's going on.

***

Spencer Oliver, the Democrat staffer whose phone was bugged in Watergate and who later became chief counsel of the House International Affairs Committee, came to believe that former CIA Director Bush and CIA veterans attached to the White House were the hidden hands behind all facets of the Iran-Contra scandal: the Nicaraguan contra operation, the Iranian arms initiative and the propaganda-driven "Project Democracy." The key players, Oliver believed, were not the government officials who became household names during the scandal – Oliver North, Robert McFarlane, John Poindexter, etc. – but the ex-CIA men, the likes of Donald Gregg and Walter Raymond, who coalesced around Vice President Bush's office and mostly stayed out of the spotlight.

"Gregg and Walt Raymond were running [Iran-Contra] out of Bush's office, the whole thing," Spencer Oliver said in an interview. "The whole thing a plan devised in the CIA. ... Gregg and Raymond were the guys who were operating it. ...Raymond was put there to run it on the NSC and Gregg was there to run it out of the Vice President's office," while both were reporting back to Bush. Yet, the congressional Iran-Contra committee never looked too closely at Bush's role and never deposed the Vice President, a lapse that Oliver still considers "shocking."

The congressional Iran-Contra report, which was issued in November 1987, dealt with Bush only in passing. The report blamed the scandal largely on "confusion and disarray at the highest levels of Government" and on "pervasive dishonesty and inordinate secrecy" from zealous operatives, such as North, Poindexter and the then-dead CIA Director William Casey.

"The Vice President attended several meetings on the Iran initiative, but none of the participants could recall his views," the congressional report said. "The Vice President said he did not know of the contra resupply operation." The committee accepted that story though noting that Bush's "National Security Adviser, Donald Gregg, was told in early August 1986 by a former colleague that North was running the Contra resupply operation. ... Gregg testified that he did not consider these facts worthy of the Vice President's attention and did not report them to him, even after the Hasenfus airplane was shot down (in October 1986) and the Administration had denied any connection with it."[2] Bush had been one of the administration officials falsely insisting that there was no U.S. government connection to the flight.

Even without examining the facts in any detail, the conclusion that an experienced intelligence officer like Gregg would have said nothing to his boss about a front-page story, like the shooting down of a contra supply plane in Nicaragua, stretches credulity. As the evidence dribbled out about what Bush and his office actually knew, the claim of Bush's ignorance took on the appearance of a brazen cover story, like the husband caught in bed with another woman, simply declaring: "Woman? What woman?"

Indeed, the evidence suggests that Bush's relationship to the contra resupply operation appears to have dated back at least to December 1983 when Bush met in Panama with General Manuel Noriega. The dictator's aide, Colonel Robert Diaz-Herrara, told me that at that meeting, Bush complained about Panama's drug money laundering and pressed for Panama's help against the Nicaraguan Sandinistas. Diaz-Herrara paraphrased Bush's two-part message as: "We will be behind you as long as you behave yourself. We are aware of some of your unscrupulous activities, and those do not bother us so much. But you must stop your support for Cuba and Nicaragua, and get firmly behind the contra effort. That is the principal U.S. objective in Central America."

In a separate interview, Jose Blandon, another top Noriega aide, agreed that Bush had complained about Panamanian money laundering and had sought support for the U.S. anti-Sandinista cause. Neither Diaz-Herrara nor Blandon asserted that Bush explicitly linked the two issues. But Blandon said former Israeli Mossad officer Michael Harrari, who directed Noriega's security detail, put the two issues together and suggested that Noriega reduce U.S. pressure on the drug issue by offering to help the Americans on Nicaragua. Blandon said Noriega instructed him to contact Gregg's office, leading to Panama's covert support to contras fighting on the southern front in Costa Rica. According to a stipulation of fact in Oliver North's Iran-Contra trial, Noriega gave $100,000 to contras fighting on the southern front in July 1984. For his part, Gregg emphatically denied Blandon's claims.

But there was other corroboration about Gregg's contra supply role. Two conservative American arms dealers, who spoke on condition of anonymity, told me that when Congress began shutting down CIA assistance in 1984, Gregg oversaw the original network for funneling non-U.S. government aid to the contras. The arms dealers, whose contra-supply roles were verified by official investigations, gave me a hand-drawn chart of the operation's structure, with Bush and Gregg at the top. The contra support network employed CIA-trained Cuban exiles, including Felix Rodriguez (using the code name "Max Gomez"), and Honduran intelligence officers to distribute the military equipment in the region.

Some of the contra weapons passed through a warehouse called the Arms Supermarket located in San Pedro Sula, Honduras, the flow chart said. "The 'Arms Warehouse' was started with 'seed money' of approximately $14 million, from the CIA," read the text accompanying the flow chart. "Later, it was believed that funds relating to narcotics traffic found its way into inventory in the warehouse." A copy of the flow chart also was obtained by investigators for special prosecutor Lawrence Walsh. I found a copy in the Iran-Contra files at the National Archives in College Park, Maryland.

The two U.S. arms dealers said primary responsibility for contra resupply was later passed on to North, who kept Rodriguez and some other Cubans in the operation. But North also brought in former CIA logistical experts, such as Richard Secord and Thomas Clines, a move that created friction with the earlier team and led eventually to Rodriguez complaining to Gregg in August 1986. Buttressing that account, the Iran-Contra investigations found that Rodriguez called Gregg after each contra delivery. But Gregg still insisted that he didn't learn of the contra resupply operation until August 1986 and even then did not inform Bush.

Bush said he first learned about the secret White House operation to support the contras in December 1986, when he was informed by Republican Senator David Durenberger, then chairman of the Senate Intelligence Committee. To buy that story, however, would require believing that Bush, the ex-CIA chief and a self-proclaimed foreign-policy expert, remained in the dark about a two-year-long White House operation to supply guns and other materiel to the contras, even as his national security adviser was in regular contact with one of the principals, Felix Rodriguez, who also knew Bush personally from their days together at the CIA. Bush dated the Durenberger meeting as December 20, 1986, two and a half months *after* one of the contra supply planes was shot down over Nicaragua and nearly a month *after* Attorney General Edwin Meese III announced discovery of the diversion of Iran arms profits to the contras.

The other possibility would be to conclude that Bush was simply lying because to admit even limited knowledge of the illegal contra supply operation might have exposed other even more damaging secrets, possibly including links between the contras and drug trafficking. Bush may have concluded that denying all knowledge made more sense than cooperating with investigators piecing together who knew what and when. As the Iran-Contra scandal unfolded in fall 1986, Bush also claimed that he was "not in the loop" on the Iran arms sales, an assertion that was later disproved by contemporaneous notes which showed Bush favoring the controversial project.

Bush's claim of ignorance about the contra supply operation came under renewed skepticism when a White House memo surfaced listing the topic of Bush's August 1986 meeting with Gregg and Rodriguez as "resupply of the contras." Still, Bush, Gregg and Rodriguez stuck to their story that contra resupply was not discussed. (In 1989, in sworn Senate testimony, Gregg suggested that the reference might have been a typo that should have read "resupply of the copters," a supposed reference to helicopters used in El Salvador, an explanation that prompted an incredulous *New York Times* editorial entitled "the Iran-Copter Affair.")

Iran-Contra special prosecutor Walsh punched another hole in the Gregg-Bush denial when Colonel James Steele, the U.S. military adviser to El Salvador, flunked a polygraph test while denying his own role in shipping weapons to the contras. Confronted with those results and incriminating notes from North's diaries, "Steele admitted not only his participation in the arms deliveries but also his early discussion of these activities with Donald Gregg," Walsh wrote in his 1997 memoirs, *Firewall*.[3] In other words, Steele was acknowledging a cover-up at the highest levels of the U.S. government.

Though evidence and logic pointed to the involvement of Bush's vice presidential office, Bush and his subordinates were able to fend off any serious challenge to their denials. That was mostly because anyone who pursued that line of inquiry suffered a pounding from Bush's media allies and congressional Republicans. *The Washington Times, The Wall Street Journal*'s editorial page and other conservative news outlets fired off salvo after salvo against Senator John Kerry and special prosecutor Lawrence Walsh, the two leading government investigators who doubted Bush's word.

The Bush team also lobbed some shells at troublesome journalists. At *Newsweek*, I co-authored an article in the May 23, 1988, edition that challenged the Gregg-Bush contra account. The story infuriated the White House, which complained bitterly to senior *Newsweek* editors. Later, *Newsweek*'s Washington Bureau Chief Evan Thomas took me aside and told me that Editor Maynard Parker was livid with me because of the story. Parker, who was known as a fairly open supporter of Reagan-Bush foreign policies, had attended a dinner party hosted by Richard Holbrooke and sat next to Donald Gregg, who had spent much of the evening complaining about me, Thomas said. I had ruined the editor's evening.

Even when – or maybe especially when – Bush found himself in a corner on what appeared to be an obvious lie, he was a master at turning the tables on his critics. Coming to Bush's defense was an impressive network of friends in high places. They rarely failed him. All the favors that Bush had done for his friends, including sending thoughtful handwritten notes, meant that a phalanx of Bush defenders would suddenly appear. When that happened, it was wise not to ask too many more questions.

"Using power to frustrate your enemy is as old as politics itself," Spencer Oliver told me. "In every level of government, anywhere in the world, people try to avoid being caught with their hands in the cookie jar. They try to limit and avoid scandal. And they always cry foul when somebody comes after them."

The Republicans took this lesson to heart in the 1970s, Oliver said. "The Watergate scandal, the hearings and the bringing down of the President, focused everybody's attention on wrongdoing in high places and the Republicans probably decided at some point that you had to protect yourself from wrongdoing being exposed by either influencing the media or influencing the prosecutors or the congressional oversight committees," Oliver said.

To achieve that protection, the Republicans realized that a major investment was necessary. "The biggest weapon in American politics is money because you can use money to influence people, to influence the media, to influence campaigns, to influence individuals, to bribe people." Oliver said. So, the conservatives, who were emerging as the dominant force in the Republican Party, tapped resources wherever they could – from William Simon's coalition of like-minded foundations to Sun Myung Moon's mysterious rivers of cash – to build their Counter-Establishment.

Richard Nixon's Watergate operations marked another historic change with the entry of CIA veterans directly into the U.S. political process, Oliver said. "The first hint that I remember of the CIA being involved in domestic politics would have been '72 when they tried to use the CIA to cover up Watergate, say it was a CIA operation," Oliver said. "Howard Hunt, Jim McCord, these were ex-CIA guys, and the Cubans were guys who had worked for the CIA at the Bay of Pigs. You train these people to do things. Then after you finish using them, they've still got the skills you gave them."

Oliver's observation also applied to other CIA intelligence officers, such as Donald Gregg and Walter Raymond. They didn't suddenly lose their intelligence skills when they went to work at the White House in the 1980s. Neither did George H.W. Bush.

***

In 1987, having fended off the first wave of the Iran-Contra investigation – the congressional committee's probe – George H.W. Bush took aim at winning the Presidency on his own. But doubts about Bush's leadership abilities and suspicions about his Iran-Contra role hindered his campaign. By summer 1988, Democratic nominee Michael Dukakis enjoyed a lead in the polls that had swelled to 17 points.

Judging that Bush would have trouble erasing his high negatives, Dukakis steered away from the lingering questions about Bush's Iran-Contra involvement. Instead, the Massachusetts governor chose to present himself as a plucky man of the people and stuck with his catchy slogan, "Good jobs for good wages." Bush, however, counter-attacked with a desperate but effective strategy. He tried to act like a regular guy, eating pork rinds and talking like Clint Eastwood. Then, Bush moved to negate his own high negatives by elevating those of Dukakis.

Bush and his political advisers scored big with the story about Willie Horton, a black convict who had raped a white woman while on a Massachusetts prison furlough program that Dukakis had supported as governor. Bush also made a big show about pledging the flag at the end of his acceptance speech at the Republican convention, highlighting Dukakis's veto of a compulsory pledge-of-allegiance law for Massachusetts schools. Bush also promised "Read my lips: no new taxes." His campaign pounced on Dukakis, too, when the hapless governor donned a helmet and took a ride in a tank. In effect, Bush changed his image from preppy wimp to belligerent bully.

Dukakis, a relative outsider to Washington, apparently hoped the national press corps would put Bush back on the defensive by excavating Bush's relationship with the drug-trafficking Noriega and Bush's hidden role in the Iran-Contra Affair. But the press corps wasn't willing to dig deeper into those issues. After watching fellow reporters get bruised whenever they scratched away at Reagan-Bush secrets for eight years, the mainstream press shied away from any adversarial posture regarding Bush. With Dukakis playing it safe and the press corps avoiding confrontation, Bush realized that he could continue stonewalling.

In the one case when a major journalist – CBS News' anchor Dan Rather – did challenge Bush on his implausible Iran-Contra story on January 25, 1988, Bush struck back hard. Prepped by media consultant Roger Ailes, Bush responded to Rather's persistent questioning by mocking the CBS anchor for his infamous desertion of the CBS News set in September 1987. Though the rejoinder had no relevance to Bush's misleading statements about the Iran-Contra scandal, it worked. The bulk of the national media applauded Bush's counter-attack against Rather, not Rather's tough questioning of Bush over the Iran-Contra facts.[4]

On Election Night 1988, Bush won a resounding victory, turning his earlier 17-point deficit into a solid eight-percentage-point win in the popular vote and a 426-111 landslide in the Electoral College. "The people have spoken," Bush declared, although it wasn't clear exactly what they were trying to say, given the paucity of meaningful debate about the issues. The people apparently didn't want their taxes raised (although Bush would renege on that promise); they liked pledging the flag; and they didn't want furloughed black prisoners raping white women. But except for that, Bush's mandate was muddled.

What was crystal clear, however, was that George H.W. Bush knew how to win, even if he had to play dirty. Four years later, however, Bush faced another challenge from a more talented opponent.

***

In 1991, in the glow of victory from the Persian Gulf War, George H.W. Bush basked in historically high approval ratings and his reelection seemed assured. But a weak economy, a soaring budget deficit and a vague platform for the future eroded his standing. Bush was dogged, too, by old questions about his Iran-Contra truthfulness and new questions about his pre-war contacts with Saddam Hussein. Also, the independent candidacy of billionaire Texan Ross Perot was eating away at Bush's support among populist conservatives.

In summer 1992, Arkansas Governor Bill Clinton, who called himself the Comeback Kid for his ability to rebound from adversity, topped off his Democratic presidential nomination with a photogenic bus tour with his running mate Al Gore. The tour pushed Clinton into a double-digit lead over the incumbent President. Bush was back where he was four years earlier, playing catch-up.

As the election clock ticked down, Bush's operatives saw little hope for their own comeback unless they could find a "silver bullet," a Clinton scandal so vile that it would take out the Comeback Kid once and for all. Republican operatives began considering the options and planning how to get a clean shot at the Democratic candidate. There was also a possibility that a burst of smaller scandals, timed toward the end of the campaign, would do the job, another type of "October Surprise."

By summer, rumors were circulating that Clinton may have done something during his year as a Rhodes scholar at Oxford in England that would disqualify him as a presidential candidate. One rumor was that Clinton may have tried to renounce his citizenship because of his opposition to the Vietnam War. There seemed to be no basis for the suspicion, but some Bush operatives thought that it wouldn't be too hard to inject fresh doubts about Clinton's behavior, given his mixed and modest track record with the American people. He had already faced questions about his marital infidelity.

The "renunciation" story began to take shape on July 30, 1992, when Michael Hedges, a reporter for Moon's *Washington Times*, submitted a Freedom of Information Act request to the FBI. The FOIA sought FBI records on Clinton's anti-war activities in the 1960s and 1970s. It fit with the vague rumors that Clinton had tried to gain citizenship from another country to avoid the draft.

The rumor attracted the interest of a still-embittered Richard Nixon, who had remained a behind-the-scenes adviser to Republicans even in his years of political exile. On August 28, after the Republican Convention, Nixon brought up the "renunciation" rumor in a conversation with his biographer, Monica Crowley. "The only way we can win now is if Clinton collapses, and I think he is too smart to do that," Nixon said. "The only things that would be self-destructive would be bombshells, like a letter showing that he asked to renounce his American citizenship during Vietnam, an illegitimate child, things like that."[5]

Whether Nixon had simply heard the rumor or whether he was pushing the dirty trick, the "renunciation" story clearly was making the rounds. In early September, Hedges approached his friend, Republican activist David Tell, to request help from the Bush administration for an expedited search of Clinton's files. Tell, a thin and intense young man, was director of opposition research for the Bush reelection campaign. In that position, Tell headed the division that dug up dirt on opponents, a dark art known in political circles as "oppo." Already, Tell had investigated a number of rumors about Clinton, even probing the work record of Clinton's mother when she was a nurse in Louisiana.

On September 16, 1992, Tell typed a memo about Hedges's FOIA request and took it to Bush's campaign manager Fred Malek. With Malek's blessing, Tell sent the memo to Robert Teeter, chairman of the Bush reelection campaign. Teeter, in turn, passed on the gist of Tell's memo to the so-called "core group" of top White House officials and campaign insiders who jointly were coordinating President Bush's reelection strategy.

The political potential of the renunciation rumor didn't escape James Baker, then-White House chief of staff. Baker, a smooth-talking Texas lawyer who had run Bush's campaign in 1988, knew the story could shatter Clinton's career. Though highly regarded in Washington for his political acumen, Baker had left his fingerprints on some of the nastiest political dirty tricks in recent history. Not only did he oversee the dismantling of Michael Dukakis in 1988, but Baker was a chief suspect in the theft of President Carter's debate briefing book in 1980, a ploy that had given Ronald Reagan a crucial advantage in a pivotal presidential debate. Baker personified the winning-is-everything school of politics.

After the "core group" meeting on September 16, 1992, Baker discussed *The Washington Times*' FOIA request with top aides Janet Mullins and Margaret Tutwiler. Baker then personally took the issue to White House legal counsel C. Boyden Gray, a lanky patrician who was another Bush loyalist. Gray recalled that Baker wanted to know if the White House could speed up the FBI response to the FOIA on "this alleged renunciation or proposed renunciation of citizenship."

The excitement over the possible "silver bullet" was energizing others, too, in the senior echelon of the Bush administration. Gray contacted Timothy Flanigan, assistant attorney general for the Office of Legal Counsel at the Justice Department. The two officials hashed over the possibilities. Flanigan advised Gray that the FBI likely would rebuff any pressure to speed up the FOIA request – and that release of such personal material would violate the Privacy Act. Gray mused that perhaps someone could examine Clinton's passport files on national security grounds. But Flanigan explained that claiming the search was needed to justify granting Clinton a national security clearance would be a hard sell since Clinton already had a national security clearance.

Bush himself was caught up in the excitement about the possibility of damaging Clinton with disclosures about his student trips, according to an interview he had with federal investigators who later examined the incident. Bush acknowledged that he was "nagging" his aides to press the investigation into Clinton's student travels to the Soviet Union and Czechoslovakia. Bush also expressed strong interest in rumors that Clinton had sought to renounce his U.S. citizenship.

Bush described himself as "indignant" that his aides failed to discover more about Clinton's student activities. But Bush stopped short of taking responsibility for the apparently illegal searches of Clinton's records. "Hypothetically speaking, President Bush advised that he would not have directed anyone to investigate the possibility that Clinton had renounced his citizenship because he would have relied on others to make this decision," the FBI interview report read. "He [Bush] would have said something like, 'Let's get it out' or 'Hope the truth gets out.'"

On September 25, 1992, with only about five-and-a-half weeks left before the November 3 election, Baker was back on the phone to one of Gray's deputies, John Schmitz. Baker was pressing for an answer on the FOIA question. At 6:08 that evening, according to Baker's notes, Gray called Baker back. Gray passed on the bad news that expedited handling of the FOIA wouldn't fly. Baker then gave Gray more details about the suspicion that Clinton had written a letter while at Oxford asking how he could renounce his country and become a British citizen.

"Holy Cow, maybe I'd better take another look at it," Gray responded, according to Baker's memo to the file. In the same memo, Baker wrote to himself that he was asking Gray to do nothing that was not "completely legal."

While Gray re-examined the prospects of pushing the FBI, Baker turned his attention to similar FOIAs submitted by journalists at the State Department. Baker instructed his aide, Janet Mullins, to ask Steven Berry, assistant secretary of state for legislative affairs, about progress on those inquiries. Mullins talked to Berry before September 30, according to their recollections.

Eventually, the high-level White House interest was communicated to State Department official Elizabeth Tamposi, a Bush political appointee who saw the White House interest as a green light to move ahead with the legally questionable search. On the night of September 30, Tamposi dispatched three aides to the federal records center in Suitland, Maryland. They searched Clinton's passport file as well as his mother's, presumably because they thought it might contain some references to Clinton. In a later press interview, Tamposi would assert that she ordered the search after Berry had pressured her to "dig up dirt on Clinton" for the Bush White House.

But the search found no letter renouncing citizenship. All the State Department officials discovered was a passport application with staple holes and a slight tear in the corner. Though the tear was easily explained by the routine practice of stapling a photo, money order or routing slip to the application, Tamposi seized on the ripped page to justify a new suspicion, that a Clinton ally at the State Department had removed the renunciation letter. Tamposi shaped that speculation into a criminal referral which was forwarded to the Justice Department. Thin as the case was, the Bush reelection effort now had its official action so the renunciation rumor could be turned into a public issue.

Within hours of the criminal referral, someone from the Bush camp leaked word about the confidential FBI investigation to reporters at *Newsweek* magazine. The *Newsweek* story about the tampering investigation hit the newsstands on October 4, 1992. The article suggested that a Clinton backer might have removed incriminating material from Clinton's passport file, precisely the spin that the Bush people wanted.

Immediately, Bush took the offensive, using the press frenzy over the tampering story to attack Clinton's patriotism on a variety of fronts, including his student trip to Moscow in 1970. With his patriotism challenged, Clinton saw his once-formidable lead shrink. Panic spread through the Clinton campaign.

The Bush camp upped the ante again, putting out new suspicions that Clinton might have been a KGB "agent of influence." Moon's *Washington Times* headlined that allegation on October 5, a story that attracted President Bush's personal interest. "Now there are stories that Clinton ... may have gone to Moscow as [a] guest of the KGB, but who knows how that will play," Bush wrote in his diary on October 5, 1992. The entry was typical of Bush's self-serving complaint that the news media didn't hold the Democrat to account for his actions.

The story created an opportunity for both the conservative and mainstream media to reprise other questions about Clinton's draft avoidance and other "character" issues. Indeed, the passport story and the related suspicions about Clinton's patriotism might have doomed Clinton's election, except that Spencer Oliver from his post on the House International Affairs Committee smelled a rat.

"In *Newsweek*, there was this little story – two paragraphs – that there were rumors about damaging information in Clinton's passport file," Oliver said in an interview about the Bush administration's search. "I said you can't go into someone's passport file. That's a violation of the law, only in pursuit of a criminal indictment or something. But without his permission, you can't examine his passport file. It's a violation of the Privacy Act." Though Oliver didn't know it at the time, his understanding of the law matched up with the opinion of the State Department counsel's office.

After consulting with House committee chairman Dante Fascell and a colleague on the Senate Foreign Relations Committee, Oliver dispatched a couple of investigators to the National Archives warehouse in Suitland,

Maryland. Oliver's assistants "came back and said there were these guys out there, and they left their cards," Oliver said. The brief congressional check had discovered that State Department political appointees had gone out to Suitland at night to search through Clinton's records. Oliver's assistants also found that the administration's suspicion rested on a very weak premise, the staple holes. The discovery of the late-night search soon found its way into an article in *The Washington Post.*

Yet still sensing that the loyalty theme had the capacity to undermine Clinton's standing with the American people, Bush continued to stoke the fire. On CNN's "Larry King Live" on October 7, Bush suggested anew that there was something sinister about a possible Clinton friend tampering with Clinton's passport file. "Why in the world would anybody want to tamper with his files, you know, to support the man?" Bush wondered before a national TV audience. "I mean, I don't understand that. What would exonerate him – put it that way – in the files?"

Bush's suggestion, obviously, was that whatever was removed would have done the opposite from exonerating Clinton. The next day, in his diary, Bush ruminated suspiciously about Clinton's Moscow trip: "All kinds of rumors as to who his hosts were in Russia, something he can't remember anything about."

But the GOP attack on Clinton's loyalty prompted some Democrats to liken Bush to Senator Joseph McCarthy, who built a political career in the early days of the Cold War challenging people's loyalties without offering proof. On October 9, the FBI complicated Bush's strategy further by rejecting the criminal referral. The FBI concluded that there was no evidence that anyone had removed anything from Clinton's passport file.

At that point, Bush began backpedaling: "If he's told all there is to tell on Moscow, fine," Bush said on ABC's "Good Morning America." "I'm not suggesting that there's anything unpatriotic about that. A lot of people went to Moscow, and so that's the end of that one."

But documents I later obtained from the National Archives revealed that privately Bush was not so ready to surrender the loyalty theme. His speechwriters were preparing a string of "zingers" that could be used to stun Clinton during the first presidential debate on October 11. The day before the debate, Bush prepped himself with one-liners designed to spotlight doubts about Clinton's loyalty if the right opening presented itself.

"It's hard to visit foreign countries with a torn-up passport," read one of the scripted lines. Another zinger read: "Contrary to what the Governor's been saying, most young men his age did not try to duck the draft. ... A few did go to Canada. A couple went to England. Only one I know went to Russia." If Clinton had criticized Bush's use of a Houston hotel room as a legal residence, Bush was ready to hit back with another Russian reference: "Where is your legal residence, Little Rock or Leningrad?"

But the October 11 presidential debate – which also involved Reform Party candidate Ross Perot – did not go as Bush had hoped. Bush did raise the loyalty issue in response to an early question about character, but the incumbent's message was lost in a cascade of inarticulate sentence fragments.

"I said something the other day where I was accused of being like Joe McCarthy because I question – I'll put it this way, I think it's wrong to demonstrate against your own country or organize demonstrations against your own country in foreign soil," Bush said. "I just think it's wrong. I – that – maybe – they say, 'well, it was a youthful indiscretion.' I was 19 or 20 flying off an aircraft carrier and that shaped me to be commander-in-chief of the armed forces, and – I'm sorry but demonstrating – it's not a question of patriotism, it's a question of character and judgment."

Clinton countered by challenging Bush directly. "You have questioned my patriotism," the Democrat shot back. Clinton then unloaded his own zinger: "When Joe McCarthy went around this country attacking people's patriotism, he was wrong. He was wrong, and a senator from Connecticut stood up to him, named Prescott Bush. Your father was right to stand up to Joe McCarthy. You were wrong to attack my patriotism."

Many observers rated Clinton's negative comparison of Bush to his father as Bush's worst moment in the debate. An unsettled Bush didn't regain the initiative for the remainder of the evening.

Although stung by the passport-ploy failure, the Bush campaign quietly continued pursuing derogatory information about Clinton's student travels. Tamposi contacted the U.S. embassies in London and Oslo and ordered searches of consular files in those countries. Only the London embassy complied and found nothing. Representative Bob Dornan, a loose-tongued Republican from California, also tried to keep the focus on Clinton's college trip to Moscow and to communist-ruled Eastern Europe in late 1969 and early 1970. Dornan, alleged that the KGB had given Clinton a ride into Prague, Czechoslovakia, from the airport.

In the days after the presidential debate, phone records revealed a flurry of calls from Bush's campaign headquarters to Czechoslovakia. There were also fax transmissions on October 14 and 15. On October 16, what appears to have been a return call was placed from the U.S. Embassy in Prague to the office of Bush's ad man Sig Rogich, who was handling anti-Clinton themes for the campaign. Another call went to Bush's National Security Council.

Following these exchanges, stories about Clinton's 1970 Prague trip began popping up in Czech newspapers. On October 24, three Czech newspapers ran similar stories about Clinton's Czech hosts. The *Cesky Denik* story had an especially nasty headline: "Bill Was With Communists." The Czech articles soon blew back to the United States. Reuters distributed a summary and, over three consecutive days, *The Washington Times* ran articles about Clinton's Czech trip. The Clinton campaign responded that

Clinton had entered Czechoslovakia under normal procedures for a student and stayed with the family of his Oxford friend.

The Czech trip stories took another turn in January 1994, a year after Clinton took office. The Czech news media disclosed that former Czech intelligence officials were saying that in 1992, the Czech secret police, called the Federal Security and Information Service (FBIS), had collaborated with the Bush reelection campaign to dig up dirt on Clinton.

The centrist newspaper *Mlada Fronta Dnes* reported that during the American presidential campaign, the FBIS gave the Republicans internal data about Clinton's Moscow-Prague trips and supplied background material about Clinton's "connections" inside Czechoslovakia. Derogatory information also allegedly was funneled through officials at the U.S. Embassy and was leaked to cooperative journalists. If true, the allegations meant that the Bush administration had enlisted a foreign secret police force to help influence the outcome of an American presidential election.[*]

***

Looking back on the 1992 presidential campaign, Spencer Oliver concluded that Bush's reelection strategy boiled down to highlighting examples of alleged personal wrongdoing by Clinton and thus disqualifying him for the Presidency.

"The pattern of Republican campaigns in modern times has been to destroy your opponent by finding some flaw or some weakness or some position that they've taken that you can exploit," Oliver said. "Negative research was at its height during that time. ... They had all these guys down in Arkansas. ... They apparently had a line of attack that was going to be Whitewater, Gennifer Flowers and what turned out to be Passportgate, to question his patriotism and to make it appear as though that in the anti-war days he had done some terrible things that were unpatriotic. They were going to unleash these things: Whitewater, Passport, Gennifer Flowers and women stuff. ...

"Because they were caught violating the law by going into Clinton's passport file, they had to go back in their hole, it put them on the defensive. And the strategy was totally disrupted."

***

---

[*] When I interviewed Rogich about the unexplained phone calls, he told me that he knew nothing about Clinton's trip to Prague or about any 1992 phone call received from the U.S. Embassy in Prague. But he said six to eight people worked in his office.

Although the Bush reelection campaign failed to come up with a "silver bullet" to take out Clinton, the cumulative effect of the suspicions raised about the Arkansas governor took a toll on his popularity. Bush, the supposedly gracious preppy and world statesman, switched into what he called "campaign mode." He began resorting to insults against Clinton and Gore.

"Listen to Governor Clinton and Ozone Man," Bush shouted at one campaign stop. "This guy [Gore] is so far off in the environmental extreme, we'll be up to our neck in owls and out of work for every American. This guy's crazy. He is way out, far out. Far out, man." Bush added, "My dog Millie knows more about foreign affairs than these two bozos."

As the election grew near, Bush gained ground on Clinton, pulling effectively even in the polls heading into the final weekend. Then, on the Friday before the election, Bush and his reelection team, which had hoped to deliver an October Surprise knockout blow to Clinton, suffered one of their own.

Iran-Contra special prosecutor Lawrence Walsh filed a second obstruction-of-justice indictment against former Defense Secretary Caspar Weinberger. Walsh said the new filing was required by the courts because a previous one had left out some documentary support, which included Weinberger's notes that made clear that Bush indeed had been inside the loop on the Iran-Contra scandal. The document made Bush out to be a liar and denied him the high ground for questioning the integrity of his opponent. Ironically, the Bush reelection campaign denounced the indictment as a political dirty trick.

In a three-way race, Clinton pulled ahead to win the Presidency with 43 percent to Bush's 37 percent and Perot's 19 percent. Clinton garnered 370 electoral votes to Bush's 168.

*** *** ***

In the days after Bush's defeat, the passport case took some unexpected turns.

On November 10, *The Washington Post* published a story claiming that the State Department also had searched the passport files of Ross Perot. Though the story apparently was inaccurate – Perot's files had been moved for safekeeping but not searched – Bush demanded that acting Secretary of State Lawrence Eagleburger fire the official in charge, Elizabeth Tamposi. "I told Larry Eagleburger we had to get rid of the person that did it," Bush wrote in his diary.

Angered by her dismissal, Tamposi revised her earlier statements to State Department Inspector General Sherman Funk. Tamposi claimed that she had conducted the Clinton passport search at the behest of White House officials, particularly Baker's aide Janet Mullins. Tamposi's new assertions prompted Funk to expand his inquiry of the case. Fearing a spreading scandal, a distraught Baker contacted Bush on November 16. According to Bush's diary, Baker was "worried that it's going to end up on his door step."

Baker grew depressed, blaming himself for the passport disaster and the reelection loss. On November 20, 1992, at 10:30 a.m., a despondent Baker visited Bush. "Jim Baker came in here ... deeply disturbed and read to me a long letter of resignation all because of this stupid passport situation," Bush wrote in his diary. But Bush rejected Baker's offer to resign.

Brushing aside Baker's fears, Bush remained hopeful that no independent counsel would be appointed, especially since that law was set to expire on December 15. Plus, Attorney General William Barr had rejected other appointments in Bush-connected cases. In December, however, Janet Mullins refused to answer questions and Inspector General Funk referred the case to the Justice Department. Barr concluded that he had no choice but to submit a special prosecutor request to a newly reconstituted three-judge panel that selects independent counsels.

The Bush administration was lucky, however, because Supreme Court Chief Justice William Rehnquist had ousted a moderate Republican, Judge George MacKinnon, who had picked Lawrence Walsh, another moderate Republican, to investigate the Iran-Contra scandal. With Republicans furious at Walsh's persistence, Rehnquist replaced MacKinnon as head of the three-judge panel with Judge David Sentelle, one of President Reagan's conservative judicial appointees. Sentelle also was a protégé of Senator Jesse Helms, one of the most conservative Republicans in the U.S. Congress.

On the U.S. Court of Appeals in Washington, Sentelle had teamed with Judge Laurence Silberman to overturn the felony convictions of Oliver North in 1990. Sentelle also had provided one of the two votes in 1991 to throw out the convictions of North's boss, National Security Adviser John Poindexter. Walsh had come to view these Reagan-Bush loyalists on the U.S. Court of Appeals as "a powerful band of Republican appointees [who] waited like the strategic reserves of an embattled army."

Sentelle, who had named his daughter Reagan after the President, was a key figure in those "strategic reserves." But Sentelle also was an unusual choice to head the three-judge panel because the special prosecutor law stated that "priority shall be given to senior circuit judges and retired judges." The law's recommendation recognized that older judges would be less vulnerable to career concerns or political pressure. Unlike MacKinnon, Sentelle was a junior judge – in his 40s – with a history of partisanship. Before donning his black robes, Sentelle had been a Republican Party activist, serving as chairman of the Mecklenburg County Republican Party and as a Reagan delegate to the 1984 GOP national convention. Even after his appointment to the federal bench, Sentelle engaged in public writings harshly critical of liberals. In an article for the winter 1991 issue of the *Harvard Journal of Law and Public Policy*, Sentelle accused "leftist heretics" of wishing to turn the United States into "a collectivist, egalitarian, materialistic, race-conscious, hyper-secular, and socially permissive state."

To investigate the Passportgate case, Sentelle recruited a fellow Reagan appointee, former U.S. Attorney Joseph diGenova, to act as the independent counsel. DiGenova was named in a sealed order on December 14, the day before the law was to lapse. (In subsequent Senate testimony, Judge Sentelle explained that his policy in selecting special prosecutors to investigate President Clinton and Democrats was to find Republicans "who had been active on the other side of the political fence." But Sentelle had followed the opposite approach when picking diGenova, a Republican, to investigate potential crimes by a Republican administration.[6])

Though diGenova's appointment was made under court seal, an order that barred disclosure of the investigation, diGenova promptly alerted the Bush White House. According to a White House phone log, diGenova called presidential counsel Boyden Gray at 2:40 p.m. on December 16. DiGenova left an "urgent" message which read: "Not at liberty to give subject b/c [because] of court order."

When I asked diGenova about the unusual message, he said he called to inform Gray that a subpoena for White House records would be forthcoming. DiGenova also recalled that he had contacted Gray only after word of the appointment had appeared in *The Washington Post*. I informed diGenova, however, that the *Post* story didn't break until the evening of December 17, more than a day after the phone call.

DiGenova called me back a few days later with a more formal answer: "One of the first things I did was to call the White House counsel's office to advise him [Gray] that there was a criminal investigation and he was to protect and preserve documents in the White House. ... They had to know there was an investigation."

Whatever diGenova's intention, however, the call did not spur Gray to issue an immediate order to White House staff about protecting records. According to another document I obtained, Gray notified the White House staff about the need to "preserve and maintain documents" only on December 21, five days after diGenova's early warning and only after the White House had received formal notification of the Passportgate investigation.

Later, diGenova's investigation did find that some relevant White House files were erased, but it was not clear if the erasures occurred between the time of diGenova's first call on December 16 and Gray's letter to the staff on December 21. At least some of the erasures were later recovered through technical means.

While diGenova's early call may not have prompted an immediate protection order, the call apparently did reassure Gray that the White House had little to worry about. On December 17, after President Bush heard about the independent counsel appointment, he called Gray, and Gray "said that the special prosecutor [diGenova] is a good and fair person and that the thing is

mainly at the State Department – the handling of the Clinton matter,"
according to Bush's diary.

Despite those assurances, Baker still fretted about the scandal's threat to
his reputation and Bush fumed about the negative press coverage. In his diary
on December 22, the President complained about "an ugly editorial by Mary
McGrory, and it will have Jim Baker climbing the wall." McGrory's column
had suggested that Baker was a natural suspect in the passport case because
"he is known as a meticulous and totally-in-control manager." To Bush,
McGrory's observations were "the meanest, nastiest, ugliest column. She has
destroyed me over and over again."

***

In the weeks after Bush's defeat, Republicans undertook a series of actions to
ensure that the investigations of the Reagan-Bush era – from its 1980 origins
in the murky October Surprise case through the Iran-Contra and Iraqgate
cases – did not outlive George H.W. Bush's Presidency.

The issue had gained new urgency when Bush's White House counsel
belatedly informed Walsh about the existence of a Bush diary that was
covered by earlier document production demands and should have been
turned over years before. These notes from 1986 and 1987 were not delivered
until December 11, 1992. Privately, Walsh was considering a possible
indictment of the ex-President for a crime similar to the one allegedly
committed by Weinberger.

Already the Republicans were stepping up their counterattack against
Walsh. Rehnquist had ousted Walsh's principal supporter on the three-judge
panel that oversaw special prosecutors, by replacing George MacKinnon
with David Sentelle. Senate Minority Leader Robert Dole of Kansas had
fired off a letter on November 9 demanding that Walsh fire James
Brosnahan, a San Francisco lawyer who had been brought in to try the
Weinberger case. Dole attacked Brosnahan's past involvement in Democratic
politics.

On November 11, four GOP senators demanded a special prosecutor to
investigate Walsh, particularly over whether the Weinberger indictment had
been timed for political reasons, though there was no evidence that was the
case. "It is time for Mr. Walsh and his staff to plead guilty to playing politics
for their taxpayer-funded inquisitions," Dole said. By December, Dole was
demanding a list of all Walsh's employees so the Republicans could conduct
personal investigations of each "employee's objectivity and impartiality."
Dole also obtained information about the staff's pay levels. "With the
election over, maybe the Walsh political operatives will decide to pack it in,"
Dole said. "The only mischief left for them is more humiliating courtroom
defeats."

Facing a suddenly expanding Iran-Contra probe that had broken through a six-year cover-up, Bush resorted to the ultimate weapon in his arsenal. On Christmas Eve 1992, Bush dealt the Iran-Contra investigation a fatal blow by pardoning Weinberger and five other Iran-Contra defendants, including CIA men Duane Clarridge, Clair George and Alan Fiers. It ranked as possibly the first time in U.S. history that a President had granted pardons in a case where he himself was a possible defendant.

A furious Walsh said Bush's action "demonstrates that powerful people with powerful allies can commit serious crimes in high office – deliberately abusing the public trust – without consequence." However, the Washington press corps mostly greeted the pardons warmly. It was a sign that in the 20 years since Watergate, the national press corps had been housebroken.

Washington Post columnist Richard Cohen spoke for many of his colleagues when he defended Bush's Iran-Contra pardons. Cohen said his view was colored by how impressed he was when he would see Weinberger in the Georgetown Safeway store, pushing his own shopping cart. "Based on my Safeway encounters, I came to think of Weinberger as a basic sort of guy, candid and no nonsense – which is the way much of official Washington saw him," Cohen wrote. "Cap, my Safeway buddy, walks, and that's all right with me."[7]

There would be one final chapter to the Iran-Contra Affair, however. After Bush left office in 1993, the ex-President reneged on an understanding that he would submit to a full-scale interview with Walsh about Bush's real involvement in the scandal. Walsh had postponed the questioning until after the presidential election to spare Bush the distraction. But once out of office, Bush refused to cooperate. Signaling the widespread disdain for Walsh's long Iran-Contra probe, the nation's news media barely mentioned Bush's non-testimony.

"My immediate instinct was to use the grand jury and subpoena Bush," Walsh wrote in his memoirs *Firewall*. "In this I was alone. The staff unanimously opposed the use of the grand jury, arguing that to do so would exaggerate public expectations and would appear retaliatory."

Walsh's staff, unlike their octogenarian boss, had futures to worry about. The Republicans had already made clear that they were prepared to conduct individual investigations of each member of the prosecution team. That could have meant career ruin for ambitious lawyers, just as it had for journalists who were too persistent. Walsh saw no choice but to fold his tent. "I gave up," Walsh said. "We then turned our full attention to our final report."

With President Clinton in office, interest in pursuing evidence of historic Republican crimes almost vanished. Clinton wrote in his 2004 memoirs, *My Life*, that he "disagreed with the [Iran-Contra] pardons and could have made more of them but didn't." Clinton cited several reasons for giving his predecessor a pass. "I wanted the country to be more united, not more divided, even if that split would be to my political advantage," Clinton wrote. "Finally, President Bush had given decades of service to our country, and I thought we should allow him to retire in peace, leaving the matter between him and his conscience."[8]

Spencer Oliver, who was at the nexus of several investigations into Reagan-Bush wrongdoing, urged the incoming Clinton administration to choose the harder path of truth and justice over the sentimentality of letting George H.W. Bush carry his secrets off into the sunset. Unlike Clinton and many of his newcomers, Oliver had stood at the front lines facing the Republican abuses of power for years.

"They were naïve," Oliver said of the Clinton crowd. "There was nobody in the upper echelons of the Clinton campaign who had ever been involved in any of the investigations – the oversight [committees], Iran-Contra or Watergate or anything like that. Clinton didn't know anything about that. He just assumed all that stuff was just politics. ... He was not going to get down in the gutter like they did. Clinton wanted to be magnanimous in victory. They just got taken in."

When Oliver protested Clinton plans to put a neoconservative Democrat into a key transition slot, Clinton aide Samuel Berger defended the choice because the fellow had helped deliver some hard-line "Scoop Jackson Democrats." Oliver said Berger's position was that "we don't want to hold any grudges. We won. We need to be gracious and magnanimous." Oliver disagreed: "I said, 'That's very naïve, Sandy. Those of us, who have been sitting up here on the Hill in the trenches for the last ten years on the receiving end of this stuff, know a lot better what these guys are all about, and if you're not careful, you'll end up with a one-term administration.'"

Within Washington's mainstream political culture, the Iran-Contra investigation was set aside as a trivial matter, with special prosecutor Walsh judged a kind of strange obsessive. *Washington Post* writer Marjorie Williams delivered that judgment in a *Washington Post* Sunday magazine article, which read: "In the utilitarian political universe of Washington, consistency like Walsh's is distinctly suspect. It began to seem ... rigid of him to care so much. So un-Washington. Hence the gathering critique of his efforts as vindictive, extreme. Ideological. ... But the truth is that when Walsh finally goes home, he will leave a perceived loser."[9]

***

Even in the Passportgate affair, in which Clinton and his mother were the victims of Republican abuses of their privacy rights, the Democrats demurred as a conservative Republican "independent counsel" gave the Bush administration a clean bill of health.

Luckily, too, for the Bush legacy, diGenova was hiring his Passportgate staff in early 1993 just as the House October Surprise Task Force was disbanding. DiGenova snapped up six veterans of that staff. The retreads included Michael Zeldin, a Democrat who had served in the Reagan-Bush Justice Department, and associate independent counsel David Laufman, who had worked for the CIA.

As part of the investigation, diGenova conducted two formal interviews with former President Bush at his office in Houston. Handwritten notes from the first interview on October 23, 1993, stated that diGenova first assured Bush that his staff lawyers were "all seasoned prof[essional] prosecutors who know what a real crime looks like. ... [This is] not a gen[eral] probe of pol[itics] in Amer[ica] or dirty tricks, etc., or a general license to rummage in people's personal lives."

The FBI's typewritten report of the interview noted that Bush acknowledged his personal interest in turning up derogatory information about Clinton and having it released, but he denied giving a direct order for the passport search. "Although he [Bush] did not recall tasking Baker to research any particular matter, he may have asked why the campaign did not know more about Clinton's demonstrating," the FBI interview report stated. As for hearing about the FOIA requests before the passport search, "President Bush remembered a general discussion that people were trying to get some information ... although he could provide no details as to who may have mentioned this to him. ...

"The President advised that ... he probably would have said, 'Hooray, somebody's going to finally do something about this.' If he had learned that *The Washington Times* was planning to publish an article, he would have said, 'That's good, it's about time.' ... Based on his 'depth of feeling' on this issue, President Bush responded to a hypothetical question that he would have recommended getting the truth out if it were legal."

Bush said he could not recall if he had heard about the passport search before it appeared in the press. But he added that he might have indirectly encouraged his subordinates to pursue those anti-Clinton rumors. "The President added that he would not have been concerned over the legality of the issue but just the facts and what was in the files," the FBI wrote.

"President Bush advised that if he had made some informal statement, although a staffer may have considered the President to have a one-track mind [on the topic], James Baker would not be motivated by such a casual or visceral comment because he would protect the President from rushing off to do something which could cause problems later. Although Baker would go along with the President's decision on major issues, President Bush did not think Baker would be motivated to follow up on something the President was nagging about. He [Bush] doubted Baker would have tasked anyone to follow up. ... The President stated that Baker would not have been driven by the President to find out about the [Clinton] FOIA requests although Baker may have said that the President had expressed an interest, suggesting that they get something on it."

Bush clearly was disappointed that the searches uncovered so little. "The President described himself as being indignant over the fact that the campaign did not find out what Clinton was doing," the FBI report stated.

Near the end of the interview, Bush voiced his "bitterness" toward several individuals whom he felt contributed to his 1992 defeat. They included Iran-Contra special prosecutor Walsh; one of Walsh's deputies, James Brosnahan; and Ross Perot. According to interview notes, Bush added that Perot was a "bastard" and "dangerous." As the interview ended, two of diGenova's assistants – Lisa Rich and Laura Laughlin – asked Bush for autographs.

After the Bush interviews, diGenova began work on his final report. Despite the evidence that Clinton's files had been exploited to influence the outcome of a presidential election, diGenova concluded that there was no wrongdoing by anyone in the Bush administration. DiGenova added "that certain White House personnel may have indirectly encouraged the search for Clinton's passport files by making inquiry about the status of responses to [FOIA] requests." As for the Oval Office, diGenova "found no evidence that President Bush was involved in this matter." [10]

DiGenova reserved his toughest criticism for State Department Inspector General Sherman Funk for suspecting that a crime had been committed in the first place. DiGenova castigated Funk for "a woefully inadequate understanding of the facts."

John Duncan, a senior lawyer in Funk's office, protested diGenova's findings of no criminal wrongdoing. "Astoundingly, [diGenova] has also concluded that no senior-level party to the search did anything improper whatever," Duncan wrote. "The Independent Counsel has provided his personal absolution to individuals who we found had attempted to use their U.S. Government positions to manipulate the election of President of the United States." [11]

***

On the historical question of secret Reagan-Bush military support for Iraq, the Clinton administration again took a dive.

In January 1995, Clinton's Justice Department issued a report clearing the Reagan-Bush administration of all suspicion of wrongdoing. The Clinton investigators, led by John M. Hogan, an assistant to Attorney General Janet Reno, expressed confidence in their conclusion that they "did not find evidence that U.S. agencies or officials illegally armed Iraq." But the review noted, curiously, that the CIA had withheld an unknown number of documents that were contained in "sensitive compartments" that were denied to the investigators.

Two weeks later, Hogan and his team looked gullible when former Reagan-Bush national security official Howard Teicher submitted a sworn affidavit in federal court in Miami, confirming many of the Iraqgate allegations of secret arms sales. The Teicher affidavit was the first public account by a Reagan insider that the covert U.S.-Iraq relationship had included arranging third-country shipments of weapons to Saddam Hussein's regime.

Teicher, who had been on Reagan's National Security Council staff, traced the U.S. tilt to Iraq to a turning point in the Iran-Iraq War in 1982 when Iran gained the upper hand and fears swept through the U.S. government that Iran's army might slice through Iraq to the oil fields of Kuwait and Saudi Arabia.

"In the Spring of 1982, Iraq teetered on the brink of losing its war with Iran," Teicher wrote. "The Iranians discovered a gap in the Iraqi defenses along the Iran-Iraq border between Baghdad to the north and Basra to the south. Iran positioned a massive invasion force directly across from the gap in the Iraqi defenses. An Iranian breakthrough at the spot would have cutoff Baghdad from Basra and would have resulted in Iraq's defeat. ... In June 1982, President Reagan decided that the United States could not afford to allow Iraq to lose the war to Iran."

Teicher wrote that he helped draft a secret national security decision directive that Reagan signed to authorize covert U.S. assistance to Saddam Hussein's military. "The NSDD, including even its identifying number, is classified," Teicher wrote.

The effort to arm the Iraqis was "spearheaded" by CIA Director William Casey and involved his deputy, Robert Gates, according to Teicher's affidavit. "The CIA, including both CIA Director Casey and Deputy Director Gates, knew of, approved of, and assisted in the sale of non-U.S. origin military weapons, ammunition and vehicles to Iraq," Teicher wrote.

Teicher said he also went to Iraq with Rumsfeld in 1984 to convey a secret Israeli offer to assist Iraq after Israel had concluded that Iran was becoming a greater danger. "I traveled with Rumsfeld to Baghdad and was present at the meeting in which Rumsfeld told Iraqi Foreign Minister Tariq Aziz about Israel's offer of assistance," Teicher wrote. "Aziz refused even to accept the Israelis' letter to Hussein offering assistance because Aziz told us that he would be executed on the spot by Hussein if he did so."

Another key player in Reagan's Iraq tilt was then-Vice President George H.W. Bush, according to Teicher's affidavit. "In 1986, President Reagan sent a secret message to Saddam Hussein telling him that Iraq should step up its air war and bombing of Iran," Teicher wrote. "This message was delivered by Vice President Bush who communicated it to Egyptian President Mubarak, who in turn passed the message to Saddam Hussein.

"Similar strategic operational military advice was passed to Saddam Hussein through various meetings with European and Middle Eastern heads of state. I authored Bush's talking points for the 1986 meeting with Mubarak and personally attended numerous meetings with European and Middle East heads of state where the strategic operational advice was communicated."

Teicher's affidavit represented a major break in the historical mystery of U.S. aid to Iraq. But it complicated a criminal arms-trafficking case that Clinton's Justice Department was prosecuting against Teledyne Industries and a salesman named Ed Johnson. They had allegedly sold explosive pellets to Chilean arms manufacturer Carlos Cardoen, who used them to manufacture cluster bombs for Iraq. The prosecutors took their fury out on Teicher, insisting that his affidavit was unreliable and threatening him with dire consequences for coming forward. Yet, while deeming Teicher's affidavit false, the Clinton administration also declared the document a state secret, classifying it and putting it under court seal. A few copies, however, had been distributed outside the court and the text was soon posted on the Internet.

After officially suppressing the Teicher affidavit, the Justice Department prosecutors persuaded the judge presiding in the Teledyne-Johnson case to rule testimony about the Reagan-Bush policies to be irrelevant. Unable to mount its planned defense, Teledyne agreed to plead guilty and accept a $13 million fine. Johnson, the salesman who had earned a modest salary in the mid-$30,000 range, was convicted of illegal arms trafficking and given a prison term.

While the Clinton administration protected the Reagan-Bush legacy, that generosity did Clinton little good when it came to the possibility of a reciprocal bipartisanship. From Clinton's first days, the Republicans and their conservative allies did whatever they could to destroy his Presidency while humiliating him and his wife, Hillary Clinton. Again, the conservative news media played a key part, switching almost overnight from an aggressive defense to an equally aggressive offense.

Spencer Oliver watched with amazement as the new Clinton team didn't even staff key offices with loyalists. "They left a lot of people in place in the government who were hardcore Republican operatives," Oliver said. "Their loyalties were not to Clinton at all. ... The whole first three years of the Clinton administration, everything they did wrong was leaked, everything, every peccadillo, every mistake, whether it was the White House Travel Office, Hillary's (health care) task force, whatever it was. They never really took control of the government."[*]

---

[*] After Representative Dante Fascell retired at the start of 1993, Spencer Oliver left his congressional job and was named secretary general of the parliamentary assembly of the Organization for Security and Cooperation in Europe. He moved to Copenhagen, Denmark, where the assembly is based.

Chapter 18: Ties That Bind

On January 28, 1995, a beaming Reverend Jerry Falwell told his Old Time Gospel Hour congregation news that seemed heaven sent. The rotund televangelist hailed two Virginia businessmen as financial saviors of debt-ridden Liberty University, the fundamentalist Christian school that Falwell had made the crown jewel of his Religious Right empire.

"They had to borrow money, hock their houses, hock everything," said Falwell. "Thank God for friends like Dan Reber and Jimmy Thomas." Falwell's congregation rose as one to applaud. The star of the moment was Daniel Reber, who was standing behind Falwell. Thomas was not present.

Reber and Thomas earned Falwell's public gratitude by excusing the Lynchburg, Virginia, school of about one-half of its $73 million debt. In the late 1980s, that flood of red ink had forced Falwell to abandon his Moral Majority political organization and the debt nearly drowned Liberty University in bankruptcy. Reber and Thomas came to Falwell's rescue in the nick of time. Their non-profit Christian Heritage Foundation of Forest, Virginia, snapped up a big chunk of Liberty's debt for $2.5 million, a fraction of its face value. Thousands of small religious investors who had bought church construction bonds through a Texas company were the big losers.

But Falwell was joyous. He told local reporters that the moment was "the greatest single day of financial advantage" in the school's history. Left unmentioned in the happy sermon was the identity of the bigger guardian angel who had appeared at the propitious moment to protect Falwell's financial interests. Falwell's secret benefactor was the Reverend Sun Myung Moon, the self-proclaimed South Korean Messiah who is controversial with many fundamentalist Christians because of his strange Biblical interpretations and his alleged brainwashing of thousands of young Americans, often shattering their bonds with their biological families, replaced by Moon and his wife as the True Parents.

Covertly, Moon had helped bail out Liberty University through one of his front groups which funneled $3.5 million to the Reber-Thomas Christian Heritage Foundation, the non-profit that had purchased the school's debt. I discovered this Moon-Falwell connection while looking for something else: how much Moon's Women's Federation for World Peace had paid former President George H.W. Bush for a series of speeches in Asia in 1995. I obtained the federation's Internal Revenue Service records but discovered that Bush's undisclosed speaking fee was buried in a line item of $13.6 million for conference expenses.

There was, however, another listing for a $3.5 million "educational" grant to the Christian Heritage Foundation. A call to the Virginia corporate records office confirmed that the foundation was the one run by Reber and Thomas. In a subsequent interview, the Women Federation's vice president Susan Fefferman confirmed that the $3.5 million grant had gone to "Mr. Falwell's people" for the benefit of Liberty University. "It was Dan Reber," she said. But she could not recall much else about the grant, even though it was by far the largest single grant awarded by the federation that year.

For details on the grant, Fefferman referred me to Keith Cooperrider, the federation's treasurer. Cooperrider was also the chief financial officer of Moon's *Washington Times* and a longtime Unification Church functionary. Cooperrider did not return calls seeking comment. Falwell and Reber also failed to respond to my calls, though Falwell later defended his acceptance of the money by saying it had no influence on his ministry.

"If the American Atheists Society or Saddam Hussein himself ever sent an unrestricted gift to any of my ministries," Falwell said, "be assured I will operate on Billy Sunday's philosophy: The Devil's had it long enough, and quickly cash the check."[1]

But the public record also reveals that Falwell solicited Moon's help in bailing out Liberty University. In a lawsuit filed in the Circuit Court of Bedford County – a community in southwestern Virginia – two of Reber's former business associates alleged that Reber and Falwell flew to South Korea on January 9, 1994, on a seven-day "secret trip" to meet "with representatives of the Unification Church." The court document states that Reber and Falwell were accompanied to South Korea by Ronald S. Godwin, who had been executive director of Falwell's Moral Majority before signing on as vice president of Moon's *Washington Times*.

According to Bedford County court records, Reber, Falwell and Godwin also had discussions at Liberty University in 1993 with Dong Moon Joo, one of Moon's right-hand men and president of *The Washington Times*. Though Reber was queried about the purposes of the Moon-connected meetings in the court papers, he settled the business dispute before responding to interrogatories or submitting to a deposition. He denied any legal wrongdoing.

But Moon's secret financial ties to Falwell raised some sensitive political questions since the bail-out came at a time when Falwell was collaborating with other conservatives who were producing videos that accused President Bill Clinton of murder and cocaine trafficking. The videos

– "Circle of Power" and "The Clinton Chronicles" – were produced by Pat Matrisciana and Larry Nichols and were distributed nationwide by Falwell's Liberty Alliance. Reaching hundreds of thousands of viewers, the videos helped stoke the fires of the "Clinton scandals," which kept the Clinton administration on the political defensive for much of its eight years and helped create the hostile environment that made the Clinton impeachment possible in 1998.

Did the $3.5 million from Moon's front group give Falwell the means to become a national pitchman for the conspiracy-mongering videos? Indeed, did Moon help to bankroll the scandal mongering as part of a design to cripple the Clinton Presidency and pave the way for an administration more to Moon's liking?

When the *Roanoke Times & World News* interviewed Falwell about the Liberty University bail-out, the televangelist sat at his desk in front of two life-size, full-color cutouts of Bill and Hillary Clinton, whom he jokingly called his "advisers." The cut-outs were gifts from Liberty staffers in recognition of Falwell's success in distributing the Clinton-bashing videos.[2]

Although the most serious allegations in the videos were proven false,[3] the Christian Right's Citizens for Honest Government continued to peddle the allegations of Clinton-connected cocaine smuggling through the Mena, Arkansas, airport in another video, "The Mena Cover-up." In a promotional letter, the group's president, Pat Matrisciana, declared that "with Bill Clinton in the White House, it is entirely possible – even probable – that U.S. government policy at the highest levels is being controlled by the narcotics kingpins in Colombia."

The irony of the allegation, however, was that Falwell's financial angel – Sun Myung Moon – was the one with mysterious connections to South American drug lords dating back at least to his cozy relations with Bolivia's Cocaine Coup government in the early 1980s. Moon, whose history also included close ties to the Asian *yakuza* crime organization and longstanding allegations of money laundering, had achieved extraordinary influence at the highest levels of the U.S. government by funneling hundreds of millions of dollars into conservative causes.

Still, the Mena accusations against Clinton were kept alive through the 1990s by conservatives although a two-year investigation by the Republican-controlled House Banking Committee failed to turn up any incriminating evidence. "We haven't come up with anything to support these allegations concerning then-Governor Clinton," committee spokesman David Runkel told me. But the committee held off on publishing a long-promised report that would have formally cleared Clinton.

Falwell reached a conclusion, too, that the "Clinton Chronicles" may have been unfair, but he still refused to apologize to Clinton. On CNBC's "Rivera Live" on March 25, 1998, Falwell said, "If I had it to do all over again, I wouldn't do it, and I'm sorry I did." But he immediately sought to push the blame back onto Clinton. "The fact is the President has over these last five years, there's just a continual cloud. And – I would think that he himself would want to get this behind him and deal with it forthrightly."

* * *

By the mid-1990s, Sun Myung Moon represented a potential embarrassment to the American Right for another reason: Moon had grown harshly anti-American after his political ally, George H.W. Bush, was ousted from office. The conservatives were lucky that few American news outlets were interested in the increasingly bizarre comments from the South Korean benefactor of U.S. conservative causes.

In earlier years, though he privately disdained America's concept of individual liberty, Moon publicly stressed his love for the United States. On September 18, 1976, for instance, Moon staged a red-white-and-blue flag-draped rally at the Washington Monument, declaring that "I not only respect America, but truly love this nation."

Even years later, Unification Church recruiters would show that video to young Americans. One recruit, New York University freshman John Stacey, was impressed with the patriotic images after he was shown the video by the Moon front, Collegiate Association for Research of Principles (CARP). "American flags were everywhere," recalled Stacey, a thin young man from central New Jersey. "The first video they showed me was Reverend Moon praising America and praising Christianity." In 1992, Stacey considered himself a patriotic American and a faithful Christian.

Stacey soon joined the Unification Church and rose to become a Pacific Northwest leader in CARP. "They liked to hang me up because I'm young and I'm American," Stacey told me. "It's a good image for the church. They try to create the all-American look."

But Stacey gradually discovered a different reality. At a 1995 leadership conference at a church compound in Anchorage, Alaska, Stacey met face-to-face with Moon who was sitting on a throne-like chair while a group of American followers, many middle-aged converts from the 1970s, sat at his feet like children. "Reverend Moon looked at me straight in the eye and said, 'America is Satanic. America is so Satanic that even hamburgers should be considered evil, because they come from America,'" Stacey said. "Hamburgers! My father was a butcher, so that bothered me. ... I started feeling that I was betraying my country."

Moon's criticism of Jesus also unsettled Stacey. "In the church, it's very anti-Jesus," Stacey said. "Jesus failed miserably. He died a lonely death. Reverend Moon is the hero that comes and saves pathetic Jesus. Reverend Moon is better than God. ... That's why I left the Moonies. Because it started to feel like idolatry. He's promoting idolatry."

After years in the sunlight of acceptance from the Reagan-Bush administrations, Moon's entered years of eclipse as his influence faded during the Clinton administration and his hostility toward the United States grew. "America has become the kingdom of individualism, and its people are individualists," Moon preached in Tarrytown, N.Y., on March 5, 1995. "You must realize that America has become the kingdom of Satan."

Moon also blamed his followers for failing him. "If Father were to complain about his course of life during the past 40 years," Moon said during a speech on January 2, 1996, speaking of himself in the third person, "imagine how much he would have been able to complain. ... Many people didn't accomplish their missions. If Father had begun to complain about his followers and the evil world that didn't accept him, what kind of miserable life Father would have. Do you understand?"

In a speech to his followers on August 4, 1996, Moon vowed that the church's eventual dominance over the United States would be followed by the liquidation of American individualism and the establishment of Moon's theocratic rule. "Americans who continue to maintain their privacy and extreme individualism are foolish people," Moon declared. "The world will reject Americans who continue to be so foolish. Once you have this great power of love, which is big enough to swallow entire America, there may be some individuals who complain inside your stomach. However, they will be digested."

During the same sermon, Moon decried assertive American women. "American women have the tendency to consider that women are in the subject position," he said. "However, woman's shape is like that of a receptacle. The concave shape is a receiving shape. Whereas, the convex shape symbolizes giving. ... Since man contains the seed of life, he should plant it in the deepest place. Does woman contain the seed of life? Absolutely not. Then if you desire to receive the seed of life, you have to become an absolute object. In order to qualify as an absolute object, you need to demonstrate absolute faith, love and obedience to your subject. Absolute obedience means that you have to negate yourself 100 percent."

Though Moon had downplayed his provocative sexual beliefs since coming to America, sometimes the old themes popped up. After Moon spoke in Minneapolis on October 26, 1996, a reporter for the *Unification News*, an internal newsletter, commented that "what the audience heard was not the usual things that one would expect to hear from a minister. Reverend Moon's talk included a very frank discussion of the purpose, role and true value of the sexual organs."[4]

On May 1, 1997, Moon told a group of followers that "the country that represents Satan's harvest is America."[5] Moon also declared that "Satan created this kind of Hell on Earth," the United States. He again denounced American women as having "inherited the line of prostitutes. ... American women are even worse because they practice free sex just because they enjoy it."

Lashing out at the United States again, Moon decried American tolerance of homosexuals, whom he likened to "dirty dung-eating dogs." For Americans who "truly love such dogs," Moon said, "they also become like dung-eating dogs and produce that quality of life."[6]

***

In fall 1996, one of Sun Myung Moon's forays into the high-priced world of media and politics was in trouble. South American journalists were writing scathingly about Moon's plan to open a regional newspaper that the 77-year-old founder of the Korean-based Unification Church hoped would give him the same influence in Latin America that *The Washington Times* had in the United States.

As publication day ticked closer for Moon's *Tiempos del Mundo*, leading South American newspapers recounted unsavory chapters of Moon's history, including his links with South Korea's fearsome intelligence service and with violent anticommunist organizations. In the early 1980s, Moon had used friendships with the military dictators in Argentina and Uruguay to invest in those two countries. Moon was such a pal that Argentine generals gave him an honorary award for siding with Argentina's junta when it invaded the Falklands Islands.[7] Moon also bought large tracts of agricultural lands in Paraguay. *La Nacion* reported that Moon had discussed these business ventures with Paraguay's ex-dictator Alfredo Stroessner.[8]

Moon's disciples fumed about these critical stories and accused the Argentine news media of trying to sabotage Moon's plans for an inaugural gala in Buenos Aires on November 23. "The local press was trying to undermine the event," complained the *Unification News*.[9]

Given the controversy, Argentina's elected president, Carlos Menem, decided to reject Moon's invitation. But Moon had a trump card to play in his bid for South American respectability: the endorsement of an ex-President of the United States, George H.W. Bush. Agreeing to speak at the newspaper's launch, Bush flew aboard a private plane, arriving in Buenos Aires on November 22. Bush stayed at Menem's official residence, the Olivos, though Bush's presence didn't change Menem's mind about attending the gala.

Still, as the biggest VIP at the inaugural celebration, Bush saved the day, Moon's followers gushed. "Mr. Bush's presence as keynote speaker gave the event invaluable prestige," wrote the *Unification News*. "Father [Moon] and Mother [Mrs. Moon] sat with several of the True Children [Moon's offspring] just a few feet from the podium" where Bush spoke. Before about 900 Moon guests at the Sheraton Hotel, Bush lavished praise on Moon.

"I want to salute Reverend Moon, who is the founder of *The Washington Times* and also of *Tiempos del Mundo*," Bush declared. "A lot of my friends in South America don't know about *The Washington Times*, but it is an independent voice. The editors of *The Washington Times* tell me that never once has the man with the vision interfered with the running of the paper, a paper that in my view brings sanity to Washington, D.C. I am convinced that *Tiempos del Mundo* is going to do the same thing" in Latin America.

Bush then held up the colorful new newspaper and complimented several articles, including one flattering piece about his wife Barbara. Bush's speech was so effusive that it surprised even Moon's followers. "Once again, heaven turned a disappointment into a victory," the *Unification News* exulted. "Everyone was delighted to hear his compliments. We knew he would give an appropriate and 'nice' speech, but praise in Father's presence was more than we expected. ... It was vindication. We could just hear a sigh of relief from Heaven."

While Bush's assertion about Moon's newspaper as a voice of "sanity" may be a matter of opinion, Bush's vouching for *The Washington Times'* editorial independence simply wasn't true. Almost since it opened in 1982, a string of senior editors and correspondents have resigned, citing the manipulation of the news by Moon and his subordinates. The first editor, James Whelan, resigned in 1984, confessing that "I have blood on my hands" for helping Moon's church achieve greater legitimacy.

But Bush's boosterism was just what Moon needed in South America. "The day after," the *Unification News* observed, "the press did a 180-degree about-turn once they realized that the event had the support of a U.S. President." With Bush's help, Moon had gained another beachhead for his worldwide business-religious-political-media empire.

After the event, Menem told reporters from *La Nacion* that Bush had claimed privately to be only a mercenary who did not really know Moon. "Bush told me he came and charged money to do it," Menem said.[10] But Bush was not telling Menem the whole story. By fall 1996, Bush and Moon had been working in political tandem for at least a decade and a half. The ex-President also had been earning huge speaking fees as a front man for Moon for more than a year.

In September 1995, Bush and his wife, Barbara, gave six speeches in Asia for the Women's Federation for World Peace, a group led by Moon's wife, Hak Ja Han Moon. In one speech on September 14 to 50,000 Moon supporters in Tokyo, Bush insisted that "what really counts is faith, family and friends." Mrs. Moon followed the ex-President to the podium and announced that "it has to be Reverend Moon to save the United States, which is in decline because of the destruction of the family and moral decay."[11]

In summer 1996, Bush was lending his prestige to Moon again. Bush addressed the Moon-connected Family Federation for World Peace in

Washington, an event that gained notoriety when comedian Bill Cosby tried to back out of his contract after learning of Moon's connection. Bush had no such qualms.[12]

Throughout these public appearances for Moon, Bush's office refused to divulge how much Moon-affiliated organizations have paid the ex-President. But estimates of Bush's fee for the Buenos Aires appearance alone ran between $100,000 and $500,000. Sources close to the Unification Church have put the total Bush-Moon package in the millions, with one source telling me that Bush stood to make as much as $10 million total from Moon's organization.

The senior George Bush may have had a political motive as well. By 1996, sources close to Bush were saying the ex-President was working hard to enlist well-to-do conservatives and their money behind the presidential candidacy of his son, George W. Bush. Moon was one of the deepest pockets in right-wing circles.

                                    ***

Moon's endless jingle of deep-pocket cash caused many conservatives – not only the senior George Bush – to turn a deaf ear toward Moon's anti-American diatribes, even as Republicans lashed out at Bill Clinton and Al Gore for accepting campaign contributions from supposedly mysterious Asian sources.

With unintended irony, Moon's *Washington Times* often led the way in criticizing alleged foreign donations to the Clinton-Gore team as it ran for reelection in 1996. "More than a million dollars of this foreign money is believed to have been contributed to the Democrats, putting the election up for auction," charged *Times'* editor Wesley Pruden in a typical column.[13] No one in the mainstream news media bothered to point out that Moon was losing an estimated $1 million of mysterious Asian money on *The Washington Times* and its sister publications *each week*.

In the 1990s, seeing his church membership decline in the United States along with his access to the Executive Branch, Moon's bitterness led him to shift his personal base of operations to a luxurious estate in Uruguay, where the church had been investing tens of millions of dollars since the early 1980s.

In a sermon on January 2, 1996, Moon was unusually blunt about how he expected the church's wealth to buy influence among the powerful in South America, just as it did in Washington. "Father has been practicing the philosophy of fishing here," Moon said, through an interpreter who spoke of Moon in the third person. "He [Moon] gave the bait to Uruguay and then the bigger fish of Argentina, Brazil and Paraguay kept their mouths open, waiting for a bigger bait silently. The bigger the fish, the bigger the mouth. Therefore, Father is able to hook them more easily."

As part of his business strategy, Moon explained that he would dot the continent with small airstrips and construct bases for submarines which could evade Coast Guard patrols. His airfield project would allow tourists to visit "hidden, untouched, small places" throughout South America, he said. "Therefore, they need small airplanes and small landing strips in the remote countryside. ... In the near future, we will have many small airports throughout the world." Moon wanted the submarines because "there are so many restrictions due to national boundaries worldwide. If you have a submarine, you don't have to be bound in that way."

(As strange as Moon's submarine project might sound, a cable from the U.S. Embassy in Japan, dated February 18, 1994, cited press reports that a Moon-connected Japanese company, Toen Shoji, had bought 40 Russian submarines. The subs were supposedly bound for North Korea where they were to be dismantled and melted down as scrap.)

Moon also recognized the importance of media in protecting his curious operations, which sounded a lot like an invitation to drug traffickers. He boasted to his followers that with his vast array of political and media assets, he will dominate the new Information Age. "That is why Father has been combining and organizing scholars from all over the world, and also newspaper organizations – in order to make propaganda," Moon said.

With his criminal record, Moon would have seemed a natural attraction for U.S. government scrutiny. But Moon may have purchased insurance against any intrusive investigation by buying so many powerful American politicians that Washington's power centers can no more afford the scrutiny than he can.

Even as he turned his back on the United States in the mid-1990s, Moon remembered to keep up some of his important friendships in the United States. In 1997, his Washington Times Foundation made a $1 million-plus donation to George H.W. Bush's presidential library in Texas.[14]

***

Despite his confidence about hooking fish in South America, Moon's relocation to Uruguay didn't go entirely without a hitch. More evidence surfaced about Moon's alleged South American money laundry.

In 1996, the Uruguayan bank employees union blew the whistle on one scheme in which some 4,200 female Japanese followers of Moon allegedly walked into the Moon-controlled Banco de Credito in Montevideo and deposited as much as $25,000 each. The money from the women went into the account of an anonymous association called Cami II, which was controlled by Moon's Unification Church. In one day, Cami II received $19 million and, by the time the parade of women ended, the total had swelled to about $80 million. It was not clear where the money originated, nor how many other times Moon's organization has used this tactic – sometimes known as "smurfing" – to transfer untraceable cash into Uruguay. Authorities did not push the money-laundering investigation, apparently out of deference to Moon's political influence and fear of disrupting Uruguay's secretive banking industry.[15]

Still, Opus Dei, a powerful Roman Catholic group, and some investigative journalists kept up pressure for a fuller examination of financial irregularities at Moon's bank. Sometimes, the critics found their work a risky business. In January 1997, only two months after the money-laundering flap, Pablo Alfano, a reporter for *El Observador* who had been investigating Moon's operations, was kidnapped by two unidentified men. The men claimed not to belong to Moon's Unification Church, but threatened Alfano at gunpoint unless he revealed his sources on Moon's operations.

One gunman shoved a revolver into Alfano's mouth and warned "this is no joke." After holding Alfano for 30 minutes, the gunmen returned the reporter to his house, with a warning that they knew his movements and those of his family. Despite the threats, the reporter said he refused to disclose his sources. But the message was clear: he should drop his investigation.[16]

Other critics condemned Moon's heavy-handed tactics. "The first thing we ought to do is clarify to the people [of Uruguay] that Moon's sect is a type of modern pirate that came to the country to perform obscure money operations, such as money laundering," said Jorge Zabalza, who was a leader of the Movimiento de Participacion Popular, part of Montevideo's ruling left-of-center political coalition. "This sect is a kind of religious mob that is trying to get public support to pursue its business."

On September 18, 1998, Uruguay's central bank intervened to seize control of the management of Moon's Banco de Credito. The action followed a warning a day earlier that the bank was violating the nation's liquidity rules by running massive debts and was in need of recapitalization. Instead, Moon-connected companies took out an additional $35 million in loans, leaving the bank effectively devoid of assets. Uruguay's bank controller put the bank's accumulated debt at $161 million.[17]

Moon's need to "crater" one of his principal financial institutions was not the sign of an up-and-up businessman who simply supported political projects because he had plenty of extra money and a strong sense of civic duty. The events in Uruguay might reasonably have prompted more questions in the United States about how the South Korean theocrat could continue lavishing hundreds of millions of dollars on U.S. conservative publications and causes. But those follow-up questions were never asked. Moon apparently had hooked too many large-mouthed fish in both South and North America.

Chapter 19: Moon's Generation Next

In August 1995, a thin dark-haired Asian woman furtively led her five children in an escape from an elegant mansion on an 18-acre estate overlooking the Hudson River north of New York City. Fearful of her tyrannical husband, the woman was abandoning a life as a modern-day princess who had "wanted for nothing," a pampered existence with docile American servants tending to her every need.

But her husband's violent behavior, made worse by a cocaine addiction and strange sexual habits, finally drove the woman to flight. She took her children from Irvington, New York, to Massachusetts and hid out with relatives. The woman's story bubbled briefly to the surface weeks later when she filed for a divorce in Middlesex Probate Court in Massachusetts. But the case still received little attention, even though it held the key to unlocking secrets of a troubling international scandal involving power, money and sex.

The woman was Nansook Moon, described by friends as resembling a Korean Faye Dunaway. Nansook also was the daughter-in-law of the Reverend Sun Myung Moon. At 15, Nansook was picked by Moon to be the bride of Hyo Jin Moon, the eldest son from Moon's second marriage. Then 19, Hyo Jin was considered Moon's heir apparent – the future overseer of the church's vast business empire and its secret network of political connections. On one level, the Nansook case challenged Moon's peculiar theology which makes him the all-wise Messiah and his immediate family the embodiment of human perfection.

Yet, inside the church, the Moon children gained a reputation as spoiled rich kids, buying whatever they wished and waited upon by worshipful American church members. When one daughter wanted to ride in Olympic equestrian events, Moon built a horse-riding facility in Deer Park, New York, for $10 million. When Hyo Jin fancied himself a heavy-metal rock musician, Moon snapped up New York City's Manhattan Center, an old opera house with a recording studio.

But more important to American politics is how the Nansook case strikes at the hypocrisy of "pro-family" conservatives who have accepted Moon's financial largesse and tolerated Moon's expanding political influence. The Nansook case also implicates Moon's organization in a wide variety of financial irregularities, including money laundering. In a sworn affidavit – and a later book – Nansook said the price for her life of luxury was tolerating Hyo Jin's violent outbursts and being part of what she regarded as a criminal enterprise.

"From very early in our marriage, Hyo Jin has abused drugs and alcohol and is an addict as a result," Nansook wrote in the affidavit. "He has a ritual of secreting himself in the master bedroom, sometimes for hours, sometimes for days, drinking alcohol, using cocaine and watching pornographic films. ... When he emerges he is more angry and more volatile." Nansook described a pattern of abuse which included Hyo Jin beating her in 1994 when she disrupted one of his cocaine parties. "He punched me in the nose and blood came rushing out," Nansook wrote. "He then smeared my blood on his hand, licked his hand and said, 'It tastes good. This is fun.'" At the time, she was seven months pregnant.

On another occasion, Nansook said he forced her to stand naked in front of him for hours because "I needed to be humiliated." Meanwhile, Nansook complained that her in-laws did little to confront Hyo Jin. "Although Hyo Jin's family knew of his addictions and his abuse of me and the children, I received very little emotional or physical support from them," Nansook wrote. "I was constantly at the mercy of Hyo Jin's erratic and cruel behavior."

To finance his personal and business activities, Hyo Jin received hundreds of thousands of dollars in unaccounted cash, Nansook said. "On one occasion, I saw Hyo Jin bring home a box about 24 inches wide, 12 inches tall and six inches deep," she wrote in her affidavit. "He stated that he had received it from his father. He opened it. ... It was filled with $100 bills stacked in bunches of $10,000 each for a total of $1 million in cash! He took this money and gave $600,000 to the Manhattan Center, a church recording studio that he ostensibly runs. He kept the remaining $400,000 for himself. ... Within six months he had spent it all on himself, buying cocaine and alcohol, entertaining his friends every night, and giving expensive gifts to other women."

Another time, a Filipino church member gave Hyo Jin $270,000 in cash, according to Nansook. She added that Hyo Jin also ordered the Manhattan Center to cover his credit-card bills which often exceeded $5,000 a month and that he instructed employees to buy drugs for him with the company's money.

After fleeing with the children, Nansook said she feared that Hyo Jin would "hunt me down and kill me." To protect her, Associate Justice Edward M. Ginsburg barred Hyo Jin from approaching Nansook and the children. Taking into account Hyo Jin's jet-set lifestyle, Ginsburg also ordered Hyo Jin to pay $8,500 a month in support payments and $65,000 for Nansook's legal fees. Ginsburg ruled that Hyo Jin "had access to cash in any amount requested on demand" from "commingled" church and personal money. Ginsburg noted, too, that Hyo Jin received $84,000 a year from a family trust and earned a regular salary from the Manhattan Center.

On July 17, 1996, when Hyo Jin failed to pay Nansook's legal fees, he was held in contempt of court and jailed in Massachusetts. To free Hyo Jin, the Unification Church's vaunted legal team sprang into action. The lawyers developed a strategy that portrayed Hyo Jin as a man of no means. They filed a bankruptcy petition on his behalf in federal court in Westchester County, New York. As part of those filings, Hyo Jin's lawyers submitted evidence that on August 5, 1996, three weeks after his jailing, Hyo Jin was severed from the Swiss-based True Family Trust. The lawyers also submitted a document showing that as of August 9, Hyo Jin had lost his $60,000-a-year job at Manhattan Center Studios "due to certain medical problems."

Nansook's lawyers denounced the bankruptcy maneuver as a devious scheme to spare Hyo Jin from his financial obligations. To corroborate Nansook's statements about Hyo Jin's access to nearly unlimited money, her lawyers secured testimony from a former Manhattan Center official and Unification Church member, Madelene Pretorious. At a court hearing, Pretorious testified that in December of 1993 or January of 1994, Hyo Jin Moon returned from a trip to Korea "with $600,000 in cash which he had received from his father. ... Myself along with three or four other members that worked at Manhattan Center saw the cash in bags, shopping bags."

On another occasion, Hyo Jin's parents gave him $20,000 to buy a boat, Pretorious recalled. There was a time, too, when Hyo Jin dipped into Manhattan Center funds to give $30,000 in cash to one of his sisters. The center also gave Hyo Jin cash several times a week to cover personal expenses, ranging from bar tabs to a Jaguar automobile, Pretorious said.

But Hyo Jin Moon won the legal round anyway. A judge ruled that the federal bankruptcy claim, no matter how dubious, overrode the Massachusetts contempt finding. Hyo Jin was released from jail. After that, the Moon family stepped up negotiations with Nansook to prevent more embarrassing disclosures.

***

As those legal battles were playing out, I met with Pretorious at a suburban Boston restaurant. A law school graduate from South Africa, the 34-year-old full-faced brunette said she was recruited by the Unification Church through the student front group CARP in San Francisco in 1986-1987.

In 1992, Pretorious went to work at the Manhattan Center and grew concerned about the way cash, brought to the United States by Asian members, would circulate through the Moon business empire as a way to launder it. The money would then go to support the Moon family's lavish life style or be diverted to other church projects. At the center of the financial operation, Pretorious said, was One-Up Corporation, a Delaware-registered holding company that owned Manhattan Center and other Moon enterprises including New World Communications, the parent company of *The Washington Times*.

"Once that cash is at the Manhattan Center, it has to be accounted for," Pretorious said. "The way that's done is to launder the cash. Manhattan Center gives cash to a business called Happy World which owns restaurants. ... Happy World needs to pay illegal aliens. ... Happy World pays some back to the Manhattan Center for 'services rendered.' The rest goes to One-Up and then comes back to Manhattan Center as an investment."

Hyo Jin Moon did not respond to interview requests sent through his divorce lawyer and the church. Church officials also were unwilling to discuss Hyo Jin's case. But Hyo Jin was forced to produce documents and discuss his financial predicament in the bankruptcy proceedings.

In a bankruptcy deposition on November 15, 1996, Hyo Jin sounded alternately confused and petulant. "All I like was guns and music," he volunteered at one point. "I'm a boring person." But Hyo Jin confirmed that he had received hundreds of thousands of dollars in cash at the Manhattan Center that was not reported as taxable income.

"[In] 1993, I received some cash, yes," he said. "At that time around 300, 500 Japanese members were touring America and they stopped by to see the progress that was happening at Manhattan Center, because it was well known within the inner ... church community that I was doing a project, a cultural project. And they came and I presented a slide show, and they were inspired by that prospect and actual achievement at that time, so they gave donations. ... It was given to me. It was a donation to me."

"Did you report that gift to the taxing authorities?" a lawyer asked.

"It was [a] gift," Hyo Jin responded. "I asked [Rob Schwartz, the center's treasurer] whether I should. He said I didn't have to. You have to ask him." When pressed for clarification about this tax advice, his lawyer counseled Hyo Jin not to answer. "I'm taking that advice," Hyo Jin announced. "My lawyer's advice not to answer it."

Hyo Jin said that in November 1994, he took a leave from the Manhattan Center to undergo treatment for "my addiction problem." He checked into the Betty Ford Center.

"Who paid for it?" a lawyer asked.

"I have no idea," he responded. "Somebody did."

Hyo Jin also recalled a stay in the Henry Hazelton addiction center in West Palm Beach, Florida. "I got kicked out," he said. "I was there for three weeks, I got kicked out ... because I wasn't cooperating."

Commenting on Moon's family problems and other cracks in the leadership, one close church associate sighed, "The inner empire is crumbling."

However, former Unification Church leader Steven Hassan said the greatest danger from Moon's organization is that it will outlive Moon, since it has grown so immense and powerful that other leaders will step forward to lead it. "There are groups out there that want to use this organization," Hassan said. "It's a multi-billion-dollar international conglomerate."

***

John Stacey, a former CARP leader in the Pacific Northwest, was another Unification Church member who described Moon's organization as dependent on money arriving from overseas. Stacey told me that the fund-raising operations inside the United States barely covered the costs of local offices, with little or nothing going to the big-ticket items, such as *The Washington Times*. Stacey added that the church-connected U.S. businesses are mostly money losers.

"These failing businesses create the image of making money ... to cover his back," Stacey said of Reverend Moon. "I think the majority of the money is coming from an outside source."

Another member who quit a senior position in the church confirmed that virtually none of Moon's American operations makes money. Instead, this source, who declined to be identified by name, said hundreds of thousands of dollars are carried into the United States by visiting church members. The cash is then laundered through domestic businesses.

Another close church associate, who also requested anonymity out of fear of reprisals, said cash arriving from Japan was used in one major construction project to pay "illegal" laborers from Asia and South America. "They [the church leaders] were always waiting for our money to come in from Japan," this source said. "When the economy in Japan crashed, a lot of our money came from South America, mainly Brazil."

***

In Nansook Moon's 1998 memoirs, *In the Shadow of the Moons*, Moon's ex-daughter-in-law – writing under her maiden name Nansook Hong – alleged that Moon's organization had engaged in a long-running conspiracy to smuggle cash into the United States and to deceive U.S. Customs agents

"The Unification Church was a cash operation," Nansook Hong wrote. "I watched Japanese church leaders arrive at regular intervals at East Garden [the Moon compound north of New York City] with paper bags full of money, which the Reverend Moon would either pocket or distribute to the heads of various church-owned business enterprises at his breakfast table.

"The Japanese had no trouble bringing the cash into the United States; they would tell Customs agents that they were in America to gamble at Atlantic City. In addition, many businesses run by the church were cash operations, including several Japanese restaurants in New York City. I saw deliveries of cash from church headquarters that went directly into the wall safe in Mrs. Moon's closet."

Mrs. Moon pressed her daughter-in-law into one cash-smuggling incident after a trip to Japan in 1992, Nansook Hong wrote. Mrs. Moon had received "stacks of money" and divvied it up among her entourage for the return trip through Seattle, Nansook Hong wrote. "I was given $20,000 in two packs of crisp new bills," she recalled. "I hid them beneath the tray in my makeup case. ... I knew that smuggling was illegal, but I believed the followers of Sun Myung Moon answered to higher laws."[1]

U.S. currency laws require that cash amounts above $10,000 be declared at Customs when the money enters or leaves the country. It is also illegal to conspire with couriers to bring in lesser amounts when the total exceeds the $10,000 figure, a process called "smurfing."

In the Shadow of the Moons raised anew the question of whether Moon's money laundering – from mysterious sources in both Asia and South America – has made him a conduit for illicit foreign money influencing the U.S. government and American politics. Moon's spokesmen have denied that he launders drug money or moves money from other criminal enterprises. They attribute his wealth to donations and business profits, but have refused to open Moon's records for public inspection.

Chapter 20: Dynastic Succession

For many Republicans, there was a color of illegitimacy the last two times Democrats controlled the White House in the Twentieth Century, as if the proper order had somehow been disrupted. Richard Nixon, after all, had won a resounding reelection in 1972 before his Presidency came undone in the Watergate scandal, enabling Jimmy Carter to slip past Gerald Ford in 1976. But that was nothing compared to how conservatives viewed the election of Bill Clinton in 1992. He was seen as an interloper, a fraud and – as Republican Senate leader Bob Dole put it – a "pretender," a word fittingly derived from the notion of dynastic succession. To Republicans, Clinton was a pretender to the throne.

Clinton also was seen as the conniving charmer who epitomized the situational morals of the Baby Boom generation. These conservatives cared little that his biography was really the stuff of the American Dream: rising from a hardscrabble life in Arkansas, a son whose father died before his birth, a survivor of a household marred by domestic violence, an achiever who gained entrance to prestigious colleges and a Rhodes scholarship, and a successful politician and governor who ultimately won election as President of the United States. Conservatives still hated Bill Clinton.

Though George H.W. Bush had turned off some conservatives by reneging on his "no-new-taxes" pledge and by advocating a "New World Order" internationalism, he had at least fought in World War II and served Ronald Reagan loyally as Vice President. To these conservatives, Clinton was simply unfit to sit in the same office where Reagan and Bush had governed; the very thought was offensive. Clinton's bipartisan gesture of letting George H.W. Bush leave Washington with his dignity intact – by looking the other way on the intersecting scandals that crisscrossed Bush's final years in the White House – would win Clinton no friends on the Right.

Through the 1990s, as the conservative news media grew and thrived, Clinton found himself repeatedly on the defensive. *The Washington Times* battered him regularly on the newsstands. Rush Limbaugh pummeled Clinton daily for three hours on the radio, reaching an estimated 30 million listeners and earning the talk show host an honorary membership in the Republican freshman class when the GOP won control of the Congress in 1994. ("Rush is as responsible for what happened here as much as anyone," said conservative strategist Vin Weber.)

Other conservative outlets stepped to the fore as well. *The American Spectator*, one of the magazines supported by right-wing foundations, gained prominence along with its star "investigative" writer David Brock. International media magnate Rupert Murdoch also expanded his U.S. news operation by launching *The Weekly Standard* magazine and the Fox News Network on cable TV. Matt Drudge's *Drudge Report* became a phenomenon on the Internet, publishing gossip about the Clintons and giving conservatives a new way to put scandal stories into play.

Washington's mainstream news outlets also continued their drift to the right. Indeed, journalists often used the Clinton administration as a stage to demonstrate they could be tougher on a Democrat than a Republican, a way to shed the longstanding "liberal press" label. Beyond that, the Establishment news media shared much of the conservative disdain for Clinton as a political climber who didn't know his place.

Society writer Sally Quinn explained this contempt for Clinton in a candid *Washington Post* column after the disclosure in 1998 of Clinton's sexual dalliance with young White House aide Monica Lewinsky. The lengthy Style-section article argued that the Washington "insiders" were angrier with Clinton than most Americans were because the President had soiled "their home" and had violated a sort of Washington tribal code by dishonoring the White House.[1]

"Washington has been brought into disrepute by the actions of the President," wrote Quinn, taking little note of the many sex scandals and more serious crimes of state that had preceded Clinton to the White House.

With no apparent sense of irony, Quinn tried to put Clinton's sexual escapades in historical context by interviewing Tish Baldrige, social secretary at John F. Kennedy's White House. "Now it's all sleaze and dirt," Baldrige groused about Clinton. "We all feel terribly let down. It's very emotional. We want there to be standards. We're used to standards. When you think back to other Presidents, they all had a lot of class."

Quinn demurred on the "standards" and "class" that may have been on display during Kennedy's infamous peccadilloes, including one affair reportedly with a Mafia don's girlfriend, nude romps at the White House pool and alleged procurement of prostitutes. Some of Kennedy's sexual activities apparently were known to his close friend, former *Washington Post* executive editor Ben Bradlee, who became Quinn's husband.

Quinn appeared equally oblivious to other aspects of the Establishment's double standards, including her own. Quinn failed to mention her affair with her boss Bradlee when he was married to someone else. But Quinn insisted that the anger against Clinton was not primarily about sex, nor even about extramarital sex. It was really about the failure to keep illicit sexual affairs secret.

"Sex is acceptable as long as it's discreet," longtime political operative David Gergen explained. Professor Roger Wilkins, one of the few black members of the Washington Establishment, added "with a chuckle, 'God knows, most people in Washington have led robust sexual lives.'"

Quinn also traced the Establishment's grievances with Clinton back to a perceived insult in Clinton's first inaugural address in 1993. In the speech, the new President described the capital as "a place of intrigue and calculation [where] powerful people maneuver for position and worry endlessly about who is in and who is out, who is up and who is down, forgetting those people whose toil and sweat sends us here and pays our way."

The comment apparently stuck in the craw of Washington's elites, including Quinn. "With that [comment], the new President sent a clear challenge to an already suspicious Washington Establishment," wrote Quinn. In her article, she countered Clinton's vision of a self-absorbed ruling class by recalling a heart-warming anecdote about a bipartisan get-together of Washington celebrities – from government and media – to raise money for spina bifida research, a party sponsored by CNN's Judy Woodruff and the *Wall Street Journal*'s Al Hunt, whose son suffers from the disease.

The event drew some Clinton figures who, according to Quinn, had graduated into insider status – Rahm Emanuel, Madeleine Albright and Donna Shalala. Respected Republicans were there, too: the likes of Senator John McCain of Arizona and Representative Bob Livingston of Louisiana, whose political career would crash the next month when he admitted to his own sexual indiscretions. Federal Reserve Board Chairman Alan Greenspan, who is married to NBC's Andrea Mitchell, attended as did PBS's Jim Lehrer and *New York Times* columnist Maureen Dowd, "all behaving like the pals that they are," people "with genuine affection" for one another, Quinn wrote.

Similarly, Quinn saw only a shining moral city on the hill when looking back at the Reagan-Bush era. She quoted Muffie Cabot, a social secretary to President and Mrs. Reagan, describing Clinton's Washington as "a demoralized little village" where people are "so disillusioned." Summing up the Establishment's view of Clinton, Quinn wrote that these elites are sticklers for the truth. "The lying offends them," Quinn said.

Then, missing the irony again, Quinn cited a famous comment by Secretary of State George Shultz during his Iran-Contra testimony in July 1987. "For both politicians and journalists, trust is the coin of the realm," Quinn wrote, paraphrasing Shultz. But Quinn omitted what had followed Shultz's remark. After assuring his congressional listeners that "trust is the coin of the realm," Shultz misled them about his knowledge of the Iran-Contra arms shipments to Iran.

When Iran-Contra prosecutor Lawrence Walsh confronted Shultz with documentary evidence of his false testimony, Shultz "admitted that significant parts of his testimony to Congress had been completely wrong," according to the Iran-Contra report.[2] Nevertheless, the well-liked Shultz remained a respected member of the Washington Establishment renowned for his honesty.

Another well-respected Washington insider, according to Quinn, was Whitewater special prosecutor Kenneth Starr, who expanded his financial probe of Clinton to include questions about the President's honesty regarding his sex life. "Ken Starr is not seen by many Washington insiders as an out-of-control prudish crusader," Quinn wrote. "Starr is a Washington insider, too. He has lived and worked here for years. ... He has many friends in both parties. Their wives are friendly with one another and their children go to the same schools."

Quinn made clear, too, that she had no tolerance for those who saw Clinton as a victim of conservative dirty tricks. To Quinn, Clinton was just the classic case of a boorish guest who overstayed his welcome and didn't have the sense to pack his bags. "Privately, many in Establishment Washington would like to see Bill Clinton resign and spare the country, the Presidency and the city any more humiliation," Quinn wrote.

***

David Brock, whose articles had helped set the "Clinton scandals" in motion, had a different take on what he had wrought. Toward the end of the decade, Brock came to regret his role as a right-wing media hit man and began criticizing his former allies.

Brock's introduction to the political wars of Washington came in 1986 as the Reagan-Bush administration was taking heat over the Iran-Contra disclosures. "This is the cauldron I stepped into when, at age 23, I entered the grand marble and brass lobby of the *Washington Times* building," Brock wrote in his 2002 memoirs, *Blinded by the Right*.

Brock started his Washington career writing for Reverend Moon's *Washington Times*, but his career as a conservative journalist always was complicated by the fact that he was gay and the "family values" conservatives viewed homosexuality as a sin and a perversion. Still, Brock made the most of his first big journalistic opportunity: the 1991 confirmation hearing for Clarence Thomas, who had been nominated by President George H.W. Bush to fill a vacancy on the U.S. Supreme Court.

Given Thomas's thin qualifications and hard-line conservative views, he already was facing stiff opposition when a former aide, Anita Hill, testified that Thomas had subjected her to crude sexual harassment, a charge Thomas angrily denied. The Thomas confirmation hearings deteriorated even further, into a tawdry exchange of ugly charges with Republican senators depicting Hill as delusional and scaring off another potential woman witness who claimed to have had similar experiences with Thomas.

With the conservative attack apparatus fully in gear against Hill and the Democrats, Thomas eked out a narrow victory in the Senate. Still, Thomas's reputation was in tatters, a situation that gave Brock his career opening. In an article for the conservative *American Spectator*, Brock trashed Anita Hill as "a little bit nutty and a little bit slutty." Brock skyrocketed to fame and fortune as the exemplar of conservative investigative journalism

Beyond admitting now that he unfairly maligned Hill to protect Thomas, Brock added new details about how the smear campaign against Hill enlisted leading conservatives, including key judges on the federal bench. One of those judges was U.S. Appeals Court Judge Laurence Silberman, who had played a role in the October Surprise controversy in 1980, oversaw the Reagan-Bush intelligence transition team that trashed that the CIA's analytical division and was one of two judges who overturned Oliver North's Iran-Contra felony convictions in 1990.

"Though the confirmation battle had been won, Thomas's closest friends knew that a full-scale defense of Thomas would help confer legitimacy on his Supreme Court tenure," Brock wrote. George H.W. Bush's White House passed along some psychiatric opinion that Anita Hill suffered from "erotomania," Brock wrote, but some of the more colorful criticism of Hill came from the federal appeals court judge. "Silberman speculated that Hill was a lesbian 'acting out,'" Brock wrote. "Besides, Silberman confided, Thomas would never have asked Hill for dates: She had bad breath."

After Brock expanded his assault on Hill into a best-selling book, *The Real Anita Hill*, Silberman and his wife Ricky along with other prominent conservatives joined a celebration at the Embassy Row Ritz-Carlton, Brock wrote. Also in attendance was U.S. Appeals Court Judge David Sentelle, the other judge who had voted to reverse North's Iran-Contra convictions.[*]

Brock said conservative activists felt their perceived enemy – the "liberal media" – justified the creation of a separate right-wing media as well as their harsh attacks on mainstream reporters or witnesses, like Hill, who came forward with information unfavorable to the conservative cause. "We needed our own media, our own reporters, and our own means of getting out our side of the story," Brock wrote.

***

In late 1993, again writing for the *American Spectator*, cobbled together a wacky set of allegations from state troopers who had guarded Clinton as Arkansas governor. Some of the tales were unlikely as well as tasteless. The

---

[*] In 1992, Sentelle was named head of the three-judge panel for picking independent counsels. In 2004, President George W. Bush appointed Silberman to head a commission to examine the use of intelligence in the build-up to the Iraq War.

troopers charged, for instance, that Hillary Clinton would call the governor's mansion from her law office "and order the troopers to fetch feminine napkins" for her. One trooper, Larry Patterson, claimed that he witnessed Vincent Foster fondling Mrs. Clinton's breasts at a party, while "she just stood there cooing, 'Oh Vince. Oh Vince.'"

Other stories were simply false. Brock quoted Patterson as claiming that Clinton was so furious in 1988 about his poorly received speech at the Democratic convention that he "refused to endorse [nominee Michael Dukakis] until a few weeks before the election." If Brock had checked, he would have discovered that Clinton's convention speech was the nominating address for Dukakis.

Brock turned these tales into another national media event in December 1993. The so-called Troopergate charges smashed the modern taboo against prying into the private life of a sitting American President.

Troopergate also enhanced Brock's standing as a hero to the Right. In February 1994, I covered the Conservative Political Action Conference in Washington where Brock spoke to a packed banquet hall of cheering activists. At the same hotel, Paula Jones introduced herself to the world. She had been mentioned in Brock's Troopergate article only as "Paula," a woman who had met with Clinton in a hotel room. At a news conference, she identified herself as that woman and said Clinton had crudely propositioned her. She suggested that she might file a lawsuit.

Four years later, in 1998, Paula Jones's lawsuit had created a courtroom context for putting Clinton on the spot about his private life – and Clinton's evasive responses about Lewinsky had created the congressional pretext for impeachment. Brock came to regret his participation in the earlier conservative hit pieces. His personal distress over hiding his homosexuality also contributed to his decision to denounce the conservative tactics.

In the April 1998 issue of *Esquire*, Brock published an apology to Clinton, but Brock's remorse couldn't turn back the clock. By then, the Clinton scandals had flowed into the mainstream press as legitimate news. As Sally Quinn described, the Establishment press held Clinton in almost as much contempt as the conservatives did. When Clinton survived impeachment in 1999 by winning acquittal in the Senate, many journalists in Quinn's Establishment shared the bitter disappointment. They felt Clinton had beaten the rap. They resented Al Gore for standing by the embattled President. They longed for the golden days of the Reagan-Bush era.

The stage was set for Campaign 2000.

***

On the stump, Texas Governor George W. Bush bounded toward voters, flashing a smile, shaking hands and kissing babies. His jovial big-man-on-campus confidence was contagious. To many observers, the younger George

Bush was "a natural," a politician with an easy manner, a common touch and the look of a winner.

Though he offered no comprehensive domestic policy and demonstrated only a rudimentary knowledge of world affairs, Bush floated – more than battled – into his position as the front runner to succeed Bill Clinton in the White House. Yet, it was always clear that in his near-effortless jockeying for the inside track, the Texas governor's greatest asset was not what he said or what his experience was, but who he was – or more precisely, who his father was. Only the public perception of former President Bush as an honorable man could explain how quickly Governor Bush took control of Campaign 2000; early in the campaign, a CBS News poll found 60 percent of Americans with a favorable view of former President Bush and only 17 percent with an unfavorable view.

"People just automatically say, 'If this guy is George and Barbara Bush's son, we don't have any question about those personal qualities that we were fooled on by Clinton,'" explained Robert M. Teeter, President Bush's campaign manager in 1992.[3]

Indeed, without the glow of the Bush name, it is hard to imagine that the joshing-backslapping Texas governor would have been the odds-on favorite to win the White House or even be viewed as serious presidential timber. As Marilyn Quayle bitterly told *The Arizona Republic*, "the caricature they made of Dan [Quayle] in '88 is George W. It's him. It wasn't true about Dan. But it is him. ... A guy that never accomplished anything. ... Everything he got, Daddy took care of."

In relying on his father's good name, George W. Bush could count himself lucky, too, that a series of investigations into his father's alleged wrongdoing were sidetracked in the late 1980s and early 1990s, dead-ended by both Republicans and senior Democrats. As memories of those many unanswered questions faded, Americans were left with the hazy impression of President George H.W. Bush as a "kinder and gentler" sort of fellow, remembered best from comedian Dana Carvey's imitation of him as an inarticulate preppie-president, with jerking hand gestures, saying, "Not gonna do it. Wouldn't be prudent." Bush's son was seen in the same benign light as he stressed his "compassionate conservatism" and struggled with the names of foreign nationalities from "Grecians" to "Kosovians."

But the younger George Bush had a darker side – like his father – that occasionally broke through the public façade. In early April 1986, for instance, George W. Bush was miffed at a prediction by the *Wall Street Journal's* Al Hunt that Representative Jack Kemp – rather than then-Vice President Bush – would win the GOP nomination in 1988. At a Dallas restaurant, Bush spotted Hunt having dinner with his wife, Judy Woodruff, and their four-year-old son. Bush stormed up to the table and started cursing out Hunt.

"You [expletive] son of a bitch," Bush yelled. "I saw what you wrote. We're not going to forget this."[4]

Bush supporters have sought to excuse his behavior that occurred before his 40th birthday on the grounds that Bush was still drinking heavily in those days. But even later, George W. Bush demonstrated a startling lack of compassion. In an obscenity-laced 1999 interview with conservative writer Tucker Carlson for *Talk* magazine, Bush ridiculed convicted murderer Karla Faye Tucker and her unsuccessful plea to Bush to spare her life. Asked about Karla Faye Tucker's clemency appeal, Bush mimicked what he claimed was the condemned woman's message to him. "With pursed lips in mock desperation, [Bush said]: 'Please don't kill me.'"

Other times, Bush displayed a sense of humor that made jokes at the expense of his friends. Lining up for a photo at an event in Texas, Bush fingered the man next to him and announced, "He's the ugly one!" Spotting a reporter, Bush offered the explanation that he was only kidding an old buddy.[5]

In one of the campaign's most memorable moments, Bush uttered an aside to his running mate Dick Cheney about *New York Times* reporter Adam Clymer. "There's Adam Clymer – major league asshole – from the *New York Times*," Bush said as he was waving to a campaign crowd from a stage in Naperville, Illinois.

"Yeah, big time," responded Cheney. Their voices were picked up on an open microphone.

While many of Bush's backers found his biting humor refreshing – the sign of a "politically incorrect" politician – some critics saw it reflecting an aristocratic condescension toward the commoners. In olden times, kings felt free to ridicule their subjects, who knew that any insubordination in return would be most unwelcome. Bush seemed to enjoy the same one-sided delivery of put-downs.

Some critics offered a more comprehensive criticism of Bush's behavior, contending that Bush's clumsy use of words – his gaffes, his mispronunciations, his poor grammar – fit with a dynastic sense of entitlement. "Although the GOP machine has spun his elementary goofs as signs of kinship with the Common Man, they are in fact an insult to the people," wrote Mark Crispin Miller in *The Bush Dyslexicon*.

"Every bit of broken English, every flash of comfy ignorance, reminds us of a privilege blithely squandered: Bush attended Phillips Andover Academy, then Yale – Olympian institutions that would never have admitted him if he were not a Bush," Miller continued. "However, he was both too limited and too secure to take full advantage of an opportunity that countless brighter, poorer folks have worked for, prayed for, and then been denied. Bush did the minimum at Yale, mainly partying and making good connections. ...

"Thus, in the matter of his education, this President, despite his folksy pretense, is something of an anti-Lincoln – one who, instead of learning eagerly in humble circumstances, learned almost nothing at the finest institutions in the land. When he comments on how many hands he's 'shaked,' or frets that quotas 'vulcanize' society, ... he is, of course, flaunting not his costly education but his disdain for it – much as some feckless prince, with a crowd of beggars watching from the street, might take a few bites from the feast laid out before him, then let the servants throw the rest away."[6]

***

Certainly, George W. Bush's early life contrasted with Bill Clinton's upbringing and even George H.W. Bush's formative life experiences. The elder George Bush was a stellar student-athlete at Andover and Yale. His son was a mediocre performer, at best. The elder volunteered for combat in World War II, flew missions off aircraft carriers and parachuted from a burning plane. During the Vietnam War, the younger Bush slipped past other applicants to snare a treasured spot in the Texas Air National Guard.

While both George Bushes had the benefit of coming from blue-blood Yankee stock and making friends in the secretive Yale fraternity, Skull and Bones, the elder George Bush struck out for Texas after college and ran a moderately successful oil business. He entered politics, won a House seat and built a sparkling resumé of high-profile posts, including U.N. ambassador and CIA director. The younger Bush ran for a Texas congressional seat in 1978 and lost. He then ran through a string of business failures.

Through his twenties and thirties, Bush drank heavily and could be surly when drunk. In one famous incident, a 26-year-old George W. Bush had taken his younger brother Marvin out drinking during a holiday visit to his parent's house in the Washington area. After getting intoxicated, George careened his car homeward through the residential neighborhood. "Drunk and driving erratically, George W. barreled the car into a neighbor's garbage can, and the thing affixed itself to the car wheel," wrote his biographer Bill Minutaglio in *First Son*. "He drove down the street with the metal garbage can noisily banging and slapping on the pavement right up until he made the turn and finally started rolling up and onto the driveway of his parents' home in the pleasant, family-oriented neighborhood they had just moved into."

When George H.W. Bush demanded to talk with his son, George W. was neither contrite nor apologetic. Instead he threatened his father. "I hear you're looking for me," said George W. "You wanna go mano a mano right here?"[7]

Clouds also have hung over Bush's stint in the Texas Air National Guard, which he entered as an alternative to fighting in the war in Vietnam. "My first impulse and first inclination was to support the country," Bush recalled in an interview about his backing for the war that he opted to avoid.[8] Bush said no one to his knowledge helped him get into the National Guard. "I asked to become a pilot," Bush said. "I met the qualifications, and ended up becoming an F-102 pilot."[9]

George W. Bush jumped over other candidates to get into the so-called "champagne unit," where the offspring of other privileged Texas families, including the son of Texas Senator Lloyd Bentsen, also served. Bush made the cut despite having the lowest acceptable score for entry.

Bush's service record in the Guard has been another source of mystery. After failing to take a mandatory physical in 1972 – a year after the Guard began testing for drug use – Bush was suspended from flying. He also arranged to transfer to an Alabama unit so he could work on Senator William Blount's reelection campaign, but his appearances at Guard duty there were spotty at best. Bush also got permission to quit the Guard eight months early so he could attend Harvard Business School in fall 1973.

"In his final 18 months of military service in 1972 and 1973, Bush did not fly at all," the *Boston Globe* reported. "And for much of that time, Bush was all but unaccounted for." Bush responded through a spokesman that he had "some recollection" of attending drills that year, "but maybe not consistently."[10]

Besides the heavy drinking, the younger George Bush apparently also abused cocaine, though he never exactly admitted it. During his presidential run in 2000, he slid away from the question by asserting that he could have cleared his father's White House personnel requirement that set time limits on how far back an applicant would have to admit illegal drug use.

***

Despite little experience in the oil-drilling business, the 32-year-old Bush in 1979 launched Arbusto Energy, naming the Midland, Texas-based company after the Spanish word for bush. He got financial help from his uncle Jonathan Bush, a Wall Street financier who raised $3 million for the venture. James Bath, a friend from the National Guard, also invested $50,000 for a five percent stake. At the time, Bath was the sole U.S. business representative for Salem bin Laden scion of the wealthy Saudi bin Laden family and half-brother of Osama bin Laden, who soon would be heading to Afghanistan to help Islamic fundamentalists resist the Soviet invasion. Though responsible for investments for Salem bin Laden, Bath has insisted that the $50,000 for Arbusto came from his own personal funds.[*]

By 1982, Arbusto had gained a reputation for drilling dry holes and the name itself became a joke since the company was becoming "a bust." Deeply in debt, Bush tried to take the company public to raise additional cash.[11]

---

[*] Salem bin Laden died in a 1988 plane crash in Texas.

First, however, Bush needed help in clearing some debts. In stepped Philip Uzielli, a New York investor and friend of James Baker III. Uzielli agreed to buy a ten percent stake in Arbusto for $1 million, though the company was valued at less than $400,000. In a 1991 interview, Uzielli recalled the investment as a major money loser. "Things were terrible," he said.[12]

But Bush did take the company public, renamed Bush Exploration, though falling well short of his target of raising $6 million. The offering only brought in $1.14 million largely due to declining oil prices and waning interest in the industry among investors. The new infusion of money perked up the business but only for another couple of years. "We didn't find much oil and gas," said Bush's Chief Financial Officer Michael Conaway. "We weren't raising any money."[13]

Bush, whose father at the time was Vice President, gained a second reprieve when Cincinnati investors, William DeWitt Jr. and Mercer Reynolds III, offered to let Bush Exploration merge with their oil exploration company, Spectrum 7. In the merger, DeWitt and Reynolds each got 20.1 percent and Bush got 16.3 percent, plus the titles of chairman and chief executive officer and a $75,000 salary.[14]

Bush's family ties were a plus. Spectrum 7 President Paul Rea said Bush's name was a definite "drawing card" for investors.[15] As oil prices continued their collapse, however, Spectrum 7 lost $400,000 in a six-month period in 1986 and owed more than $3 million.[16]

In September 1986, Harken Energy Corporation tossed Bush his third lifeline. Harken's owner Alan Quasha agreed to acquire Spectrum 7 by paying one share of publicly traded Harken stock for five shares of nearly worthless Spectrum 7 shares.[17] Bush got $600,000 worth of Harken stock options, a $120,000-a-year consulting contract and a seat on Harken's board of directors.[18]

While bringing little experience in running a successful company, Bush did give Harken publicity because of his name. After working on his father's 1988 presidential campaign, Bush also brought a set of connections to key figures in the new administration, including the most important one, his dad. By 1989, Harken was scouting out oil investments in the Middle East, where family ties are considered crucial. In January 1990, in a surprise decision, Bahrain granted exclusive offshore oil drilling rights to Harken, a company that had never drilled outside Texas, Louisiana, and Oklahoma and had never drilled offshore.[19] Harken stock rose more than 22 percent to $5.50 from $4.50 a share.

Soon, Bush was angling to join an investment group that was trying to buy the Texas Rangers baseball team. Major League Baseball Commissioner Peter Ueberroth lent a hand to the President's son by bringing in a second investment group headed by billionaire Richard Rainwater, who agreed to the deal but set strict limits on Bush's participation. Named one of two "managing partners," Bush was granted little role in running the team.[20]

To finance his stake, Bush decided to sell two-thirds of his holdings in Harken. He pressed ahead with this decision though he knew that Harken was struggling financially and was planning to sell shares in two subsidiaries to avert bankruptcy. Outside lawyers from the Haynes and Boone law firm advised Harken officers and directors on June 15, 1990, that if they possessed any negative information about the company's outlook, a stock sale might be viewed as illegal trading. Bush, who had attended a meeting four days earlier on the plan to sell off the two subsidiaries, went ahead anyway.

On June 22, 1990, Bush sold 212,140 shares to a still-unidentified buyer who spared Bush the trouble of selling on the open market, which likely would have tanked Harken's lightly traded stock and meant less money for Bush. The sale also preceded Harken's disclosure of more than $23 million in losses for the second quarter, which caused the stock to fall 20 percent before recovering for a time.[21]

To make matters worse, Bush missed deadlines by up to eight months for disclosing four stock sales to the Securities and Exchange Commission. After the missed deadlines were noted in published reports in 1991, the SEC opened an insider-trading investigation. At the time, Bush's father was President of the United States and appointed the SEC chairman. George W. Bush denied any wrongdoing in the Harken stock sales. He insisted that he had sold into the "good news" of Harken landing offshore drilling rights in Bahrain. Bush's lawyers also argued that he had cleared the stock sale with the Haynes and Boone lawyers, a claim that proved to be important in the SEC's decision to close the investigation on August 21, 1991, without ever interviewing Bush.

But what the SEC didn't know at the time was that the Haynes and Boone lawyers had sent Bush and other Harken officials that letter warning against selling shares if they knew about the company's financial troubles. One day after the investigation was closed, Bush's lawyer Robert W. Jordan delivered the warning letter to the SEC. Asked years later about the letter, SEC investigators said they had no memory of reading it. "The SEC investigation apparently never examined a key issue raised in the memo: whether Bush's insider knowledge of a plan to rescue the company from financial collapse by spinning off two troubled units was a factor in his decision to sell," the *Boston Globe* reported.[22]

Bush also has been less than forthcoming about why he missed the deadlines for reporting that stock sale and three others. For years, he claimed publicly that he had sent the reports in on time and the SEC had lost them, a sort of the bureaucrats-ate-my-stock-sale-reports argument. The issue resurfaced again in 2002 when Bush positioned himself as a friend of embattled shareholders and demanded that corporate officers reveal their stock sales almost immediately. Asked why he had not lived up to his own admonition, Bush shifted the blame to Harken's lawyers for the late filings.

He then changed his story again to say that he simply didn't know what had happened. He never apologized for claiming falsely for years that it had been the SEC's fault.[23]

On June 22, 1990, Bush made $848,560 on his Harken stock sale. He used $606,000 of his profits to buy a 1.8 percent stake in the Texas Rangers baseball team. Then, after Bush helped engineer public financing for a new baseball stadium in Arlington, Texas, he sold his interest in the Rangers for $14.9 million, more than 20 times his original investment.[24] The success of his Texas Rangers investment was even more dramatic when compared with what happened to the Harken stock that Bush sold for $4 a share. A dozen years later, each of those shares would have been worth two cents.

***

The All-American image of owning a Major League baseball team boosted Bush's political image, too. In 1994, he parlayed his fame as the public face of the Texas Rangers – and as the son of a respected former President – into a run for the Texas governorship. Besides his father's positive reputation and financial contacts, the younger George Bush benefited from having learned the lessons of hardball politics at his father's knee in the 1988 and 1992 presidential campaigns.

In his father's presidential race in 1988, Bush termed himself the campaign's "enforcer," demanding loyalty from the staff and likening his role to Robert Kennedy's in 1960. "Because of the access I had to George Bush, I had the ability – and I think I used it judiciously – I had the ability to go and lay down some behavior modification," George W. Bush said.[25]

Bush also picked up techniques for appealing to the Christian Right through subtle messaging. Doug Wead, a political adviser to the senior George Bush in 1987, had written a series of memos to the then-Vice President on how to communicate with evangelical Christians. Wead's motto was "signal early and signal often," meaning that sprinkling speeches with references to God and meeting with celebrity evangelicals sent a message to this important political group that would pass over the heads of non-evangelicals.

Wead found George W. to be an avid fan of the memos. "George would read my memos, and he would be licking his lips saying, 'I can use this to win in Texas,'" Wead said.[26] Later, Bush would demonstrate that he could use Wead's strategies to win by attracting evangelicals throughout the South and across the country.

In the 1988 campaign, George W. Bush also grew close to political strategist Lee Atwater, a legendary master of ruthless politics. Atwater's critics said his tactics included "baiting gays and blacks and scaring the holy hell out of nervous white voters," according to Bush biographer Bill

Minutaglio in *First Son.* "George W. would grow to love Lee Atwater," Minutaglio wrote.[27] (Atwater died in 1991 at age 40.)

When challenging popular Democratic Governor Ann Richards in 1994, George W. Bush reached into the old bag of Atwater's tricks, painting Richards as soft on crime, much as Atwater had skewered Michael Dukakis for the Willie Horton furlough. The strategy – along with the nationwide anti-Clinton backlash of 1994 – helped Bush defeat Richards with 54 percent of the Texas vote to her 45 percent. Four years later, Bush cruised to re-election with 69 percent of the vote.

Bush's Atwater-style politics carried over to the fight for the Republican presidential nomination in 2000 when Bush's campaign targeted Senator John McCain of Arizona for personal attacks. By late October 1999, McCain, who spent five years in a North Vietnamese prisoner-of-war camp during the Vietnam War, had narrowed Bush's lead in the polls and the Bush assault began. "Apparently the memo has gone out from the Bush campaign to start attacking John McCain, something that I'd hoped wouldn't happen," McCain said.[28]

Bush's negative attacks intensified after McCain won the New Hampshire primary. To undercut McCain, Bush's campaign ran a misleading ad lambasting the senator for not supporting breast cancer research. The ad cited an omnibus spending bill, which McCain voted against not because of the breast cancer research but because of the enormous spending included in the overall legislative package. There were also rumors about McCain undergoing Communist brainwashing while in a North Vietnamese prison camp, and mysterious "push-pull" calls to Southern voters asked if they would be less likely to vote for McCain if they knew he had a black child, without explaining that McCain had adopted the child from Bangladesh.

To burnish his conservative credentials before the key South Carolina primary, Bush spoke at Bob Jones University and avoided criticizing the school's racist and anti-Catholic policies. After nailing down South Carolina, Bush shifted gears again, issuing a rare apology for not having criticized prejudice at Bob Jones University, a contrition that played well in the upcoming primaries in the North. After securing the Republican nomination, Bush renewed his pledge to run a positive general election campaign.

***

The news media's disdain for Bill Clinton and respect for George H.W. Bush brought George W. Bush generally favorable news coverage. Bush won even more gentle treatment by rubbing shoulders with the press and giving individual reporters nicknames. "Stretch" seemed to be a favorite that he would attach to tall reporters.

By contrast, the Washington press corps was relentless in its criticism of Vice President Al Gore, who became a sort of whipping boy for journalists annoyed that Clinton had survived impeachment. Indeed, to read the major newspapers and to watch the TV pundit shows during parts of Campaign 2000, one couldn't avoid the impression that many journalists had decided that Gore was unfit to be elected President. The lopsided coverage was a sign of how far the Republicans had come in changing the national media environment in the quarter century since Watergate.

Across the board – from *The Washington Post* to *The Washington Times,* from *The New York Times* to the *New York Post,* from NBC's cable networks to the traveling campaign press corps – journalists didn't even disguise their contempt for Gore. At one early Democratic debate, a gathering of about 300 reporters in a nearby press room hissed and hooted at Gore's answers.

More broadly, every perceived Gore misstep, including his choice of clothing, was treated as a new excuse to put him on a psychiatrist's couch and find him wanting. Journalists called him "delusional," "a liar" and "Zelig." Yet, to back up these sweeping denunciations, the media relied on a series of distorted quotes and tendentious interpretations of his words, at times following scripts written by the national Republican leadership.

In December 1999, for instance, the news media generated dozens of stories about Gore's supposed claim that he discovered the Love Canal toxic waste dump in upstate New York in the late 1970s. "I was the one that started it all," he was quoted as saying. This "gaffe" then let pundits recycle other situations in which Gore allegedly exaggerated his role or, as some writers put it, told "bold-faced lies." But behind these examples of Gore's "lies" often was very sloppy journalism.

The Love Canal flap started when *The Washington Post* and *The New York Times* misquoted Gore on a key point and cropped out the context of another sentence to give readers a false impression of what he meant. The error was then exploited by national Republicans and amplified endlessly by the rest of the news media, even after the *Post* and *Times* grudgingly filed corrections.

Almost as remarkable, though, is how the two newspapers finally agreed to run corrections. They were effectively shamed into doing so by high school students in New Hampshire who heard Gore's original comment. The error also was cited by an Internet site called *The Daily Howler*, edited by a stand-up comic named Bob Somerby.[29]

The Love Canal controversy began on November 30, 1999, when Gore was speaking to a group of high school students in Concord, New Hampshire. He was exhorting the students to reject cynicism and to recognize that individual citizens can effect important changes. As an example, he cited a high school girl from Toone, Tennessee, a town that had experienced problems with toxic waste. She brought the issue to the attention of Gore's congressional office in the late 1970s.

"I called for a congressional investigation and a hearing," Gore told the students. "I looked around the country for other sites like that. I found a little place in upstate New York called Love Canal. Had the first hearing on that issue, and Toone, Tennessee – that was the one that you didn't hear of. But that was the one that started it all."

After the congressional hearings, Gore said, "we passed a major national law to clean up hazardous dump sites. And we had new efforts to stop the practices that ended up poisoning water around the country. We've still got work to do. But we made a huge difference. And it all happened because one high school student got involved."

The context of Gore's comment was clear. What sparked his interest in the toxic-waste issue was the situation in Toone: "That was the one that you didn't hear of. But that was the one that started it all." After learning about the Toone situation, Gore looked for other examples and "found" a similar case at Love Canal. He was not claiming to have been the first one to discover Love Canal, which already had been evacuated. He simply needed other case studies for the hearings.

The next day, *The Washington Post* stripped Gore's comments of their context and gave them a negative twist. "Gore boasted about his efforts in Congress 20 years ago to publicize the dangers of toxic waste," the *Post* said. "'I found a little place in upstate New York called Love Canal,' he said, referring to the Niagara homes evacuated in August 1978 because of chemical contamination. 'I had the first hearing on this issue.' ... Gore said his efforts made a lasting impact. 'I was the one that started it all,' he said."[30] *The New York Times* ran a slightly less contentious story with the same false quote: "I was the one that started it all."[31]

The Republican National Committee spotted Gore's alleged boast and was quick to fax around its own take. "Al Gore is simply unbelievable – in the most literal sense of that term," declared Republican National Committee Chairman Jim Nicholson. "It's a pattern of phoniness – and it would be funny if it weren't also a little scary." The GOP release then doctored Gore's quote a bit more. After all, it would be grammatically incorrect to have said, "I was the one that started it all." So, the Republican handout fixed Gore's grammar to say, "I was the one who started it all."

In just one day, the key quote had transformed from "that was the one that started it all" to "I was the one that started it all" to "I was the one who started it all." But instead of taking the offensive against these misquotes, Gore tried to head off the controversy by clarifying his meaning and apologizing if anyone got the wrong impression. But the fun was just beginning. The national pundit shows quickly picked up the story of Gore's new exaggeration.

"Let's talk about the 'love' factor here," chortled Chris Matthews of CNBC's "Hardball." "Here's the guy who said he was the character Ryan O'Neal was based on in 'Love Story.' ... It seems to me ... he's now the guy who created the Love Canal [case]. I mean, isn't this getting ridiculous? ... Isn't it getting to be delusionary?"

Matthews turned to his baffled guest, Lois Gibbs, the Love Canal resident who is widely credited with bringing the issue to public attention. She sounded confused about why Gore would claim credit for discovering Love Canal, but defended Gore's hard work on the issue. "I actually think he's done a great job," Gibbs said. "I mean, he really did work, when nobody else was working, on trying to define what the hazards were in this country and how to clean it up and helping with the Superfund and other legislation."[32]

The next morning, *Post* political writer Ceci Connolly highlighted Gore's boast and placed it in his alleged pattern of falsehoods. "Add Love Canal to the list of verbal missteps by Vice President Gore," she wrote. "The man who mistakenly claimed to have inspired the movie 'Love Story' and to have invented the Internet says he didn't quite mean to say he discovered a toxic waste site."[33]

That night, CNBC's "Hardball" returned to Gore's Love Canal quote by playing the actual clip but altering the context by starting Gore's comments with the words, "I found a little town..."

"It reminds me of Snoopy thinking he's the Red Baron," laughed Chris Matthews. "I mean how did he get this idea? Now you've seen Al Gore in action. I know you didn't know that he was the prototype for Ryan O'Neal's character in 'Love Story' or that he invented the Internet. He now is the guy who discovered Love Canal."

Matthews compared Gore to "Zelig," the Woody Allen character whose face appeared at an unlikely procession of historic events. "What is it, the Zelig guy who keeps saying, 'I was the main character in 'Love Story.' I invented the Internet. I invented Love Canal."

Former Labor Secretary Robert Reich, who favored Gore's rival, former Senator Bill Bradley, added, "I don't know why he feels that he has to exaggerate and make some of this stuff up."

The following day, Rupert Murdoch's *New York Post* elaborated on Gore's pathology of deception. "Again, Al Gore has told a whopper," the *Post* wrote. "Again, he's been caught red-handed and again, he has been left sputtering and apologizing. This time, he falsely took credit for breaking the Love Canal story. ... Yep, another Al Gore bold-faced lie."

The editorial continued: "Al Gore appears to have as much difficulty telling the truth as his boss, Bill Clinton. But Gore's lies are not just false, they're outrageously, stupidly false. It's so easy to determine that he's lying, you have to wonder if he wants to be found out. Does he enjoy the embarrassment? Is he hell-bent on destroying his own campaign? ... Of course, if Al Gore is determined to turn himself into a national laughingstock, who are we to stand in his way?"

On ABC's "This Week" pundit show, there was head-shaking amazement about Gore's supposed Love Canal lie. "Gore, again, revealed his Pinocchio problem," declared former Clinton adviser George Stephanopoulos. "Says he was the model for 'Love Story,' created the Internet. And this time, he sort of discovered Love Canal."

A bemused Cokie Roberts chimed in, "Isn't he saying that he really discovered Love Canal when he had hearings on it after people had been evacuated?"

"Yeah," added Bill Kristol, editor of Murdoch's *Weekly Standard.* Kristol then read Gore's supposed quote: "I found a little place in upstate New York called Love Canal. I was the one that started it all."[34]

The Love Canal controversy soon moved beyond the Washington-New York power axis. On December 6, *The Buffalo News* ran an editorial entitled, "Al Gore in Fantasyland," that echoed the words of RNC chief Nicholson. It stated, "Never mind that he didn't invent the Internet, serve as the model for 'Love Story' or blow the whistle on Love Canal. All of this would be funny if it weren't so disturbing."

The next day, Sun Myung Moon's *Washington Times* judged Gore crazy. "The real question is how to react to Mr. Gore's increasingly bizarre utterings," the *Times* wrote. "Webster's New World Dictionary defines 'delusional' thusly: 'The apparent perception, in a nervous or mental disorder, of some thing external that is actually not present ... a belief in something that is contrary to fact or reality, resulting from deception, misconception, or a mental disorder.'"

The editorial denounced Gore as "a politician who not only manufactures gross, obvious lies about himself and his achievements but appears to actually believe these confabulations."

But *The Washington Times'* own credibility was shaky. For its editorial attack on Gore, the newspaper not only printed the bogus quote, "I was the one that started it all," but attributed the quote to the Associated Press, which had actually quoted Gore correctly, ("That was the one...").

Yet, while the national media was excoriating Gore, the Concord students were learning more than they had expected about how media and politics work in modern America. For days, the students pressed for a correction from *The Washington Post* and *The New York Times.* But the prestigious papers balked, insisting that the error was insignificant.

"The part that bugs me is the way they nit pick," said Tara Baker, a Concord High junior. "They should at least get it right."[35]

When the David Letterman show made Love Canal the jumping off point for a joke list: "Top 10 Achievements Claimed by Al Gore," the students responded with a press release entitled "Top 10 Reasons Why Many Concord High Students Feel Betrayed by Some of the Media Coverage of Al Gore's Visit to Their School."[36]

The Web site, *The Daily Howler*, also was hectoring a "grumbling editor" at the *Post* to correct the error. Finally, on December 7, a week after Gore's comment, the *Post* published a partial correction, tucked away as the last item in a corrections box. But the *Post* still misled readers about what Gore actually said.

The *Post* correction read: "In fact, Gore said, 'That was the one that started it all,' referring to the congressional hearings on the subject that he called." The revision fit with the *Post's* insistence that the two quotes meant pretty much the same thing, but again, the newspaper was distorting Gore's clear intent by attaching "that" to the wrong antecedent. From the full quote, it's obvious the "that" refers to the Toone toxic waste case, not to Gore's hearings.

Three days later, *The New York Times* followed suit with a correction of its own, but again without fully explaining Gore's position. "They fixed how they misquoted him, but they didn't tell the whole story," commented Lindsey Roy, another Concord High junior.

While the students voiced disillusionment, the two reporters involved showed no remorse for their mistake. "I really do think that the whole thing has been blown out of proportion," said Katharine Seelye of the *Times*. "It was one word."

The *Post's* Ceci Connolly even defended her inaccurate rendition of Gore's quote as something of a journalistic duty. "We have an obligation to our readers to alert them [that] this [Gore's false boasting] continues to be something of a habit," she said.[37]

The half-hearted corrections also did not stop newspapers around the country from continuing to use the bogus quote. A December 9 editorial in the Lancaster, Pennsylvania, *New Era* even published the polished misquote that the Republican National Committee had stuck in a press release: "I was the one who started it all."

The *New Era* then went on to psychoanalyze Gore. "Maybe the lying is a symptom of a more deeply-rooted problem: Al Gore doesn't know who he is," the editorial stated. "The Vice President is a serial prevaricator."

In the *Milwaukee Journal Sentinel,* writer Michael Ruby concluded that "the Gore of '99" was full of lies. He "suddenly discovers elastic properties in the truth," Ruby declared. "He invents the Internet, inspires the fictional hero of 'Love Story,' blows the whistle on Love Canal. Except he didn't really do any of those things."[38]

The National Journal's Stuart Taylor Jr. cited the Love Canal case as proof that President Clinton was a kind of political toxic waste contaminant. The problem was "the Clintonization of Al Gore, who increasingly apes his boss in fictionalizing his life story and mangling the truth for political gain. Gore – self-described inspiration for the novel *Love Story*, discoverer of Love Canal, co-creator of the Internet," Taylor wrote.[39]

On December 19, GOP chairman Nicholson was back on the offensive. Far from apologizing for the RNC's misquotes, Nicholson was reprising the allegations of Gore's falsehoods that had been repeated so often that they had taken on the color of truth: "Remember, too, that this is the same guy who says he invented the Internet, inspired Love Story and discovered Love Canal."

More than two weeks after the *Post* correction, the bogus quote was still spreading. *The Providence Journal* lashed out at Gore in an editorial that reminded readers that Gore had said about Love Canal, "I was the one that started it all." The editorial then turned to the bigger picture: "This is the third time in the last few months that Mr. Gore has made a categorical assertion that is – well, untrue. ... There is an audacity about Mr. Gore's howlers that is stunning. ... Perhaps it is time to wonder what it is that impels Vice President Gore to make such preposterous claims, time and again."[40]

On New Year's Eve, a column in Moon's *Washington Times* returned again to the theme of Gore's pathological lies. Entitled "Liar, Liar; Gore's Pants on Fire," the column by Jackie Mason and Raoul Felder concluded that "when Al Gore lies, it's without any apparent reason. Mr. Gore had already established his credits on environmental issues, for better or worse, and had even been anointed 'Mr. Ozone.' So why did he have to tell students in Concord, New Hampshire, 'I found a little place in upstate New York called Love Canal. I had the first hearing on the issue. I was the one that started it all.'"[41]

The characterization of Gore as a clumsy liar continued into the New Year. Again in Moon's *Washington Times,* R. Emmett Tyrrell Jr. put Gore's falsehoods in the context of a sinister strategy: "Deposit so many deceits and falsehoods on the public record that the public and the press simply lose interest in the truth. This, the Democrats thought, was the method behind Mr. Gore's many brilliantly conceived little lies. Except that Mr. Gore's lies are not brilliantly conceived. In fact, they are stupid. He gets caught every time ... Just last month, Mr. Gore got caught claiming ... to have been the whistle-blower for 'discovering Love Canal.'"[42]

It was unclear where Tyrrell got the quote, "discovering Love Canal," since not even the false quotes had put those words in Gore's mouth. But Tyrrell's description of what he perceived as Gore's strategy of flooding the public debate with "deceits and falsehoods" might fit better with what the news media and the Republicans had been doing to Gore.

Beyond Love Canal, the other prime examples of Gore's "lies" – inspiring the male lead in *Love Story* and working to create the Internet – also stemmed from a quarrelsome reading of his words, followed by exaggeration and ridicule rather than a fair assessment of how his comments and the truth matched up.

The earliest of these Gore "lies," dating back to 1997, was Gore's comment about a media report that he and his wife Tipper had served as models for the lead characters in the sentimental bestseller and movie, *Love Story*. When the author, Erich Segal, was asked about Gore's impression, he stated that the preppy hockey-playing male lead, Oliver Barrett IV, indeed was modeled after Gore and Gore's Harvard roommate, actor Tommy Lee Jones. But Segal said the female lead, Jenny, was not modeled after Tipper Gore.[43]

Rather than treating this distinction as a minor point of legitimate confusion, the news media concluded that Gore had willfully lied. The media made the case an indictment against Gore's honesty. In doing so, however, the media repeatedly misstated the facts, insisting that Segal had denied that Gore was the model for the lead male character. In reality, Segal had confirmed that Gore was, at least partly, the inspiration for the character, Barrett, played by Ryan O'Neal.

Some journalists seemed to understand the nuance but still could not resist disparaging Gore's honesty. For instance, in its attack on Gore over the Love Canal quote, the *Boston Herald* conceded that Gore "did provide material" for Segal's book, but the newspaper added that it was "for a minor character."[44] That, of course, was untrue, since the Barrett character was one of *Love Story's* two principal characters

The media's treatment of the Internet comment followed a similar course. Gore's statement may have been poorly phrased, but its intent was clear: he was trying to say that he worked in Congress to help develop the Internet. Gore wasn't claiming to have "invented" the Internet or to have been the "father of the Internet," as many journalists have asserted.

Gore's actual comment, in an interview with CNN's Wolf Blitzer that aired on March 9, 1999, was as follows: "During my service in the United States Congress, I took the initiative in creating the Internet."

Republicans quickly went to work on Gore's statement. In press releases, they noted that the precursor of the Internet, called ARPANET, existed in 1971, a half dozen years before Gore entered Congress. But ARPANET was a tiny networking of about 30 universities, a far cry from today's "information superhighway," ironically a phrase widely credited to Gore.

As the media clamor arose about Gore's supposed claim that he had invented the Internet, Gore's spokesman Chris Lehane tried to explain. He noted that Gore "was the leader in Congress on the connections between data transmission and computing power, what we call information technology. And those efforts helped to create the Internet that we know today."[45] There was no disputing Lehane's description of Gore's lead congressional role in developing today's Internet. But the media was off and running.

Routinely, the reporters lopped off the introductory clause "during my service in the United States Congress" or simply jumped to word substitutions, asserting that Gore claimed that he "invented" the Internet which carried the notion of a hands-on computer engineer. Whatever imprecision may have existed in Gore's original comment, it paled beside the distortions of what Gore clearly meant. While excoriating Gore's phrasing as an exaggeration, the media engaged in its own exaggeration.

With the Love Canal controversy, the media pattern of distortion had returned with a vengeance. The national news media put a false quote into Gore's mouth and then extrapolated from it to the point of questioning his sanity. Even after the quote was acknowledged to be wrong, the words continued to be repeated, again becoming part of Gore's "record."

At times, the media jettisoned any pretext of objectivity. According to various accounts of the first Democratic debate in Hanover, New Hampshire, reporters openly mocked Gore as they sat in a nearby press room and watched the debate on television. Several journalists later described the incident, but without overt criticism of their colleagues. As *The Daily Howler* observed, *Time*'s Eric Pooley cited the reporters' reaction only to underscore how Gore was failing in his "frenzied attempt to connect."

"The ache was unmistakable – and even touching – but the 300 media types watching in the press room at Dartmouth were, to use the appropriate technical term, totally grossed out by it," Pooley wrote. "Whenever Gore came on too strong, the room erupted in a collective jeer, like a gang of 15-year-old Heathers cutting down some hapless nerd." *Hotline*'s Howard Mortman described the same behavior as the reporters "groaned, laughed and howled" at Gore's comments.

Later, during an appearance on C-SPAN's "Washington Journal," *Salon.com*'s Jake Tapper cited the Hanover incident, too. "I can tell you that the only media bias I have detected in terms of a group media bias was, at the first debate between Bill Bradley and Al Gore, there was hissing for Gore in the media room up at Dartmouth College. The reporters were hissing Gore, and that's the only time I've ever heard the press room boo or hiss any candidate of any party at any event."[46]

Traditionally, journalists pride themselves in maintaining deadpan expressions in such public settings, at most chuckling at a comment or raising an eyebrow, but never demonstrating derision for a public figure. What the behavior at Dartmouth indicated was that the reporters saw no career danger in openly ridiculing Gore. Indeed, many may have sensed that resisting the group behavior might have opened them to suspicions of holding private sympathies for Gore.

Reasons for this media contempt for Gore varied. Conservative outlets, such as Moon's *Washington Times* and Murdoch's media empire, clearly favored the election of a Republican to the White House. In the mainstream press, many reporters may have felt that savaging Gore protected them from the "liberal" label that can so damage a reporter's career. Others simply might have been venting residual anger over President Clinton's survival of the Monica Lewinsky scandal. They might have felt that Gore's destruction would be a fitting end to the Clinton administration.

Yet, the national media's prejudice against Gore – including fabrication of damaging quotes and misrepresentation of his meanings – raised a troubling question: How could voters have any hope of expressing an informed judgment when the media intervened to transform one of the principal candidates – an individual who, by all accounts, was a well-qualified public official and a decent family man – into a national laughingstock?

***

As Campaign 2000 progressed, the national news media continued to apply two starkly different standards for judging how George W. Bush and his running mate, Dick Cheney, handled the truth versus how Al Gore did. Bush and Cheney could utter misleading statements and even outright falsehoods with little or no notice. By contrast, Gore's comments were fly-specked to support the media's "theme" – reinforced by the Republicans – that Gore was an inveterate liar.

Besides the cases of Love Canal, *Love Story* and the Internet, the news media mocked Gore's description of his work as a boy on the family farm (Gore's version turned out to be true), the degree of danger he faced in Vietnam (the reporters had no way to know), his alleged misrepresentation of his father's civil rights record (again the press was being unfair), and his alleged exaggeration that his sister worked as a Peace Corps "volunteer" (she had, although not in a foreign setting).

Yet because of this pattern of contentious journalism, the press canards became the backdrop – a kind of accepted reference point – for Lyin' Al. That meant that when Gore made any misstatement, no matter how innocuous, such as remembering inaccurately being at a Texas disaster scene in 1998 with the director of the Federal Emergency Management Administration when he actually was with the director's deputy, the news media reprised the litany of Gore-as-serial-exaggerator stories.

By contrast to the front-page treatment given Gore's FEMA mistake, the press shrugged its shoulders at dubious statements by Bush and Cheney, even when they appeared calculated to mislead the public. At the vice presidential debate, for instance, Cheney depicted himself as a self-made multi-millionaire from his years as CEO and chairman of Halliburton Company. As for his success in the private sector, Cheney told Democratic nominee Joe Lieberman that "the government had absolutely nothing to do with it."

After months of hypercritical coverage of Al Gore for supposedly puffing up his resumé, one might have expected the media to jump all over this falsehood. But the big newspapers and major television networks offered no challenge to Cheney's comment. Bloomberg News, a business wire, was one of the few outlets that took note of the variance between Cheney's statement and the facts.

"Cheney's reply left out how closely Dallas-based Halliburton's fortunes are linked to the U.S. government," said an article by Bloomberg News reporter John Rega. The article noted that Halliburton was a leading defense contractor (with $1.8 billion in contracts from 1996-99) and a major beneficiary of federal loan guarantees (another $1.8 billion in loans and loan guarantees from the U.S.-funded Export-Import Bank during Cheney's years). The article also cited internal Ex-Im Bank e-mails showing that Cheney personally lobbied bank chairman James Harmon for a $500 million loan guarantee for Russia's OAO Tyumen Oil Company. The Ex-Im loan guarantee helped finance Halliburton's contract with Tyumen.

In further contradiction of Cheney's self-made-man claim, Bloomberg News quoted from a 1997 speech that Cheney gave to the Ex-Im Bank. "I see that we have in recent years been involved in projects in the following (countries) supported, in part, through Ex-Im activities: Algeria, Angola, Colombia, the Philippines, Russia, the Czech Republic, Thailand, China, Turkey, Turkmenistan, Kuwait, India, Kenya, the Congo, Brazil, Argentina, Trinidad and Tobago, Venezuela, Indonesia, Malaysia and Mexico," Cheney said. "Export financing agencies are a key element in making this possible, helping U.S. businesses blend private sector resources with the full faith and credit of the U.S. government."[47]

Fresh from his debate pronouncement about his self-reliance, Cheney took the offensive resuming his attacks on Gore for alleged exaggerations. "He [Gore] seems to have a compulsion to embellish his arguments or … his resumé," Cheney said on October 6. "He seems to have this uncontrollable desire periodically to add to his reputation, to his record, things that aren't true. That's worrisome and I think it's appropriate for us to point that out."

Normally, hypocrisy is a big story. Yet, Cheney's own resumé polishing was barely mentioned in the major media. The media maintained this position even as the former Defense Secretary went out of his way to defend his self-made man statement in later comments on National Public Radio. There, he insisted that the government contracts with Halliburton had predated his arrival at the company in 1995.

"We did do some" work for the government, Cheney told NPR interviewer Bob Edwards on October 11. "The fact is the company I worked for won a competitive bid before I ever got there. So it's not as though this were some kind of gift."[48] Yet, contrary to Cheney's suggestion that he was not responsible for bringing in Halliburton's government business, Halliburton actually moved up the list of Pentagon contractors during Cheney's tenure, reaching 17 in 1999.

While giving Bush and Cheney virtually a free pass on their statements, the news media occasionally and uncritically took note of how well the Republicans had portrayed Gore as a liar. *The New York Times* described what it called "a skillful and sustained 18-month campaign by Republicans to portray the Vice President as flawed and untrustworthy," according to an article on October 15.[49]

In one example, the *Times* noted that the Republicans successfully portrayed Gore as a liar for having talked about his work on the family's farm as a boy. Republican National Chairman Jim Nicholson mocked Gore as a pampered city boy misrepresenting his past. "Friends later told reporters that Mr. Gore's father had kept him on a backbreaking work schedule during summers on the family farm," the *Times* said.

But the cumulative effect of the imbalanced coverage was to leave tens of millions of Americans believing that Gore was a pathological liar, while they saw Bush as maybe a little slow intellectually but a "straight shooter" and a regular guy. When Americans went to vote on November 7, many voters said in exit polls that Gore's lack of honesty was why they went with Bush. A later study by pollster Stan Greenberg found that the biggest reason people decided not to vote for Gore was his "exaggerations and untruthfulness."

Chapter 21: Electoral Coup

In the days before the November 7 election, Republicans feared a situation that hadn't occurred for more than a century in U.S. politics: that one candidate would win the national popular vote while the other would walk away with a majority in the Electoral College, giving him the Presidency but not a mandate.

Their concern, however, was that George W. Bush would be the popular vote winner while Al Gore would prevail in the Electoral College. The expectation was that Green Party candidate Ralph Nader might siphon off millions of votes from Gore nationwide, but not enough in key states to keep them out of Gore's column. That could allow Gore to amass the 270 electoral votes needed for winning the Presidency.

After eight years of battling Bill Clinton, some of these Republicans were not prepared to accept Gore snaking away with the White House if Bush got more votes nationwide. According to scattered press reports in the run-up to the election, advisers to the Bush campaign were weighing the possibility of challenging the legitimacy of a popular-vote loser gaining the White House.

"The one thing we don't do is roll over – we fight," said one Bush aide, according to an article by Michael Kramer in the *New York Daily News* on November 1, a week before the election. The article reported that "the core of the emerging Bush strategy assumes a popular uprising, stoked by the Bushies themselves, of course. In league with the campaign – which is preparing talking points about the Electoral College's essential unfairness – a massive talk-radio operation would be encouraged."

"We'd have ads, too," said a Bush aide, "and I think you can count on the media to fuel the thing big-time. Even papers that supported Gore might turn against him because the will of the people will have been thwarted." The article added that "local business leaders will be urged to lobby their customers, the clergy will be asked to speak up for the popular will and Team Bush will enlist as many Democrats as possible to scream as loud as they can." The planning had gotten so detailed that the Bush advisers were reportedly considering names of front groups. "You think 'Democrats for Democracy' would be a catchy term for them?" asked a Bush adviser.

The Bush strategy also planned to lobby members of the Electoral College, the 538 electors who are picked by the campaigns and state party organizations to go to Washington for what is normally a ceremonial function, Kramer's article said. Many of the electors are not legally bound to a specific candidate.

Another article describing the Republican thinking appeared in *The Boston Herald* on November 3. It also quoted Republican sources outlining plans to rally public sentiment against Gore if he won the Electoral College but lost the popular vote. "The Bush camp, sources said, would likely challenge the legitimacy of a Gore win, casting it as an affront to the people's will and branding the Electoral College as an antiquated relic," said the article by Andrew Miga. "One informal Bush adviser, who declined to be named, predicted Republicans would likely benefit from a storm of public outrage if Bush won the popular vote but was denied the presidency."

The article quoted the Bush adviser as saying: "That's what America is all about, isn't it. I'm sure we would make a strong case."

The November 7 election turned out differently, however.

***

Al Gore ended up winning the national popular vote by about 544,000 votes, a number that exceeded the victory margins of John Kennedy in 1960 and Richard Nixon in 1968. Gore also appeared to have been the choice of voters in the pivotal state of Florida, which would have given him a clear majority in the Electoral College.

But thousands of votes in Democratic strongholds were spoiled. Elderly Jewish voters were confused by a "butterfly" ballot in West Palm Beach, causing them to vote accidentally for right-wing candidate Pat Buchanan. Antiquated punch-card machines functioned poorly in some low-income African-American precincts, leaving many ballots unreadable by vote-counting machines. Later, it was also discovered that thousands of predominantly African-American voters had been falsely identified by the state as felons and purged from the voting lists. Some were turned away from the polls on Election Day.

Still, the preliminary counts of unspoiled ballots in Florida showed George W. Bush clinging to a tiny lead of less than 1,000 votes out of six million cast. If Bush could hang on to that thin edge, he would defeat Gore in the Electoral College by a narrow 271-to-266 margin, even while losing the national popular vote. So, with Bush's younger brother Jeb the sitting governor of Florida and Bush's state chairman, Katherine Harris, the secretary of state in charge of certifying the results, the Bush team moved quickly to prevent any thorough statewide recount. Partial recounts in some counties chipped away at Bush's lead, which dwindled to less than 600 votes.

The Republicans, who had been gearing up to protest the trampling of democracy if Gore had won the Electoral College and lost the popular vote, changed their tune, too. Gone was the talk of challenging the Electoral College as an anti-democratic relic. Gone was a principled stand in defense of the expressed will of the American people. The new "theme" was that Gore was trying to steal the election by "inventing" votes in Florida. The conservative news media – on TV, in print, on the Internet and on the radio – rallied the Republican faithful to defend Bush's "victory," while the mainstream press corps acted as if the election were essentially a tie and that Bush was somehow a better choice for the country.

For his part, Gore discouraged street demonstrations by his supporters and pursued recounts under rules prescribed in Florida law. Bush followed a very different two-pronged strategy. He used legal challenges to block any court-ordered recounts and unleashed Republican activists to disrupt recounts that were taking place. To direct the war against the recount, the Bush campaign brought onboard former President Bush's longtime confidante, James Baker, who had overseen George H.W. Bush's presidential campaigns in 1988 and 1992. Planeloads of Republican legislators and congressional staffers were deployed to Florida as early as mid-November.

"We now need to send reinforcements," the Bush campaign said in an appeal to Republicans on November 18. "The campaign will pay airfare and hotel expenses for people willing to go." These reinforcements – many of them Republican staffers from Capitol Hill – added an angrier tone to the dueling street protests already underway between supporters of Bush and Gore. The new wave of Republican activists injected "venom and volatility into an already edgy situation," wrote reporter Jake Tapper in his 2002 book, *Down and Dirty*.[1]

"This is the new Republican Party, sir!" Brad Blakeman, Bush's campaign director of advance travel logistics, bellowed into a bullhorn to disrupt a CNN correspondent interviewing a Democratic congressman. "We're not going to take it anymore!"

The street battle reached its apex when the Miami-Dade canvassing board tried to conduct a recount on November 22. After learning the board was starting an examination of 10,750 disputed ballots that had not been counted, Representative John Sweeney, a New York Republican, called on Republican troops to "shut it down." Brendan Quinn, executive director of the New York GOP, told about two dozen Republican operatives to storm the room on the 19th floor where the canvassing board was meeting.[2]

"Emotional and angry, they immediately make their way outside the larger room in which the tabulating room is contained," Tapper wrote. "The mass of 'angry voters' on the 19th floor swells to maybe 80 people," including many of the Republican activists from outside Florida. News cameras captured the chaotic scene outside the canvassing board's offices. The protesters shouted slogans and banged on the doors and walls. The unruly protest prevented official observers and members of the press from reaching the room. Miami-Dade county spokesman Mayco Villafana was pushed and shoved. Security officials feared the confrontation was spinning out of control.

The canvassing board suddenly reversed its decision and canceled the recount. "Until the demonstration stops, nobody can do anything," said David Leahy, Miami's supervisor of elections, although the canvassing board members would later insist that they were not intimidated into stopping the recount.[3]

While the siege of the canvassing board office was underway, county Democratic chairman Joe Geller stopped at another office seeking a sample ballot. He wanted to demonstrate his theory that some voters had intended to vote for Gore but instead marked an adjoining number that represented no candidate. As Geller took the ballot marked "sample," one of the Republican activists began shouting, "This guy's got a ballot!"

In *Down and Dirty*, Tapper wrote: "The masses swarm around him, yelling, getting in his face, pushing him, grabbing him. 'Arrest him!' they cry. 'Arrest him!' With the help of a diminutive DNC aide, Luis Rosero, and the political director of the Miami Gore campaign, Joe Fraga, Geller manages to wrench himself into the elevator. "Rosero, who stays back to talk to the press, gets kicked, punched. A woman pushes him into a much larger guy, seemingly trying to instigate a fight. In the lobby of the building, a group of 50 or so Republicans are crushed around Geller, surrounding him. ...

"The cops escort Geller back to the 19th floor, so the elections officials can see what's going on, investigate the charges. Of course, it turns out that all Geller had was a sample ballot. The crowd is pulling at the cops, pulling at Geller. It's insanity! Some even get in the face of 73-year-old Representative Carrie Meek. Democratic operatives decide to pull out of the area altogether."[4]

Bush and his top aides said nothing publicly to discourage these disruptive tactics, while privately encouraging the practices. *The Washington Post* reported that "even as the Bush campaign and the Republicans portray themselves as above the fray," national Republicans actually had joined in and helped finance the raucous protests.[5]

The Wall Street Journal added more details, including the fact that Bush offered personal words of encouragement to the rioters in a conference call to a Bush campaign-sponsored celebration on the night of Thanksgiving Day, one day after the canvassing board assault. "The night's highlight was a conference call from Mr. Bush and running mate Dick Cheney, which included joking reference by both running mates to the incident in Miami, two [Republican] staffers in attendance say," according to the *Journal*.

Crooner Wayne Newton serenaded the staffers by singing "Danke Schoen," German for thank-you very much.[6]

The *Journal* also reported that the assault on the canvassing board – dubbed the Brooks Brothers Riot because of the preppy clothing of some protesters – was led by national Republican operatives "on all expense-paid trips, courtesy of the Bush campaign." After their success in Dade, the rioters moved on to Broward, where the protests remained unruly but failed to stop that count.

"Behind the rowdy rallies in South Florida this past weekend was a well-organized effort by Republican operatives to entice supporters to South Florida," with DeLay's Capitol Hill office taking charge of the recruitment, the *Journal* reported. About 200 Republican congressional staffers signed on. They were put up at hotels, given $30 a day for food and "an invitation to an exclusive Thanksgiving Day party in Fort Lauderdale," the article said. The *Journal* reported that there was no evidence of a similar Democratic strategy to fly in national party operatives. "This has allowed the Republicans to quickly gain the upper hand, protest-wise," the *Journal* said.

The Bush campaign also worked to conceal its hand. "Staffers who joined the effort say there has been an air of mystery to the operation. 'To tell you the truth, nobody knows who is calling the shots,' says one aide. Many nights, often very late, a memo is slipped underneath the hotel-room doors outlining coming events," the *Journal* reported.

On November 25, the Bush campaign issued "talking points" to justify the Miami protest, calling it "fitting, proper" and blaming the canvassing board for the disruptions. "The board made a series of bad decisions and the reaction to it was inevitable and well justified," the Bush campaign said.[7]

Meanwhile, another recount in Broward County had whittled down Bush's lead. Gore was gaining slowly in Palm Beach's recount, too, despite constant challenges from Republican observers. To boost Bush's margin back up, Republican Secretary of State Harris allowed Nassau County to throw out its recounted figures that had helped Gore. Then, excluding a partial recount in Palm Beach and with Miami shut down, Harris certified Bush the winner by 537 votes.

Bush partisans cheered their victory and began demanding that Bush be called the president-elect. Soon afterwards, Bush appeared on national television to announce himself the winner and to call on Gore to concede defeat. "Now," Bush said, "we must live up to our principles. We must show our commitment to the common good, which is bigger than any person or any party."

To many Gore supporters, the aborted recount in Miami changed the course of the Florida events, preventing Gore from narrowing Bush's small lead. The Miami assault also represented an escalation of tactics, demonstrating the potential for spiraling political violence if the recount battle dragged on. The Republicans were putting down a marker that they were prepared to do what was necessary to win, regardless of what the voters wanted.

The Washington Post's columnist Richard Cohen spoke for many in the Washington Establishment when he argued that the deepening national divisions could only be resolved if Al Gore gave up. Cohen wrote: "Given the present bitterness, given the angry irresponsible charges being hurled by both camps, the nation will be in dire need of a conciliator, a likable guy who will make things better and not worse. That man is not Al Gore. That man is George W. Bush."[8]

Cohen's column fit with the pattern of the mainstream media to condemn both sides equally for the acrimony while placing the primary onus on Gore to resolve the impasse by surrendering. Meanwhile, the conservative media heaped the blame overwhelmingly on Gore, who supposedly was trying to "steal" the election. The reality, which was documented later in political filings with the Internal Revenue Service, was that Bush outspent Gore four-to-one on the recount battle, including picking up the expenses of Republican protesters who had rioted in Miami.

The payments were documented in hundreds of pages of Bush committee records released grudgingly to the IRS on July 15, 2002. The records showed that the Bush recount committee spent a total of $13.8 million. By contrast, the Gore recount operation spent $3.2 million, about one quarter of the Bush total. Bush, a vocal critic of the legal profession and what he calls "frivolous lawsuits," spent more just on lawyers – $4.4 million – than Gore did on his entire effort.

According to the documents, the Bush organization also put on the payroll about 250 staffers, spent about $1.2 million to fly operatives to Florida and elsewhere, and paid for hotel bills adding up to about $1 million. To add flexibility to the travel arrangements, a fleet of corporate jets was assembled, including planes owned by Enron Corporation, then run by Bush backer Kenneth Lay, and Halliburton Company, where Dick Cheney had served as chairman and chief executive officer.

Only a handful of the Brooks Brothers rioters were publicly identified, some through photographs published in *The Washington Post*. Jake Tapper's book, *Down and Dirty*, provided a list of 12 Republican operatives who took part in the Miami riot. Half of those individuals received payments from the Bush recount committee, according to the IRS records.

The Miami protesters who were paid by Bush's recount committee were: Matt Schlapp, a Bush staffer who was based in Austin and received $4,276.09; Thomas Pyle, a staff aide to House Majority Whip Tom DeLay, $456; Michael Murphy, a DeLay fund-raiser, $935.12; Garry Malphrus, House majority chief counsel to the House Judiciary subcommittee on criminal justice, $330; Charles Royal, a legislative aide to Representative Jim DeMint of South Carolina, $391.80; and Kevin Smith, a former GOP House staffer, $373.23. Three of the Miami protesters were later hired as members of Bush's White House staff, the *Miami Herald* reported. They included Schlapp, a special assistant to the President; Malphrus, deputy director of the President's Domestic Policy Council; and Joel Kaplan, another special assistant to the President.[9]

The Bush committee records showed, too, that Bush's operation paid for the hotel where the Republican protesters celebrated at the Thanksgiving Day party. According to the IRS documents, the Bush recount committee paid $35,501.52 to the Hyatt Regency Pier 66 in Fort Lauderdale, where the party was held. A number of miscellaneous expenses, reported by the Bush recount committee, also appear to have gone for party items, such as lighting, sound systems and even costumes. Garrett Sound and Lighting in Fort Lauderdale was paid $5,902; Beach Sound Inc. in North Miami was paid $3,500; and the House of Masquerades, a costume shop in Miami, had three payments totaling $640.92, according to the Bush records.

***

Despite the rioting, Gore continued to pursue his legal strategy, seeking court-ordered recounts. After two more weeks of delays and courtroom arguments, Gore's strategy finally appeared to have paid off. On December 8, the Florida Supreme Court, on a split vote, ordered a statewide recount to examine all ballots that had been kicked out by machines for supposedly having no choice for President.

The next day, facing a deadline of December 12 for certification of Florida's electors, vote counters across the state began examining these so-called "under-votes." Although not known at the time, canvassers also were told to collect so-called "over-votes," ballots that had been rejected because they had more than one name entered, which sometimes meant that voters both checked the name of their preference and wrote in his name. In such cases, Florida law allowed for counting "over-votes."

In the first few hours of the December 9 recount, the counters found scores of ballots with clear votes for President that had been missed by the machines. Other ballots were set aside for a judicial determination about whether a vote was registered or not. With Bush's lead at less than 200 votes and slipping, Bush played his trump card. He turned to his five conservative allies on the U.S. Supreme Court.

By a 5-4 majority, the court – for the first time in U.S. history – stopped the counting of votes cast by American citizens for President. The majority consisted of Justices William Rehnquist, Anthony Kennedy, Sandra Day O'Connor, Clarence Thomas and Antonin Scalia. In a written explanation, Scalia made clear that the purpose of the extraordinary injunction was to prevent Bush from losing his lead and having "a cloud" cast over the "legitimacy" of his Presidency if the court decided to throw out the new votes. Scalia maintained that a count of Florida's votes that showed Bush to be the loser – when the court might later make him the winner – undermined the need for "democratic stability."

Three days later, only two hours before the December 12 deadline was to expire, the same five justices issued a complex ruling that reversed the Florida Supreme Court's recount order. The justices cited a hodgepodge of "constitutional" issues, including complaints about the lack of consistent standards in the Florida recount. After having delayed any remedy up to the deadline, Bush's five allies then demanded that any revised plan and recount be completed within two hours, a patently impossible task.

The five conservatives also may have taken some perverse pleasure in applying "equal protection" arguments to prevent the recount. Historically, Supreme Court liberals have used "equal protection" principles to strike down discrimination against African-Americans and other minorities. Now, the five conservative justices were hoisting the liberals on their own petard. The "equal protection" argument asserted that the votes of other Florida citizens would be diluted if the ballots that had been kicked out by voting machines were counted using standards that varied from county to county.

The irony of the argument was that in wealthier voting precincts, new optical scanners were used to count votes and did the counting so efficiently that few of the votes cast for President were missed. In poorer precincts, where African-Americans and retired Jewish voters were concentrated, older punch-card systems were used which failed to record thousands of votes. Just as poor neighborhoods ended up with older textbooks in their schools, they got stuck with antiquated voting machines. In effect, the "equal protection" argument was used to extend special protection to the well-to-do. The Florida Supreme Court had sought to ameliorate this imbalance by ordering hand examinations of ballots statewide. The U.S. Supreme Court stopped it.

Besides this perverse use of "equal protection," the U.S. Supreme Court relied on reasoning that – if applied fully – would have judged the entire Florida election unconstitutional. While excluding the hand recounts ordered by the Florida Supreme Court, the U.S. Supreme Court allowed the inclusion of earlier hand recounts done in Republican areas that had boosted Bush's total by hundreds of votes.

Also left in Florida totals were scores of overseas absentee ballots, heavily favoring Bush, that were counted after some Republican counties waived legal requirements almost entirely. Supposedly to avoid disenfranchising U.S. military personnel, ballots were accepted even though they lacked signatures, witnesses and dates. In a couple of cases, overseas ballots were faxed in and counted clearly in violation of state law.[10] In two other cases in Seminole and Martin counties, Republicans were allowed to fix errors on absentee ballot applications also in violation of state law. The state courts ruled, however, that these ballots should be counted, despite the irregularities, because the sanctity of the vote was more important than technical voting rules. Those situations all favored Bush.

Given the lack of consistent standards throughout Florida and the waiving of technical legal requirements in other cases, a logical extension of the U.S. Supreme Court's logic would be that the entire presidential election in the Florida should be thrown out as unconstitutional. Or the U.S. Supreme Court would have agreed that the best, though imperfect, remedy would have been to conduct as full and fair a recount as possible. But Bush and his advisers prevented the latter outcome, first by turning to violent protests and then to political allies on the U.S. Supreme Court.

In a dissenting opinion on December 12, Justice John Paul Stevens, an appointee of President Gerald Ford, said the majority's action in blocking the Florida recount "can only lend credence to the most cynical appraisal of the work of judges throughout the land." Justices Stephen Breyer and Ruth Bader Ginsburg, appointees of President Bill Clinton, said in another dissent, "Although we may never know with complete certainty the identity of the winner of this year's presidential election, the identity of the loser is perfectly clear. It is the nation's confidence in the judge as an impartial guardian of the rule of law."

The prevailing mood in the U.S. news media was one of relief. Campaign 2000 had gone into extra innings, tiring out many of the correspondents who had pushed themselves to the physical limit in their coverage of the campaign up to November 7. There was also a sense that Bush would be a better President to bring the country together, given how furious the conservatives had shown themselves to be during the recount battle. Many journalists, too, seemed to reflect the attitude of Ralph Nader's Green Party campaign that there wasn't much difference between Gore and Bush anyway. Plus, Bush was seen as likely to bring back the "adults" – his father and his father's advisers – who were expected to guide the inexperienced son through the challenges of the Presidency.

***

George W. Bush was inaugurated the 43rd President of the United States on a cold and rainy day, January 20, 2001. He was the first popular-vote loser in 112 years – since Benjamin Harrison – to ascend to the Presidency.

Along with the thousands of well-dressed Republican celebrants, tens of thousands of protesters surged close to the parade route down Pennsylvania Avenue. Many shouted slogans, such as "Selected, not elected!," "Shame!," "Gore got more!," and "Hail to the thief!" Eggs were thrown at the presidential limousine. Fearing a riot, the Secret Service sped up the car carrying Bush, who scrapped the tradition of getting out of the limousine to walk the final block to the White House.

Presumably out of a desire to restore political unity behind the new President, the national news media played down the demonstrations. (Many American viewers were shocked to see the scenes for the first time when they were included in Michael Moore's anti-Bush documentary, "Fahrenheit 9/11," in 2004.)

It would be ten months after the Inauguration for a consortium of major news organizations to finish their own unofficial recount of the Florida ballots. The outcome was delayed by the September 11, 2001, terrorist attacks on the World Trade Center and the Pentagon. When editors could turn their attention to the recount project again in November, they faced new pressures because of the public's demand for even greater unity after the murders of about 3,000 people. Polls showed a rally-'round-the-President phenomenon.

The news executives, therefore, faced a dilemma. Their recount had discovered that if all legally cast votes were counted, Gore would have won Florida, regardless of what standard was used to judge the punch-card ballots, whether dimpled, hanging or fully punched-through chads. The key was that Gore gained a surprising number of votes from the so-called "over-votes" where his name was both marked and written in. If the news stories were written straight, they would have stated that a full recount of legal Florida ballots would have made Al Gore the winner; that George W. Bush not only lost the national popular vote but he wasn't even the choice of Florida voters. In other words, the wrong guy was in the White House. By any chad measure, Gore won.

But stories written that way would have invited a furious reaction from Republicans against the "liberal" news media. Other Americans would likely lash out at the press for presenting news that would only divide the country at a moment of deep national crisis. While facing a dangerous enemy, George Bush would have his legitimacy as the leader of the Free World called into question. And to what end? There was no way for the events of December 2000 to be rewritten. What was done was done.

Some Democrats might say that Bush shouldn't be bailed out by the news media after having created the problem in the first place. He could have agreed to Gore's early request for a full Florida recount or he could have accepted the judgment of the Florida Supreme Court and let the recount proceed. Journalistic purists also might argue that the only duty the press has in a democracy is to tell the people the truth as fully and fairly as possible, not protect them from unpleasant information. But the real world of journalism is different. Editors and news executives don't operate in an ivory tower. They must weigh a complex set of priorities, which can include the public reaction to their decisions and the consequences on their careers.

So, the major newspapers and news networks chose to write the story as if George W. Bush really had won the Florida election. The news organizations structured their stories on the ballot review to support headlines such as "Florida Recounts Would Have Favored Bush."[11] *Post* media critic Howard Kurtz took the spin one cycle further with a story headlined, "George W. Bush, Now More Than Ever," in which Kurtz ridiculed as "conspiracy theorists" those who thought Gore had won.

"The conspiracy theorists have been out in force, convinced that the media were covering up the Florida election results to protect President Bush," Kurtz wrote. "That gets put to rest today, with the finding by eight news organizations that Bush would have beaten Gore under both of the recount plans being considered at the time."

Kurtz also mocked those who believed that winning an election by getting the most votes was important in a democracy. "Now the question is: How many people still care about the election deadlock that last fall felt like the story of the century – and now faintly echoes like some distant Civil War battle?" he wrote. In other words, the elite media's judgment was in: "Bush won, get over it." Only "Gore partisans" – as both *The Washington Post* and *The New York Times* called critics of the Florida election tallies – would insist on looking at the fine print.

Buried deeper in the stories or referenced in subheads was the fact that the actual results of the statewide review of 175,010 disputed ballots determined that Gore was the winner, even ignoring the "butterfly ballot" and other irregularities that cost him thousands of votes. "Full Review Favors Gore," *The Washington Post* said in a box on page 10, showing that under all standards applied to the ballots, Gore came out on top. *The New York Times'* graphic revealed the same outcome. Counting fully punched chads and limited marks on optical ballots, Gore won by 115 votes. With any dimple or optical mark, Gore won by 107 votes. With one corner of a chad detached or any optical mark, Gore won by 60 votes. Applying the standards set by each county, Gore won by 171 votes. Still, the headlines and leads to the stories highlighted hypothetical, partial recounts that supposedly favored Bush.

The news organizations opted for the pro-Bush leads by focusing on two partial recounts that were proposed – but not completed – in the chaotic environment of November and December 2000. The articles made much of Gore's decision to seek recounts in only four counties and the Florida Supreme Court's decision to examine only "under-votes," those rejected by voting machines for supposedly lacking a presidential vote. A recurring theme in the articles was that Gore was to blame for his defeat, even if he may have actually won the election.

"Mr. Gore might have eked out a victory if he had pursued in court a course like the one he publicly advocated when he called on the state to 'count all the votes,'" *The New York Times* wrote, suggesting that Gore was both hypocritical and foolish. *The Washington Post* recalled that Gore "did at one point call on Bush to join him in asking for a statewide recount" with a mutual pledge to accept the results without further legal challenge, but that Bush rejected the proposal as "a public relations gesture."

In the days that followed the release of the recount study, it turned out that the major newspapers were wrong in another way. They had assumed that the Florida Supreme Court's ruling would not have counted the "over-votes," but a document, revealed by *Newsweek* magazine, showed that the judge in charge of the recount was planning to include legal "over-votes" in the tally, too. A memo from the presiding judge, Terry Lewis, to a county canvassing board showed that he was instructing the county boards to collect "over-votes" that had been rejected for indicating two choices for President when, in reality, the voters had made clear their one choice.

"If you would segregate 'over-votes' as you describe and indicate in your final report how many where you determined the clear intent of the voter," wrote Judge Terry Lewis, "I will rule on the issue for all counties." Lewis's memo to the chairman of the Charlotte County canvassing board was written on December 9, 2000, just hours before Bush succeeded in getting five Republican justices on the U.S. Supreme Court to stop the Florida recount.

Lewis, who had been named by the Florida Supreme Court to oversee the statewide recount, said in an interview with the Orlando *Sentinel* that he might well have expanded the recount to include those "over-votes." Indeed, he would have had little choice but to count any legitimate votes once they were recovered by the counties and submitted to him. The "over-votes" in which voters marked the name of their choice and also wrote in his name would be even more clearly legal votes under Florida law than the "under-votes" which were kicked out for failing to register a choice that could be read by voting machines. The key to accepting a vote as legal in Florida, as in many other states, is if the clear intent of the voter can be ascertained.

So, it was no longer obvious at all that the state-ordered recount would have favored Bush. It also appeared likely that the interference by the U.S. Supreme Court was decisive – and that the judgment of the major news outlets about Bush as the legitimate winner was wrong. Again, a Bush had gotten the benefit of the doubt.

Chapter 22: September 11

In the months and years before 9/11, the capability of Americans to conduct the serious business of democracy had already weakened to a dangerous degree. The U.S. news media – which had set the world standard in the 1970s by exposing the crimes of Watergate, the abuses at the CIA and the truth in the Pentagon Papers – had been transformed. On one side was an aggressive conservative news media that promoted a strong ideological agenda and helped to organize conservatives politically nationwide. On the other side was a mainstream press corps that had been intimidated by decades of accusations about "liberal bias." Too many journalists who had resisted those pressures had lost jobs or had seen their careers damaged.

One result of these trends, combined with other commercial pressures, was the trivialization of the national news. Personal scandal, especially when a Democrat was involved, was the safest topic for almost everyone in national journalism. So, as al-Qaeda was readying its deadly attacks on New York and Washington, the national news media was obsessed with the disappearance of Capitol Hill intern Chandra Levy, who'd had an affair with Representative Gary Condit, a California Democrat.

On August 1, in a classic sequence that looked like a scene from a movie parody, the major TV news networks made a madcap dash of helicopters and satellite trucks to Fort Lee, Virginia, south of Richmond. The spare-no-expense race was in reaction to an anonymous tip published on a Web site that Levy's body had been "shrink-wrapped" and buried in a Fort Lee parking lot. The next day, the tip turned out to be a hoax, but the networks still broadcast live stand-ups from Fort Lee. Fox News – which had devoted hours and hours of daily coverage to the Chandra Levy case, even consulting psychics – did its Fort Lee updates under the slogan, "Fox on Top."

The pretense behind the media's interest in Levy's disappearance was always a heartfelt concern to help her parents find their missing daughter. It was a fortunate byproduct that the disappearance gave the TV news shows a chance to gossip about the young woman's sexual affair with Condit. The Chandra Levy case also brought the old cast from the Monica Lewinsky scandal back in force, with conservatives such as Ann Coulter and William Bennett reprising their roles as the nation's moral arbiters. In one dissonant question, CNN interviewer Larry King asked Bennett about hypocrisy on the part of Republicans who had embraced Condit as a conservative "Blue Dog" Democrat before the Chandra scandal and then disowned him. Bennett, the author of the book, *The Death of Outrage*, explained the moral relativism: "Look, hypocrisy is better than no standards at all."[1]

As the Chandra obsession wore on, some media defenders blamed the excessive coverage on the summer news doldrums, not on a national news media permanently adrift. But it would soon be obvious that a major storm of news was brewing just over the horizon, if the press corps had bothered to look. Counter-terrorism experts such as White House aide Richard Clarke were desperately trying to get the Bush administration to focus on a gathering terrorist threat. According to Clarke, CIA Director George Tenet was running around Washington with his "hair on fire," warning about an imminent attack. Tenet told the 9/11 Commission that "the system was blinking red."[2]

"Threat reports surged in June and July, reaching an even higher peak of urgency," the 9/11 Commission Report said. "The headline of a June 30 briefing to top officials was stark: 'Bin Laden Planning High-Profile Attacks.' The report stated that Bin Laden operatives expected near-term attacks to have dramatic consequences of catastrophic proportions." By late June, there were stirrings of mutiny among counter-terrorism officials against their superiors in the Bush administration, the 9/11 Commission Report said.

Counter-terrorism staffers tried to shock administration officials out of their lethargy by using blunter and blunter language. The Senior Executive Intelligence Brief on June 30 contained an article addressing doubts that still existed among top officials; it was entitled, "Bin Laden Threats Are Real." But, still, senior officials didn't share the alarm. National Security Council staff aide Stephen "Hadley told Tenet in July that Deputy Secretary of Defense Paul Wolfowitz questioned the reporting. Perhaps Bin Laden was trying to study U.S reactions," the 9/11 Commission Report said, summarizing Wolfowitz's doubts. "Tenet replied that he had already addressed the Defense Department's questions on this point; the reporting was convincing."[3]

Some top counter-terrorism officials discussed quitting to dramatize their alarm. "To give a sense of his anxiety at the time, one senior official in the Counterterrorist Center told us that he and a colleague were considering resigning in order to go public with their concerns," the 9/11 Commission Report said.[4] Amid such intense feelings, an alert press corps can almost always discover divisions inside a government. Though much of the information was classified, a commitment of only a fraction of the journalistic resources that were being applied to the Chandra Levy case could have pried loose details of the battle going on inside the Bush administration.

Plus, if journalists had paid more attention to the behind-the-scenes drama over the rising threat level, terrorism might have become a bigger issue for George W. Bush and his political advisers in August when he withdrew for a month-long vacation to his Texas ranch. Bush might have paid more heed to the Presidential Daily Brief on August 6, which contained the warning "Bin Laden Determined To Strike in US." Instead, George W. Bush cleared brush at the ranch, went fishing and devoted his energies to philosophical deliberations over stem-cell research. After weeks of soul-searching, he gave a nationally televised speech, delivering his judgment that existing cells from fetuses could be used but not new ones. Some commentators hailed Bush's stem-cell decision as "Solomon-like" and proof he had more *gravitas* than his critics admitted.

Later examinations of the Bush administration's pre-September 11 actions showed that Bush's vacation and his concentration on stem-cell ethics coincided with his administration losing focus on terrorism. *The New York Times* reported that "the White House's impulse to deal more forcefully with terrorist threats within the United States peaked July 5 and then leveled off until September 11." The administration also had other priorities. On September 6, for example, Defense Secretary Donald Rumsfeld threatened a presidential veto of a proposal by Senator Carl Levin, a Michigan Democrat, to transfer money from strategic missile defense to counter-terrorism.[5]

Asked about the administration's failure to respond more aggressively to the August 6 warning, Bush's National Security Adviser Condoleezza Rice said she could think of nothing that she would have done differently. "I would like very much to know what more could have been done given that it was an urgent problem," Rice told Ed Bradley of CBS News' "60 Minutes." "I don't know, Ed, how, after coming into office, inheriting policies that had been in place for at least three of the eight years of the Clinton administration, we could have done more than to continue those policies while we developed more robust policies."[6]

But counter-terrorism coordinator Clarke said a lot more could have been done if Bush had ordered high-level meetings to "shake the trees" and possibly dislodge some of the clues that did exist within the federal bureaucracy about al-Qaeda's plans. FBI agents, for instance, were suspicious about Middle Easterners taking flight-training classes in the United States and one such al-Qaeda member, Zacarias Moussaoui, was arrested in Minnesota.

Clarke said high-level interest from Bush could have forced more attention to these pieces of the puzzle at the FBI, CIA, Customs, the Immigration and Naturalization Agency, and other federal offices. Indeed, after September 11, FBI officials did come forward with evidence they had about suspicious training on aircraft and the fact that two known al-Qaeda operatives had entered the United States although the CIA was not alerted. Either of those bits of evidence combined with other clues might have enabled U.S. authorities to break up the plot, much as alert police work headed off the al-Qaeda bombings planned for the Millennium celebration at the start of 2000.

Attorney General John Ashcroft told the 9/11 Commission that he "assumed the FBI was doing what it needed to do. He acknowledged that in retrospect, this was a dangerous assumption. He did not ask the FBI what it was doing in response to the threats and did not task it to take any specific action. He also did not direct the INS ... to take any specific action."

The 9/11 Commission said, "In sum, the domestic agencies never mobilized in response to the threat. They did not have direction, and did not have a plan to institute. The borders were not hardened. Transportation systems were not fortified. Electronic surveillance was not targeted against a domestic threat. State and local law enforcement were not marshaled to augment the FBI's efforts. The public was not warned."[7]

The commission, however, didn't blame Bush or other senior officials for failing to thwart the mass murders committed by al-Qaeda operatives at the World Trade Center, at the Pentagon and in a field in Pennsylvania. The commission's findings prompted Clarke to pen a *New York Times* Op-Ed article entitled "Honorable Commission, Toothless Report."[8] Michael F. Scheuer, the CIA officer who led the unit that tracked al-Qaeda leader Osama bin Laden, went even further, attacking the 9/11 Commission for not fingering the "bureaucratic cowards" who let down the country. The commission's report, Scheuer wrote, "seems to deliberately ignore those who were clearly culpable of negligence or dereliction."[9] (The 9/11 Commission's vice chairman was former Representative Lee Hamilton.)

***

Almost from the minute that the second plane struck the World Trade Center's south tower, George W. Bush was in dire need of having the perceptions of the American people managed. The reality was that Bush – with his very thin qualifications to be President – flunked his first big test. Not only had he failed to react vigorously to the terror threat warnings as they rose in the summer, but he froze in indecision when White House chief of staff Andrew Card whispered in his ear that "America is under attack." For about seven minutes, he sat almost motionless in a second-grade classroom at the Emma E. Booker Elementary School in Sarasota, Florida.

Bush was using the school as a backdrop to promote his education initiatives. The plan was to read a children's book, *My Pet Goat.* But before entering the classroom shortly before 9 a.m., Bush and Card were informed by political adviser Karl Rove that a plane had crashed into the World Trade Center. "The President's reaction was that the incident must have been caused by pilot error," Card told the 9/11 Commission.

Less than three months after the attacks, Bush gave a different account of what he knew and how he knew it before entering the classroom. At a town hall meeting in Orlando on December 4, Bush claimed to have watched the first plane hit the north tower on television. He said, "I was sitting outside the classroom, waiting to go in, and I saw an airplane hit the tower – the TV was obviously on. And I used to fly myself, and I said, 'Well, there's one terrible pilot.'" But the *Wall Street Journal* would later report that the television in the room where Bush waited was unplugged. Plus, there was no footage shown of the first plane hitting the tower until late on the night of September 11.[10]

At 9:05 a.m., with Bush seated in the classroom, Card walked over and whispered in his ear, "A second plane hit the second tower. America is under attack." The chief of staff then left the commander-in-chief seated in the classroom.

At that moment, the nation was in desperate need of decisive leadership. Two national landmarks were in flames. Some people in the buildings were leaping to their deaths rather than be burned alive. A third plane, American Flight 77, flying from Dulles to Los Angeles had been hijacked over Ohio about 11 minutes earlier. The hijackers were swinging it around as a flying bomb headed for Washington, D.C. A fourth plane, United Flight 93, *en route* from Newark, New Jersey, to San Francisco, would be seized by hijackers about 30 minutes after Card whispered in Bush's ear. It, too, would take aim at Washington.

While the circumstances were extraordinary, crisis-management jobs – of which the Presidency is one of the most demanding – test the people who hold them in moments of crisis. The situations are by definition chaotic and unpredictable. Fast thinking is a prerequisite. Facts must be assembled quickly. The right people must be moved into place. Even in the fog of partial information, judgments must be clearheaded. From police to firefighters, from military officers to doctors, professionals are judged by how they perform under these pressures. Crisis managers who fail at such moments are often removed from the line of command or are washed out of their professions. That may seem harsh, but it is the nature of their jobs. Often, lives are at stake, which was certainly the case on September 11.

Perhaps the worst reaction from a crisis manager is to freeze, which is what Bush did. For about seven minutes, after being told "America is under attack," he sat in a second-grade classroom reading a children's story. His aides in the school were equally nonplussed. None of them interrupted the photo op to excuse the President so he could handle a national crisis. An uncut videotape of the classroom scene showed that Bush – after having been told "America is under attack" – listened to children read the story about a pet goat and asked the children questions.

That it took the President seven minutes to react was a fact that few Americans knew until the 9/11 Commission in early 2004 compiled a detailed chronology of the actions of the key players. When Michael Moore showed footage from the seven minutes in his documentary, "Fahrenheit 9/11," Bush's indecision – measured by a clock superimposed in the corner – was a shocking revelation to millions of Americans.

Almost immediately on September 11, a cover-up of Bush's performance began, with the White House staff trying to shrink the time of Bush's inaction. The national news media, which had representatives present in the classroom, played along, making no big deal out of Bush's nearly disqualifying behavior. The thinking again seemed to be that criticism of Bush at a time of crisis would hurt the nation.

Card, who had relayed word of the attack to Bush, later claimed that "not that many seconds later, the President excused himself from the classroom, and we gathered in the holding room and talked about the situation." As for the reason for even that brief delay, Card said Bush's "instinct was not to frighten the children by rushing out of the room."[11]

Bush himself offered a slightly different excuse for his failure to cut short the book reading. Under questioning by the 9/11 Commission, Bush said "his instinct was to project calm, not to have the country see an excited reaction at a moment of crisis. The press was standing behind the children; he saw their phones and pagers start to ring. The President felt he should project strength and calm until he could better understand what was happening."[12]

But Bush's explanation had holes. How was he going to better understand what was happening by staying seated and reading a children's story? Why couldn't he have maintained a sense of calm by quietly explaining that something had come up that the President needed to address and that the teacher would finish the book reading? Nobody was suggesting that Bush jump out of his seat and run screaming from the classroom. But there were alternatives to staying seated for seven minutes.

After finally leaving the classroom, Bush said he wanted to return to Washington, but was persuaded for security reasons to fly to airfields in Louisiana and then Nebraska before returning to Washington in the evening. White House officials insisted at the time that Bush's decision was driven by a credible terrorist threat against Air Force One. But White House spokesman Dan Bartlett later acknowledged that there was no credible threat, only misunderstood rumors.

In explaining Bush's delay in returning to Washington until after 4 p.m., political adviser Rove said there were still reports about civilian jetliners aloft until then and thus still a threat to Air Force One. But Benjamin Sliney, the top Federal Aviation Administration official responsible for air-traffic control, said the agency informed the White House and the Pentagon at 12:16 p.m. that there were no more hijacked planes in the air and all commercial planes were out of U.S. airspace, the *Wall Street Journal* reported.[13]

There were additional discrepancies about what orders Bush actually issued that day. Bush told the town-hall meeting in Orlando that "one of the first acts I did was to put our military on alert." But the *Journal* reported that the evidence was that Air Force General Richard Myers, the acting head of the Joint Chiefs of Staff, made the decision to raise the U.S. defense level to Defcon III, the highest state of military threat since the 1973 Arab-Israeli War.[14]

Federal officials, interviewed by the *Journal*, said the government's emergency response plans were implemented by lower-level officials, not by Bush, despite Bush's assertion in a nationally televised speech on the night of September 11 that he gave the orders. FBI spokesman Paul Bresson said the so-called "Conplan" was activated without any input from Bush or the White House. A former White House official told the *Journal* that Bush was not involved until he signed a disaster declaration on September 14.[15]

After September 11, a stunned nation rallied around the President, expressing its unity by voicing approval of Bush's performance, regardless of how shaky it may have been. The world also rallied to America's side, even countries that had differed with Bush's approach to international problems, such as his opposition to the Kyoto treaty on global warming.

Spontaneous displays of sympathy and solidarity occurred in all corners of the planet. My second-oldest son Nathaniel was in Copenhagen, Denmark, and joined a pilgrimage to the U.S. Embassy where Danes covered the sidewalk with flowers and other memorabilia, such as a New York Yankees cap. Similar scenes occurred in dozens of countries. The French paper *Le Monde* ran a cover story with the banner headline, "We Are All Americans." More substantively, there was new cooperation in sharing intelligence about the al-Qaeda terrorists and in dealing with their protectors in Afghanistan, the Taliban.

For his part, Bush started talking tough about "smoking out" al-Qaeda or bringing in Osama bin Laden "dead or alive." He also broadened America's goals, defining the task ahead as not just the defeat of the al-Qaeda killers but the destruction of terrorism and the eradication of "evil." Bush began to see the "war on terror" as part of his religious calling. "I think, in [Bush's] frame, this is what God has asked him to do," a close acquaintance told *The New York Times*. "It offers him enormous clarity." According to this acquaintance, Bush believes "he has encountered his reason for being, a conviction informed and shaped by the President's own strain of Christianity," the *Times* reported.[16]

Bush offended some Muslim sensibilities by calling the U.S. counterattack a "crusade," a word that has a European connotation of chivalrous knights in shining armor driving the infidels out of the Holy Lands, but conjures up very different memories in the Islamic world, of a bloody Christian holy war against Arabs. In 1099, the Crusaders massacred many of the inhabitants of Jerusalem. Osama bin Laden pounced on Bush's gaffe to rally Islamic fundamentalists. A typed statement attributed to bin Laden called the coming war "the new Christian-Jewish crusade led by the big crusader Bush under the flag of the cross."

Beyond lacking sensitivity toward Islamic historical grievances, Bush also showed little understanding of the recent checkered history of U.S. anti-terrorism campaigns. While calling his war on terror a new kind of conflict, the reality was that his father was Vice President when Ronald Reagan made combating terrorism a top priority of U.S. foreign policy, replacing the Carter administration's emphasis on human rights. Reagan committed his administration to the war on terrorism in the wake of the Islamic revolution in Iran and the radical Arab nationalism of Libya's Muammar Qaddafi. Reagan created special counter-terrorism task forces and authorized the CIA to hunt down suspected terrorists in preemptive attacks.

The war on terrorism even led the Reagan-Bush administration to engage in terrorism itself. For instance, in a 1985 strike against Hizbollah leader Sheikh Fadlallah, CIA Director Casey helped finance an operation that included the hiring of operatives who detonated a car bomb outside the Beirut apartment building where Fadlallah lived.

As described by Bob Woodward in *Veil*, "the car exploded, killing 80 people and wounding 200, leaving devastation, fires and collapsed buildings. Anyone who had happened to be in the immediate neighborhood was killed, hurt or terrorized, but Fadlallah escaped without injury. His followers strung a huge 'Made in the USA' banner in front of a building that had been blown out."[17]

***

Military retaliation against al-Qaeda and their Taliban protectors in Afghanistan was an obvious first step after the September 11 attacks. But Bush and his senior advisers turned their attention as well to preparing for war against another old nemesis, Iraq's Saddam Hussein. Counter-terrorism chief Richard Clarke asserted in his book, *Against All Enemies*, and in testimony before the 9/11 Commission that Iraq had been a Bush administration obsession since the first days, while al-Qaeda had not been viewed as an urgent priority.

The day after the September 11 attacks, Clarke said Bush confronted him in the White House Situation Room and demanded that Clarke investigate Saddam Hussein's involvement. "See if Saddam did this," Bush said, according to Clarke. "See if he's linked in any way." Clarke said he told Bush that the evidence was clear that al-Qaeda was behind the attacks, not Iraq. Indeed, the Islamic fundamentalists in al-Qaeda considered Hussein's secular regime an enemy.

After Clarke described this conversation in 2004, White House spokesman Scott McClellan sought to poke a hole in Clarke's credibility by telling reporters that Bush didn't recall the conversation and that no records showed Bush to be in the Situation Room at that time. However, Clarke's former deputy, Roger Cressey, corroborated that the conversation between Bush and Clarke had occurred.[18] The White House subsequently acknowledged that Clarke and Bush did have a conversation in the Situation Room on September 12, 2001.

Bush's first Treasury Secretary Paul O'Neill said he also witnessed the administration's early interest in ousting Hussein's government in Iraq. In Ron Suskind's *The Price of Loyalty*, O'Neill described the first NSC meeting at the White House only a few days into Bush's Presidency. The message from Bush was "find a way to do this," according to O'Neill, who was forced out of his job in December 2002. There was even a map for a post-war occupation, marking how Iraq's oil fields would be carved up.

In fall 2001, the U.S. and its allies drove the Taliban from power with relative ease and disrupted al-Qaeda (though failing to capture Osama bin Laden and Taliban leader Mullah Omar). The Bush administration simultaneously moved its planning for war with Iraq into high gear. A secretive Pentagon office, named the Office of Special Plans, was created to finalize strategies for invading Iraq and preparing for the post-war period. The Office of Special Plans "was given a nondescript name to purposefully hide the fact that although the administration was publicly emphasizing diplomacy at the United Nations, the Pentagon was actively engaged in war planning and postwar planning," the *Washington Post* reported in an article quoting senior Defense Department officials Douglas J. Feith and William J. Luti.[19]

In May 2002, Air Force Lieutenant Colonel Karen Kwiatkowski was among the career military officers pulled into the war planning at the Office of Special Plans. "I was 'volunteered' to enter what would be a well-appointed den of iniquity," Kwiatkowski wrote about her experiences. "The education I would receive there was like an M. Night Shyamalan movie – intense, fascinating and frightening. While the people were very much alive, I saw a dead philosophy – Cold War anti-communism and neo-imperialism – walking the corridors of the Pentagon. It wore the clothing of counter-terrorism and spoke the language of a holy war between good and evil."

Kwiatkowski said Bush's political appointees overwhelmed the judgments of career specialists. "This seizure of the reins of U.S. Middle East policy was directly visible to many of us working in the Near East South Asia policy office, and yet there seemed to be little any of us could do about it," she wrote. Beyond the loss of control to neoconservative ideologues, Kwiatkowski and her fellow officers were troubled by how the American people were being manipulated.

"Many of us in the Pentagon, conservatives and liberals alike, felt that this agenda, whatever its flaws or merits, had never been openly presented to the American people," she wrote. "Instead, the public story line was a fear-peddling and confusing set of messages, designed to take Congress and the country into a war of executive choice, a war based on false pretenses." Kwiatkowski went public with her observations after retiring from the Air Force in July 2003.[20]

Investigative reporter Seymour Hersh also discovered the work of this small group of neoconservative ideologues at the Pentagon's Office of Special Plans, organized by deputy Defense Secretary Wolfowitz and called the Cabal. Hersh quoted a former Bush administration intelligence official as saying he quit because "they were using the intelligence from the CIA and other agencies only when it fit their agenda. They didn't like the intelligence they were getting, and so they brought in people to write the stuff. They were so crazed and so far out and so difficult to reason with – to the point of being bizarre. Dogmatic, as if they were on a mission from God."

Hersh found, too, that Wolfowitz and other key neoconservatives at the Pentagon were disciples of the late political philosopher Leo Strauss, who believed that some deception of the population is necessary in statecraft. "The whole story is complicated by Strauss's idea – actually Plato's – that philosophers need to tell noble lies not only to the people at large but also to powerful politicians," said Stephen Holmes, a law professor at New York University.[21]

***

By the late summer and early fall of 2002, the administration's war talk was heating up. Bush and his subordinates were startling the American people with references to "mushroom clouds" from hypothetical Iraqi nuclear bombs. A more immediate threat, the Bush administration said, came from Iraq's deadly chemical weapons and biological toxins that could be handed to terrorists to inflict death and destruction on U.S. cities. Bush expounded on his new doctrine of "preemptive war," the elimination of foreign governments that he deemed a "gathering" threat to U.S. security.

The White House spelled out Bush's policy in a September 20, 2002, report on "national security strategy." In justifying the departure from traditional U.S. policy, the White House said, "the only path to peace and security is the path of action." The report stated, "We must be prepared to stop rogue states and their terrorist clients before they are able to threaten or use weapons of mass destruction against the United States and our allies and friends." While the administration depicted this new threat as unprecedented, with the U.S. no longer protected by its two oceans, the reality was that at least since the development of Soviet intercontinental missiles in the 1950s, Americans have lived with threats far more immediate than anything that Iraq could present.

But along with the administration's alarming rhetoric came a domestic political corollary that choked off any meaningful debate. Indeed, critics who challenged Bush's vision were often baited as disloyal by the powerful conservative news media and its growing legion of allies in the mainstream press. This "politics of preemption" got a test run after former Vice President Al Gore delivered a comprehensive critique of the so-called "Bush Doctrine" on September 23, 2002.

Speaking at the Commonwealth Club in San Francisco, Gore laid out his concern that Bush was using the war on terror to rush into a war against Iraq. Gore, who supported the Persian Gulf War in 1990-1991, said he was not opposing efforts to oust Saddam Hussein. Rather, the Tennessee Democrat criticized Bush's failure to enlist the international community as his father did in 1990.

"I am deeply concerned that the course of action that we are presently embarking upon with respect to Iraq has the potential to seriously damage our ability to win the war against terrorism and to weaken our ability to lead the world in this new century," Gore said. "To put first things first, I believe that we ought to be focusing our efforts first and foremost against those who attacked us on September 11. ... Great nations persevere and then prevail. They do not jump from one unfinished task to another. ... If you're going after Jesse James, you ought to organize the posse first, especially if you're in the middle of a gunfight with somebody who's out after you."

But rather than welcome a vigorous debate on the Bush Doctrine's merits and shortcomings, conservative commentators treated Gore and others raising questions as dishonest, unpatriotic and even unhinged. Gore got whacked from all angles, variously portrayed as seeking cheap political gain and committing political suicide.

Helped by the fact that Gore's speech received spotty television coverage – MSNBC carried excerpts live and C-SPAN replayed the speech later that night – Bush partisans were free to distort Gore's words and then dismiss his arguments as "lies" largely because few Americans actually heard what he said. Republican National Committee spokesman Jim Dyke called Gore a "political hack." An administration source told *The Washington Post* that Gore was simply "irrelevant," a theme that would be repeated often in the days after Gore's speech.[22]

Other slurs came from conservative opinion-makers. "Gore's speech was one no decent politician could have delivered," wrote *Washington Post* columnist Michael Kelly. "It was dishonest, cheap, low. It was hollow. It was bereft of policy, of solutions, of constructive ideas, very nearly of facts – bereft of anything other than taunts and jibes and embarrassingly obvious lies. It was breathtakingly hypocritical, a naked political assault delivered in tones of moral condescension from a man pretending to be superior to mere politics. It was wretched. It was vile. It was contemptible."[23]

"A pudding with no theme but much poison," declared another *Post* columnist, Charles Krauthammer. "It was a disgrace – a series of cheap shots strung together without logic or coherence."[24] At *Salon.com*, Andrew

Sullivan penned an attack that termed Gore "The Opportunist." By contrast, columnist William Bennett portrayed the speech as "Al Gore's Political Suicide" in an Op-Ed piece for the *Wall Street Journal*. Gore had "made himself irrelevant by his inconsistency" and had engaged in "an act of self-immolation" by daring to criticize Bush's policy, Bennett wrote.[25]

When the conservative pundits addressed Gore's actual speech, his words were selectively edited, reprising the news media's favorite "Lyin' Al" theme of the presidential campaign. Kelly, for instance, wrote that Gore was lying when he said "the vast majority of those who sponsored, planned and implemented the cold-blooded murder of more than 3,000 Americans are still at large, still neither located nor apprehended, much less punished and neutralized."

To Kelly, this comment was "reprehensible" and "a lie." Kelly continued, "The men who 'implemented' the 'cold-blooded murder of more than 3,000 Americans' are dead; they died in the act of murder on September 11. Gore can look this up." Kelly added that most of the rest were in prison or on the run. But Gore clearly was talking about the likes of Osama bin Laden and Taliban leader Mullah Omar, who had not been located. Plus, even the Bush administration expressed frustration at the failure of Afghan and Pakistani forces to cut off escape routes for al-Qaeda and the Taliban during the U.S. invasion of Afghanistan. As for the continuing potency of al-Qaeda, the administration itself had cited the group's resurgence. In September 2002, Attorney General John Ashcroft and Homeland Security chief Tom Ridge raised the terrorist threat warning in the U.S. from yellow to orange.

As Bob Somerby, editor of *The Daily Howler* media-criticism Web site, pointed out, radio talk show host Rush Limbaugh and Fox News' Brit Hume led the way on another front, accusing Gore of lying about his position on the Persian Gulf War in 1991. That claim was advanced by snipping off a portion of Gore's September 23 remarks to create a phony contradiction with a statement he made in 1991, Somerby wrote.

On Fox News' "Special Report" on September 24, Hume played a clip of Gore's Commonwealth Club speech in which Gore, who had voted in the U.S. Senate to support President George H.W. Bush's intervention to oust Iraqi forces from Kuwait, said "I felt betrayed by the first Bush administration's hasty departure from the battlefield." Then, Hume played a comment by Gore on April 18, 1991, in which Gore defended the first President Bush's decision not to march to Baghdad and added, "It was universally accepted that our objective was to push Iraq out of Kuwait, and it was further understood that when this was accomplished, combat should stop."

Juxtaposed, these two statements were made to appear as contradictions, another Gore "lie." Hume's panel of pundits jumped at the opportunity to draw that conclusion. Hume asked, "How do we explain that, as against what he said yesterday?"

"It's inexplicable," said Bill Sammon of *The Washington Times*, "It's puzzling why he would flip-flop on something so easily checkable."

"He invented the Internet," smirked pundit Morton Kondracke. "He's got a bad memory."

But as Somerby pointed out, Hume had created Gore's "contradiction" by omitting a key phrase from Gore's speech, relating to which battlefield Gore was referring. The fuller Gore quote read, "I felt betrayed by the first Bush administration's hasty departure from the battlefield, even as Saddam began to renew his persecution of the Kurds of the North and the Shiites of the South – groups we had encouraged to rise up against Saddam."

Gore made similar points in April 1991, when he criticized the elder Bush for leaving the anti-Hussein forces in the lurch. Gore said Bush's handling of the post-war insurrections "revives the most bitter memories of humankind's worst moments."[26] It would be clear to any honest reader that Gore's two comments were about different aspects of the Iraqi conflict. But Gore's critique of the younger George Bush's emerging Iraq War policy would be overwhelmed by the pundits' rhetorical sleights of hand. Bush and his allies made clear that any disagreement would open a dissenter to personal attacks, including challenges to his sanity and patriotism.

Though George W. Bush's political adviser Karl Rove appears to have masterminded this political strategy to question the patriotism of Iraq War skeptics, Bush himself joined in during a campaign speech in Trenton, New Jersey, on September 23. Bush declared that Democratic opposition to deleting labor protections from the law creating a new Department of Homeland Security meant that the Democratic-controlled Senate "is more interested in special interests in Washington, and not interested in the security of the American people."

The normally mild-mannered Senate Majority Leader Tom Daschle fumed that Bush's shot was a punch below the belt. Daschle demanded an apology in the name of many Democrats who had fought for their country, including Senator Daniel Inouye of Hawaii who lost an arm in World War II and Senator Max Cleland of Georgia who lost both legs and one arm in Vietnam. Many other Democratic leaders served the country in war, including Senator John Kerry who won the Silver Star in Vietnam and Daschle who served as an intelligence officer in the U.S. Air Force Strategic Air Command during the Vietnam War.

By contrast, both Bush and Dick Cheney avoided national military service in Vietnam, Bush by joining the Texas Air National Guard and Cheney by taking advantage of five separate draft deferments. But Bush refused to apologize and the press corps turned on Daschle for his intemperate behavior. Moon's *Washington Times* pictured the South Dakota Democrat as headless in an editorial cartoon. Another *Washington Times* cartoon drew Gore as Pinocchio because of his supposedly dishonest criticism of Bush's Iraq policy. Rather than addressing the substance of the criticism, the conservative media simply ascribed bad political motives.

Little attention was paid to how the strategy of striking another country before it actually threatened the United States required the U.S. government not only to accurately analyze another country's capabilities but to read the minds of that country's leaders, assessing possible intentions and potential motives. Like some worldwide version of "predictive crime," as portrayed in the Tom Cruise movie "Minority Report," these evaluations then would become the basis for "defensive" action before any offensive action occurs.

Senator Robert Byrd, known for his scholarship on constitutional issues, argued in a Senate floor speech on October 3 that the Bush Doctrine represented a rewriting of the U.S. Constitution that augured a new era of international chaos. The West Virginia Democrat said Bush's resolution seeking broad powers to wage war in the Middle East was "a product of presidential hubris. This resolution is breathtaking, breathtaking in its scope. It redefines the nature of defense. It reinterprets the Constitution to suit the will of the Executive Branch. This Constitution, which I hold in my hand, is amended without going through the constitutional process of amending this Constitution."

Byrd, who was first elected to the U.S. Senate in 1958, said Bush's policy of preemptive war represented "an unprecedented and unfounded interpretation of the president's authority under the Constitution of the United States, not to mention the fact that it stands the Charter of the United Nations on its head." Other countries, Byrd noted, could be expected to cite the U.S. precedent in justifying strikes at their own enemies, which might be considered potential threats sometime in the future.

***

In the weeks before the 2002 congressional elections, Bush demanded from Congress authority to use force if necessary to protect against Iraq's weapons of mass destruction. To secure congressional approval, the administration also agreed to seek the United Nations' support. Some senators, including John Kerry, said they voted for the resolution so they wouldn't undercut Bush's ability to gain a U.N. consensus for a united front in dealing with Iraqi disarmament. But Bush already had his mind set on invading Iraq.

After getting approval from Congress, Bush immediately sought to soften up opposition from the French and the Germans. His conservative base heaped hatred on the two traditional allies as a way to pressure the U.N. Security Council to sanction a U.S. invasion of Iraq. But the French, German and other key countries held firm, insisting that a new round of weapons inspections precede any rush to war.

After Iraq agreed to accept the return of U.N. return inspectors for unfettered searches of suspected Iraqi weapons sites, Bush and his allies soon were turning up the heat on chief U.N. weapons inspector Han Blix and his inspection team. Their failure to find WMD also brought them in for ridicule. In one TV routine, right-wing comic Dennis Miller likened Blix and his inspectors to the cartoon characters in "Scooby Doo," racing around pointlessly in their vans. Meanwhile, conservative news outlets carried accusations that Blix was incompetent, corrupt and possibly sympathetic to Saddam Hussein.

Despite the bullying, Bush could muster only four out of 15 votes on the U.N. Security Council, causing him to withdraw a resolution to authorize war. It was a diplomatic defeat of historic proportions, though the embarrassing vote count was barely reported by the U.S. news media. Bush pressed ahead with Great Britain and a handful of other countries in a "coalition of the willing." He forced the U.N. inspectors to leave Iraq a couple of days before the invasion was to start.

In his book, *Disarming Iraq*, Blix wrote that on March 16, 2003, he received blunt advice from a Bush administration official to withdraw the U.N. inspectors. "Although the inspection organization was now operating at full strength and Iraq seemed determined to give it prompt access everywhere, the United States appeared as determined to replace our inspection force with an invasion army," Blix wrote.[27] For Bush, the die had long since been cast for war.

Asked later whether he had consulted his father about the decision to go to war, Bush told author Bob Woodward that "I can't remember a moment where I said to myself, maybe he can help me make the decision. ... You know, he is the wrong father to appeal to in terms of strength. There is a higher father that I appeal to."[28]

Chapter 23: To War

On the night of March 19, 2003 – already March 20 in the Middle East – George W. Bush launched the invasion of Iraq. Senior administration officials were filled with optimism that Saddam Hussein's government would collapse in the opening hours as the United States blasted selected targets with a "shock and awe" bombardment from the skies. Sitting with a panel of ex-generals, NBC anchor Tom Brokaw said, "One of the things that we don't want to do is to destroy the infrastructure of Iraq because in a few days we're going to own that country." The administration expressed high hopes, too, that once U.S. troops entered Iraq and captured some Iraqi scientists that the elusive WMD stockpiles would quickly be discovered.

But the war didn't go as predicted. The "shock and awe" bombing campaign destroyed some government buildings – and created impressive pyrotechnics for the television news shows – but the Iraqis didn't just throw up their hands and surrender. Indeed, there was surprising resistance as coalition forces advanced into southern towns such as Umm Qasr, Nasiriya and Basra, which were expected to fall easily. Coalition forces also didn't run across any of the WMD stockpiles that had supposedly been moved toward the front lines for use against U.S. troops.

Some well-placed U.S. military analysts whom I spoke with during the early days of the invasion were alarmed, fearing that the stiffer-than-expected resistance and the absence of WMD meant that Bush might have already "lost" the war, politically if not militarily, and that a lengthy occupation of a hostile country might lay ahead. These analysts felt that only if U.S. troops were welcomed by the Iraqi population and did find the WMD stockpiles would the net benefits of the invasion outweigh the net negatives.

Otherwise, the analysts worried that the cost of ousting Saddam Hussein would be so high that "victory" could constitute a strategic defeat for the United States, with higher-than-expected battlefield casualties and political hatred swelling around the world, especially in the Middle East. These analysts saw the possibility that U.S. forces might find themselves trapped in a predicament like Israeli troops faced in occupying the Gaza Strip, only worse since Iraq is much larger, the size of California.[1]

So, behind the patriotic flag-waving in the U.S. news media and the confident predictions of administration spokesmen, a chilling realization began to spread in Washington that Bush's Iraq invasion might become the mother of all presidential miscalculations – an extraordinary blend of Bay of Pigs-style wishful thinking with a "Black Hawk Down" reliance on U.S. military technology against an alien culture far from the United States. But Iraq had the potential to be worse than either the Bay of Pigs fiasco in Cuba in 1961 or the bloody miscalculations in Somalia in 1993. In both those cases, the U.S. government exercised the tactical flexibility to extricate itself from military misjudgments without grave strategic damage.

The CIA-backed Bay of Pigs invasion left a small army of Cuban exiles in the lurch when the rosy predictions of popular uprisings against Fidel Castro failed to materialize. The botched "Black Hawk Down" raid in Mogadishu cost the lives of 18 U.S. soldiers, but President Clinton cut U.S. losses and withdrew. Similarly, President Ronald Reagan pulled out U.S. forces from Lebanon in 1983 after a suicide bomber killed 241 Marines who were part of a force that had entered Beirut as peacekeepers but found itself drawn into the middle of a brutal civil war.

But no one believed that Bush – confident of his "gut" judgments – would admit to mistakes and rethink his decisions. As author Bob Woodward observed in his book, *Bush at War*, "his instincts are almost his second religion."[2] Once Bush has decided what to do, there is little room for doubt or second thoughts, His aides simply assemble arguments to support or to sell the decision, and those who question either the decision or the arguments are brushed aside.

Yet, by the first week of the Iraq War, it was clear that Bush had misgauged perhaps the biggest question: "Would the Iraqis fight?" Because Bush had cut himself off from internal dissent at the CIA and the Pentagon, he had underestimated how difficult it would be to conquer and subdue a nation as large and as unruly as Iraq. Bush hadn't listened when some intelligence analysts and field generals warned against the danger of wishful thinking.

General Eric Shinseki, who was the Army's top general, had sounded a discordant note by telling Congress that he foresaw the need for several hundred thousand soldiers in post-war Iraq, an estimate that was laughed off by Deputy Defense Secretary Paul Wolfowitz, who called it "way off the mark." Wolfowitz and other civilian Pentagon officials instead conjured up visions of happy Iraqi welcoming U.S. troops as liberators who had saved Iraq from the clutches of dictator Saddam Hussein.

Confident that the high-tech U.S. army could do much more with less than its predecessors, Bush also rushed the invasion without the full U.S. force in place. Once Turkey balked at letting the Army's Fourth Division use Turkish territory to open a northern front, Bush had the option of delaying the war by a month to transfer the division's armor and equipment to Kuwait.

The extra month also might have helped the U.S. diplomatic position by giving the U.N. more time to hunt for weapons of mass destruction and by addressing some French and German concerns. But Bush, who had pronounced himself tired of diplomatic games, lurched ahead. Before his TV speech announcing the start of the war, he pumped his fist in the air and exclaimed about himself, "Feel good!"

The new watchword was a "rolling start," which meant that the invasion would begin before a full complement of U.S. forces was in place. So, American generals, who had wanted an invasion force of 500,000 troops and then settled for a force half that size, were told to launch the war with only about 130,000 troops.

As the Iraq invasion progressed, the expected shower of rose petals gave way to a grim reality of ambushes and suicide bombs. Still, Bush and his team insisted that their pre-war judgments about the Iraqi civilians welcoming U.S. "liberators" were correct. The new explanation was that the people were just kept in check by fear of Saddam Hussein's "goons" – as Fox News reported – or "death squads" – as Defense Secretary Donald Rumsfeld said. Later, "foreign terrorists" and Iraqi "dead-enders" were blamed for the continued resistance to the U.S. presence, though other analysts recognized that the U.S. invasion had sparked an explosion of Iraqi nationalism and Islamic rejection of Western occupation.

On the battlefield, rather than throwing down their arms, the Iraqi army sometimes fought heroically though hopelessly against the technologically superior U.S. forces. *Christian Science Monitor* reporter Ann Scott Tyson interviewed U.S. troops with the 3rd Infantry Division who were deeply troubled by their task of mowing down Iraqi soldiers who kept fighting even in suicidal situations.

"Even as U.S. commanders cite dramatic success in the three-week-old war, many look upon the wholesale destruction of Iraq's military and the killing of thousands of Iraqi fighters with a sense of regret," Tyson reported. "They voice frustration at the number of Iraqis who stood their ground against overwhelming U.S. firepower, wasting their lives and equipment rather than capitulating as expected."

"They have no command and control, no organization," said Brigadier General Louis Weber. "They're just dying."

Commenting upon the annihilation of Iraqi forces in one-sided battles, Lieutenant Colonel Woody Radcliffe said, "We didn't want to do this. Even a brain-dead moron can understand we are so vastly superior militarily that there is no hope. You would think they would see that and give up." In one battle around Najaf, U.S. commanders ordered air strikes to kill the Iraqis *en masse* rather than have U.S. soldiers continue to kill them one by one.

"There were waves and waves of people coming at them (the U.S. soldiers) with AK-47s, out of this factory, and they (the U.S. soldiers) were killing everyone," said Radcliffe. "The commander called and said, 'This is not right. This is insane. Let's hit the factory with close air support and take them (the Iraqis) out all at once.'"

This slaughter of young Iraqis troubled front-line U.S. soldiers. "For lack of a better word, I felt almost guilty about the massacre," one soldier said privately. "We wasted a lot of people. It makes you wonder how many were innocent. It takes away some of the pride. We won, but at what cost?"[3]

Bush seemed to share none of these regrets. Commenting about the Iraqi soldiers to his war council, Bush said they "fight like terrorists," according to a *New York Times* report on how Bush saw the war.[4] Later, Bush acknowledged that the resistance was stiffer than expected. "Shock and awe said to many people that all we've got to do is unleash some might and people will crumble," Bush said in an interview with NBC's Tom Brokaw after Baghdad finally fell. "And it turns out the fighters were a lot fiercer than we thought. ...The resistance for our troops moving south and north was significant resistance."[5]

***

A quick discovery of Iraqi chemical or biological weapons might have buttressed Bush's international standing by showing that Hussein's regime was in defiance of the U.N. The Security Council's majority might have looked naïve in thinking that inspections would have worked. But the promised WMD discoveries never materialized.

Instead, as the carnage mounted, Washington witnessed a precipitous decline in U.S. standing with the rest of the world. For instance, in Spain, whose government was part of Bush's "coalition of the willing," 91 percent of Spaniards opposed the U.S. invasion, according to polls. The Pew Global Attitudes Project found that majorities in every country surveyed except the U.S. felt that the Iraq War hurt, rather than helped, the worldwide fight against terrorism. In the seven countries that were surveyed that did not take part in the Iraq War, disapproval of the war hovered at around 85 percent.

But in the United States, Bush benefited from near shoulder-to-shoulder support for the war in the major U.S. news media. The cable news channels, in particular, competed to demonstrate the greatest degree of "patriotism." The "fair and balanced" Fox News broadcast showed stirring sequences of American and British soldiers being interviewed about the war while a harmonica soundtrack in the background played "The Battle Hymn of the Republic."

Fox's super-patriotic tone apparently helped it outpace its chief rivals, MSNBC and CNN, in the ratings war. Though lagging in the Nielsen ratings, MSNBC and CNN did not trail Fox by much in branding their own news in red-white-and-blue. Like Fox, MSNBC used a logo superimposing the American flag on scenes of Iraq. To avoid a discordant message in the run-up to war, MSNBC also dumped a show hosted by war critic Phil Donahue. For its part, CNN adopted Bush's name for the war – "Operation Iraqi Freedom" – as the title for much of its coverage, even when the scenes showed Iraqis being rounded up and handcuffed.

As U.S. forces captured Baghdad after three weeks of fighting and toppled Hussein's statue in Firdos Square, the news networks intensified their competition for the hearts and minds of American TV viewers. MSNBC began presenting Madison-Avenue-style montages of the Iraq War. One showed U.S. troops in heroic postures moving through Iraq. The segment ended with an American boy surrounded by yellow ribbons for his father at war, and the concluding slogan, "Home of the Brave." Another MSNBC montage showed Iraqis rejoicing after Hussein's statue fell. The stirring pictures ended with the slogan, "Let Freedom Ring."

The Wall Street Journal took note of the dueling coverage presented by domestic CNN versus its CNNI Network, which broadcasts to international viewers. While domestic CNN focused on happy stories, such as the rescue of U.S. prisoner-of-war Jessica Lynch, CNNI carried more scenes of wounded civilians overflowing Iraqi hospitals. "During the Gulf War in 1991, [CNN] presented a uniform global feed that showed the war largely through American eyes," the *Journal* reported. "Since then, CNN has developed several overseas networks that increasingly cater their programming to regional audiences and advertisers."[6]

Left unsaid by the *Journal*'s formulation of how CNN's overseas affiliates "cater" to foreign audiences was the flip side of that coin, that domestic CNN was freer to shape a version of the news that was more pleasing to Americans and to U.S. advertisers – largely by leaving out scenes of Iraqi suffering.

As unprofessional as much of the U.S. media's war coverage was, flag-waving journalism worked in the ratings race. While MSNBC remained in third place among U.S. cable news outlets, it posted the highest ratings growth in the lead-up to war and during the actual fighting, up 124 percent compared with a year earlier. Fox News, the industry leader, racked up a 102 percent gain and No. 2 CNN rose 91 percent.[7]

U.S. cable news networks and talk radio often went beyond boosting the war to act as the Bush administration's public enforcers. On MSNBC, Republican host Joe Scarborough accused actors Sean Penn and Tim Robbins of whining when their war criticism led to retaliations against their careers. "Sean Penn is fired from an acting job and finds out that actions bring about consequences. Whoa, dude!" chortled Scarborough, who cited Penn's skepticism about Iraq's WMD stockpiles as justification for depriving Penn of work.[8]

To some foreigners, the uniformity in the U.S. war coverage had the feel of a totalitarian state. "There have been times, living in America of late, when it seemed I was back in the Communist Moscow I left a dozen years ago," wrote Rupert Cornwell in the London-based *Independent*. "Switch to cable TV and reporters breathlessly relay the latest wisdom from the usual unnamed 'senior administration officials,' keeping us on the straight and narrow. Everyone, it seems, is on-side and on-message. Just like it used to be when the hammer and sickle flew over the Kremlin."

Cornwell traced this lock-step U.S. coverage to the influence of Fox News, which "has taken its cue from George Bush's view of the universe post-11 September – either you're with us or against us. Fox, most emphatically, is with him, and it's paid off at the box office. Not for Fox to dwell on uncomfortable realities like collateral damage, Iraqi casualties, or the failure of the U.S. troops to protect libraries and museums."[9]

There was also the question of whether Bush's attacks crossed the line into war crimes. One U.S. bombing of a neighborhood restaurant where Hussein was mistakenly believed to be eating, killed 14 civilians, including seven children. "When the broken body of the 20-year-old woman was brought out torso first, then her head," the Associated Press reported, "her mother started crying uncontrollably, then collapsed." The London *Independent* cited this restaurant attack as one that represented "a clear breach" of the Geneva Conventions ban on bombing civilian targets.

But the restaurant bombing attracted little interest from U.S. television news networks on the lookout for upbeat stories. "American talking heads, playing the what-if game about Saddam's whereabouts, never seemed to give the issue (of the errant bombing) any thought," wrote Eric Boehlert in a report on the U.S. war coverage for *Salon.com*. "Certainly they did not linger on images of the hellacious human carnage left in the aftermath."

Hundreds of other civilian deaths were equally horrific. Saad Abbas, 34, was wounded in an American bombing raid, but his family sought to shield him from the greater horror. The bombing had killed his three daughters – Marwa, 11; Tabarek, 8; and Safia, 5 – who had been the center of his life. "It wasn't just ordinary love," his wife said. "He was crazy about them. It wasn't like other fathers."[10]

The horror of the war was captured, too, in the fate of 12-year-old Ali Ismaeel Abbas, who lost his two arms when a U.S. missile struck his Baghdad home. Ali's father, his pregnant mother and his siblings were all killed. As he was evacuated to a Kuwaiti hospital, becoming a symbol of U.S. compassion for injured Iraqi civilians, Ali said he would rather die than live without his hands. For its part, the Bush administration announced that it had no intention of tallying the number of Iraqi civilians who were killed in the war. Some estimates exceeded 10,000.

Stretched thin controlling the California-sized country, U.S. troops also couldn't stop widespread looting after the fall of Hussein's government. Among the destroyed buildings was the central library where ancient Arabic texts were stored. The national museum – one of the prides of the Islamic world – was ransacked with many priceless antiquities stolen and others smashed.

"They lie across the floor in tens of thousands of pieces, the priceless antiquities of Iraq's history," wrote Robert Fisk of London's *Independent* newspaper. "The looters had gone from shelf to shelf, systematically pulling down the statues and pots and amphorae of the Assyrians and the Babylonians, the Sumerians, the Medes, the Persians and the Greeks and hurling them on to the concrete. "Our feet crunched on the wreckage of 5,000-year-old marble plinths and stone statuary and pots that had endured every siege of Baghdad, every invasion of Iraq throughout history only to be destroyed when Americans came to 'liberate' the city."[11]

As Marines and other front-line combat troops were forced into controlling anti-American demonstrations, killings of civilians followed. In the northern city of Mosul, Marines fired into angry crowds, killing 17 Iraqis in the city's main square, the director of the city's hospital said. Marines said they had been fired upon, but Mosul residents denied those claims – and Islamic fundamentalists began to emerge as the chief political beneficiaries of the swelling hostility.[12]

"We must be united and support each other against the Anglo-American invasion," declared Sheik Ibrahim al-Namaa, a rising leader in Mosul, where the looting of that city's ancient treasures also fed anger over the U.S. occupation. "We must try to put an end to this aggression."[13]

"You are the masters today," another Islamic leader, Ahmed al-Kubeisy, said about the Americans. "But I warn you against thinking of staying. Get out before we kick you out."[14]

The Bush administration, however, had no intention of withdrawing U.S. military forces for the foreseeable future. Though eager to hand over a limited "sovereignty" to a pro-U.S. government of Iraqis, the administration viewed Iraq as a site for military bases that could be used to project American power throughout the Middle East. American military officials wanted four bases in Iraq, including one at the international airport outside Baghdad and one near Nasiriya in the south, senior administration officials told *The New York Times*. "There will be some kind of a long-term defense relationship with a new Iraq, similar to Afghanistan," one official said.[15]

***

Bush's first term may have reached its heroic peak on May 1, 2003, when Bush donned a flight suit and landed on the deck of the U.S.S. Abraham Lincoln. The aircraft carrier circled offshore, delaying its return to port in San Diego, California, after its 10-month tour in the Persian Gulf so the President could have a dramatic backdrop for a televised speech declaring victory in Iraq. Though the ship was within helicopter range of the coast, Bush opted for an arrival on a military jet, which he helped co-pilot.

After landing, Bush swaggered around the deck in his Top Gun outfit with his flight helmet under his arm and posed for photos with the crew members. In his later speech, standing under a banner that read "Mission Accomplished," Bush declared that "major combat" in Iraq was over. His political adviser Karl Rove undoubtedly envisioned the scene as a killer 30-second commercial for Bush's 2004 campaign.

"U.S. television coverage ranged from respectful to gushing," observed *New York Times* columnist Paul Krugman. "Nobody seemed bothered that Mr. Bush, who appears to have skipped more than a year of the National Guard service that kept him out of Vietnam, is now emphasizing his flying experience."[16]

Indeed, the likes of MSNBC's Chris Matthews used the occasion to praise Bush's manliness in contrast to Democratic presidential candidates, including Senator John Kerry, a decorated Vietnam War veteran. "Imagine Joe Lieberman in this costume, or even John Kerry," Matthews said on MSNBC on May 1. "Nobody looks right in the role Bush has set for the presidency-commander-in-chief, medium height, medium build, looks good in a jet pilot's costume or uniform, rather has a certain swagger, not too literary, certainly not too verbal, but a guy who speaks plainly and wins wars. I think that job definition is hard to match for the Dems."

When some Democrats criticized the photo op, Bush's aides mounted a mini-cover-up of the facts. The White House first lied about the reasons for the jet flight, insisting that it was necessary because the ship was outside helicopter range. As it turned out, the ship was only 30 miles offshore and slowed down to give Bush an excuse to use the jet.

A later *New York Times* article revealed that Bush had personally collaborated on the jet landing idea and that the imagery was choreographed by a White House advance team led by communications specialist Scott Sforza, who arrived on the carrier days earlier. The carrier landing was just one scene in a deliberate pattern of images sought by the White House to burnish Bush's heroic image. At an economic speech in Indianapolis, people sitting behind Bush were told to take off their ties so they'd look more like ordinary folks, WISH-TV reported. At a speech at Mount Rushmore in South Dakota, cameramen were given a platform that offered up Bush's profile as if he were already carved into the mountain with Washington, Jefferson, Lincoln and Theodore Roosevelt.[17]

But the TV media and the American people shrugged off concerns about whether Bush had used the U.S.S. Abraham Lincoln and its crew as props. When Democrats demanded a cost accounting, MSNBC posed its question-of-the-day this way: "President Bush's Flight Flap. Much Ado About Nothing?"[18] A *New York Times*/CBS News poll found 59 percent of the American people agreeing that use of the carrier was appropriate and saying that Bush was not seeking political gain.

The Top Gun scene, however, would come back to haunt Bush. In November 2003, as the Iraqi insurgency gained strength and the U.S. death toll kept rising, Bush tried to shift responsibility for the "Mission

Accomplished" banner to the crewmen. "The 'Mission Accomplished' sign, of course, was put up by the members of the U.S.S. Abraham Lincoln, saying that their mission was accomplished, " Bush told reporters. "I know it was attributed somehow to some ingenious advance man from my staff. They weren't that ingenious, by the way."

Later White House officials acknowledged that the banner had been created at their direction, though they insisted that the idea had come from the crew. On April 30, 2004, Bush amended the explanation further. "A year ago, I did give the speech from the carrier, saying that we had achieved an important objective, that we'd accomplished a mission, which was the removal of Saddam Hussein."[19] So, apparently, the "Mission Accomplished" idea was Bush's all along – referring not to the crew's mission but to Bush's mission of ousting Saddam Hussein, though he had put the blame on the crewmen when he was under pressure in November 2003.

***

At times during the Iraq War, facts and reality diverged so sharply that it seemed as if the U.S. population had been transported into a kind of fictional "Matrix," like in the science-fiction movie about a false but pleasing imagery that prevented people from seeing the ugly reality around them. Many Americans so enjoyed the TV-driven nationalism of the Iraq War that they didn't want it spoiled by troubling facts. During the conflict, they objected when news outlets showed mangled bodies or wounded children or U.S. POWs. Only positive images were welcome.

According to polls, majorities of Americans also believed a pattern of supposed "facts" that weren't facts: they thought WMD stockpiles had been discovered and that Iraq's government was complicit in the September 11 terror attacks. Other Americans said they simply didn't care that Bush may have misled the world with his pre-war claims.

Some of the confusion could be blamed on the U.S. news media – from Fox News to *The New York Times* – which repeatedly trumpeted supposed WMD discoveries and played down later stories showing that the original reports were bogus. Bush also declared vindication prematurely when two mobile labs were discovered in May 2003. U.S. intelligence jumped to the conclusion that they were labs for producing biological weapons.

"Those who say we haven't found the banned manufacturing devices or banned weapons are wrong," Bush declared, referring to the mobile labs. "We found them."[20] Only later did it turn out that the labs were for producing hydrogen for artillery weather balloons.

Tom Tomorrow's "This Modern World" cartoon captured the notion of an American *faux* reality in a strip called "The Republican Matrix." In the cartoon's drawings, clueless Americans parrot back Bush administration messages as the cartoon asks, "What is the Republican Matrix? It is an illusion that engulfs us all...a steady barrage of images which obscure reality. It is a world born anew each day...in which there is nothing to be learned from the lessons of the past...a world where logic holds no sway...where up is down and black is white...where reality itself is a malleable thing...subject to constant revision. In short, it's their world."

The cartoon ends with a frame showing Bush, Vice President Cheney and Defense Secretary Rumsfeld in sunglasses like those worn by the anti-human "agents" in the "Matrix" movies. "What should we do today, fellas?" Bush asks. "Any damn thing we want, George," answers Cheney.

Among U.S. politicians, ailing Senator Robert C. Byrd, shaking as he stood on the Senate floor, was one of the few voices addressing the dangers to democracy and to U.S. troops that resulted from pervasive government lying.

"No matter to what lengths we humans may go to obfuscate facts or delude our fellows, truth has a way of squeezing out through the cracks, eventually," the West Virginia Democrat said on May 21, 2003. "But the danger is that at some point it may no longer matter. The danger is that damage is done before the truth is widely realized. The reality is that, sometimes, it is easier to ignore uncomfortable facts and go along with whatever distortion is currently in vogue."

Byrd continued, "Regarding the situation in Iraq, it appears to this senator that the American people may have been lured into accepting the unprovoked invasion of a sovereign nation, in violation of long-standing international law, under false pretenses. ...The run up to our invasion of Iraq featured the President and members of his Cabinet invoking every frightening image they could conjure, from mushroom clouds, to buried caches of germ warfare, to drones poised to deliver germ-laden death in our major cities."

"The tactic was guaranteed to provoke a sure reaction from a nation still suffering from a combination of post traumatic stress and justifiable anger after the attacks of 9/11. It was the exploitation of fear. It was a placebo for the anger. ... Presently our loyal military personnel continue their mission of diligently searching for WMD. They have so far turned up only fertilizer, vacuum cleaners, conventional weapons and the occasional buried swimming pool. They are misused on such a mission and they continue to be at grave risk," Byrd said.

"But the Bush team's extensive hype of WMD in Iraq as justification for a pre-emptive invasion has become more than embarrassing," Byrd said. "It has raised serious questions about prevarication and the reckless use of power. Were our troops needlessly put at risk? Were countless Iraqi civilians killed and maimed when war was not really necessary? Was the American public deliberately misled? Was the world?"

***

By summer 2003, reality was intruding on the Bush administration's pleasant expectations about Iraq. The U.S. death toll continued to climb as Iraqi insurgents used ambushes and explosive devices to kill American soldiers, often one or two a day. Bush kept up his macho posturing, calling U.S. troops "plenty tough" to handle the situation and taunting Iraqi fighters to "bring 'em on."

Increasingly, it looked like the fall of Saddam Hussein's government was not a victory after all, but only the start of a new phase of the war. In an interview with *Newsday*, an Iraqi militia fighter said, "We have many more people and we're a lot better organized than the Americans realize. We have been preparing for this for a long time, and we're much more patient than the Americans. We have nowhere else to go."

American troops began to complain about the worsening dangers, compounded by the brutal 120-degree summer heat and their need to wear flak jackets and Kevlar helmets. "Make no mistake, the level of morale for most soldiers that I've seen has hit rock bottom," said an officer from the Army's 3rd Infantry Division, according to an article in the *Christian Science Monitor*.[21]

Soon the number of U.S. soldiers killed since May 1, 2003, and Bush's declared end of "major combat" had exceeded the 138 Americans who had died during the invasion.

***

Commemorating the first anniversary of the invasion of Iraq, George W. Bush gave the American people a glimpse of his vision of the future: a grim world where a near endless war is waged against forces of evil by forces loyal to Bush, representing what is good.

"There is no neutral ground – no neutral ground – in the fight between civilization and terror, because there is no neutral ground between good and evil, freedom and slavery, and life and death," Bush said on March 19, 2004. "The terrorists are offended not merely by our policies; they're offended by our existence as free nations. No concession will appease their hatred. No accommodation will satisfy their endless demands."

So to Bush, the "war on terror" was a fight to the finish. Eliminate everyone who would or might engage in terrorism before they destroy civilization and impose slavery on everyone else. To Bush's many supporters, this black-and-white analysis represented "moral clarity." To others around the world, it had taken on the look of madness.

At least in his public rhetoric, Bush still refused to accept what counter-insurgency experts have taught for decades, that confronting terrorism requires both targeting those who perpetrate the crimes and addressing the root causes – poverty, powerlessness, humiliation – that drive young people to strap on explosives and blow themselves up.

According to counter-insurgency experts, the only route to success is to remove as many causes of the broader political anger as possible, then isolate the hard-core enemy and gradually transform a war into a police action. A major part of defeating terrorism, therefore, involved addressing legitimate grievances that may be stoking the flames of hatred, which require making practical concessions and reasonable accommodations, just the things that Bush ruled out.

Three years into his Presidency, Bush saw crushing terrorism – or "evil" as he put it – as a religious and historic duty that must be carried out regardless of the costs. In his March 19 speech, Bush employed quasi-religious language when he said the war on terror "is an inescapable calling of our generation." The concept of a "calling" has a powerful meaning among Bush's fundamentalist Christian political base, suggesting a divine duty. In other words, Bush's strategy was not really about a practical means to reduce tensions, resolve political differences and isolate hard-core enemies. It was about the opposite, escalating a low-intensity conflict into a full-scale war with a goal of not simply prevailing over a foe but eradicating evil itself.

In a healthy democracy, Bush's speech would have been cause for alarm, possibly outrage, certainly a fierce debate. But Bush's grim vision was greeted with remarkably little comment in the United States even though it could have calamitous real-life consequences: generations of young Americans dying in a worldwide version of the Hundred Years War; the U.S. national treasury drained; and the Founding Fathers' grand experiment of a democratic republic ended.

Bush's "moral clarity" grew fuzzier in other ways by spring 2004, as the principal justifications for the U.S. invasion – Iraq's alleged possession of WMD and Saddam Hussein's supposed working relationship with al-Qaeda – weren't borne out by the evidence. Bush shifted his defense of the Iraq War to a humanitarian justification. "There are no longer torture chambers or rape rooms or mass graves in Iraq," Bush said on April 30. However, U.S. forces were soon facing their own allegations of rape, torture and mass killings.

Retaliating for the gruesome killing of four American security contractors in Fallujah, U.S. forces bombarded the rebellious city with 500-pound bombs and raked its streets with cannon and machine-gun fire. The U.S. assault transformed a soccer field into a fresh mass grave for hundreds of Iraqis – many of them civilians. There were so many dead that the soccer field became the only place to bury the bodies, city officials said.

Worldwide press attention also turned to evidence that U.S. guards had tortured and sexually abused Iraqi prisoners held at the Abu Ghraib prison, the same prison that Saddam Hussein's henchmen had used. U.S. guards photographed repulsive scenes of naked Iraqis forced into sexual acts and humiliating postures while a U.S. servicewoman gleefully gestured at their genitals, according to pictures first shown on CBS News's "60 Minutes II."

Investigative journalist Seymour Hersh disclosed in *The New Yorker* that a 53-page classified Army report concluded that the prison's military police were urged on by intelligence officers seeking to break down the Iraqis before interrogation. The abuses, occurring from October to December 2003, included use of a chemical light or broomstick to sexually assault one Iraqi, the report said. Witnesses also told Army investigators that prisoners were beaten and threatened with rape, electrocution and dog attacks. At least one Iraqi died during interrogation.

"Numerous incidents of sadistic, blatant and wanton criminal abuses were inflicted on several detainees," said the report written by Army Major General Antonio M. Taguba.

One victim who faced torture at Abu Ghraib under both Saddam Hussein's regime and the U.S. occupation said the physical abuse from Hussein's guards was preferable to the sexual humiliation employed by the Americans. Dhia al-Shweiri told the Associated Press that the Americans were trying "to break our pride."[22]

After publication of the Abu Ghraib photos, Bush said he "shared a deep disgust that those prisoners were treated the way they were treated." He added that "their treatment does not reflect the nature of the American people."

Politically, however, the bloody occupation of Iraq continued to erode U.S. international standing, adding to anti-American anger across the Middle East and around the globe. Even traditional U.S. backers were becoming unnerved at what many Arabs saw as a Christian zealot who thinks he's guided by the Almighty inflicting death and destruction on an Islamic nation. Egyptian President Hosny Mubarak, considered one of the staunchest U.S. allies, cancelled a meeting with Bush and said current U.S. policies have created "hatred of Americans like never before in the region."

"There was no hatred of Americans," Mubarak said, but "after what has happened in Iraq, there is unprecedented hatred." He said, "The despair and feeling of injustice are not going to be limited to our region alone. American and Israeli interests will not be safe, not only in our region but anywhere in the world."

Conclusion: Broken Toys

On July 26, 2004, the second night of the Democratic National Convention in Boston, Fox News anchor Bill O'Reilly brought Michael Moore onto the "O'Reilly Factor" for a confrontation. O'Reilly challenged the documentary maker to apologize to George W. Bush for accusing the President of lying about the pre-war dangers from Iraqi weapons of mass destruction. O'Reilly acknowledged that Bush's WMD claims had been false but argued that Bush had made his assertions in good faith. In other words, Bush was not a liar; he had simply acted on bum information.

Not surprisingly, Moore refused to apologize, noting that more than 900 American soldiers had died in Iraq because Bush sent them into harm's way for a bogus reason. Moore said Bush was the one who should apologize to those soldiers and to the American people. O'Reilly went on badgering Moore through much of the segment, but neither media star backed down.

What was extraordinary about the encounter, however, was how it demonstrated the role that the conservative media apparatus has long played for both George Bushes. Normally, news organizations don't rally to the defense of politicians who have misled the American people as significantly as George W. Bush had on Iraq or as George H.W. Bush had on the Iran-Contra and other scandals of the 1980s. The offending pols are sometimes allowed to make their own case – explaining how their false statements weren't exactly lies – but rarely would a journalist make the case for them. At least those were the rules of the game 30 years ago at the time of Watergate.

But the rules changed with the development of the conservative media-political infrastructure, with the George Bushes two of its principal beneficiaries. While Democrats and liberals could expect to be skewered over minor or even imagined contradictions, Republicans – especially the Bushes – would find themselves surrounded by a phalanx of ideological bodyguards. Not only would O'Reilly and his fellow conservative media personalities defend George W. Bush over his false statements about Iraq, they could be counted on to go on the offensive against anyone who dared criticize him. That was true during the run-up to war when they wouldn't permit a serious debate about the WMD and other issues – and it was true after the invasion.

But the defense of George W. Bush's honesty about Iraq – that he didn't intentionally mislead the nation to war – misses the larger context of his presentation of the Iraq evidence. From the start, Bush engaged in a pattern of hyping the case for war that consistently exaggerated or misrepresented the evidence. Bush wasn't as much presenting the evidence to the American people so a thorough and thoughtful debate could be held about going to war; he was making the case for war, always spinning a more clear-cut story than the evidence supported, always applying a worst-case scenario for the facts implicating Iraq while excluding mitigating evidence.

Beyond the WMD issue, Bush repeatedly juxtaposed references to Osama bin Laden, al-Qaeda, terrorism and Iraq. Though Bush may never have said explicitly that Iraq was implicated in the September 11 attacks, the repetition created the impression of a linkage that the facts didn't support. According to polls, that was exactly the inference drawn by a large majority of Americans, that Saddam Hussein was somehow involved in the terror attacks. The inference was not an accident.

Bush's pattern of connecting Hussein to Islamic fundamentalist terrorism continued even after the invasion. In an interview with Fox News anchor Brit Hume on September 23, 2003, Bush associated Hussein with Ansar al-Islam, which Bush said was "very active [in Iraq] during Saddam's period – that's the terrorist organization." The implication was clear: that the Hussein regime was in league with this terrorist group. But just because Ansar al-Islam was active in Iraq, did that mean that Hussein's government was complicit in the group's activities? Contrary to Bush's suggestion, intelligence experts have noted that Ansar al-Islam was supported by Hussein's Iranian enemies. It also operated outside the area of Iraq that Hussein effectively controlled. Indeed, Ansar al-Islam's base was in an area to the north protected against Hussein's military operations by a U.S. "no-fly zone," distinctions that Bush appeared to understand.

"And their camp there in the north," Hume said about Ansar al-Islam.

"Yes, it is, northeast," Bush replied. Still, for public consumption, he left a misleading impression about the relationship between Hussein's secular government and this Islamic fundamentalist group.

Just months after the invasion, Bush even began rewriting the history of the Iraq War to make his actions seem more defensible. According to Bush's revised version, Hussein had refused to cooperate with U.N. demands for weapons inspections, leaving the U.S. and its "coalition of the willing" no choice but to invade Iraq in defense of the U.N.'s disarmament resolutions and to protect the United States from Iraq's WMD.

On July 14, 2003, seated next to U.N. Secretary General Kofi Annan, Bush said about Hussein, "we gave him a chance to allow the inspectors in, and he wouldn't let them in. And, therefore, after a reasonable request, we decided to remove him from power." Bush reiterated that war-justifying claim on January 27, 2004, when he said, "We went to the United Nations, of course, and got an overwhelming resolution – 1441 – unanimous resolution, that said to Saddam, you must disclose and destroy your weapons programs, which obviously meant the world felt he had such programs. He chose defiance. It was his choice to make, and he did not let us in."

Defense Secretary Donald Rumsfeld spun the same historical point in an Op-Ed article in *The New York Times* on March 19, 2004, the war's first anniversary. "In September 2002, President Bush went to the United Nations, which gave Iraq still another 'final opportunity' to disarm and to prove it had done so," Rumsfeld wrote. He added that "Saddam Hussein passed up that final opportunity" and then rejected a U.S. ultimatum to flee. "Only then, after every peaceful option had been exhausted, did the President and our coalition partners order the liberation of Iraq," Rumsfeld wrote.

At other points, Washington pundits have joined Bush in arguing that one of the strongest reasons to believe that Hussein did possess weapons of mass destruction was his supposed refusal to allow U.N. inspections of suspected WMD sites even in the face of a threatened U.S. invasion. In an interview at the 2004 Democratic National Convention, ABC News anchor Ted Koppel, considered one of the more thoughtful television journalists, showed that he had bought into this Bush administration spin point.

"It did not make logical sense that Saddam Hussein, whose armies had been defeated once before by the United States and the Coalition, would be prepared to lose control over his country if all he had to do was say, 'All right, U.N., come on in, check it out, I will show you, give you whatever evidence you want to have, let you interview whomever you want to interview,'" Koppel said in an interview with Amy Goodman, host of "Democracy Now."

But as anyone with a memory of those historic events should know, Iraq did let the U.N. weapons inspectors in and gave them freedom to examine any site they wished. Iraqi officials, including Hussein, also declared publicly that they didn't possess weapons of mass destruction, contrary to the repetition of the question posed by Bush's defenders that: "Well, if Saddam Hussein didn't have WMD, why didn't he say so?" The history is clear – or should be – that it was the Bush administration that forced the U.N. inspectors out of Iraq so the United States and its coalition could press ahead with the invasion.

Yet, through repetition the Bush administration's favored narrative of the war has sunk in as a *faux* reality for Washington journalists, including Koppel, that Bush bent over backwards to avoid the invasion and was forced to attack because Hussein's intransigence made it look like the dictator was hiding something. While Koppel's response to Amy Goodman might be viewed as a case of Koppel trying to spin the facts himself to dodge responsibility for his lack of pre-war skepticism, he clearly had gotten the idea for his misleading explanation from the Bush administration.

Bush stretched the truth again when he used the September 11 catastrophe as part of his excuse for reneging on a promise to run balanced budgets. As he began to amass record federal deficits, Bush claimed that he had given himself an escape hatch during the 2000 campaign. In speech after speech in the months after the September 11 attacks, Bush recounted his supposed caveat from the campaign, that he would keep the budget balanced except in event of war, recession or national emergency. Bush then delivered the punch line: "Little did I realize we'd get the trifecta."

The joking reference to the trifecta – a term for a horseracing bet on the correct order of finish for three horses – always got a laugh from his listeners, although some families of the September 11 victims found the joke tasteless. But beyond the question of taste, Bush's trifecta claim about having set criteria for going back into deficit spending appears to have been fabricated. Neither the White House nor independent researchers could locate any such campaign statement by Bush, although Al Gore had made a comment similar to the one Bush was claiming for himself.

In his sometimes brazen pattern of deception, Bush apparently sensed no danger from being called to account. After all, Bush had Fox News and other conservative news outlets covering his flanks. Indeed, critics, such as Michael Moore, who have tried to apply the L-word to Bush's dissembling are the ones who are confronted with demands that *they* apologize to the President, not that he express any regret for misleading the American people.

This built-in protection on questions of stretching the truth has let Bush and his allies safely step out of their glass houses to hurl stones at critics for supposedly lying. When former Treasury Secretary Paul O'Neill questioned Bush's leadership in Ron Suskind's *The Price of Loyalty*, the White House portrayed O'Neill as a disgruntled flake who couldn't be trusted. Later when White House counter-terrorism chief Richard Clarke asserted in *Against All Enemies* that Iraq was a Bush obsession after he took office while al-Qaeda was not, senior congressional Republicans and the conservative news media savaged Clarke's credibility, even suggesting that he be charged with perjury.

Senate Majority Leader Bill Frist went to the Senate floor on March 26, 2004, to accuse Clarke of leaving out much of his criticism about Bush in July 2002 when Clarke gave classified testimony to the House and Senate intelligence committees. Clarke, then a special adviser to the President, said he told the truth in his congressional testimony though he had stressed the positive as a White House representative. He also noted that the testimony occurred before the invasion of Iraq, which solidified Clarke's assessment that Bush was bungling the war on terror.

But in a scathing Senate speech, Frist demanded that Clarke's sworn Capitol Hill testimony be declassified and examined for discrepancies from his testimony to the 9/11 Commission. "Loyalty to any administration will be no defense if it is found that he has lied to Congress," the Tennessee Republican said.

Conservatives also tossed the L-word freely at Senator John Kerry when he emerged as the presumptive Democratic nominee to challenge Bush. A case in point was Kerry's off-hand remark on March 8, 2004, that he had spoken with foreign "leaders" who hoped he would defeat Bush. Quickly, the Republican attack machine began churning out suggestions that Kerry had lied and might be un-American to boot. "Kerry's imaginary friends have British and French accents," said Republican National Chairman Ed Gillespie on March 11, setting out the themes that Kerry was both delusional and suspect for hanging out with foreigners.

The story switched into high gear when Sun Myung Moon's *Washington Times* blared the results of its investigation of Kerry's remarks across the front page of its March 12 issue. Though it was well known that many foreign leaders were troubled by Bush's unilateral foreign policy and favored someone else in the White House, *The Washington Times* acted as if Kerry's claim was so strange that it merited some major sleuthing.

The article asserted that Kerry "cannot back up foreign 'endorsements,'" in part because he declined to identify the leaders whom he had spoken with in confidence about Bush. Kerry had "made no official foreign trips since the start of last year," the newspaper wrote. Plus, "an extensive review of Mr. Kerry's travel schedule domestically revealed only one opportunity for the presumptive Democratic presidential nominee to meet with foreign leaders here," the article said.[1]

The point was obvious: Kerry was a liar. The possibility that Kerry might have talked to anyone by phone or used some other means of communication apparently was not contemplated by Moon's newspaper.

"Mr. Kerry has made other claims during the campaign and then refused to back them up," *The Washington Times* wrote. Then came the ridicule: "Republicans have begun calling Mr. Kerry the 'international man of mystery,' and said his statements go even beyond those of former Vice President Al Gore, who was besieged by stories that he lied or exaggerated throughout the 2000 presidential campaign."

Soon, Bush was personally suggesting that Kerry was a liar. "If you're going to make an accusation in the course of a campaign, you've got to back it up," Bush said. Vice President Dick Cheney added even uglier implications that Kerry may have engaged in acts close to treason. "We have a right to know what he is saying to them that makes them so supportive of his candidacy," Cheney said.

The Washington Times also kept stirring the pot. On March 16, it quoted Senator John Sununu, a New Hampshire Republican, as saying "I think there's a real question as to whether or not the claim was a fabrication." That same day, again implying that Kerry perhaps suffers from mental illness,

Bush's campaign chief Ken Mehlman accused the Massachusetts senator of living in a "parallel universe." Mehlman then made a preemptive strike to protect Bush from any Kerry counter-attack against Bush's lies. Mehlman said Kerry already had shown a "willingness to try to project onto the President what are his own weaknesses."[2]

The Republican allegations against Kerry reverberated through the TV pundit shows for a week. But the larger absurdity of the controversy was that Kerry's comment about many foreign leaders privately wishing for Bush's defeat was certainly true. For instance, the newly elected Spanish Prime Minister Jose Luis Rodriguez Zapatero had called Bush's Iraq War a "disaster" and has said he favored new U.S. leadership.

***

Some liberal activists wonder why Democratic leaders are often so circumspect about what they say. Why, these activists ask, don't the Democrats just let it fly like the Republicans do? The cautious tone turns off much of the Democratic base while leaving many independent voters questioning whether the Democrats really know what they stand for.

The Democratic-defensive dynamic, however, is another consequence of the media-political infrastructure that Republicans and conservatives have spent three decades – and billions of dollars – creating. Especially since liberals have failed to match the investment and dedication, the Right-Wing Machine has given Republicans a powerful advantage – and one that does not seem likely to go away. As long as conservatives, such as Sun Myung Moon and Rupert Murdoch, continue to pour vast sums into this media-political apparatus, the Republicans can expect to be protected when they make missteps. At the same time, Democrats can expect to pay a high price even for innocuous mistakes.

The conservative infrastructure also has helped the Republicans achieve a unity that often has been lacking on the Democratic side. Conservatives can tune in Fox News, listen to Rush Limbaugh, pick up *The Washington Times* or consult dozens of other well-financed media outlets to hear the latest pro-Republican "themes," often coordinated with the Republican National Committee or Bush's White House. The liberals lack any comparable media apparatus, and the committed liberal outlets that do exist are almost always under-funded and often part-time. Only in 2004 have liberals launched a rudimentary – and cash-strapped – talk-radio network, called Air America, to begin competing with the dominant right-wing talk shows.

This media imbalance has turned the concept of an independent watchdog press into a "broken toy" of the American political process. Another "broken toy" is the tradition of objective analysis in the U.S. intelligence community.

During George W. Bush's administration, in particular, the CIA has become a conveyor belt for propaganda with senior officials often delivering to Bush the information that they think he wants, with his wishes made clear by his public speeches and visits to the Langley headquarters by Vice President Dick Cheney.

Politicized intelligence is another problem that dates back at least to the mid-1970s when then-CIA Director George H.W. Bush allowed Paul Wolfowitz and other members of Team B into the CIA's analytical division to challenge its tempered assessment of the Soviet Union. Slanting of intelligence became a way of life at the CIA during the reign of William Casey and Robert Gates from 1981 to 1993 – and was not corrected during President Bill Clinton's administration. By 2001, when Bush arrived, the behavior was deeply entrenched. Careerism was rewarded; objectivity in the face of political pressure was punished.

While some Washington insiders respond to criticism about their factual errors by suggesting that historians will correct the mistakes, there are growing warning signs that history may become the next "broken toy" unable to fulfill its responsibilities. The week-long hagiography of Ronald Reagan after his death in June 2004 revealed the same patterns that have become apparent in U.S. intelligence analysis and in U.S. journalism. To maintain their mainstream credibility, some popular historians filled the hours of TV time with uncritical discussions about Reagan's legacy. Indeed, rather than the historians supplying a more accurate account of Reagan's Presidency, they arguably did a worse job in telling a straight story than the journalists had done in the 1980s.

The notion that documents will emerge in a timely way to fill in crucial gaps also may be more wishful thinking. Immediately after taking office in January 2001, George W. Bush stopped the legally required release of documents from the presidencies of Ronald Reagan and George H.W. Bush. Then, after the September 11 terrorist attacks as a stunned nation rallied around him, Bush issued an even more sweeping secrecy order. He granted former Presidents and Vice Presidents or their surviving family members the right to stop release of historical records, including those related to "military, diplomatic or national security secrets." Bush's order stripped the Archivist of the United States of the power to overrule claims of privilege from former Presidents and their representatives.[3]

By a twist of history, Bush's order eventually could give him control over both his and his father's records covering 12 years of the Reagan-Bush era and however long Bush's own presidential term lasts, potentially a 20-year swath of documentary evidence. Under Bush's approach, control over those two decades worth of secrets could eventually be put into the hands of Bush's daughters, Jenna and Barbara, a kind of dynastic control over U.S. history that would strengthen the hand of Bush apologists even more in controlling how history gets to understand this era.

***

Many of these changes over the past three decades have come gradually, failing to cause alarm, as with a frog not recognizing the danger of sitting in water slowly being brought to a boil. Many of the events may seem on the surface disconnected, although many of the central characters have reappeared throughout the course of the drama and others were understudies of earlier characters, carrying on their mentors' tactics and strategies.

But viewed as a panorama of 30 years, a continuity becomes apparent. What one sees is an evolution of a political system away from the more freewheeling democracy of the 1970s toward a more controlled system in which consensus is managed by rationing information and in which elections have become largely formalities for the sanctioning of power rather than a valued expression of the people's will.

Privately – and sometimes publicly – Bush insiders celebrated this transformation of the United States from what George W. Bush used to call a "humble" nation into a modern-day empire driven by a quasi-religious certainty in its own righteousness. In some political quarters, it became fashionable to suggest that God picked George W. Bush to be President. On December 23, 2001, NBC News Washington bureau chief Tim Russert joined New York Mayor Rudy Giuliani, Cardinal Theodore McCarrick and First Lady Laura Bush in ruminating about whether divine intervention had put George W. Bush in the White House to handle the 9/11 crisis.

Russert asked Mrs. Bush if "in an extraordinary way, this is why he was elected." Mrs. Bush disagreed with Russert's suggestion that "God picks the President, which he doesn't." But Giuliani thought otherwise. "I do think, Mrs. Bush, that there was some divine guidance in the President being elected. I do," the mayor said. McCarrick also saw some larger purpose. "I think I don't thoroughly agree with the First Lady. I think that the President really, he was where he was when we needed him," the cardinal said. Theologically speaking, it was less clear why God didn't simply let Bush actually be elected, rather than forcing him to get a U.S. Supreme Court ruling to stop the vote count in Florida.

Senior administration officials also have suggested that God chose the United States to establish an empire that would carry out His political wishes. In a Christmas card to political friends in late 2003, Vice President Cheney cited a quote from Benjamin Franklin, who said at the Constitutional Convention in 1787, "And if a sparrow cannot fall to the ground without His notice, is it probable that an empire can rise without His aid?" Though Cheney offered no explanation for this peculiar Christmas message – some Franklin experts said Cheney had taken the quote out of context – the implication seemed to be that God was guiding America's emergence as an empire.[4]

Yet, as empires have discovered throughout history, the occupation of foreign peoples abroad and the assertion of constant threats at home endanger democratic freedoms. In the days after the September 11 attacks, Attorney General John Ashcroft ordered the arrests of hundreds of Arabs and other Islamic people inside the United States for, as Ashcroft put it, the legal equivalent of "spitting on the sidewalk." The mass detentions, often for minor visa violations or as "material witnesses," swept up large numbers of students and taxi drivers, but netted no one who was implicated in the September 11 attacks. The only person charged in the United States in connection with the attacks, Zacarias Moussaoui, was already in detention when the attacks occurred. (While rounding up the "usual suspects," the Bush administration also helped facilitate the rapid departure of well-connected Saudis, including members of the bin Laden family who underwent at most cursory questioning.)[5]

To the American people, Ashcroft also made clear that the post-September 11 period was no time to criticize the Bush administration over curtailment of democratic freedoms. The Attorney General admonished those who fret over "the phantoms of lost liberty" because those who would make such complaints only serve to "aid terrorists – for they erode our national unity and diminish our resolve." Signs of dissent "give ammunition to America's enemies, and pause to America's friends," Ashcroft said at congressional hearings in December 2001.

Bush also asserted virtually unlimited authority as President, according to a series of administration legal opinions. Bush declared that he had the power to arrest and indefinitely imprison anyone he deemed an "enemy combatant," no need for charges or a trial. Bush's lawyers also claimed for him the right to order the torturing of anyone in U.S. government custody and the power to kill his international enemies whenever he judged that necessary, even if civilian bystanders also would die. In effect, Bush claimed that no law can infringe on his inherent power to do whatever he wishes as commander-in-chief. It was a declaration of personal authority unprecedented in scope – and it was not just theoretical.

In June 2002, Bush ordered U.S. citizen Jose Padilla detained indefinitely, incommunicado, without formal charges and without constitutional rights, simply on Bush's assertion that the alleged al-Qaeda operative was an "enemy combatant." In August 2002, the Justice Department asserted that international laws against torture don't apply to interrogations of al-Qaeda suspects. Around the same time, White House lawyers asserted that the President has the right to wage war without authorization from Congress. And during the early days of the U.S. invasion of Iraq in 2003, Bush authorized the bombings of civilian targets, including a restaurant, merely on the belief that Iraqi dictator Saddam Hussein or other Iraqi leaders might be there.

The Wall Street Journal, which obtained a draft of the torture memo, summarized its contents this way: "The President, despite domestic and international laws constraining the use of torture, has the authority as commander-in-chief to approve almost any physical or psychological actions during interrogation, up to and including torture." The *Journal* also reported that "a military lawyer who helped prepare the report said that political appointees heading the working group sought to assign to the President virtually unlimited authority on matters of torture – to assert 'presidential power at its absolute apex,' the lawyer said."[6]

***

The slow unveiling of this autocratic political system for the United States has been accompanied by new signs of resistance, however. Many old-time conservatives have begun to share the alarm that liberals long have felt about the implications of George W. Bush's assertions of sweeping executive power and his vision of an unchallengeable American Empire.

The anti-empire forces – including the likes of conservative Pat Buchanan and liberal Howard Dean – maintained that Bush and his neoconservatives have endangered the traditions of the American democratic Republic, which values personal liberty and imposes constitutional limits on a President's authority. The anti-empire forces have asserted that they have the traditions of America on their side, as long as the American people are not frightened into trading their freedoms for what they may perceive as greater security.

But the anti-imperial groupings emphasized different arguments. Conservative commentator Buchanan complained that neoconservative ideologues had won over Bush and were pushing strategies that were in the interests of hard-liners in Israel's Likud Party who oppose ending Israel's occupation of Palestinian territories. "We charge that a cabal of polemicists and public officials seek to ensnare our country in a series of wars that are not in America's interests," Buchanan wrote in *The American Conservative.*[7]

Former Vermont Governor Dean, one of the few Democratic presidential contenders who opposed Bush's Iraq War resolution, stressed the need for more international cooperation. "This unilateral approach to foreign policy is a disaster," Dean wrote in explaining his opposition to the Bush Doctrine. "All of the challenges facing the United States – from winning the war on terror and containing weapons of mass destruction to building an open world economy and protecting the global environment – can only be met by working with our allies. A renegade, go-it-alone approach will be doomed to failure, because these challenges know no boundaries."[8]

Beyond internal divisions, the anti-empire/pro-republic forces also lack a consistent means for reaching a broad cross-section of the American people. This media deficit puts the Bush critics at a particular disadvantage because their arguments require explanation of historical context and acceptance of the frustrating work of diplomacy. On the other hand, Bush's argument is easier to grasp: kill the bad guys.

Still, the Bush critics have struck a chord with millions of Americans who understand that violence alone rarely solves problems. Many Americans also share an abhorrence of empire, recognizing that it is inimical to freedom and democracy. Others simply distrust Bush's judgment, seeing him as The Man Who Knows Too Little, like the character in the Doonesbury cartoon who dons a Roman helmet and declares, "Pox Americus!"

Leading news organizations, including *The New York Times* and *The Washington Post*, also appear to have learned some lessons from the Bush administration's manipulation of information in the run-up to the Iraq War. After writing limited self-criticisms of their handling of the WMD issue, the *Times* and the *Post* showed new skepticism when a conservative veterans group, Swift Boat Veterans for Truth, attacked John Kerry's war record after he emerged as the presidential nominee of the Democratic Party and pulled ahead of Bush in opinion polls in August 2004.

The major newspapers pointed out the solid documentary record supporting Kerry's commendations for his Silver Star and Bronze Star as well as the inconsistencies in claims made by the anti-Kerry veterans. But many other elements of the national press corps, especially conservative news outlets and the cable news networks, treated the anti-Kerry charges as credible, continuing the long-established pattern of spinning the news in ways most favorable to the Bushes.

***

To understand how the United States got to where it is today, one must recognize that the changes have not been sudden. The terrorist attacks on September 11, 2001, may have ignited the fire that has driven the United States in the direction of a more authoritarian system. But the kindling was put in place over three decades. It also seems likely that many of the conservatives who set the United States off in this political direction in the 1970s had no idea where the journey would end. Their original thinking was more defensive than offensive.

The elder George Bush started out as a kind of Mr. Fix-it with gold-plated connections in both the Eastern Establishment and the Texas Oil World. He knew how to defuse a scandal and hide the incriminating evidence. He worked diligently, though ultimately unsuccessfully, to protect Richard Nixon from Watergate. He was more successful in getting the CIA off the front pages for Gerald Ford in 1976. Bush's cover-up skills enhanced his own power during the Reagan-Bush era of 1981 to 1993 and saved the family name so his sons could build their own political careers.

In the 1990s, the younger George Bush entered a political world where the conservatives were already in the ascendancy and the liberals were on the run. His contribution was an intuitive grasp of how hardball Republican strategies, aggressive conservative news outlets and mystical Christian fundamentalism could blend into a potent political coalition and consolidate the Right's dominance of U.S. government power.

Bush picked up useful lessons during his father's 1988 presidential campaign from the likes of Doug Wead, who taught Bush how to signal to the Christian fundamentalists, and Lee Atwater, who passed on the tricks for turning a decent opponent into a national laughingstock.

Given the shortcomings of other presidential candidates in 1999 and 2000, Bush became the darling of the conservative news media and a favorite of many mainstream journalists. His easygoing style, which conceals a fierce competitiveness, made Bush a sellable commodity to the American people, especially to white men.

Add the fear and the sense of victimization from the 9/11 attacks and a new political model suddenly lay open as a possibility for the United States. It would be a post-modern authoritarian system that would rely less on traditional repression of political opponents than on a sophisticated media to intimidate and marginalize dissidents.

The new system would be the sum of the parts gradually arising out of the ruins of Watergate. At its core would be the intelligence concept of "perception management," not so much Orwellian as post-Orwellian. While Orwell's *1984* envisioned sophisticated torture to extract confessions and mass speeches to stir up ethnic hatreds, this new system would rely on ridicule to make those who get in the way objects of derision, outcasts whose very names draw eye-rolling chuckles and knee-slapping guffaws. Think of Michael Dukakis, Bill Clinton and Al Gore – or any number of lesser-known public figures who objected to the rush to war in Iraq.

George W. Bush was perhaps the perfect candidate for exploiting this transformation. Lacking a deep appreciation for the American constitutional system of checks and balances, Bush wasn't personally repulsed by the notion of shifting to a more authoritarian structure of governance and silencing meaningful dissent. Indeed, he was attracted to the idea.

After claiming the Presidency in December 2000, Bush once joked, "If this were a dictatorship, it would be a heck of a lot easier – so long as I'm the dictator." It is hard to imagine that any other American President would have said such a thing.

NOTES

Chapter 2

[1] See Robert Parry, *Lost History* (Arlington, VA: The Media Consortium, 1999)

Chapter 3

[1] See Kevin Philips, *American Dynasty* (New York: Viking, 2004), pp. 21-23
[2] Ibid., pp. 24-25
[3] Ibid., p. 39
[4] Ibid., p. 39
[5] See J. Anthony Lukas, *Nightmare* (Athens, OH: Ohio University Press, 1999), pp. 110-111
[6] Ibid., p. 111
[7] See Herbert S. Parmet, *George Bush* (New Brunswick: Transaction Publishers, 2002), p. 140
[8] Ibid., pp. 142-143
[9] Ibid., pp. 143-145
[10] Lukas, *Nightmare*, p. 111
[11] Parmet, *George Bush*, pp. 142-143
[12] See H.R. Haldeman, *The Haldeman Diaries* (New York: G.P. Putnam's Sons, 1994), p. 210
[13] Ibid., p. 217
[14] Parmet, *George Bush*, p. 157
[15] See Stanley I. Kutler, *Abuse of Power* (New York: The Free Press, 1997), p. 8
[16] Ibid., p. 9
[17] Ibid., p. 20
[18] Lukas, *Nightmare*, p. 199
[19] Ibid., p. 38
[20] See Jim Hougan, *Secret Agenda* (New York: Random House, 1984), pp. 107-115
[21] Lukas, *Nightmare*, pp. 201-202
[22] Ibid., p. 202
[23] Ibid., p. 151
[24] *The New York Times* (December 12, 1972)

[25] *The New York Times* (June 15, 1972)

[26] Lukas, *Nightmare*, p. 203

[27] Kutler, *Abuse of Power*, p. 40

[28] Lukas, *Nightmare*, pp. 206-209

[29] *The New York Times* (September 22, 1972)

[30] *The New York Times* (December 7, 1972)

[31] *The New York Times* (December 11, 1972)

[32] *The New York Times* (December 7, 1972)

[33] Parmet, *George Bush*, p. 157

[34] Ibid., p. 158

[35] "Bush with Gold," *Looking Forward*, pp. 120-121

[36] *The New York Times* (April 18,1973)

[37] *The New York Times* (April 20, 1973)

[38] Ibid.

[39] *The New York Times* (April 23, 1974)

[40] *The Washington Post* (April 8, 1973)

[41] Haldeman, *The Haldeman Diaries*, p. 651

[42] *The Washington Post* (May 1, 1973)

[43] Lukas, *Nightmare*, p. 339

[44] *The Washington Post* (July 25, 1973)

[45] Ibid.

[46] Ibid.

[47] Ibid.

[48] *The Washington Post* (January 22, 1976)

[49] See John Loftus and Mark Aarons, *The Secret War Against the Jews* (New York: St. Martin's Press, 1994), pp. 369-370

[50] *The New York Times* (April 23, 1974)

[51] *The New York Times* (January 31, 1974)

[52] *The Washington Post* (April 30, 1974)

[53] See Bob Woodward and Carl Bernstein, *The Final Days* (New York: Simon & Schuster, 1976), p. 369

[54] Lukas, *Nightmare*, p. 561

[55] Parmet, *George Bush*, pp. 171-72

[56] Ibid., p. 180

Chapter 4

[1] See Kathryn S. Olmstead, *Challenging the Secret Government* (Chapel Hill: The University of North Carolina Press, 1996), p. 12

[2] Parmet, *George Bush*, p. 188-191

[3] *The New York Times* (November 12, 1975)

[4] Parmet, *George Bush*, p. 190

[5] *The New York Times* (November 9, 1975)

[6] Parmet, *George Bush*, pp. 192-194

[7] *The New York Times* (January 31,1976)

[8] Olmstead, *Challenging the Secret Government*, p. 161

[9] Ibid., pp.161-162

[10] Ibid., pp. 163-164
[11] Ibid., p. 173
[12] See Robert Parry, *Fooling America* (New York: William Morrow & Company, 1992), p. 50
[13] Parmet, *George Bush*, p. 194
[14] Anne Hessing Cahn and John Prados, "Team B: The Trillion Dollar Experiment," *The Bulletin of Atomic Scientists* (April 1993)
[15] Ibid.
[16] Ibid.
[17] Ibid.
[18] Parmet, *George Bush*, p. 199
[19] Cahn and Prados, "Team B: The Trillion Dollar Experiment," *The Bulletin of Atomic Scientists* (April 1993)
[20] Ibid.
[21] See Robert Gates, *From the Shadows* (New York: Simon & Schuster, 1996), p. 106
[22] Ibid., p. 108
[23] Ibid.
[24] Cahn and Prados, "Team B: The Trillion Dollar Experiment," *The Bulletin of Atomic Scientists* (April 1993)
[25] Parmet, *George Bush*, pp. 195-196
[26] See Peter Kornbluh, *The Pinochet File* (New York: The New Press, 2003), Document 4, p. 237
[27] Ibid., pp. 214-216
[28] Ibid., p. 222
[29] Ibid., p. 349
[30] Ibid., p. 326
[31] Ibid., pp. 322-323
[32] Ibid., p. 333
[33] Ibid., pp. 336-337
[34] See Marguerite Feitlowitz, *A Lexicon of Terror* (New York: Oxford University Press, 1998), p. 6
[35] Ibid., 42-44
[36] Ibid., 28
[37] Marta Gurvich, "Baby-Snatching: Argetine Dirty War Secret," Consortiumnews.com
[38] Kornbluh, *The Pinochet File*, p. 340
[39] Ibid., p. 342
[40] Ibid., pp. 348-349
[41] Ibid., p. 343
[42] Ibid., pp. 343-351
[43] See John Dinges and Saul Landau, *Assassination on Embassy Row* (New York: Pantheon Books, 1980), p. 384
[44] Ibid.
[45] Ibid., p. 385
[46] *The New York Times* (September 23, 1976)
[47] Parry, *Fooling America*, p. 52

[48] Kornbluh, *The Pinochet File*, p. 353
[49] Ibid.
[50] Dinges and Landau, *Assassination on Embassy Row*, p. 386
[51] Kornbluh, *The Pinochet File*, p. 346
[52] Ibid., p. 355
[53] Parry, *Fooling America*, p. 55
[54] Ibid.

Chapter 5

[1] *The New York Times* (November 5, 1976)
[2] William M. Hammond, *The Military and the Media: 1962-1968* (Washington, DC: Center of Military History, United States Army, 1988), p. 387
[3] See David Halberstam, *The Fifties* (New York: Ballantine Books, 1993); Also see Taylor Branch, *Parting the Waters* (New York: Touchstone, 1989)
[4] "The Myth of the Liberal Media," *Extra!* (July/August 1998)
[5] See Sidney Blumenthal, *The Rise of the Counter-Establishment* (New York: Times Books, 1986), p. 61
[6] Ibid., p. 65
[7] Ibid.
[8] Ibid., p. 66
[9] Ibid., p. 67
[10] FBI records obtained through a Freedom of Information Act request by Larry Zilliox, a Virginia private investigator
[11] See Nansook Hong, *In the Shadow of the Moons* (New York: Little, Brown & Company, 1998), pp. 196-197
[12] Ibid., pp. 26-27
[13] Robert Parry, "Dark Side of Rev. Moon: Generation Next," Consortiumnews.com
[14] See David E. Kaplan and Alec Dubro, *Yakuza* (Reading, Massachusetts: Addison Wesley Publishing Company, 1986), p. 68-81
[15] Ibid., 80
[16] See Robert Boettcher, *Gifts of Deceit* (New York: Holt, Rinehart & Winston, 1980), pp.4-5
[17] Ibid., p. 344
[18] FBI records obtained through a Freedom of Information Act request by Larry Zilliox, a Virginia private investigator
[19] Ibid.
[20] The Washington Post (September 17, 1984)

Chapter 6

[1] See David Rockefeller, *Memoirs* (New York: Random House, 2002), pp. 365-366
[2] Ibid., p. 160
[3] Rockefeller, *Memoirs*, p. 366
[4] Ibid., p. 367
[5] Ibid., p. 368
[6] Rockefeller, *Memoirs*, p. 369

[7] See Kai Bird, *The Chairman* (New York: Simon & Schuster, 1992), p. 652

[8] Rockefeller, *Memoirs*, p. 371

[9] See Robert Parry, *Trick or Treason* (New York: Sheridan Square Press, 1993), p. 213

[10] Ibid.

[11] Rockefeller, *Memoirs*, 374-375

[12] See Seymour Hersh, *The Price of Power* (New York: Simon & Schuster, 1983), pp. 21-22

[13] See Anna Chennault, *The Education of Anna*, New York, Times Books, 1980, p. 190

[14] See Hersh, *The Price of Power*, pp. 21-22

[15] See Clark Clifford, *Counsel to the President* (New York: Anchor Books, 1991), p. 581

[16] *The Washington Post* (May 28, 1995)

[17] See Anthony Summers, *The Arrogance of Power* (New York: Viking, 2000), p. 297

[18] Ibid., p. 299

[19] Ibid., pp. 299-301

[20] Ibid., p. 302

[21] Ibid., pp. 305-306

[22] See Nguyen Cao Ky, *Buddha's Child*, (New York, St. Martin's Press, 2002)

Chapter 7

[1] Parmet, *George Bush*, p. 221

[2] Parry, *Trick or Treason*, p. 77

[3] See Gary Sick, *October Surprise* (New York: Times Books, 1991), pp. 52-54

[4] Parry, *Trick or Treason*, p. 250

[5] Ibid., p. 251

[6] Sick, *October Surprise*, pp. 55-56

[7] Ibid., p. 33

[8] Rockefeller, *Memoirs*, p. 374

[9] See Miles Copeland, *The Game Player* (London, Aurum Press, 1989), p. 256

[10] See Ari Ben-Menashe, *Profits of War* (New York: Sheridan Square Press, 1992), p. 48

[11] Ibid., p. 53

[12] Ibid., pp. 55-57

[13] Ibid., p. 53-59

[14] Parry, *Trick or Treason*, p. 252

[15] Sick, *October Surprise*, pp. 34-35

[16] Ibid., p. 34

[17] See *Final Report of the Independent Counsel for Iran/Contra Matters, Vol. I*, p. 501

[18] Parry, *Trick or Treason*, p. 287

[19] Ibid., pp. 81-83

Chapter 8

[1] Parry, *Trick or Treason*, p. 142
[2] Ibid., p. 291
[3] Sick, *October Surprise*, p. 101
[4] Parry, *Trick or Treason*, p. 126
[5] Ibid., pp. 292-293
[6] Ben-Menashe, *Profits of War*, pp. 71-74
[7] Sick, *October Surprise*, p. 100

Chapter 9

[1] *The Wall Street Journal* (October 21, 1980)
[2] Parry, *Trick or Treason*, p. 119
[3] Ibid.
[4] *The Washington Post* (November 28, 2003)
[5] Ben-Menashe, *Profits of War*, pp. 74-75
[6] Ibid., p. 75
[7] Parry, *Trick or Treason*, pp. 317-319
[8] Ibid., p. 318
[9] Ibid., pp. 319-320
[10] David Corn, *Blond Ghost* (New York: Simon and Schuster, 1994), p. 358
[11] *The New York Times* (October 24, 1980)
[12] Corn, *Blond Ghost*, p. 359
[13] See Ed Rollins, *Bare Knuckles and Back Rooms* (New York: Broadway Books, 1996), pp. 214-215
[14] Parry, *Trick or Treason*, p. 260
[15] Ibid.

Chapter 10

[1] Parry, *Trick or Treason*, 100-101
[2] Ibid., pp. 160-161
[3] Ibid., p. 161
[4] Ibid., pp. 162-163
[5] Ibid., p. 68
[6] Ibid.
[7] See Steven Emerson and Jesse Furman, "What October Surprise? The Conspiracy that Wasn't," *The New Republic* (November 18, 1991)
[8] See Robert Friedman, *The Nation* (May 15, 1995)
[9] See "Making of a Myth, the October Surprise: It Wasn't Treason but a Conspiracy Theory Run Wild," *Newsweek* (November 11, 1991)
[10] Parry, *Trick or Treason*, p. 237
[11] Ibid., p. 239
[12] Parry, *Lost History*, Chapters 1-2
[13] Parry, *Trick or Treason*, p. 269
[14] See Peter Maas, *Manhunt* (New York: Random House, 1986), p. 247
[15] Parry, *Trick or Treason*, p. 281

[16] Ibid., pp. 282-283
[17] Ibid., p. 284
[18] Ibid., p. 285
[19] Ibid., p. 285
[20] Ibid., p. 288

Chapter 11

[1] Parry, *Trick or Treason*, p. 303
[2] Ibid., pp. 38-39
[3] Ibid., pp. 294-296
[4] Ibid., p. 296
[5] Ibid., pp. 302-303
[6] Joint Report of the Task Force to Investigate Certain Allegations Concerning the Holding of American Hostages by Iran in 1980, p. 78
[7] Ibid., p. 168
[8] Parry, *Trick or Treason*, pp. 314-315

Chapter 12

[1] *The New York Times* (January 24, 1993)
[2] Parry, *Trick or Treason*, p. 302

Chapter 13

[1] Gates, *From the Shadows*, pp. 190-191
[2] Mark Perry, *Eclipse* (New York: William Morrow & Company, 1992), p. 317
[3] Gates, *From the Shadows*, p. 192
[4] See Melvin A. Goodman, "Ending the CIA's Cold War Legacy," *Foreign Policy* (Spring 1997)
[5] Ibid.
[6] *Nomination of Robert M. Gates, Select Committee on Intelligence of the United States Senate, Volume III*, pp. 83-84
[7] Gates, *From the Shadows*, p. 204
[8] Ibid., pp. 204-205
[9] *Nomination of Robert M. Gates, Select Committee on Intelligence of the United States Senate, Volume III*, p. 85
[10] Ibid.
[11] Ibid.
[12] Ibid., pp. 86-87
[13] Ibid., pp. 87-88
[14] Ibid., p. 82
[15] *Nomination of Robert M. Gates, Select Committee on Intelligence of the United States Senate, Vol. II*, p. 725
[16] *Nomination of Robert M. Gates, Select Committee on Intelligence of the United States Senate, Vol. III*, pp. 9-22

[17] Goodman, "Ending the CIA's Cold War Legacy," *Foreign Policy* (Spring 1997)
[18] Gates, *From the Shadows*, p. 207
[19] *Nomination of Robert M. Gates, Select Committee on Intelligence of the United States Senate, Vol. II*, pp. 714-729
[20] Ibid., p. 714
[21] See George P. Schultz, *Turmoil and Triumph* (New York: Scribner's Sons, 1993), p. 864
[22] Goodman, "Ending the CIA's Cold War Legacy," *Foreign Policy* (Spring 1997)
[23] Ibid.
[24] Ibid.
[25] "Truth, War and Consequences," *Frontline*, PBS (October 1993)
[26] *The Washington Post* (July 13, 2004)
[27] *The New York Times* (July 10, 2004)
[28] See Seymour Hersh, "The Stovepipe," *The New Yorker* (October 27, 2003)
[29] *The O'Reilly Factor*, Fox News (June 12, 2003)
[30] See Joseph Wilson, *The Politics of Truth* (New York: Carroll & Graf Publishers, 2004), pp. 1-2
[31] Ibid., p. 2
[32] Ibid.
[33] *The New York Times* (October 2, 2003)
[34] *The Washington Times* (October 2, 2003)
[35] *The Washington Times* (October 6, 2003)

Chapter 14

[1] See Michael T. Klare and Peter Kornbluh, *Low-Intensity Warfare* (New York: Pantheon Books, 1988), pp. 14-15
[2] *The Tampa Tribune* (December 25, 1980)
[3] See Ray Bonner, *Weakness and Deceit* (New York: Random House, 1984), p. 341-343
[4] *The New York Times* (February 26, 1999)
[5] *The Washington Post* (February 26, 1999)
[6] *The Washington Post* (October 16, 1981)
[7] *The New York Times* (June 5, 1988)
[8] Hodel, "Evita, Swiss & the Nazis," *Consortiumnews.com* (January 7, 1999)
[9] See Peter Dale Scott and Jonathan Marshall, *Cocaine Politics* (Berkeley: University of California Press, 1991), p. 45
[10] See Michael Levine, *The Big White Lie* (New York: Thunder's Mouth Press, 1993), p. 56
[11] Ibid., p. 58

Chapter 15

[1] See Christopher Dickey, *With the Contras* (New York: Simon & Schuster, 1987)
[2] Parry, *Lost History*, p. 72

Chapter 16

[1] See Scott Anderson and Jon Lee Anderson, *Inside the League* (New York: Dodd, Mead & Company, 1986), p. 46

[2] Ibid.

[3] See Henrik Kruger, *The Great Heroin Coup* (Montreal: Black Rose Books, 1993)

[4] See Samuel Blixen, "Rev. Moon's Uruguayan Money Laundry," *Consortiumnews.com* (August 19, 1998)

[5] Anderson, *Inside the League,* p. 106

[6] See Robert Parry, "Dark Side of Rev. Moon: Drug Allies," *Consortiumnews.com* (October 13, 1997)

[7] Scott and Marshall, *Cocaine Politics,* p. 46

[8] An English translation of Kai Hermann's article was published in *Covert Action Information Bulletin* (Winter 1986)

[9] Martin Andersen, *Dossier Secreto* (Boulder, CO: Westview Press, 1993), p. 291

[10] Anderson, *Inside the League,* pp. 105-106

[11] Hermann, *Covert Action Information Bulletin* (Winter 1986)

[12] Ibid.

[13] *The Boston Globe* (April 20, 1988); Ross Gelbspan later described his investigation in a book, *Break-ins, Death Threats and the FBI* (Cambridge, MA: South End Press, 1991)

[14] *Regardie's* (November 1988)

[15] Anderson, *Inside the League,* p. 129

[16] *Clarin* (July 7, 1996)

[17] *The Washington Times* (April 11, 1986)

[18] *The Washington Times* (August 13, 1986)

[19] *The Washington Times* (January 21, 1987)

[20] *Drug, Law Enforcement and Foreign Policy – the Kerry Report* (December 1988)

[21] Parry, *Lost History*

[22] Ibid., p. 198

[23] The contra drug evidence, which was uncovered during internal CIA and Justice Department investigations, is detailed in Parry's *Lost History*, Chapters 10 and 11.

[24] *The Washington Post* (January 6, 1983)

[25] See Andrew Ferguson, *American Spectator* (September 1987)

[26] See *Common Cause Magazine* (Fall 1993)

[27] *The Washington Post* (October 15, 1989)

[28] *The Sand Diego Union-Tribune* (April 9,1989)

[29] *The Washington Times* (May 17, 1992)

Chapter 17

[1] See Murray Waas and Craig Unger, "In the Loop: Bush's Secret Mission," *The New Yorker* (November 2, 1992)

[2] *Report of the Congressional Committees Investigating the Iran-Contra Affair* (November 1987), p. 21

[3] See Lawrence E. Walsh, *Firewall* (New York: W.W. Norton & Company, 1997), p. 262

[4] Parry, *Fooling America*, pp. 42-43

[5] See Monica Crowley, *Nixon off the Record* (New York: Random House, 1996), p. 112

[6] See Robert Parry, "Picking Prosecutors," *Consortiumnews.com* (April 17, 1999)

[7] *The Washington Post* (December 30, 1992)

[8] See Bill Clinton, *My Life* (New York: Alfred A. Knopf, 2004), p. 457

[9] *The Washington Post* (April 11, 1993)

[10] *Final Report of the Independent Counsel in Re: Janet G. Mullins,* Vol. I, p. 378

[11] *Final Report of the Independent Counsel in Re: Janet G. Mullins,* Vol. II, pp. 292-311

Chapter 18

[1] See "Moon-Related Funds Filter to Evangelicals," *Christianity Today* (Posted on Web, February 9, 1998)

[2] *The Roanoke Times & World* (February 6, 1995)

[3] See Joe Conason and Gene Lyons, *The Hunting of the President* (New York: St. Martin's Press, 2000), p. 142

[4] See *Unification News* (December 1996)

[5] See *Unification News* (June 1997)

[6] *The Washington Post* (Nov. 23-24, 1997)

[7] UPI (November 16, 1984)

[8] *La Nacion* (November 19, 1996)

[9] *Unification News* (December 1996)

[10] *La Nacion* (November 26, 1996)

[11] *The Washington Post* (September 15, 1995)

[12] *The Washington Post* (July 30, 1996)

[13] *The Washington Times* (October 18, 1996)

[14] *The Washington Post*, (November 24, 1997)

[15] See Samuel Blixen, "Rev. Moon's Uruguayan Money Laundry," *Consortiumnews.com* (August 19, 1998)

[16] Foreign Broadcast Information Service (January 30, 1997)

[17] See Samuel Blixen, "Rev. Moon's Bank Scam," *Consortiumnews.com* (November 6, 1998)

Chapter 19

[1] Hong, *In the Shadow of the Moons*, pp. 172-173

Chapter 20

[1] *The Washington Post* (November 2, 1998)

[2] See *Final Report of the Independent Counsel for Iran/Contra Matters*, p. 352

[3] *The New York Times* (July 24, 1999)

[4] *The Washington Post* (July 25, 1999)

[5] *The New York Times* (August 22, 1999)

[6] See Mark Crispin Miller, *The Bush Dyslexicon* (New York: W.W. Norton & Company, 2002), p. 14-15

[7] See Bill Minutaglio, *First Son* (New York: Three Rivers Press, 1999), pp. 147-148

[8] *The New York Times* (July 11, 2000)

[9] Associated Press (July 5, 1999)

[10] *The Boston Globe* (May 23, 2000)

[11] *The Washington Post* (July 30, 1999)

[12] Ibid.

[13] Ibid.

[14] See *Harper's Magazine* (February 2000)

[15] *The Washington Post* (July 30, 1999)

[16] *Harper's Magazine* (February 2000); Minutaglio, *First Son*, p. 207

[17] *The Washington Post* (July 30, 1999)

[18] See *Harper's Magazine* (February 2000)

[19] Ibid.

[20] Ibid.

[21] See Sam Parry, "Bush's Life of Deception," *Consortiumnews.com* (November 4, 2002)

[22] *The Boston Globe* (October 30, 2002); also, see *The Washington Post* (November 1, 2002)

[23] Ibid.

[24] Minutaglio *First Son*, p. 322

[25] Ibid., p. 216

[26] See *GQ Magazine* (September 2003)

[27] Minutaglio, *First Son*, p. 217

[28] Associated Press (October 26, 1999)

[29] See *The Daily Howler*, www.dailyhowler.com

[30] *The Washington Post* (December 1, 1999)

[31] *The New York Times* (December 1, 1999)

[32] *Hardball*, CNBC (December 1, 1999)

[33] *The Washington Post* (December 2, 1999)

[34] *This Week*, ABC (December 5, 1999)

[35] Associated Press (December 14, 1999)

[36] *The Boston Globe* (December 26, 1999)

[37] Associated Press (December 14, 1999)

[38] *Milwaukee Journal Sentinel* (December 12, 1999)

[39] See Stuart Taylor Jr., *National Journal* (December 18, 1999)

[40] *The Providence Journal* (December 23, 1999)

[41] *The Washington Times* (December 31, 1999)

[42] *The Washington Times* (January 7, 2000)

[43] *The New York Times* (December 14, 1997)

[44] *The Boston Herald* (December 5, 1999)

[45] Associated Press (March 11, 1999)

[46] *The Daily Howler*, http://www.dailyhowler.com/h121499_1.shtml (December 14, 1999)

[47] Bloomberg News (October 6, 2000)
[48] *Morning Edition*, NPR (October 11, 2000)
[49] *The New York Times* (October 15, 2000)

Chapter 21

[1] See Jake Tapper, *Down and Dirty* (New York: Little, Brown, 2001), p. 260
[2] Ibid., pp. 260-261
[3] Ibid., p. 264
[4] Ibid., pp. 265-266
[5] *The Washington Post* (November 27, 2000)
[6] *The Wall Street Journal* (November 27, 2000)
[7] Tapper, *Down and Dirty*, p. 277
[8] *The Washington Post* (November 24, 2000)
[9] *The Miami Herald* (July 14, 2002)
[10] See "Bending the Rules Boosted Bush Totals," *Salon.com* (December 11, 2000)
[11] *The Washington Post* (November 12, 2001)

Chapter 22

[1] CNN (July 10, 2001)
[2] See National Commission on Terrorist Attacks Upon the United States, *The 9/11 Commission Report* (New York: W.W. Norton & Company, 2004), p. 259
[3] Ibid.
[4] Ibid., pp. 259-260
[5] *The New York Times* (April 4, 2004)
[6] *60 Minutes*, CBS (March 28, 2004)
[7] *9/11 Commission Report*, p. 265
[8] *The New York Times* (July 25, 2004)
[9] *The New York Times* (Aug. 17, 2004)
[10] *The Wall Street Journal* (March 22, 2004)
[11] Ibid.
[12] *9/11 Commission Report*, p. 38
[13] *The Wall Street Journal* (March 22, 2004)
[14] Ibid.
[15] Ibid.
[16] *The New York Times* (September 22, 2001)
[17] Bob Woodward, *Veil* (New York: Simon & Schuster, 1987), p. 397
[18] *The New York Times* (March 23, 2004)
[19] *The Washington Post* (March 13, 2004)
[20] See Karen Kwiatkowski, "The New Pentagon Papers," *Salon.com* (March 10, 2004)
[21] See Seymour Hersh, "Selective Intelligence," *The New Yorker* (May 12, 2003)
[22] *The Washington Post* (September 24, 2002)
[23] *The Washington Post* (September 25, 2002)
[24] *The Washington Post* (September 27, 2002)
[25] *The Wall Street Journal* (September 26, 2002)

[26] *The New York Times* (April 13, 1991), as cited by Somerby in his column of September 26, 2002

[27] See Hans Blix, *Disarming Iraq* (New York: Pantheon Books, 2004), p. 3

[28] See Bob Woodward, *Plan of Attack* (New York: Simon & Schuster, 2004), p. 421

Chapter 23

[1] See Robert Parry, "Bay of Pigs Meets Blackhawk Down,"*Consortiumnews.com* (March 30, 2003)

[2] Bob Woodward, *Bush at War* (New York: Simon & Schuster, 2003), p. 342

[3] See Ann Scott Tyson, "US troops' anguish: Killing outmatched foes," *Christian Science Monitor* (April 11, 2003)

[4] *The New York Times* (April 14, 2003)

[5] *NBC Nightly News*, NBC (April 25, 2003)

[6] *The Wall Street Journal* (April 11, 2003)

[7] *The Wall Street Journal* (April 21, 2003)

[8] Transcript, MSNBC (May 18, 2003)

[9] *Independent* (April 23, 2003)

[10] *The New York Times* (April 14, 2003)

[11] *Independent* (April 13, 2003)

[12] *The New York Times* (April 17, 2003)

[13] *The New York Times* (April 20, 2003)

[14] *The New York Times* (April 19, 2003)

[15] *The New York Times* (April 20, 2003)

[16] *The New York Times* (May 6, 2003)

[17] *The New York Times*, (May 16, 2003)

[18] MSNBC (May 8, 2003)

[19] *The Washington Post* (May 1, 2004)

[20] *The Washington Post* (May 31, 2003)

[21] See Ann Scott Tyson, "Troop morale in Iraq hits 'rock bottom,'" *Christian Science Monitor* (July 7, 2003)

[22] *USA Today* (May 3, 2004)

Conclusion

[1] *The Washington Times* (March 12, 2004)

[2] *The Washington Post* (March 17, 2004)

[3] *The New York Times* (January 3, 2003)

[4] *The Washington Post* (December 28, 2003)

[5] See Craig Unger, *House of Bush, House of Saud* (New York: Scribner, 2004), p. 11

[6] *The Wall Street Journal* (June 7, 2004)

[7] See Patrick Buchanan, "Whose War?," *The American Conservative* (March 24, 2003)

[8] See Howard Dean, "Bush: It's Not Just his Doctrine That's Wrong," *CommonDreams*.org (April 17, 2003)